PHILOSOPHY
and
PARAPSYCHOLOGY

PHILOSOPHY
and
PARAPSYCHOLOGY

edited by JAN LUDWIG

℞ Prometheus Books
1203 Kensington Avenue
Buffalo, New York 14215

Published 1978 by Prometheus Books
1203 Kensington Avenue, Buffalo, New York 14215

Copyright © by Prometheus Books
All Rights Reserved

Library of Congress Card Number 77-91852
ISBN 0-87975-075-8

Printed in the United States of America

Contents

Contents

SECTION IV: PRECOGNITION AND ITS PROBLEMS

SECTION V: PARAPSYCHOLOGY AND THE PHILOSOPHY OF MIND

Contents

Preface

To be provocative and useful, an anthology should not be a mere collection. I have endeavored to make this book more than a set of essays related only by a common concern with philosophical issues involving parapsychology. Through the division of the text into sections and the headings given the respective sections I have attempted to impose some organization on the general topic. More importantly, within each section I have tried to include selections that engage the reader in the process of argument and philosophical disagreement. The result, I believe, is a collection that develops some important themes in the philosophy of parapsychology, that conveys to the reader a sense of the dialectical advance of debate in this area, and that "hangs together" as a whole. To promote the latter end, I have occasionally interpolated footnotes of clarification or cross-reference, always in square brackets and signed "Ed."

On the other hand, I have made no attempt to summarize or to interpret for the reader the individual selections or the structure of the argument in a particular section of the text. Learning to do this for oneself is a crucial aspect of education in philosophy and is thus better left to the reader and perhaps to teachers who may be using this collection in their own courses for their own purposes. In my view, the editor of an anthology has a special obligation to select provocative materials for inclusion and then to organize and edit them carefully, but equally an obligation not to impose upon the reader by giving an analysis and evaluation of each selection included. An indication of my own position in regard to the philosophical issues of parapsychology is provided by the introductory essay.

Some background knowledge of experimental parapsychology is helpful in approaching certain of the selections, although on the whole I have sought to make this collection intelligible to readers who lack extensive knowledge of the parapsychological literature. In my own teaching I have suggested familiarity with such works as J. B. Rhine's *Extra-Sensory Perception* and Gardner Murphy's *Challenge of Psychical Research* as a basis for discussion of philosophical issues in parapsychology, but other works might do as well. A selection of background readings in parapsychology is included in the bibliography at the end of the book.

Potential readers examining the contents of this collection may be surprised by its entire omission of materials dealing specifically with the survival issue, that is, with questions of the possibility and even probability of the continuation, in some sense, of individual human personalities beyond bodily death. These questions have of course been hotly contested by students of parapsychology at various times in the history of the subject. Some philosophical reasons for excluding this issue from consideration here are stated in my introductory essay. A rather more pragmatic justification is the fact that materials relating to survival are already widely available, whereas the works here reprinted, many for the first time, deserve a wider readership than they would have gotten as denizens of periodical back-issue files. I have, however, included some works on the survival issue in my bibliography, which may provide the interested reader with an entry into this area of philosophical parapsychology.

ACKNOWLEDGMENTS

I wish to thank the authors and literary executors whose cooperation made possible the reprinting of the works included in this collection. I am especially grateful to Antony Flew for substantially revising his two contributions especially for this volume, to John Beloff for adding a postscript to his article, and to Stephen Braude for allowing me to include a previously unpublished paper of his. My thanks are also due to the editors and publishers who willingly granted me permission to reprint copyrighted materials; specific acknowledgment accompanies each selection.

In pursuit of works suitable for inclusion here I have received help from the reference staff of the Schaffer Library, Union College, and from my student, David Lederkramer, who aided in the literature search, an unexciting task which he performed well. A grant from the Union College Mellon Fund for Faculty Development and an appointment as a Research Fellow in the Department of the History of Science, Harvard University, although both primarily for other purposes, enabled me to spend the 1976-77 academic year at Harvard and to use the collections of the Harvard College Library. My work on this book was supported in prior years by grants from the Humanities Faculty Research Fund of Union College. For all of this support I am indeed grateful; without it this book would never have appeared.

Finally, I should like to thank all of the following: my students in "Spooks" who provoked the book and whose critical responses determined to some extent its final form; my colleagues in the Philosophy Department, Union College, who encouraged me along the way, especially Frederick Elliston and Willard Enteman; Paul Kurtz, editor of Prometheus Books, for his patient interest in publishing such a book; my bookseller friend, Wayne Somers, for his bibliographical advice and general good judgment; and my wife, Karen, who criticized and improved my writing, while constantly supporting me.

Jan Ludwig

Philosophy & Parapsychology

Matters of Fact well proved ought not to be denied, because we cannot conceive how they can be perform'd. Nor is it a reasonable method of inference,
first to presume the thing impossible, and thence to conclude that the fact
cannot be proved. On the contrary, we should judge of the Action by the evidence, and not the evidence by the measures of our Fancies about the
Action.

Joseph Glanvill—*Saducismus Triumphatus*

William James died in 1910. Yet I have before me a book that James is supposed to have dictated to its automatist/editor in the mid-nineteen-twent-
ies.' Such, according to one common view, is the stuff of parapsychology
that strains credulity.

But the embodied, ante-mortem William James took parapsychology
(or *psychical research,* as it was known in his time) seriously, as did
(and do) many other philosophers. Does this indicate merely that philosophers, like all human beings, have their intellectually weak moments, or
are there aspects of parapsychology worthy of philosophical study? There
is obviously much more to parapsychology than claims of post-mortem
authorship, and some of the other issues raised by parapsychologists are
such as to be of central concern to philosophers. Yet, given the mass of

intellectually irresponsible claims that have been held to be parapsychological, the problem is to isolate those aspects of parapsychology that most deserve the attention of serious philosophers.

The same ante-mortem James who took parapsychology seriously also introduced into philosophy the distinction between tender-minded and tough-minded thinkers.[2] James characterized the former as, among other things, "rationalistic (going by *principles*)," religious, free-willist, and dogmatical, while the latter were typically "empiricist (going by *facts*)," materialistic, irreligious, fatalistic, and skeptical. He added that members of each of the two groups "have a low opinion of each other. . . . The tough think of the tender as sentimentalists and soft-heads. The tender feel the tough to be unrefined, callous, or brutal."[3] James's distinction, and his characterization of the attitudes of the respective proponents toward one another, is especially appropriate in discussing the attitudes of philosophers toward parapsychology.

On one, perhaps prevalent view, a fellow philosopher's interest in parapsychology is persuasive evidence of tender-mindedness. On this view, philosophers who "truck with spooks" are seeking premises to support their tender-minded conclusions, among which are counted theism, mind/body dualism, the immortality of the soul, and the doctrine of human free will. Since no tough-minded philosopher accepts any of these conclusions, and since parapsychology is of interest only as a source of premises for such conclusions, it follows that parapsychology is of no intrinsic interest to tough-minded philosophers. Parapsychology is regarded as romantic and soft, with little cognitive significance.

The tough-minded philosopher is correct on some counts. Parapsychology has sometimes been used in attempts to justify the sorts of conclusions mentioned above, and it has often been so used in a careless and uncritical fashion. For example, mediumistic communications have been taken as evidence for the immortality of the soul; again, the evidence of experimental parapsychology has sometimes been held to support the existence of free will, on the grounds that no causally deterministic explanation of "correct guessing" is possible. Such inferences are clearly unwarranted, and it is well that the tough-minded philosopher makes this apparent. There is indeed much to complain about in the way in which parapsychology has been used for philosophical purposes.

It is also true that some philosophers (and parapsychologists) have placed too much credence in what are called in parapsychology "spontaneous cases," that is, largely anecdotal accounts by people from all walks of life of experiences which seem to them (and to others) to be psychical or paranormal, as, for example, visual apparitions of the dead and dying, telepathic communications from relatives or close friends, premonitory dreams, and so on. The tender-minded often take these to be the common experiences of humankind and, as such, surely indicative of something "real." But the tough-minded philosopher replies that hallucinations and chance coincidences are at least as common and much more probable. And so goes the debate.

But the tough-minded philosophers also make some mistakes. Their tendency is to reject parapsychological phenomena as "impossible," but on what grounds? Often it turns out that the data of parapsychology are impossible because they do not fit with a tough-minded view of the world; that is, parapsychology is supposed inconsistent with atheism, materialism, causal determinism, and, ultimately, with an empiricist theory of knowledge. The question-begging and often dogmatic nature of this position should be obvious. Tough-minded philosophers are hardly being empiricistic and skeptical if they hold that parapsychology is impossible because it is inconsistent with their own conclusions. But *is* parapsychology inconsistent with such conclusions?

To say that it is, is to concede too much to the tender-minded view. A careful study of the literature of parapsychology, together with a tough-minded world view, might lead quite plausibly to a reconciliation of the parapsychological evidence and tough-minded conclusions. The literature reveals a number of attempts to reconcile parapsychology with materialism and its attendant physicalistic theories of the mind.[4] Moreover, pointing out the *non sequitur* in arguing from parapsychological evidence to free will, for example, proves nothing about the truth of determinism, but it detracts nothing either. Much could be said about the extent to which parapsychology might be argued to be consistent with tough-minded conclusions, but there is a more important point to be made.

Notice that both the tough- and the tender-minded are regarding parapsychology only as a source of premises for, or potential counter-examples to, conclusions sought (often on other grounds as well) by the respective camps. Neither is treating parapsychology itself as an object for philosophical investigation; neither is admitting that parapsychology might have some philosophical interest in its own right. This is the key mistake of both the tough- and the tender-minded views, and it is a mistake with a long history. It lies at the heart of most discussions of the relevance of parapsychology to philosophy.[5] Note that there is nothing wrong *per se* in discussing the philosophical implications of parapsychology for questions in metaphysics or the philosophy of mind.[6] But it is wrong to think that such discussions are the *only* reason for philosophers to deal with parapsychology at all. And treating these issues without prior careful examination of parapsychology itself is fraught with the perils of ungrounded assumption, fallacious inference, and wasted mental effort.

False premises fail to support even the best of true conclusions. Arguments whose premises involve equivocation with respect to key terms produce fallacious conclusions. Purported arguments containing meaningless premises are not arguments at all. The moral, known to every student of elementary logic, is that unexamined premises are not worth asserting. The moral for philosophers looking to parapsychology as a source of premises is: examine parapsychology. Although this has not typically been done, it is crucial for a reasoned defense of either tough- or tender-minded conclusions in relation to parapsychological claims.

Philosophers in both camps would like their premises to be true, but where empirical claims are concerned, truth is a function of evidence. So the quality of parapsychological evidence and of the methods by which it is obtained should be of paramount importance. Moreover, in order to be true a statement must first be meaningful and unambiguous. Therefore, philosophical inquiries into the conceptual and methodological foundations of parapsychology must be regarded as logically prior to the use of parapsychological claims as premises leading to conclusions in metaphysics or the philosophy of mind. What is required, in short, is the careful study of the philosophy of parapsychology.

'Philosophy of parapsychology' is a phrase seldom used and perhaps therefore little understood. It may be explicated partially in terms of the contrast discussed above between the philosophical use of parapsychological claims and the philosophical examination of them. But the phrase 'philosophy of parapsychology' may also be clarified by analogy with such accepted phrases as 'philosophy of physics,' 'philosophy of biology,' or 'philosophy of the social sciences,' which are applied to the activities and results of extending the general analytical techniques and distinctions of the philosophy of science to a particular, specialized subject matter which is itself not philosophical, but empirical and scientific. Just as the philosophy of biology treats the concepts, methods, and theories of biology from a philosophical point of view, the philosophy of parapsychology might do the same for the research results claimed and theories advanced by parapsychologists. If the nature of explanation in biology, for example, is a legitimate and important philosophical issue, then surely the investigation of explanation in parapsychology has a right to attention from philosophers. If the inference of causal conclusions from statistical correlations is a philosophical problem of the social sciences generally, why not study it in the context of parapsychology in particular, where it arises with striking clarity? Of course any such philosophical investigation requires close familiarity with the actual methods and research results of the discipline under examination.[7] Such an enterprise also demands from its philosophical practitioners a judicious and open-minded outlook, an outlook unlike the extremes of either tough- or tender-mindedness, an outlook prepared to challenge methods and conclusions through constructive criticism.

Against my claimed analogy between the philosophy of parapsychology and the philosophy of various special sciences it might be objected that parapsychology, unlike, say, biology, is nonempirical and therefore not a science at all. The thrust of this objection might be either that parapsychology is nonempirical because its claims are not empirically falsifiable, or that it is nonempirical because it deals with "other-worldly" phenomena, with the paranormal.[8] But parapsychology as a putative science is not unfalsifiable; it is clearly possible to conceive of empirical evidence which would refute the various specific claims of experimental parapsychology. For example, it might be shown that each of the classic experiments or sets of experiments commonly accepted by parapsychologists as supporting the existence of some form of ESP or PK (psychokinesis) was *in fact* fraudulently conducted,[9] or is more plausibly interpreted as involving only known sensory means of communication. Were this sort of circumstance to occur, I think it is undeniable that the claims of parapsychology would have been falsified.[10]

In regard to the objection that parapsychology is unscientific because it treats of "other-worldly" or paranormal phenomena, the following reply seems appropriate. The proponent of such an objection appears to be trapped into accepting the idea that our existing body of scientific knowledge is both complete and correct as it stands.[11] But a moment's reflection is sufficient to reveal the untenability of such a position, since it must be acknowledged that scientific knowledge is basically open-ended, that the scientific principles and theories accepted today might be rejected on empirical grounds tomorrow. Serious study of the history of science provides an effective immunization against the all-too-common belief that science as it stands today is the final truth in matters empirical. To hold such a position is to deny a future to scientific research and, at the same time, to deny the lessons of history. There have been too many occasions in the past when the "other-worldly" has become a part of the scientist's stock in trade for such a position to be even remotely defensible.[12]

A second objection to my analogy might be to concede that although parapsychology is in principle an empirical science, it is not comparable to the other existing sciences because it possesses no well-defined and widely accepted body of theory which serves to characterize it and to distinguish it as a scientific discipline. Therefore, the objector might say, there is no subject matter for the philosopher of parapsychology to investigate. This objection has some force, in that there is no body of theory widely accepted by parapsychologists; however, there does seem to be substantial agreement among parapsychologists as regards the methodology of experimental research. One possible reply to this objection is to note that there are a number of other purportedly scientific disciplines, especially in the social sciences and including psychology proper, in which the theoretical situation is very similar in its lack of cohesiveness and pervasiveness to that which obtains in parapsychology. It might also be noted that, from a sociological point of view, parapsychology possesses many of the trappings of a science; it has its professional organizations and journals, it is recognized by wider scientific associations, such as the American Association for the Advancement of Science, and research reports by parapsychologists are (infrequently) published in prestigious scientific periodicals, such as *Nature.*

It is perhaps best to acknowledge that parapsychology is not now a theoretically highly developed science, but at the same time to insist that on methodological and sociological grounds it has a right to be treated as a potential science. Whether parapsychology will eventually develop into a full-fledged science, with its own body of theory based upon experimentally established facts, is of course one of the important questions to be raised in the philosophy of parapsychology. But clearly we can discuss such issues only by tentatively granting it the status of a possible science. This point of view is especially defensible if care is taken to limit the notion of scientific parapsychology to careful and systematic empirical investigations of such alleged phenomena as telepathy, clairvoyance, precognition, and psychokinesis, together with the theories and explanations proposed on the basis of such factual investigations. Holding to such a limited notion of parapsychology helps to legitimate its claims to scientific standing, while excluding the more fantastic and occult claims from parapsychology proper, insofar as they are not based on careful empirical research. Such a characterization of parapsychology will perhaps satisfy the critic who is wary lest superstition pose as science; at the same time it provides a reasonably well-defined subject matter for the philosopher of parapsychology to investigate.

In championing the philosophy of parapsychology I am not calling for the creation of a new area of philosophy out of whole cloth. Philosophy of parapsychology does not need to be invented—it already exists. Some of the best work by philosophers on parapsychological topics has been squarely in the philosophy of parapsychology, involving as it does the critical assessment of the concepts, theories, and experimental methods of practicing parapsychologists.[13] I think it is fair to say, however, that this sort of work has not received as much attention as the activities of philosophers attempting to defend their tough- or tender-minded metaphysics through the rejection or acceptance of parapsychological conclusions at best partially analyzed and understood. Philosophy of parapsychology, as contrasted above with applied parapsychology, does need a great deal more emphasis in the intellectual community and certainly deserves to be developed more systematically than has been the case until now.[14]

Some philosophers and parapsychologists might believe that, in defending the philosophy of parapsychology, I have advocated too narrow a conception of parapsychology. They might claim that, by construing parapsychology in such strictly empirical and narrowly scientific terms, I have ruled out of consideration certain types of evidence and certain issues which have historically been of central importance to the subject. In particular, it might be argued that I have excluded from consideration the evidence from spontaneous cases, from informal tests for telepathy and/or clairvoyance, and from mediumship. As regards spontaneous cases, my view of parapsychology does not rule them out as scientifically unsound, provided that they are well documented and empirically corroborated. In any case, I shall have more to say about spontaneous cases later in this essay. As far as informal and relatively uncontrolled "experiments" into telepathy or clairvoyance are concerned, my exclusion of them is quite intentional. It seems to me that we should evaluate the best evidence available for parapsychological phenomena, and I take this to be the evidence produced under controlled experimental conditions. If it should turn out that the experimental evidence is inadequate to support the claimed existence of ESP or PK, then I would hold that the less scientifically sound "evidence" must fall as well. My general position is perhaps a restrictive one: if no merit is to be found in the claims of scientific parapsychology, then philosophers can well afford to pay scant attention to the claims made with regard to nonscientific evidence of parapsychological phenomena. Parapsychology must, in my view, stand or fall on scientific grounds.

My exclusion of mediumistic phenomena from scientific parapsychology will particularly distress those philosophers and parapsychologists for whom the question of the possible survival of human personalities after bodily death is a central concern, since the major evidence claimed in support of survival derives from mediumistic sources. That there are philosophers and parapsychologists for whom the survival issue is of primary importance is undeniable. An examination of the philosophical and parapsychological literature soon reveals a substantial interest in the concept of survival and the evidence for it.

That the survival question has loomed so large in philosophical discussions of parapsychology seems to me unfortunate, especially when parapsychology is considered to be an empirical science. It is unfortunate because it has diverted the attention of philosophers from the consideration of important questions more central to parapsychology and because it has tended to encourage the view that parapsychology is primarily metaphysical or superstitious. Most significantly, it seems clear that survival, when identified with what has traditionally been called immortality of the individual soul, has not been, and perhaps cannot be, a subject to which scientific parapsychology has anything particularly helpful to contribute.

Souls are, after all, controversial. Whether or not humans have souls is hardly decidable on empirical grounds. But even if one assumes the existence of individual souls, what possible empirical evidence could demonstrate their post-mortem survival for the *infinite*, or even the indefinite, future?[15] Certainly parapsychology has not so far generated any such evidence and it is extremely questionable whether it could do so in principle. In any case the issue of the nature of the soul and its possible immortality is strictly philosophical, not parapsychological; it is a metaphysical issue, as Plato and Descartes well knew.[16]

If survival is not identified with personal immortality, but is rather construed as the possible continuation for a transient and finite period of fragments of an ante-mortem personality, then there might be empirical evidence for survival and parapsychology might provide at least some of it. But designing a suitable experiment to obtain such evidence would not be easy, and few, if any, such experiments have been attempted in the history of scientific parapsychology.[17] Most of the evidence for survival in this sense[18] is derived from two sources: (1) apparitions of or telepathic communications from the dead, as anecdotally reported; and (2) mediumistic phenomena, especially the much heralded "cross-correspondence" evidence.[19] But such "evidence" is of questionable reliability and has not generally been obtained under controlled conditions. It is clearly not the same sort of evidence as is claimed for the phenomena central to experimental parapsychology, such as telepathy, clairvoyance, and precognition.

Thus, even if it is conceded that empirical evidence of the transient continuation of fragments of a personality might be possible, this is not an issue which lies at the heart of scientific parapsychology and therefore it is not of fundamental importance to the philosophy of parapsychology. Insofar as the notion of survival is construed in the philosophically interesting way, namely, as involving immortality of the soul, it is not a parapsychological issue at all. Yet when survival is construed such that parapsychology might be relevant to it, the notion of survival involved is not philosophically so interesting.[20] Thus I think that the time of philosophers of parapsychology might be better spent in the analysis of issues more central to the discipline.

What, then, are some of the major issues with which the philosophy of parapsychology, as characterized above, should be concerned? In the remainder of this introductory essay, I shall indicate briefly what I take to be some of these issues and some possible approaches to them. Many of these topics are treated in greater detail in the essays included in this volume.

THE LANGUAGE OF PARAPSYCHOLOGY

The nomenclature and terminology of a given field at a particular time in its history—in effect, its "jargon"—reflects the theoretical and conceptual assumptions operative at that time. Terminological disagreements indicate a lack of consensus among practitioners as to these theoretical and conceptual commitments. The use of purportedly descriptive terms that are in fact theory-laden can create further difficulties in understanding the state of a discipline at a given time, and often effectively bars the introduction of alternative explanatory schemes for the interpretation of the existing data. It seems to me that all of these general considerations concerning language apply with special force to the current state of parapsychology.

Take the term 'parapsychology' itself. I have characterized it above as applying to the empirical, scientific investigation of apparently paranormal phenomena, such as those traditionally classed under such headings as 'telepathy,' 'clairvoyance,' 'precognition,' and 'psychokinesis.' My stress was on the empirical and systematic nature of these investigations, as contrasted with intuitive, anecdotal, literary, or even purely philosophical discussions of the paranormal. My intent was to leave open the questions whether such phenomena actually occur; whether, given their occurrence, they are physical or nonphysical in nature; and whether such phenomena, if they occur, involve the violation of currently accepted scientific laws and theories.

So my use of the term 'parapsychology' commits us to very little beyond a scientific approach to allegedly paranormal phenomena of certain sorts. It thus contrasts strikingly with some ways in which the term has been used by parapsychologists. For example, in adapting the German term 'parapsychologie' to characterize the field of his investigations, J. B. Rhine stressed in 1934 the notions: (1) that phenomena within the field, such as telepathy, clairvoyance, and various "physical" phenomena, "seem, superficially at least, to escape in a significant way certain laws of the natural world as we know it through our sciences;"[21] and (2) that "this evasion or circumvention is always a purposive or intelligent activity, as of the nature of personality in function; i.e., the 'psychic phenomenon' is characterized by the suggestion of personal agency in some form" thus bringing parapsychology "clearly within the field of Psychology."[22] Further, according to Rhine, the prefix 'para-' should not be taken "as implying that psychical research [which phrase Rhine treats as synonymous with 'parapsychology'][23] is outside the field of psychology—but simply that it is 'beside' psychology in the older and narrower conception."[24]

It is essentially this view of the meaning of 'parapsychology' that one finds in the glossary of technical terms published in the *Journal of Parapsychology* twenty-five years later: "parapsychology:—A division of psychology dealing with behavioral or personal effects that are demonstrably nonphysical (that is, which do not fall within the scope of known physical principles)."[25] But contrast with this the definition of 'parapsychology' found in the glossary appended to the current issue of the same journal: "parapsychology:—The branch of science that deals with psi communication, i.e., behavioral or personal exchanges with the environment which are extrasensorimotor—not dependent on the senses and muscles."[26] Clearly a significant shift has occurred in the manner in which the term 'parapsychology' is understood by at least some practitioners of the discipline.

I cannot discuss here the merits or defects of these and other senses of the term 'parapsychology.' But I do wish to stress the importance of investigating the uses of this and many other parapsychological terms as a means for understanding the various and shifting conceptions which underlie research and theorizing in the field. Indeed, it strikes me that a history of the evolution of key terms in parapsychology would contribute substantially to an improved appreciation of the conceptual changes and shifts in research loci which have occurred. I also wish to point out that it was the above sort of difficulty in regard to an acceptable definition of 'parapsychology' or 'psychical research' that avoided theoretical and philosophical presuppositions that led Thouless and Wiesner to recommend the neutral and noncommittal term 'psi' for use in the discussion of certain sorts of alleged phenomena and the results of research into them.[27] This term has gained currency in the last twenty-five years, especially among scientists sensitive to the theoretical commitments implicit in many uses of the more traditional terms 'parapsychology' and 'psychical research.'

Antony Flew defended the extension of the general sorts of considerations which led Thouless and Wiesner to exchange 'psi' for 'parapsychology' to support the elimination of the specific terms frequently used to describe certain sorts of experiments and research results, such as 'telepathy,' 'clairvoyance,' and 'precognition.'[28] Arguing that the use of such terms involved commitments to concepts and theories which went well beyond anything justified by the research data at hand (essentially the statistical frequencies of correct "guesses" under various controlled conditions), Flew suggested that, following Thouless and Wiesner, the term '$\psi\gamma$' replace 'ESP' and '$\psi\kappa$' replace 'PK,' with further subscripts to indicate the type of ESP. The use of such terms would make it possible to describe the correlations derived from experiments in the most neutral manner, leaving a wide open field for explanatory theorizing. As Flew put it: "What we need, therefore, is a new terminology which does not imply more than we want to imply, which is theoretically neutral, and which is not gratuitously provocative of philosophical perplexity. In the present state of our ignorance that means a terminology with the absolute minimum of implications."[29] This suggestion has not been widely followed, even though Flew provided an extended discussion of its merits from a philosophical point of view.[30]

On the other hand, John Beloff objects to the above sort of terminological proposal, not so much on the grounds that it commits us to too little , but because it implicitly commits us to the view that no explanation of parapsychological phenomena is possible at all. Characterizing this view and its consequences as "Flewism," Beloff claims that: "Its appeal is mainly to a certain type of common sense philosopher of the Anglo-American school who is deeply suspicious of anything that savours of occultism or mystery-mongering but, at the same time, is anxious to demonstrate his empirical commitment to the facts."[31]

I shall not here attempt to resolve this or any of the other philosophical debates which arise from the analysis of the language of parapsychology. My primary purpose is simply to stress the importance of such philosophical analysis for a clearer understanding of parapsychology and its claims, and, secondarily, to urge philosophers and historians of science to investigate these matters more frequently and more systematically in the future.

CHANCE, STATISTICAL CORRELATION, AND CAUSATION

Much of the early criticism of experimental parapsychology attacked the statistical methods utilized in "guessing" tests, particularly the basic "odds against chance guessing" approach of Rhine and his followers.[32] Insofar as the formal statistical techniques as such were at issue, they were by and large vindicated as standard techniques widely used in psychology and other sciences, and endorsed by professional statisticians. Some early criticisms were, however, aimed not at the formal statistics utilized but at the possibility of fallacious statistical conclusions arising from the methods used in selecting good subjects for continued testing, and from the practice of "optional stopping," which latter could be proven to give high "odds against chance" purely by chance.[33] Rhine denied these charges, while at the same time modifying his experimental designs to avoid the possibility of optional stopping. But in any case, more recent experiments by both Rhine and other investigators, especially those involving automated target selection and scoring, are designed in such a way as to avoid such criticisms.

A more radical line of attack on the statistical basis of parapsychological conclusions was to construe the experimental results themselves as a challenge to the concept of randomness underlying probability theory generally. The most notable proponent of this view was G. Spencer Brown, who argued that: "the logical form of the data derived from experiments in psychical research which depend upon statistical tests is such as to provide little evidence for telepathy, clairvoyance, precognition, psychokinesis, etc., but to give some grounds for questioning the practical validity of the test of significance used."[34] But, as Brown himself acknowledges, it is wrong to interpret this line of argument as an attack specifically aimed at parapsychology; if it succeeds, it is rather an attack on the results of all sciences and social sciences which draw conclusions using methods of statistical inference.

Another, and very different, challenge to the usual concept of randomness involves the notion of synchronicity, as presented first by Carl Jung[35] and recently further developed by Arthur Koestler.[36] Very roughly, the notion of synchronicity turns on the idea that there are some coincidences that are not chance coincidences, that these "synchronous events" are especially meaningful and important, and that it is such events that constitute the data of parapsychology. The main difficulty with this view is that the crucial notion of synchronicity in question seems never to have been formulated with sufficient clarity to distinguish synchronous events from chance coincidences that happen to be subjectively significant to some person or group of persons. And if this distinction canot be made, then the whole enterprise of interpreting parapsychology in terms of objective synchronicities in nature is without any foundation whatever.

An issue that has been discussed far less often than those just alluded to is the question how the statistical results in a typical ESP experiment are to be interpreted. Suppose a subject is able to "guess" the targets in a long series of GESP (General Extrasensory Perception)[37] runs at an average rate of ten correct per run of twenty-five targets. Assume a closed deck of twenty-five ESP (Zener) cards, five each of five different symbols. Assume also, for the sake of argument, that the experimental design is airtight, that is, no fraud, subconscious cueing, etc., is possible. The odds against a subject averaging ten "hits" per run over a series of, say, one hundred runs purely by chance are of course astronomical,[38] so it looks as if we must interpret the results in some other-than-chance terms. The conclusion usually drawn in such a case is that the subject in question has demonstrated ESP, or that ESP occurs. But what does this claim amount to?

I can think of at least four possible interpretations of the claim that ESP occurs under such conditions as those stated hypothetically above: (1) ESP is strongly correlated with high antichance scoring on such "guessing" tests; (2) ESP causes high scoring on such tests; (3) ESP is empirically, or contingently, identical to high antichance scoring; (4) the term 'ESP' means the ability to achieve high antichance scores on such tests. I do not have space to discuss these four possibilities in detail, but perhaps the following comments will suggest some possible lines of analysis of them.

Interpretation (2) above is clearly the one most often advanced by experimental parapsychologists, but is this interpretation justified by the evidence? (Assuming, you will recall, that the conditions under which the evidence is produced are unassailable.) In the first place, such an interpretation is subject to all of the philosophical doubts raised by philosophers of science in regard to the general practice, common in the social sciences, of drawing causal conclusions from mere statistical correlations. This procedure is especially questionable where there is no prior theory which warrants the prediction of such correlations or the assumption of a causal relationship among the variables. In parapsychology the latter difficulty is apparent; what we have most often in parapsychology are bare correlations in search of an explanatory theory. This difficulty is all the more obvious when we reflect upon the fact that it is difficult in parapsychology to predict or control the performance of even a given subject from one series of trials to another.

Furthermore, interpretation (2) assumes that we have independent knowledge of what ESP is and of the causal effects that it produces. To the extent that this might be held to be the case, our knowledge depends largely, if not exclusively, upon informal, anecdotal evidence of perhaps questionable scientific standing. If we have no independent scientific grounds for holding that the nature of ESP and its causal effects is understood, then it would seem unjustified to assert as an interpretation of the experimental evidence that ESP causes high scoring by the subject.

Interpretation (1) thus appears the more cautious and less theoretically questionable view of the evidence from "guessing" experiments. But it too presupposes a prior understanding of the nature of ESP, or at least an ability to identify persons possessing ESP independently of their performance as subjects in tests of the sort in question. If an empirical correlation is claimed between two variables, it must be possible to specify the two variables independently of one another. The history of experimental parapsychology reveals, however, that tests of this sort have been the primary and often the exclusive method for identifying subjects possessing ESP.

A further consideration is the fact that parapsychologists want to be in a position to claim that a person could possess ESP yet not perform well as a subject of such tests, either in certain circumstances (influence of drugs, exhaustion, illness, etc.,) or for a certain number of trials (decline effects). Thus, the possession of ESP is not a sufficient condition for high rates of scoring on such tests. (*Exercise* of ESP might be held to be such a sufficent condition, as contrasted with mere possession of ESP ability, but this is a distinction seldom, if ever, drawn in the experimental literature.) This point provides an additional difficulty with regard to at least some versions of interpretations (1) and (2), and, together with the difficulties mentioned above, effectively rules out interpretation (3). The latter is untenable, since for two empirical phenomena to be contingently identical each must be both a necessary and a sufficient condition of the other. (The problem of independent identification of ESP possession or exercise by a person also tells against interpretation (3).)

Are we then forced to adopt interpretation (4), that the term 'ESP' simply means (is defined as, is synonymous with) the ability to achieve high antichance scores on certain sorts of guessing tests? This is tantamount to an operational definition of 'ESP' in terms of the results of certain types of experiments and, as such, it is subject to the usual objections to operational definition. In particular, adopting this interpretation would commit us to the view that the term 'ESP' has no meaning in contexts other than those which provide its operationalization. This is a high price to pay for intelligibility, one which I suspect most parapsychologists would be unwilling to pay. There does seem, after all, to be some sense in which we understand the term 'ESP' in other scientific and nonscientific contexts and which leads us to construe the laboratory results as involving the exercise of ESP. In order to avoid this intuitive or prescientific connotation of the term 'ESP' the adherent of interpretation (4) should adopt a different term to characterize the experimental results in question. This is of course precisely what Flew has advocated,[39] and the result is what Beloff has dubbed "Flewism." But where does this leave us as far as our understanding of the informal, anecdotal evidence for ESP (otherwise defined) is concerned? Is this evidence somehow continuous with the laboratory evidence, or not?[40]

I cannot begin to resolve these issues of interpretation in this brief essay. Indeed, there may be other, better interpretations of the evidence which I have not even mentioned. Or perhaps a proper philosophical understanding of experimental parapsychology requires a pluralistic interpretative stance. I raise the issue because it is of fundamental importance in trying to comprehend and evaluate experimental parapsychology, and in the hope that even this brief discussion will lead to a more critical reading of the experimental conclusions presented by parapsychologists.

"SPONTANEOUS CASES" AND THEIR ROLE IN SCIENTIFIC PARAPSYCHOLOGY

It has often been held that "spontaneous cases" or anecdotal evidence, since derived from other than controlled conditions and frequently difficult or impossible to corroborate objectively, ought to have a heuristic, rather than a justificatory, status as regards the claims of scientific parapsychology. That is, carefully collected and systematically categorized spontaneous cases may suggest new lines of research or innovative experimental designs which will in turn lead to the verification of certain parapsychological claims. For example, anecdotal evidence from physical mediumship and from gambling is said to have led to controlled research into psychokinesis.[41] Another example is the laboratory research on dream telepathy by Krippner and Ullman, suggested by the large number of spontaneous cases involving information apparently acquired paranormally during dreams.[42] It is often further urged that, due to this heuristic status, the "natural history" of spontaneous cases plays a particularly important role in scientific parapsychology. That such cases have historically played such a role is no doubt true;[43] whether they should be accorded such importance is an issue open to at least some doubts, owing to certain rather striking differences between spontaneous cases and experimental evidence.

In the first place, each spontaneous case is a unique occurrence, the circumstances of which will never, and perhaps can never, be repeated.[44] In contrast, one objective of scientific parapsychology is to produce significant results under circumstances designed to be repeatable, in order that the results may be replicated by other parapsychologists. Second, experimental tests for ESP or PK involve intentional behavior on the part of either the subject or the agent (or both), while spontaneous cases seldom involve an explicit intention to communicate on the part of any of the persons involved. In spontaneous cases the percipient, in particular, is almost always a passive receiver of information, yet in experimental situations it has often been held that motivation to succeed and concentration on the task at hand on the part of the subject are crucial to a successful experimental outcome.[45] Somewhat paradoxically, the most convincing spontaneous cases are often those involving persons *not* predisposed to a belief in ESP or PK and not intending to communicate with anyone by paranormal means. Yet there is some experimental evidence that believers in ESP score higher on the usual sorts of guessing tests than do nonbelievers.[46]

Finally, in the typical experimental situation statistics involving precise "odds against chance" producing the result under tightly controlled conditions are the crux of the matter. In spontaneous cases, it is nearly always possible for the determined skeptic to "explain away" the evidence of a parapsychological phenomenon in terms of chance coincidence, or intentional fraud or unintentional misrepresentation. Whether the possibility of fraud is always an argument against the *experimental* evidence for parapsychological phenomenon is a much debated matter.[47] My own view is that, as a general claim, the argument from the possibility of fraud is scarcely more reasonable in regard to experimental parapsychology than it would be as a sweeping criticism of experiments in physics, and that the possibility of fraud in individual experiments must be evaluated on a case-by-case basis. But it does seem clear that arguments from the possibility of fraud are much more plausible when applied to the evidence claimed in spontaneous cases than when urged against (at least some) experimental results.

The intent of these remarks is not necessarily to suggest that spontaneous cases are irrelevant to scientific parapsychology. Rather I wish to advance the somewhat weaker claim that the continuity so often assumed between the phenomena evidenced in such cases and the phenomena of laboratory parapsychology is not so obviously justified when examined from a philosophically critical point of view. Further examination of the relationships between spontaneous cases and experimental results seems clearly desirable.

JAN LUDWIG

REPEATABILITY OF EXPERIMENTS

The alleged inability of parapsychologists to succeed in repeating the experimental results of other investigators has been a major criticism of parapsychology as a putative science, on the grounds that such repeatability is one hallmark of a genuine science. It is undeniable that failures to replicate experimental results have been common in the literature of scientific parapsychology, but the force of this criticism is somewhat diminished when the situation in orthodox psychology and other social sciences is also taken into consideration. For it is well known that repeatability of experiments is more difficult to accomplish in the sciences dealing with human activities than in the natural sciences, such as physics and chemistry.

Repeatability of experiments requires control of all variables relevant to the outcome of an experiment. But control of relevant variables in turn requires not only a sound experimental design and good technique, but, perhaps more importantly, an underlying theory which indicates clearly what sorts of variables are relevant to a particular type of outcome and what sorts are not. In the natural sciences, these conditions are often met, so that the physicist, for example, can have nearly total control of the experimental situation. In the social sciences, however, the experimental context is virtually never subject to such tight control, in part because the required theory is not so highly developed and in part because the social sciences involve human beings, who introduce many currently unknown sources of interference with the expected outcome. Indeed it is relatively common in the social sciences for variables believed to be spurious to be later discovered relevant to a particular result. Parapsychology, as one of the social sciences and one without a highly articulated theoretical structure, is of course particularly subject to these concerns.

But parapsychology, in contrast with most of the other social sciences, possesses another characteristic that renders the repeatability of experiments even more problematic. Most experiments in the social sciences, with perhaps some exceptions in psychology, lead to results stated in terms of the aggregate behavior of a large number of subjects. Individual idiosyncracies that inhibit the expected outcome in particular cases are effectively "cancelled out" when a statistical result over many cases is produced. Parapsychology, it seems to me, depends heavily upon the behavior of individual subjects; there is therefore more "room" for individual personality factors, physiological stress, etc., to influence the outcome of an experiment.[48] This renders a given experiment in parapsychology more difficult to replicate, not only with different subjects, but even with the same subjects at a different time. It is extraordinarily difficult, especially without a highly developed theory, to control for all the individual variables which might affect the performance of a subject at a particular time.

The import of my remarks is not to suggest that repeatability of experiments is impossible in parapsychology, nor that such repeatability is inappropriate as a measure of parapsychology's scientific standing. It is rather to urge that the criterion of repeatability imposed upon parapsychology should be a looser one appropriate to the social sciences, and that we should perhaps be more tolerant of failures to replicate results in parapsychology than we are even of such failures in other of the social sciences involving the statistical aggregation of individual behaviors. At the same time, it must be granted that successful repetition of parapsychological experiments is highly desirable and perhaps crucial to the long range acceptance of parapsychology as science.[49]

In the preceding sections I have tried to indicate what seem to me to be some important issues in the philosophy of parapsychology, as earlier characterized. There are, however, many other topics in the philosophy of parapsychology which merit serious discussion by philosophers. An issue of considerable importance is the question of the relationship of parapsychology to physics, and of the standing of parapsychology in the debate over the reducibility of all sciences to physics. J. B. Rhine, for example, has urged the incompatibility of parapsychology with "mechanistic materialism,"[50] which he takes to be the viewpoint which underlies the physical sciences, while other philosophers and parapsychologists have attempted to demonstrate that parapsychological phenomena can be explained on physical principles. Indeed, what might be termed the "paradox of J. B. Rhine" results from reflecting upon Rhine's claim to have produced experimental, scientific evidence for the existence of nonphysical phenomena. Perhaps this indicates that the level of the debate over the compatibility of parapsychology and physical theory would be raised by introducing the philosophical distinction between the linguistic or conceptual sense of scientific reduction and the ontological sense.[51] The latter involves the ontological status of entities described and theoretically presupposed by the various special sciences, while the former deals with the reducibility of a theory in one area of science to the concepts and laws comprising a theory in another scientific area. Thus, reducibility of one science to another might hold ontologically, but not conceptually. But, in any case, as Ernest Nagel has pointed out, before we can meaningfully debate the reducibility of theories one to another, the respective theories must be highly developed and unambiguously articulated.[52] Since this condition is not presently satisfied by parapsychology, it is perhaps premature even to raise the reducibility issue with respect to this discipline.

Other topics of importance in the philosophy of parapsychology include issues involving our concepts of space, time, and causality that arise particularly in connection with the parapsychological evidence for precognition,[53] and the challenges to our usual concepts of force and conservation of energy which may be posed by the claimed results of psychokinesis experiments. More intellectual effort should also be spent on the examination of parapsychology as a case study in the sociology of science. Such studies might repay dividends in terms of our understanding of the role of scientific institutions, channels of publication, and peer pressures in the development (or inhibition) of particular areas of scientific research.

It should now be clear that there is much work to be done in the philosophy of parapsychology, and that the issues involved are sufficiently important and central to the concerns of philosophers to repay the time and effort invested in the study of them. Particularly where a subject matter as controversial and, at the same time, as challenging as parapsychology is concerned, we should heed the advice of Glanvill and not rule out its claims as impossible without engaging in a careful and open-minded philosophical analysis of them. But, equally, we philosophers should not accept the conclusions of parapsychology without critically investigating them, since, as William James advises us in the essay which concludes this volume: "Tactically, it is far better to believe much too little than a little too much; . . . Better a little belief tied fast, better a small investment *salted down*, than a mass of comparative insecurity."[54] *

NOTES

1. For the curious, the book is: Margaret Underhill, *Your Infinite Possibilities* (London: Rider and Co., n.d. [c. 1925]), a prime example of the genre of post-mortem authorship.
2. See: William James, *Pragmatism* (New York: Longmans, Green, and Co., 1907), Lecture I, esp. pp. 11-13.

3. *Pragmatism,* pp. 12-13.

4. For one recent example, see: David E. Cooper, "ESP and the Materialist Theory of Mind," in Shivesh C. Thakur [editor], *Philosophy and Psychical Research* (London: George Allen & Unwin, 1976), pp. 59-80.

5. That is, most such discussions focus almost exclusively on the implications of parapsychology for traditional philosophical problems, or on parapsychology as a challenge to standard philosophical positions, as in C. D. Broad's "The Relevance of Psychical Research to Philosophy" (see pp. 43-63). The papers in Section I: "Paprapsychology and Philosoophy" provide some examples of this focus on the implications of parapsychology, as well as some attempts to urge the application of philosophical analysis to parapsychology itself, rather than exclusively discussing its implications for philosophy.

6. Some examples of such discussion appear in Section V of this book.

7. And, I would urge, some familiarity with the historical development of the discipline under philosophical examination. In the current postpositivist period, the importance of historical considerations is accepted by many philosophers of science working with the more traditional sciences, such as physics or biology. The history of parapsychology is equally important for the philosophy of parapsychology, but historians of science have by and large not yet applied their expertise to this field. For one interesting exception, see: Michael R. McVaugh and Seymour Mauskopf, "J. B. Rhine's *Extra-Sensory Perception* and Its Background in Psychical Research," *Isis* 67 (1976): pp. 160-189.

8. The term 'paranormal' is often used in discussions of parapsychology, but its meaning is seldom clear. Stephen E. Braude's essay, "On the Meaning of 'Paranormal,' " which appears on pp. 227-244, is a welcome attempt to bring some clarity to this problematic notion.

9. I stress that the experiments would have to be proven fraudulent *in fact.* Contrary to C. E. M. Hansel, I do not think it sufficient to prove the mere possibility of fraud in order to justify rejecting the parapsychological evidence. Cf., C. E. M. Hansel, *ESP: A Scientific Evaluation* (New York: Scribner's, 1966). Section II also deals with this issue.

10. That is to say, each of the particular claims that some form of ESP occurred in the context of a given experiment would have been falsified by a demonstration that fraud or sensory communication owing to inadequate experimental control produced the results. If all existing experimental claims could be thus falsified, this would show that there is (at present) no scientific evidence that ESP exists, but not, strictly speaking, that the general claim that ESP exists is false. No empirical evidence could ever in principle falsify the general claim that ESP exists (or occurs), if one has in mind conclusive falsification, since the potential favorable evidence cannot be exhausted. This is just as true of general existence claims in the physical sciences, such as "Magnetic monopoles exist," as it is of the claim that ESP exists. [For a discussion of this and related points, see: Norwood Russell Hanson, "What I Don't Believe," in Robert S. Cohen and Marx W. Wartofsky [editors], *Boston Studies in the Philosophy of Science, Volume III* (Dordrecht: D. Reidel Publishing Co., 1968), pp. 467-489.] But particular experiments claiming to demonstrate the existence of magnetic monopoles can be empirically falsified, just as the conclusions claimed in particular parapsychological experiments can be refuted on empirical grounds. And it is the empirical falsifiability of particular experimental conclusions that is at issue here, not the falsifiability of unqualified general existence claims. [My thanks to Willard Enteman for raising this point.]

11. Or that it has been finally established precisely what sorts of phenomena are acceptable as evidence in a scientific experiment. But this is also unsound; one has only to recall, for example, the insistence on the impossibility of action-at-a-distance during an earlier period in the history of physics to see the futility of assuming that acceptable types of scientific evidence can be given a closed definition, or specified by a closed set of criteria. The paper by Michael Scriven and Paul E. Meehl, "Compatability of Science and ESP" (pp. 187-190), provides some further discussion of the sorts of points I am raising here.

12. Some examples might be the alchemical doctrine of transmutation of chemical substances, the seventeenth century "speculations" concerning voyages to the moon, and the artificial creation of new life forms not found in nature. Many other examples could of course be found.

13. The papers included in Sections III and IV of this book are intended to represent work

solidly in the philosophy of parapsychology.

14. It seems to me particularly unfortunate that philosophers of science have paid relatively little attention to parapsychology, since the study of its literature reveals that many classic issues in the philosophy of science, such as the nature of explanation, the relationship of experiment to theory, the problem of induction and statistical inference, and the justification of causal claims, arise with striking clarity within parapsychology. Parapsychology also provides a nearly ideal context for discussions of the very basic question: What are the criteria which distinguish science from nonscience?

15. It might be held that human beings have souls that are metaphysically distinct from their bodies, but that souls have only a limited continuation beyond bodily death. Such a position is closely similar to the one discussed in the next paragraph.

16. Despite the empirical aspects of the Slave Boy passage in Plato's *Meno*, the conclusion reached on the basis of it depends crucially on Plato's metaphysical views. And of course it is debatable whether the passage in question proves the immortality of the soul, or merely its preexistence.

17. The only such "experiments" which come immediately to mind are the sporadic attempts to "weigh" the soul at the moment of death, and the occasional proposals to make ante-mortem arrangements for post-mortem communications through specific mediums, often involving sealed codes known only to the potential communicator. But such "experiments" have not generally been carefully conducted.

18. Actually, such evidence has usually been construed as supporting survival in the immortal soul sense, but this is clearly a mistake. At best, such evidence supports the relatively brief continuation of a personality after bodily death. To claim more for it is to introduce an unwarranted metaphysical assumption.

19. That is, messages from "beyond" involving several different mediums and sophisticated information which only makes sense when fitted together in complicated ways. For an extended discussion, with examples of the evidence from cross-correspondences, see: Gardner Murphy (with Laura A. Dale), *Challenge of Psychical Research* (New York: Harper & Row, 1961), Chapter VII.

20. There is of course some purely philosophical interest in discussions of the conceivability of individual survival, even in the more limited, transient sense. See, for example: H. H. Price, "Survival and the Idea of 'Another World'," *Proceedings of the Society for Psychical Research* 50 (1953): pp. 1-25; and Antony Flew, "Can a Man Witness His Own Funeral?", *Hibbert Journal* 54 (1956): pp. 242-250.

21. J. B. Rhine, *Extra-Sensory Perception* (Boston: Bruce Humphries, 1964), p. 3 (First published in 1934.)

22. Rhine, *Extra-Sensory Perception*, p. 4

23. Whether it is legitimate to treat 'parapsychology' and 'psychical research' as synonymous terms strikes me as a potentially interesting issue, but one which would require for its resolution a careful investigation into the history of these two terms and a systematic study of the various uses to which they have been put. On the surface at least, they do not appear synonymous, although they have often been treated as such, not only by Rhine, but by many other philosophers and parapsychologists as well.

24. Rhine, *Extra-Sensory Perception*, p. 6.

25. *Journal of Parapsychology* 23 (1959): p. 297. A glossary is appended to every issue of this journal.

26. *Journal of Parapsychology* 40 (1976), p. 356.

27. Robert H. Thouless and B. P Wiesner, "The Psi Process in Normal and 'Paranormal' Psychology," *Proceedings of the Society for Psychical Research* 48 (1946-49): pp. 177-196. Note the use of the term 'psi' in the definition of 'parapsychology' quoted above from the most recent issue of the *Journal of Parapsychology*.

28. See: Antony Flew, *A New Approach to Psychical Research* (London: Watts & Co., 1953), Chapter IX. [Revised version printed on pp. 207-226.]

29. Flew, *A New Approach to Psychical Research*, p. 116. [This book, p. 211.]

30. Flew, *A New Approach to Psychical Research*, pp. 111-117. [This book, pp. 207-212.]

31. John Beloff, "Epilogue-1977" to "Explaining the Paranormal," in this volume, pp.

367-368.

32. For an extensive bibliography of early criticism of experimental parapsychology, see: John L. Kennedy, "A Methodological Review of Extra-Sensory Perception," *Psychological Bulletin* 36 (1939): pp. 50-103. Some works dealing with the statistical basis of parapsychological research are included in the bibliography at the end of this volume.

33. See, for example: Clarence Leuba, "An Experiment to Test the Role of Chance in ESP Research," *Journal of Parapsychology* 2 (1938): pp. 217-221. Leuba does, however, appear to go too far in pushing his claims about the effects of selecting data. His position seems to require that all evidence ever generated (ever to be generated?!) anywhere must be included before any conclusion can be justifiably drawn as to the existence of ESP phenomena.

34. See: G. Spencer Brown, "Statistical Significance in Psychical Research," *Nature* 172 (1953): pp. 154-156 (quotation from p. 154); and, *Probability and Scientific Inference* (London: Longmans, Green, and Co., 1957).

35. C. G. Jung, "Synchronicity: An Acausal Connecting Principle," in C. G. Jung and W. Pauli, *The Interpretation of Nature and the Psyche* (New York: Pantheon Books, 1955).

36. See: Arthur Koestler, *The Roots of Coincidence* (New York: Random House, 1972), esp. Chapter 3; and also Koestler's contributions to: Alister Hardy, Robert Harvie, and Arther Koestler, *The Challenge of Chance* (New York: Random House, 1975).

37. "General Extrasensory Perception: ESP which could be either telepathy or clairvoyance or both." Quoted from the glossary in *Journal of Parapsychology* 40 (1976): p. 355.

38. Substantially less than 10^{-61}, using the critical ratio derived according to Rhine's now somewhat outmoded 1934 method. See Table XLIV, p. 226, of Rhine's *Extra-Sensory Perception*. Of course the exact value of such immense odds against chance is at best of academic interest.

39. See footnote 28, above.

40. I shall return to this question of the continuity between anecdotal and experimental evidence in the next section.

41. See, for example: J.B. Rhine, *The Reach of The Mind* (New York: William Sloane Associates, 1947), especially Chapter 6.

42. Compare Part I of Montague Ullman and Stanley Krippner (with Alan Vaughan), *Dream Telepathy* (New York: Macmillan, 1973).

43. Beginning with the early days of the Society for Psychical Research, which produced the monumental and now classic collection of spontaneous cases, *Phantasms of the Living*, by Edmund Gurney, Frederic W. H. Myers, and Frank Podmore (London: Rooms of the Society for Psychical Research, Trübner and Co., 1886).

44. Of course, it might be argued that, in a perhaps trivial sense, each event of any sort that ever occurs is unique, in that any other distinct event must occur at a different time or spatial location. This is not the sort of uniqueness I have in mind here. Rather, it seems to me that even the basic circumstances of a given spontaneous case, such as the person(s) involved, the nature of the information transferred, the apparent mode of transmission, the psychological and physical conditions, etc., are of such nature that they will never recur in precisely the same configuration. It is this characteristic of spontaneous cases which I wish to contrast with the ideal conditions of experimental control in parapsychology, and the corollary goal of the repeatability of experiments.

45. For example: J. B. Rhine, *Extra-Sensory Perception*, Chapter 12.

46. As reported in: Gertrude Schmeidler and R. A. McConnell, *ESP and Personality Patterns* (New Haven: Yale University Press, 1958).

47. See Section II of this book for one classic locus of this debate. See also Hansel's book referred to in footnote 9, above.

48. There have of course been group experiments in parapsychology involving the statistical aggregation of individual behaviors; for example, the sheep/goat experiments discussed in the work by Schmeidler and McConnell mentioned in footnote 46, above. But many of the classic experiments on the basis of which ESP is claimed to exist involve the performance of particular subjects, such as, for example, Basil Shackleton (Soal's work on precognition) and Hubert Pearce (the Pearce-Pratt distance tests at Duke University).

49. For further discussion of the repeatability issue, see the essays by Antony Flew, "Parapsychology Revisited: Laws, Miracles, and Repeatability," and Gardner Murphy, "The Problem of Repeatability in Psychical Research," in Section III, pp. 263-283.

50. Rhine's view is expressed in his essay, "The Science of Nonphysical Nature," *Journal of Philosophy* 51 (1954): pp. 801-810. [Reprinted on pp. 117-127.]

51. See, for instance: Carl G. Hempel, "Reduction: Ontological and Linguistic Facets," in Sidney Morgenbesser, Patrick Suppes, and Morton White [editors], *Philosophy, Science, and Method: Essays in Honor of Ernest Nagel* (New York: St. Martin's Press, 1969), pp. 179-199.

52. Ernest Nagel, *The Structure of Science* (New York: Harcourt, Brace & World, 1961), p. 345.

53. For a discussion of some of these issues, see Section IV.

54. William James, "Final Impressions of a Psychical Researcher," in his *Memories and Studies* (New York: Longmans, Green, and Co., 1912), p. 179. [Reprinted here, pp. 407-420; quotation on p. 409.]

* I would like to thank Willard Enteman and Wayne Somers for their helpful criticisms of an earlier draft of this essay.

Section 1

Parapsychology and Philosophy

C. D. Broad

The Relevance of Psychical Research to Philosophy

INTRODUCTION

I will begin this paper by stating in rough outline what I consider to be the relevance of psychical research to philosophy, and I shall devote the rest of it to developing this preliminary statement in detail.

In my opinion psychical research is highly relevant to philosophy for the following reasons. There are certain limiting principles which we unhesitatingly take for granted as the framework within which all our practical activities and our scientific theories are confined. Some of these seem to be self-evident. Others are so overwhelmingly supported by all the empirical facts which fall within the range of ordinary experience and the scientific elaborations of it (including under this heading orthodox psychology) that it hardly enters our heads to question them. Let us call these *Basic Limiting Principles*. Now psychical research is concerned with alleged events which seem *prima facie* to conflict with one or more of these principles. Let us call any event which seems *prima facie* to do this an *Ostensibly Paranormal Event*.

A psychical researcher has to raise the following questions about any ostensibly paranormal event which he investigates. (1) Did it really happen? Has it been accurately observed and correctly described? (2) Supposing that it really did happen and has been accurately observed and

Reprinted from *Philosophy*, volume 24 (1949), pp. 291-309, by permission of the Cambridge University Press.

correctly described, does it really conflict with any of the basic limiting principles? Can it not fairly be regarded merely as a strange coincidence, not outside the bounds of probability. Failing that, can it not be explained by reference to already known agents and laws? Failing that, can it not be explained by postulating agents or laws or both, which have not hitherto been recognized, but which fall within the framework of accepted basic limiting principles?

Now it might well have happened that every alleged ostensibly paranormal event which had been carefully investigated by a competent psychical researcher was found either not to have occurred at all, or to have been misdescribed in important respects, or to be a chance-coincidence not beyond the bounds of probability, or to be susceptible of an actual or hypothetical explanation within the framework of the basic limiting principles. If that had been so, philosophy could afford to ignore psychical research; for it is no part of its duty to imitate the White Knight by carrying a mousetrap when it goes out riding, on the offchance that there might be mice in the saddle. But that is not how things have in fact turned out. It will be enough at present to refer to a single instance, viz., Dr. Soal's experiments on card-guessing with Mr. Shackleton as subject, of which I gave a full account in *Philosophy* in 1944. There can be no doubt that the events described happened and were correctly reported; that the odds against chance-coincidence piled up to billions to one; and that the nature of the events, which involved both telepathy and precognition, conflicts with one or more of the basic limiting principles.

Granted that psychical research has established the occurrence of events which conflict with one or more of the basic limiting principles, one might still ask: How does this concern philosophy? Well, I think that there are some definitions of "philosophy," according to which it would not be concerned with these or any other newly discovered facts, no matter how startling. Suppose that philosophy consists in accepting without question, and then attempting to analyse, the beliefs which are common to contemporary plain men in Europe and North America, i.e., roughly the beliefs which such persons acquired uncritically in their nurseries and have since found no occasion to doubt. Then, perhaps, the only relevance of psychical research to philosophy would be to show that philosophy is an even more trivial academic exercise than plain men had been inclined to suspect. But, if we can judge of what philosophy *is* by what great philosophers have *done* in the past, its business is by no means confined to accepting without question, and trying to analyse, the beliefs held in common by contemporary European and North American plain men. Judged by that criterion, philosophy involves at least two other closely connected activities, which I call *Synopsis* and *Synthesis*. Synthesis is the deliberate viewing together of aspects of human experience which, for one reason or another, are generally kept apart by the plain man and even by the professional scientist or scholar. The object of synopsis is to try to find out how these various aspects are interrelated. Synthesis is the attempt to supply a coherent set of concepts and principles which shall cover satisfactorily all the regions of fact which have been viewed synoptically.

Now what I have called the basic limiting principles are plainly of great philosophical importance in connection with synopsis and synthesis. These principles do cover very satisfactorily an enormous range of well established facts of the most varied kinds. We are quite naturally inclined to think that they must be all-embracing; we are correspondingly loth to accept any alleged fact which seems to conflict with them; and, if we are forced to accept it, we strive desperately to house it within the accepted framework. But just in proportion to the philosophic importance of the basic limiting principles is the philosophic importance of any well-established exception to them. The speculative philosopher who is honest and competent will want to widen his synopsis so as to include these facts; and he will want to revise his fundamental concepts and basic limiting principles in such a way as to include the old and the new facts in a single coherent system.

THE BASIC LIMITING PRINCIPLES

I will now state some of the most important of the basic limiting principles which, apart from the findings of psychical research, are commonly accepted either as self-evident or as established by overwhelming and uniformly favourable empirical evidence. These fall into four main divisions, and in some of the divisions there are several principles.

(1) *General Principles of Causation.* (1.1) It is self-evidently impossible that an event should begin to have any effects before it has happened.

(1.2) It is impossible that an event which ends at a certain date should contribute to cause an event which begins at a later date unless the period between the two dates is occupied in one or other of the following ways. (i) The earlier event initiates a process of change, which continues throughout the period and at the end of it contributes to initiate the later event. Or (ii) the earlier event initiates some kind of structural modification which persists throughout the period. This begins to cooperate at the end of the period with some change which is then taking place, and together they cause the later event.

(1.3) It is impossible that an event, happening at a certain date and place, should produce an effect at a remote place unless a finite period elapses between the two events, and unless that period is occupied by a causal chain of events occurring successively at a series of points forming a continuous path between the two places.

(2) *Limitations on the Action of Mind on Matter.* It is impossible for an event in a person's mind to produce *directly* any change in the material world except certain changes in his own brain. It is true that it seems to him that many of his volitions produce directly certain movements in his fingers, feet, throat, tongue, etc. These are what he wills, and he knows nothing about the changes in his brain. Nevertheless, it is these brain-changes which are the immediate consequences of his volitions; and the willed movements of his fingers, etc., follow, if they do so, only as rather remote causal descendants.

(3) *Dependence of Mind on Brain.* A necessary, even if not a sufficient, immediate condition of any mental event is an event in the brain of a living body. Each different mental event is immediately conditioned by a different brain-event. Qualitatively dissimilar mental events are immediately conditioned by qualitatively dissimilar brain-events, and qualitatively similar mental events are immediately conditioned by qualitatively similar brain-events. Mental events which are so interconnected as to be experiences of the same person are immediately conditioned by brain-events which happen in the same brain. If two mental events are experiences of different persons, they are *in general* immediately conditioned by brain-events which occur in different brains. This is not, however, a rule without exceptions. In the first place, there are occasional but quite common experiences, occurring in sleep or delirium, whose immediate conditions are events in a certain brain, but which are so loosely connected with each other or with the stream of normal waking experiences conditioned by events in that brain that they scarcely belong to any recognizable person. Secondly, there are cases of multiple personality, described and treated by psychiatrists. Here the experiences which are immediately conditioned by events in a single brain seem to fall into two or more sets, each of which constitutes the experiences of a different person. Such different persons are, however, more closely interconnected in certain ways than two persons whose respective experiences are immediate-

ly conditioned by events in different brains.

(4) *Limitations on Ways of Acquiring Knowledge.* (4.1) It is impossible for a person to perceive a physical event or a material thing except by means of sensations which that event or thing produces in his mind. The object perceived is not the *immediate* cause of the sensations by which a person perceives it. The immediate cause of these is always a certain event in the percipient's brain; and the perceived object is (or is the seat of) a rather remote causal ancestor of this brain-event. The intermediate links in the causal chain are, first, a series of events in the space between the perceived object and the percipient's body; then an event in a receptor organ, such as his eye or ear; and then a series of events in the nerve connecting this receptor organ to his brain. When this causal chain is completed, and a sensory experience arises in the percipient's mind, that experience is not a state of acquaintance with the perceived external object, either as it was at the moment when it initiated this sequence of events or as it now is. The qualitative and relational character of the sensation is wholly determined by the event in the brain which is its immediate condition; and the character of the latter is in part dependent on the nature and state of the afferent nerve, of the receptor organ, and of the medium between the receptor and the perceived object.

(4.2) It is impossible for A to know what experiences B is having or has had except in one or other of the following ways. (i) By hearing and understanding sentences, descriptive of that experience, uttered by B, or by reading and understanding such sentences, written by B, or reproductions or translations of them. (I include under these headings messages in Morse or any other artificial language which is understood by A.) (ii) By hearing and interpreting cries which B makes, or seeing and interpreting his gestures, facial expressions, etc. (iii) By seeing, and making conscious or unconscious inferences from, persistent material records, such as tools, pottery, pictures, etc., which B has made or used in the past. (I include under this head seeing copies or transcriptions, etc., of such objects.)

Similar remarks apply, *mutatis mutandis*, to the conditions under which A can acquire from B knowledge of facts which B knows or acquaintance with propositions which B contemplates. Suppose that B knows a certain fact or is contemplating a certain proposition. Then the only way in which A can acquire from B knowledge of that fact or acquaintance with that proposition is by B stating it in sentences or other symbolic expressions which A can understand, and by A perceiving those expressions themselves, or reproductions or translations of them, and interpreting them.

(4.3) It is impossible for a person to forecast, except by chance, that an event of such and such a kind will happen at such and such a place and time except under one or other of the following conditions. (i) By making an inference from data supplied to him by his present sensations, introspections, or memories, together with his knowledge of certain rules of sequence which have hitherto prevailed in nature. (ii) By accepting from others, whom he trusts, either such data or such rules or both, and then making his own inferences: or by accepting from others the inferences which they have made from data which they claim to have had and regularities which they claim to have verified. (iii) By non-inferential expectations, based on associations which have been formed by certain repeated sequences in his past experience and which are now stimulated by some present experience.

It should be noted here that, when the event to be forecast by a person is a future experience or action of himself or of another person, we have a rather special case, which is worth particular mention, although it falls under one or other of the above headings. A may be able to forecast that he himself will have a certain experience or do a certain action, because he knows introspectively that he has formed a certain intention. He may be able to forecast that B will have a certain experience or do a certain action, because he has reason to believe, either from B's explicit statements or from other signs, that B has formed a certain intention.

(4.4) It is impossible for a person to know or have reason to believe that an event of such and such a kind happened at such and such a place and time in the past except under one or another of the following conditions. (i) That the event was an experience which he himself had during the lifetime of his present body; that this left a trace in him which has lasted until now; and that this trace can be stimulated as to give rise in him to a memory of that past experience. (ii) That the event was one which he witnessed during the lifetime of his present body; that the experience of witnessing it left a trace in him which has lasted till now; and that he now remembers the event witnessed, even though he may not be able to remember the experience of witnessing it. (iii) That the event was experienced or witnessed by someone else, who now remembers it and tells this person about it. (iv) That the event was experienced or witnessed by someone (whether this person himself or another), who made a record of it either at the time or afterwards from memory; that this record or copies or translations of it have survived; and that it is now perceptible by and intelligible to this person. (These four methods may be summarized under the heads of present memory, or testimony based on present memory or on records of past perceptions or memories.) (v) Explicit or implicit inference, either made by the person himself or made by others and accepted by him on their authority, from data supplied by present sense-perception, introspection, or memory, together with knowledge of certain laws of nature.

I do not assert that these nine instances of basic limiting principle are exhaustive, or that they are all logically independent of each other. But I think that they will suffice as examples of important restrictive principles of very wide range, which are commonly accepted today by educated plain men and by scientists in Europe and America.

GENERAL REMARKS ON PSYCHICAL RESEARCH

I turn now to psychical research. Before going into detail I will make some general remarks about its data, methods and affiliations.

(1) The subject may be, and has been, pursued in two ways. (i) As a critical investigation of accounts of events which, if they happened at all, did so spontaneously under conditions which had not been deliberately prearranged and cannot be repeated at will. (ii) As an experimental study, in which the investigator raises a definite question and prearranges the conditions so that the question will be answered in this, that, or the other way according as this, that, or the other observable event happens under the conditions. An extreme instance of the former is provided by the investigation of stories of the following kind. *A* asserts that he has had an hallucinatory waking experience of a very specific and uncommon kind, and that this experience either imitated in detail or unmistakably symbolized a certain crisis in the life of a certain other person *B*, e.g., death or a serious accident or sudden illness, which happened at roughly the same time. *A* claims that *B* was many miles away at the time, that he had no normal reason to expect that such an event would happen to *B*, and that he received no information of the event by normal means until afterwards. An extreme instance of the latter is provided by the card-guessing experiments of Dr. Soal in England or of Professor Rhine and his colleagues in U.S.A.

Intermediate between these two extremes would be any carefully planned and executed set of sittings with a trance-medium, such as the late Mr. Saltmarsh held with Mrs. Warren Elliott and described in Vol. XXXIX of the *S.P.R. Proceedings*.[2] In such cases the procedure is experimental at least in the following respects. A note-taker takes down everything that is said by sitter or medium, so that there is a permanent record from which an independent judge can estimate to a considerable extent whether the medium was "fishing" and whether the sitter was inadvertently giving hints. Various techniques are used in order to try to estimate objectively whether the statements of the medium which are alleged to concern a certain dead person do in fact fit the peculiarities of that person and the circumstances of his life to a significantly closer degree than might be expected from mere chance-coincidence. On the other hand, the procedure is non-experimental insofar as the sitter cannot ensure that the utterances of the entranced medium shall refer to pre-arranged topics or answer pre-arranged questions. He must be prepared to hear and to have recorded an immense amount of apparently irrelevant twaddle, in the hope that something importantly relevant to his investigation may be embedded in it.

(2) It seems to me that both methods are important, and that they stand in the following relations to each other. The sporadic cases, if genuine and really paranormal, are much richer in content and more interesting psychologically than the results of experiment with cards or drawings. In comparison with the latter they are as thunderstorms to the mild electrical effects of rubbing a bit of sealing wax with a silk handkerchief. But, taken in isolation from the experimentally established results, they suffer from the following defect. Any one of them separately might perhaps be regarded as an extraordinary chance-coincidence; though I do not myself think that this would be a reasonable view to take of them collectively, even if they were not supported by experimental evidence, when one considers the number and variety of such cases which have stood up to critical investigation. But, however that may be, there is no means of estimating *just how* unlikely it is that any one such case, or the whole collection of them, should be mere chance-coincidence.

Now, if there were no independent experimental evidence for telepathy, clairvoyance, precognition, etc., it would always be possible to take the following attitude towards the sporadic cases. "Certainly," it might be said, "the evidence seems watertight, and the unlikeliness of mere chance-coincidence seems enormous, even though one cannot assign a numerical measure to it. But, if the reported events were genuine, they would involve telepathy or clairvoyance or precognition. The antecedent improbability of these is practically infinite, whilst there is always a possibility of mistake or fraud even in the best attested and most carefully checked reports of any complex incident which cannot be repeated at will. And there is no coincidence so detailed and improbable that it may not happen occasionally in the course of history. Therefore, it is more reasonable to hold that even the best attested sporadic cases were either misreported or were extraordinary coincidences than to suppose that they happened as reported and that there was a causal connection between *A*'s experience and the nearly contemporary event in *B*'s life to which it seemed to correspond."

Now, whether this attitude would or would not be reasonable in the absence of experimental cases, it is not reasonable when the latter are taken into account and the sporadic cases are considered in relation to them. In card-guessing experiments, e.g., we can assign a numerical value to the most probable number of correct guesses in a given number of trials on the supposition that chance coincidence is the only factor involved. We can also assign a numerical value to the probability that, if chance coincidence only were involved, the actual number of correct guesses would exceed the most probable number by more than a given amount. We can then go on repeating the experiments, under precisely similar conditions, hundreds or thousands of times, with independent witnesses, elaborate checks on the records, and so on.

Now Dr. Soal, Professor Rhine and his colleagues, and Mr. Tyrrell, working quite independently of each other, have found that certain subjects can cognize correctly, with a frequency so greatly above chance-expectation that the odds against such an excess being fortuitous are billions to one, what another person *has been and is no longer perceiving,* what he *is contemporaneously perceiving,* and what he *will not begin to perceive until a few seconds later.* This happens under conditions where there is no possibility of relevant information being conveyed to the subject by normal sensory means, and where there is no possibility of his consciously or unconsciously inferring the future event from any data available to him at the time. It follows that the antecedent improbability of paranormal cognition, whether postcognitive, simultaneous, or precognitive, cannot reasonably be treated as practically infinite in the sporadic cases. These paranormal kinds of cognition must be reckoned with as experimentally verified possibilities, and, in view of this, it seems reasonable to accept and to build upon the best attested sporadic cases.

(3) The findings of psychical research should not be taken in complete isolation. It is useful to consider many of them in connection with certain admitted facts which fall within the range of orthodox abnormal psychology and psychiatry. The latter facts form the best bridge between ordinary

common sense and natural science (including normal psychology), on the one hand, and psychical research, on the other. As I have already mentioned in connection with Principle 3, the occurrence of dreams and delirium and the cases of multiple personality would suffice, even in the absence of all paranormal phenomena, to qualify the dogma that, if two mental events are experiences of different persons, they are always immediately conditioned by events in different brains. We can now go further than this. There are obvious and important analogies between the phenomena of trance-mediumship and those of alternating personality unaccompanied by alleged paranormal phenomena. Again, the fact of dreaming, and the still more startling facts of experimentally induced hypnotic hallucinations, show that each of us has within himself the power to produce, in response to suggestions from within or without, a more or less coherent quasi-sensory presentation of ostensible things and persons, which may easily be taken for a scene from the ordinary world of normal waking life. Cases of veridical hallucination corresponding to remote contemporary events, instances of haunted rooms, and so on, are slightly less incredible when regarded as due to this normal power, abnormally stimulated on rare occasions by a kind of hypnotic suggestion acting telepathically. It is certainly wise to press this kind of explanation as far as it will go, though one must be prepared for the possibility that it will not cover all the cases which we have to accept as genuine.

(4) If paranormal cognition and paranormal causation are facts, then it is quite likely that they are not confined to those very rare occasions on which they either manifest themselves sporadically in a spectacular way or to those very special conditions in which their presence can be experimentally established. They may well be continually operating in the background of our normal lives. Our understanding of, and our misunderstandings with, our fellowmen; our general emotional mood on certain occasions; the ideas which suddenly arise in our minds without any obvious introspectable cause; our unaccountable immediate emotional reactions towards certain persons; our sudden decisions where the introspectable motives seem equally balanced; and so on; all these may be in part determined by paranormal cognition and paranormal causal influences.

In this connection it seems to me that the following physical analogy is illuminating. Human beings have no special sensations in presence of magnetic fields. Had it not been for the two very contingent facts that there are loadstones, and that the one element (iron) which is strongly susceptible to magnetic influence is fairly common on earth, the existence of magnetism might have remained unsuspected to this day. Even so, it was regarded as a kind of mysterious anomaly until its connection with electricity was discovered and we gained the power to produce strong magnetic fields at will. Yet, all this while, magnetic fields had existed, and had been producing effects, whenever and wherever electric currents were passing. Is it not possible that natural mediums might be comparable to loadstones; that paranormal influences are as pervasive as magnetism; and that we fail to recognize this only because our knowledge and control of them are at about the same level as were men's knowledge and control of magnetism when Gilbert wrote his treatise on the magnet?

ESTABLISHED RESULTS OF PSYCHICAL RESEARCH

We can now consider in detail some well-established results of psychical research, which seem *prima facie* to conflict with one or more of our basic limiting principles.

I will begin with paranormal cognition. As I have said, the existence of this has been abundantly verified experimentally, and this fact makes it reasonable to accept the best attested and most carefully investigated of the sporadic cases as genuine instances of it. The following general remarks seem to be worth making about it.

(1) In much of the experimental work the word "cognition" must be interpreted behaviouristically, at least as regards the subject's introspectable mental processes. In Dr. Soal's experiments, e.g., the agent acts as if he often knows what card has been, or is now being, or very soon will be, looked at by the agent in an adjoining room. He does so in the following sense. He already knows that each of the cards bears a picture of one or other of a certain set of five animals. Whenever he receives a signal to inform him that the agent has just turned up a card he immediately writes down the initial letter of the name of one of these five animals. It is found that the letter thus written agrees with the name of the animal on the card which *will next* be turned up by the agent so often that the odds against such an excess of hits being a mere matter of chance are about 10^{35} to 1. Now the subject says that he writes down the initial letter "almost automatically" and that he seldom gets a mental image of the animal depicted. Again, he is not consciously aiming at guessing the nature of the card which *will next* be turned up. In the earlier experiments at least he was aiming at the card which he knew that the agent was *then* looking at.

Lastly, a whole series of 25 cards are turned up in fairly rapid succession, the average interval being about 2.5 seconds. The behaviourist character of the whole process is even more marked in Mr. Tyrrell's experiments. If there is genuine cognition, it takes place at some level which is not introspectable by the subject.

(2) A most interesting fact, which has been noted by several experimenters, is the occurrence of *significantly negative* results, i.e., scores which are so much *below* chance-expectation that the odds against getting such poor results merely by chance are enormous. In order consistently to score below chance-expectation the subject must presumably know at some level of his consciousness what the target card is, and must for some reason be impelled to write down some *other alternative*.

(3) It has been common for writers and experimenters in psychical research to subdivide paranormal cognition into telepathy, clairvoyance, precognition, etc. It should be noted, however, that the establishment of the occurrence of precognition makes it difficult in the case of many successful experiments to classify the results with confidence under any one of these heads. They are evidence for paranormal cognition of *some* kind, but it is uncertain of *which* kind.

I will now go a little further into this matter. We must allow for the following alternatives, which do not necessarily exclude each other. A causal condition of A's present paranormal cognition of x might be of any of the following kinds. (i) His own future normal cognition of x. This may be called a *precognitive autoscopic* condition. (ii) Another person's past, contemporary, or future normal cognition of x. This may be called a *telepathic* condition, and according to the temporal circumstances, it will be called *post-cognitive, simultaneous,* or *precognitive*.

Now in any actual case of paranormal cognition we can raise the question, with regard to each of these conditions or any combination of them, whether it was necessary and whether it was sufficient. It cannot have been necessary if the instance occurred in its absence. It cannot be *known* to have been sufficient, though it may in fact have been so, if others of these conditions were fulfilled in addition to it. If we could verify the occurrence of a paranormal cognition in a case where all these conditions were known to be absent, we might describe it as an instance of *pure clairvoyance*, which might be either post-cognitive, simultaneous, or precognitive. It should be noted that the word "clairvoyance," as I have just defined it, is a negative term. It denotes merely the occurrence of paranormal cognition in the absence of the autoscopic and the telepathic conditions. It is plainly difficult to imagine a case, in regard to which one could feel sure that it was purely clairvoyant. In order to be sure that *A*'s ostensible cognition of *x* was not conditioned either autoscopically or telepathically we should have to know that neither *A* himself nor anyone else would ever come to cognize *x* normally and that no one else either had cognized or was cognizing *x* normally at the time when *A*'s experience occurred. It is plain that all these negative conditions are seldom fulfilled. And, if they were, it is hard to see how *A* himself or anyone else could ascertain whether *A*'s ostensible cognition of *x* was veridical or delusive.

It does not follow that there are no cases of clairvoyance. For one or other of the autoscopic or telepathic conditions might be present in a particular case of paranormal cognition, but might either be not operating at all or be merely supplementing clairvoyance. Nor does it follow that there might not be cases in which an explanation in terms of autoscopy or telepathy, though possible, would be so far-fetched that it might be more plausible to describe them as instances of clairvoyance.

In Soal's experiments the autoscopic condition was absent; for the subject was not afterwards informed of the actual cards which had been turned up, and so could not have been autoscopically precognizing his own future state of normal information. Again, Soal interspersed among the normal runs of guesses, in which the agent took up the card and looked at it, other runs in which the agent merely touched the back of the card without looking at it. These variations were introduced sometimes with and sometimes without telling the subject. Now, in the interspersed runs the number of successful guesses sank to the level of chance-expectation, whilst in the normal runs, among which they were interspersed, it was very significantly above chance-expectation. So it would seem that, with this subject and these agents at any rate, the telepathic condition (in the precognitive form) is necessary to success.

In Mr. Tyrrell's experiments, however (*S.P.R. Proceedings,* Vol. 44)[3] the subject scored very significantly above chance-expectation under conditions where precognitive autoscopy and every kind of telepathy seem to be excluded. These experiments were of a very different nature and with a different subject. Here the agent would press one or other of five keys connected with small lamps in five light-tight boxes. The subject had to open the lid of the box in which she believed that the lamp had been lighted. Successes and failures were scored mechanically on a moving band of paper. Tyrrell introduced a commutator between the keys and the lamps. The effect of this was that the same key would light different lamps on different occasions, and that the agent would never know which lamp he was lighting when he pressed any particular key. Moreover, the automatic recorder merely marked success or failure; it did not show *which box* was responsible for any particular success. So it would not help the subject if she were precognitively aware either of her own or of the experimenter's subsequent normal perception of the record. It would seem, therefore, that there is good evidence for paranormal cognition under purely clairvoyant conditions. Good evidence under these conditions is also claimed by Professor Rhine and his colleagues.

THE ESTABLISHED RESULTS AND THE BASIC LIMITING PRINCIPLES

We are now in a position to confront our nine basic limiting principles with the results definitely established by experimental psychical research.

(1) Any paranormal cognition obtained under precognitive conditions, whether autoscopic or telepathic, seems *prima facie* to conflict with Principle 1.1. For the occurrence of the cognition seems to be in part determined by an event which will not happen until *after* it has occurred. E.g., in Soal's experiments the subject's act of writing down the initial letter of the name of a certain animal seems in many cases to be in part determined by the fact that the agent *will* a few seconds later be looking at a card on which that animal is depicted.

It also conflicts with Principle 4.3. For we should not count the forecasting of an event as an instance of *paranormal* cognition, unless we had convinced ourselves that the subject's success could not be accounted for either by his own inferences, or by his knowledge of inferences made by others, or by non-inferential expectations based on associations formed in his mind by repeated experiences of sequence in the past. Now in the case of such experiments as Dr. Soal's and Professor Rhine's all these kinds of explanation are ruled out by the design of the experiment. And in some of the best cases of sporadic precognition it seems practically certain that no such explanation can be given.

It seems to me fairly plain that the establishment of paranormal precognition requires a radical change in our conception of time, and probably a correlated change in our conception of causation. I do not believe that the modifications introduced into the notion of physical time and space by the Theory of Relativity are here relevant, except in the very general sense that they help to free our minds from inherited prejudices and to make us more ready to contemplate startling possibilities in this department. Suppose, e.g. that a person has an autoscopic paranormal precognition of some experience which he will have some time later. I do not see that anything that the Theory of Relativity tells us about the placing and dating of physical events by means of measuring-rods and clocks regulated by light-signals can serve directly to make such a fact intelligible.

(2) Paranormal cognition which takes place under conditions which are telepathic but not precognitive does not conflict with Principles 1.1 and 4.3. But it does seem *prima facie* to conflict with Principle 4.2, and also with Principle 2, 1.3, and 3.

As regards Principle 4.2, we should not count *A*'s knowledge of a contemporary or past experience of *B*'s as paranormal, unless we had convinced ourselves that *A* had not acquired it by any of the normal means enumerated in that Principle. The same remarks apply *mutatis mutandis* to *A*'s acquiring from *B* knowledge of a fact known to the latter, or to *A*'s becoming aware of a proposition which *B* is contemplating. Now, in the experimental cases of simultaneous or post-cognitive telepathy all possibilities of normal communication are carefully excluded by the nature of the experimental arrangements. And in the best of the sporadic cases there seems to be no reasonable doubt that they were in fact excluded. In many well attested and carefully investigated cases the two persons concerned were hundreds of miles apart, and out of reach of telephones and similar means of long-distance communication, at the time when the one had an experience which corresponded to an outstanding and roughly contemporary experience in the other.

If non-precognitive telepathy is to be consistent with Principle 3, we must suppose that an immediate necessary condition of *A*'s telepathic cognition of *B*'s experience is a certain event in *A*'s brain. If it is to be consistent with Principle 2, we cannot suppose that this event in *A*'s brain is produced *directly* by the experience of *B* which *A* telepathically cognizes. For Principle 2 asserts that the only change in the material world which an event in a person's mind can *directly* produce is a change in that person's own brain. If, further, it is to be consistent with Principle 1.3, the event in *B*'s brain, which is the immediate consequence in the material world of his experience, cannot *directly* raise the event in *A*'s brain which is the immediate necessary condition of *A*'s telepathic cognition of *B*'s experience. For there is a spatial gap between these two brain-events; and Principle 1.3 asserts that a finite period must elapse and that this must be occupied by a causal chain of events occurring successively at a series of points forming a continuous path between the two events.

So, if non-precognitive telepathy is to be reconciled with Principles 3, 2, and 1.3 taken together, it must be thought of as taking place in the following way. *B*'s experience has as its immediate concomitant or consequence a certain event in *B*'s brain. This initiates some kind of transmissive process which, after an interval of time, crosses the gap between *B*'s body and *A*'s body. There it gives rise to a certain change in *A*'s brain, and this is an immediate necessary condition of *A*'s telepathic cognition of *B*'s experience. I suspect that many people think vaguely of non-precognitive telepathy as a process somewhat analogous to the broadcasting of sounds or pictures. And I suspect that familiarity with the *existence* of wireless broadcasting, together with ignorance of the *nature* of the processes involved in it, has led many of our contemporaries, for completely irrelevant and invalid reasons, to accept the possibility of telepathy far more readily than their grandparents would have done, and to ignore the revolutionary consequences of the admission.

There is nothing in the known facts to lend any colour to this picture of the process underlying them. There is nothing to suggest that there is always an interval between the occurrence of an outstanding experience in *B* and the occurrence of a paranormal cognition of it in *A*, even when *B*'s and *A*'s bodies are very widely separated. When there is an interval there is nothing to suggest that it is correlated in any regular way with the distance between the two person's bodies at the time. This in itself would cast doubt on the hypothesis that, in all such cases, the interval is occupied by a causal chain of events occurring successively at a series of points forming a continuous path between the two places. Moreover, the frequent conjunction in experimental work of precognitive with non-precognitive telepathy, under very similar conditions, makes it hard to believe that the processes involved in the two are fundamentally different. But it is plain that the picture of a causal chain of successive events from an event in *B*'s brain through the intervening space to an event in *A*'s brain cannot represent what happened in *precognitive* telepathy. Then, again, there is no independent evidence for such an intermediating causal chain of events. Lastly, there is no evidence for holding that an experience of *B*'s is more likely to be cognized telepathically by *A* if he is in *B*'s neighbourhood at the time than if he is far away; or that the telepathic cognition, if it happens, is generally more vivid or detailed or correct in the former case than in the latter.

I do not consider that any of these objections singly, or all of them together, would conclusively disprove the suggestion that non-precognitive telepathy is compatible with Principles 3, 2, and 1.3. The suggested account of the process is least unplausible when *B*'s original experience takes the form of a visual or auditory perception or image, and *A*'s corresponding experience takes the form of a visual or auditory image or hallucinatory quasi-perception resembling *B*'s in considerable detail. But by no means all cases of non-precognitive telepathy take this simple form.

I can imagine cases, though I do not know whether there are any well-established instances of them, which would be almost impossible to reconcile with the three Principles in question. Suppose, e.g. that *B*, who understands Sanskrit, reads attentively a passage in that tongue enunciating some abstract and characteristic metaphysical proposition. Suppose that at about the same time his friend *A*, in a distant place, not knowing a word of Sanskrit, is moved to write down in English a passage which plainly corresponds in meaning. Then I do not see how the physical transmission theory could be stretched to cover the case.

(3) If there be paranormal cognition under purely clairvoyant conditions, it would seem to constitute an exception to Principle 4.1. For it would seem to be analogous to normal perception of a physical thing or event, insofar as it is not conditioned by the subject's own future normal knowledge of that object, or by any other person's normal knowledge of it, whether past, contemporary, or future. And yet, so far as one can see, it is quite unlike ordinary sense-perception. For it does not take place by means of a sensation, due to the stimulation of a receptor organ by a physical process emanating from the perceived object and the subsequent transmission of a nervous impulse from the stimulated receptor to the brain.

To sum up about the implications of the various kinds of paranormal cognition. It seems plain that they call for very radical changes in a number of our basic limiting principles. I have the impression that we should do well to consider much more seriously than we have hitherto been inclined to do the type of theory which Bergson put forward in connection with *normal* memory and sense-perception. The suggestion is that the function of the brain and nervous system and sense-organs is in the main *eliminative* and not productive. Each person is at each moment potentially capable of remembering all that has ever happened to him and of perceiving everything that is happening anywhere in the universe. The function of the brain and nervous system is to protect us from being overwhelmed and confused by this mass of largely useless and irrelevant knowledge, by shutting out most of what we should otherwise perceive or remember at any moment, and leaving only that very small and special selection which is likely to be practically useful. An extension or modification of this type of theory seems to offer better hopes of a coherent synthesis of normal and paranormal cognition than is offered by attempts to tinker with the orthodox notion of events in the brain and nervous system *generating sense-data.*

Another remark which seems relevant here is the following. Many contemporary philosophers are sympathetic to some form of the so-called "verification principle," i.e., roughly that a synthetic proposition is significant if and only if we can indicate what kind of experiences in assignable circumstances would tend to support or to weaken it. But this is generally combined with the tacit assumption that the only kinds of experience which could tend to support or to weaken such a proposition are sense-perceptions, introspections, and memories. If we have to accept the occurrence of various kinds of paranormal cognition, we ought to extend the verification principle to cover the possibility of propositions which are validated or invalidated by other kinds of cognitive experience beside those which have hitherto been generally admitted.

THE LESS FIRMLY ESTABLISHED RESULTS AND THE BASIC PRINCIPLES

So far I have dealt with paranormal facts which have been established to the satisfaction of everyone who is familiar with the evidence and is not the victim of invincible prejudice. I shall end my paper by referring to some alleged paranormal phenomena which are not in this overwhelmingly strong position, but which cannot safely be ignored by philosophers.

(1) Professor Rhine and his colleagues have produced what seems to be strong evidence for what they call *psycho-kinesis* under experimental conditions. The experiments take the general form of casting dice and trying to influence by volition the result of the throw. Some of these experiments are open to one or another of various kinds of criticism; and, so far as I am aware, all attempts made in England to reproduce the alleged psycho-kinetic effect under satisfactory conditions have failed to produce a sufficient divergence from chance-expectation to warrant a confident belief that any paranormal influence is acting on the dice. But the fact remains that a considerable number of the American experiments

seem to be immune to these criticisms, and that the degree of divergence from chance-expectation in these is great enough to be highly significant.

Along with these experimental results should be taken much more spectacular ostensibly telekinetic phenomena which are alleged to have been observed and photographed, under what seem to be satisfactory conditions, in presence of certain mediums. Perhaps the best attested case is that of the Austrian medium Rudi Schneider, investigated by several competent psychical researchers in England and in France between the first and the second world-wars.

We ought therefore to keep something more than an open mind towards the possibility that psycho-kinesis is a genuine fact. If it is so, we seem *prima facie* to have an exception to Principle 2. For, if psycho-kinesis really takes place in Rhine's experiments, an event in the subject's mind, viz., a volition that the dice shall fall in a certain way, seems to produce directly a change in a part of the material world outside his body, viz., in the dice. An alternative possibility would be that each of us had a kind of invisible and intangible but extended and dynamical "body," beside his ordinary visible and tangible body; and that it puts forth "pseudopods" which touch and affect external objects. (The results of Osty's experiments with Rudi Schneider provide fairly strong physical evidence for some such theory as this, however fantastic it may seem.)

(2) Lastly, there is the whole enormous and very complex and puzzling domain of trance mediumship and ostensible communications from the surviving spirits of specified persons who have died. To treat this adequately a whole series of papers would be needed. Here I must content myself with the following brief remarks.

There is no doubt that, amongst that flood of dreary irrelevance and high-falutin twaddle which is poured out by trance-mediums, there is a residuum of genuinely paranormal material of the following kind. A good medium with a good sitter will from time to time give information about events in the past life of a dead person who claims to be communicating at the time. The medium may have had no chance whatever to gain this information normally, and the facts asserted may at the time be unknown to the sitter or to anyone else who has sat with the medium. They may afterwards be verified and found to be highly characteristic of the ostensible communicator. Moreover, the style of the communication, and the mannerisms and even the voice of the medium while speaking, may seem to the sitter to be strongly reminiscent of the ostensible communicator. Lastly, there are a few cases in which the statements made and the directions given to the sitter seem to indicate the persistence of an intention formed by the dead man during his lifetime but not carried out. There are other cases in which the ostensible communicator asserts, and the nature of the communications seem to confirm, that action is being taken by him and others at and between the sittings in order to provide evidence of survival and identity.

Some of the best cases, if taken by themselves, do strongly suggest that the stream of interconnected events which constituted the mental history of a certain person is continued after the death of his body, i.e., that there are *post-mortem* experiences which are related to each other and to the *ante-mortem* experiences of this person in the same characteristic way in which his *ante-mortem* experiences were related to each other. In most of these cases the surviving person seems to be communicating only indirectly through the medium. The usual dramatic form of the sitting is that the medium's habitual trance-personality, speaking with the medium's vocal organs, makes statements which claim to be reports of what the surviving person is at the time directly communicating to it. But in some of the most striking cases the surviving person seems to take control of the medium's body, to oust both her normal personality and her habitual trance-personality, and to speak in its own characteristic voice and manner through the medium's lips.

If we take these cases at their face value, they seem flatly to contradict Principle 3. For this asserts that every different mental event is immediately conditioned by a different brain-event, and that mental events which are so interconnected as to be experiences of the same person are immediately conditioned by brain-events which occur in the same brain.

But I do not think that we ought to take the best cases in isolation from the mass of mediumistic material of a weaker kind. And we certainly ought not to take them in isolation from what psychiatrists and students of abnormal psychology tell us about alternations of personality in the absence of paranormal complications. Lastly, we ought certainly to view them against the background of established facts about the precognitive, telepathic, and clairvoyant powers of ordinary embodied human beings. There is no doubt at all that the best phenomena of trance-mediumship involve paranormal cognition of a high order. The only question is whether this, combined with alternations of personality and extraordinary but not paranormal powers of dramatization, will not suffice to account for the phenomena which *prima facie* suggest so strongly that some persons survive the death of their bodies and communicate through mediums. This I regard as at present an open question.

In conclusion I would make the following remark. The establishment of the existence of various forms of paranormal cognition has in one way helped and in another way hindered the efforts of those who seek to furnish empirical proof of human survival. It has helped, in so far as it has undermined that epiphenomenalist view of the human mind and all its activities, which all other known facts seem so strongly to support, and in view of which the hypothesis of human survival is antecedently so improbable as not to be worth serious consideration. It has hindered, in so far as it provides the basis for a more or less plausible explanation, in terms of established facts about the cognitive powers of embodied human minds, of phenomena which might otherwise seem to require the hypothesis of survival.

NOTES [Added by Editor.]

1. "Discussion: The Experimental Establishment of Telepathic Precognition," *Philosophy* 19 (1944), pp. 261-275.

2. H. F. Saltmarsh, "Report on the Investigation of Some Sittings with Mrs. Warren Elliott," *Proceedings of the Society for Psychical Research*, volume 39 (1929), pp. 47-184.

3. G. N. M. Tyrrell, "Further Research in Extra-Sensory Perception," *Proceedings of the Society for Psychical Research*, volume 44 (1936), pp. 99-167.

M. Kneale, R. Robinson, & C. W. K. Mundle

Symposium: Is Psychical Research Relevant to Philosophy?

I. ——*BY* M. KNEALE.

There are two ways in which one intellectual discipline may be relevant to another: the exponents of the one may be either the critics or the beneficiaries of the other, either the production experts or the consumers. Thus we can discuss whether philosophers should criticize the methods and arguments of psychical research, or whether they should take its results into account in pursuing their own studies. I am not going to discuss whether philosophers should act as critics to psychical research, although I think that they should. Their training fits them well for the task, and those of them who are experts in probability are particularly well-placed for criticizing the statistical methods recently used by some psychical researchers. But it is to the second question, which seems to me more difficult and more interesting, that I shall address myself. I shall, nevertheless, have some remarks to make on the critical function, for it is impossible entirely to separate the two.

The question calls for two definitions, that of psychical research and that of philosophy. The former need present no difficulty. At the present stage of development precision is impossible and a quasi-ostensive definition together with some explanation will suffice. Let me then define psychical research as the study of all those phenomena which are discussed by Mr. Tyrrell in his recent book, *The Personality of Man.* I will

Reprinted from the *Proceedings of the Aristotelian Society*, Supplementary Volume 24 (1950), pp. 173-231, by courtesy of the Editor of The Aristotelian Society. Copyright 1950 The Aristotelian Society.

explain further by saying that the phenomena are abnormal or queer in one of the following ways: Either (*a*) they are physical happenings of a sort not explicable in terms of the laws known to commonsense or science, *e.g.,* poltergeist phenomena and the physical phenomena occurring at some seances; or (*b*) they are the acquiring by human beings of information which they could not obtain in normal ways, because the events concerned are either too far separated in space and time or of such a sort as to be normally inaccessible to them. This covers the so-called mental phenomena, telepathy, clairvoyance and precognition. (I am using the current names. I don't think they are necessarily the best.)

This account of psychical research enables me to elucidate my question a little. It may be interpreted, "Should philosophers read Mr. Tyrrell's book and the works mentioned in his bibliography? Should they quote him and discuss what he says at their meetings and in their published works?" But in order to answer this question we need to know what philosophers should be doing, and so there arises the need for the second definition. This is much more troublesome, and I had hoped to avoid it, for I am inclined to think that philosophers recently have spent too much time in discussing what they should be doing rather than in doing something. However, the question lurks and cannot be ignored. I don't want to become involved in it and I don't want to shirk it. I shall try to avoid both alternatives, although with little hope of succeeding, by first saying something brief and dogmatic about the alternative views and then by adopting that interpretation of the philosopher's activity which appears least favourable to the position I shall take in this paper and arguing from that.

We have passed in this century from regarding philosophy as a peculiar non-inductive method of discovering highly general facts to thinking of it as linguistic analysis. I believe that these two views are not so different as they seem at first sight. The work done by the exponents of the two is much more similar than one would expect from their prefaces. This is because the factual enquiry is not so factual, nor the lingustic analysis so linguistic as is sometimes claimed. I hold therefore that for the purposes of this paper it does not matter so much which view one adopts as might appear at first sight. But in order to strengthen my position as much as possible I shall adopt for the purposes of the argument the position which makes it *prima facie* less plausible. I am going to maintain that philosophers should take notice of some peculiar empirical facts, and it is more difficult to maintain that empirical facts (except linguistic facts) are relevant to a linguistic enquiry than that they are relevant to a factual enquiry, however rarified. To illustrate this, it is more difficult to show that psychical research is relevant to Professor Ryle's enquiry in *The Concept of Mind* than it is to show that it is relevant to Professor Broad's enquiry in *The Mind and its Place in Nature*.

I am going to assume, then, that philosophy is a kind of linguistic analysis, but I must insist that it is the kind which not merely records usage but also criticizes and recommends new usage. This is done either because current usage involves contradictions or, more generally, because it is found inconvenient in describing the facts as we know them. For this reason empirical facts are relevant to philosophy, and philosophers have in fact always used them, both the empirical facts open to ordinary commonsense and the results of the special sciences.

It does not follow, then, that because psychical research presents empirical facts it is no concern of the philosopher, but we can still ask, "Why these particular facts?" Before trying to answer this question, I should perhaps meet another argument which might well be brought forward to show that philosophers should ignore psychical research. This is simply that there is "nothing in it," that psychical research has no peculiar facts to present. All that we have here can be found in other fields, that is, coincidence, fraud and credulity. To meet this argument fully would be to practise the critical faculty I have disclaimed: I have only two points to make in reply. First, many intelligent persons disagree with the criticism, and it is, in fact, very difficult to maintain after a real study of the evidence. Secondly, even if all the phenomena were in some sense bogus, psychical research would still be of some interest to philosophy although not in the way I think it is. The amount of gullibility involved would be of interest to the moralist and the political theorist.

But let us take for granted that psychical research has some peculiar facts to present. Why should the philosopher be concerned with them particularly? The answer in general terms is clear and has often been given. Their very queerness calls attention in an extremely forcible manner to the fact that the terminologies devised by common sense and science are not in all respects adequate for the description and explanation of all known empirical facts.

But an answer in general terms is not enough. It is necessary to produce detailed arguments to show how consideration of the facts of psychical research might lead philosophers to suggest modifications of terminologies or might cause them to suggest modifications different from those they do suggest.

In what follows, I shall try to produce some examples of such detailed argument. But before I do so I want to make one general remark. The sort of definition that I have had to give of psychical research shows that it is not, as yet, a science. Its results are not confirmed hypotheses, but simply queer empirical facts. Psychical research is what is left over when the regular sciences have marked out their territories. It is the collection of facts which physics, biology, psychology, etc., have failed to assimilate. It cannot therefore be expected that anyone should produce a philosophy of psychical research in the way in which a philosophy of physics, *i.e.,* a scheme of the interrelation of its basic terms might be produced. The different facts of psychical research are relevant to different parts of philosophical enquiry, partly to the philosophy of physics, partly to the philosophy of biology and psychology and partly to the critique of commonsense. For this reason I'm afraid, the following arguments may appear somewhat disjointed, but this is inevitable and in the nature of the case. Psychical research has a general relevance, I think, to that branch of philosophical enquiry which concerns the relationship of one scientific terminology to another and of scientific terminology in general to commonsense terminology. This I hope to point out at the end but the detailed enquiry must come first.

I shall therefore argue as follows: (*a*) The physical phenomena of psychical research call for some revision of the terminology of physics and also of the commonsense material object terminology. (*b*) The so-called mental phenomena should influence us in making recommendations for the revision of "mental" terminology and of the terminology to be used in making connections between mental and physical terms, that is, in our discussion of the "philosophy of mind" and the "mind-body problem." In this field I think that the facts of psychical research, perhaps rather surprisingly, do not, with one exception, suggest modifications which would not be suggested by other facts much more easily accessible. Their role is to throw into sharp relief certain facts which we all know perfectly well but are apt to forget as philosophers.

Let us now consider material object terminologies both at the scientific and commonsense levels. Of the former I can say very little. Professional philosophers have now almost ceased to criticize the terminology of physics, although this was once very much their field. This does not mean that there is no need for a philosophy of physics but that physicists must be their own philosophers. Nevertheless, I think that the professional philosopher might still, consistently with his modesty, point out to the physicists that they have not dealt with poltergeists and pseudopods yet. He might also point out that these phenomena are perhaps less alarming to the physicist than is sometimes supposed. Some authors (including a number of psychical researchers) have written as if to accept the genuineness of the physical phenomena of psychical research would be to deny what is already established in physics. I do not think there is so far any reason to believe this. We need not suppose that anything different will happen in physical laboratories if we accept the account of the Goligher séances[1] as literally true. Powerful mediums are not generally about in physical laboratories and the fact that queer things happen when they are about would not invalidate the laws of physics in general any more than the phenomena of magnetism invalidate the ordinary laws of mechanics for non-magnetized bodies. It may be said that this is not a fair analogy. Physics has thoroughly incorporated magnetism.

But the facts of psychical research are not only not incorporated: they even seem to be in contradiction with the most fundamental laws of physics, namely, those concerning the distribution and transference of energy. There are two points to be remembered, however. First, the phenomena of magnetism seemed at one time as rare, as mysterious, and even as magical as the facts of psychical research do now. I suppose that an obvious natural magnet is about as rare in physical nature as a good physical medium is among persons. Secondly, it is not established that the phenomena are in contradiction with the fundamental laws of physics; for, so far as I know, these phenomena have never been thoroughly investigated with a view to determining what transferences of energy they involve. This is obviously the first step, and when this is done, a fundamental revision may or may not be necessary. But if so, why not? It won't be the first time.

We might look at this in another way, Poltergeist phenomena and the like call for a decision on the scope of the term "physical science." If we decide to use the term so as to include the study of these phenomena, then we must say that there are some physical phenomena which have not yet been investigated, meaning by "physical" "such as are the concern of physical science." If we decide to use the term so as to exclude the study of them, then we must say that there are some changes in material objects in the commonsense meaning of the words which are not the concern of physical science. What we cannot do is to maintain that physical science applies universally to all changes in material objects and that it is not concerned with poltergeist phenomena. This would seem to be a philosophically unsound position involving us in the last resort in saying that the same event both is and is not a change in a material object—unless, indeed, we were prepared to recommend a revision of a commonsense terminology to the effect that objects thrown about by poltergeists are not, when thrown, material objects, a revision far too drastic to be at all advisable, since commonsense is firmly convinced that the objects thrown about by poltergeists are material objects. But some other phenomena raise questions on which commonsense is still undecided, *i.e.,* on which its terminology is still fluid. Is a pseudopod a material object or not? If we decide to say that it is, we shall have to drop some of the implications of the term "material object" as to mode of production, permanence, etc. Only further empirical investigation would enable us to determine which use is most convenient.

There is a philosophical controversy concerning material-object terms to which psychical research is not, I think, relevant, although some writers on the subject seem to have thought that it is. This is the controversy between phenomenalists and non-phenomenalists. The late Mr. Whately Carington,[2] for example, seems to hold that the facts of psychical research somehow tell in favour of phenomenalism in that they are easier to describe or account for if phenomenalism is true. The argument seems to be something like this. The sense-datum terminology recommended by phenomenalists is adequate for the description of apparitions. Therefore the terminology has a use. Let us then adopt it for describing material objects as well, and we shall then be no more puzzled by apparitions than by material objects. This, of course, will not do, for the issue between phenomenalists and anti-phenomenalists is just whether the sense-datum terminology is adequate for the description of material objects and it is quite irrelevant to this that it is adequate for the description of something else.

The so-called mental phenomena of psychical research, if relevant at all, will be relevant to what used to be called "the philosophy of mind." As an instance of this I want to consider Professor Ryle's *Concept of Mind* and especially the chapter on the imagination, and to suggest that one might have to modify some of its conclusions if one considered carefully the facts of psychical research.

Professor Ryle distinguishes two concepts, seeing and "seeing." He describes the difference as follows:—

To see is one thing; to picture or visualize is another. A person can see things only when his eyes are open, and when his surroundings are illuminated; but he can have pictures in his mind's eye, when his eyes are shut and when the world is dark. Similarly, he can hear music only in situations in which other people could also hear it; but a tune can run in his head, when his neighbours can hear no music at all. Moreover he can see only what there is to be seen and hear only what is there to be heard, and often he cannot help seeing and hearing what is there to be seen and heard; but on some occasions he can choose what pictures shall be before his mind's eye and what verses or tunes he shall go over in his head.

One way in which people tend to express this difference is by writing that, whereas, they see trees and hear music, they only 'see' in inverted commas the objects of recollection and imagination.

Now which of Professor Ryle's terms applies to the following case?

Mr. and Mrs. Clifford Pye were on holiday in Cornwall in 1933 and were travelling by bus from Wadebridge to Boscastle. As they neared Boscastle they kept a good lookout for a suitable hotel in which to stay, and just before they reached the point at which the road drops steeply down into the village the bus stopped to set down a passenger. Mr. Pye writes: "It had come to rest almost outside the gates of a rather substantial house, standing on the left-hand side of the road. It stood back from the road some twenty yards or so, there being a semi-circular drive from the gate outside which we stopped to another gate twenty five yards further. The garden front was screened from the road by a hedge over which we could just see from our seats in the bus . . . the most striking feature, however, was the lawn, where among beds of scarlet geraniums, there were several wicker or cane chairs and tables over which were standing large garden umbrellas of black and orange. . . . I called my wife's attention to the place and she immediately replied that it was just what we were looking for but before we could come to any decision, the bus moved off and in two or three minutes we were down in Boscastle."

Mr. and Mrs. Pye were not much attracted by the village of Boscastle, so, while Mr. Pye stayed with the luggage, his wife walked back up the hill and tried to book rooms at the guest-house they had seen from the bus. After nearly an hour and a half Mrs. Pye returned, looking considerably heated, and said that she had not been able to find it. . . . She seemed much astonished, and Mr. Pye said that he would point out the guest-house to her as they returned along the road. On the returning bus, just as they reached the top of the hill, Mr. Pye remarked: "It's just here on the right—about fifty yards further on—" but to [his] astonishment "there was no house . . . just empty fields running across to the cliffs by Blackapit."[3]

I am inclined to think that Professor Ryle would put this case under "seeing," and maintain that Mr. and Mrs. Pye were "seeing" but mistakenly believing that they were seeing, for he says:—

The fact that in certain conditions he fails to realize that he is not seeing but only 'seeing,' as in dreams, delirium, extreme thirst, hypnosis, and conjuring shows, does not in any degree tend to obliterate the distinction between the concept of seeing and that of 'seeing.'[4]

But this would be very odd for the experience of Mr. and Mrs. Pye has many of the characteristics of seeing as described by Professor Ryle, *e.g.,* they could only see the house when their eyes were open and they had to see it when their eyes were open. Again I think that Professor Ryle would say that "seeing" is not any kind of observing, but it would be odd to deny that Mr. Pye in the sentences quoted is reporting his observations.

Professor Ryle must, I suspect, allow at least three concepts, seeing, "seeing" and what might be called hallucinatory seeing. I think it is at least unnatural in the case of hallucinatory seeing not to use a terminology of "special status objects." It seems odd to say of Mr. and Mrs. Pye that they were not "being spectators of the resemblance of a house" but only "resembling spectators of a house."

I think that this could be developed much further and that the logic we develop for hallucinatory seeing might have repercussions upon that of Professor Ryle's "seeing," but this is not the time to develop this point.

It will be noticed that material from psychical research is not really necessary to make this point. Any really good visual hallucination, or even an eidetic image, would do as well. This, as I said before, is true in general of the mental phenomena of psychical research. They are, in a sense, not peculiar phenomena, but rather examples in peculiar settings of very common phenomena. I shall try to illustrate the point further first by reference to telepathy and secondly by reference to the much more doubtful phenomenon known as psychokinesis.

Telepathy is an example of the influencing of one person by another, a thing that can be done in a great variety of ways, *e.g.,* by talking, shouting, hitting. The curious feature in pure telepathy is that the transaction takes place apparently without any physical intermediary. One person causes another to have an image, form a belief, or experience a feeling simply by having an image, belief, or feeling himself. The images, thoughts, or feelings belong in each case solely to the private or inner lives of the persons concerned. This is of great philosophical importance because it establishes beyond any doubt that in order to say all there is to say about persons we must have a vocabulary for the inner as well as for the outer life. In other words we cannot manage with a purely behaviouristic terminology. The temptation to suppose that we can arises partly from assumption that all *transactions* between persons are describable without reference to the inner life: when they make this assumption, psychologists who are interested chiefly in transaction naturally think that the vocabulary of the inner life is superfluous. The occurrence of telepathy shows that this is not so.

Here, I think, lies the main philosophical interest of telepathy, and yet we do not really need telepathy to make the point, because we all know perfectly well that almost all transactions between persons involve their inner lives. In saying this I may seem to be crying down the philosophical interest of telepathy. Much more has often been claimed for it, but some at least of the claims are mistaken. For example, telepathy provides no answer to the question "How do we know that other people have minds or inner lives?" because, as Professor Price has already pointed out,[5] it is a causal transaction between persons, and not the direct inspection by one person of another person's inner life. A claim to such inspection would, I think, be a contradiction in terms.

There are, of course, other philosophical questions which arise in connection with telepathy. The most obvious is, "What is the best terminology in which to formulate a scientific hypothesis about the conditions of its occurrence?" Mr. Whately Carington suggested the vocabulary of unconscious mental processes which has been found useful by psychoanalysts.[6] I think that the discussion of the fruitfulness and adequacy of this terminology is a philosophical task according to the concept of philosophy adopted at the beginning of this paper.

I have said above that it is necessary to have a vocabulary to describe a person's inner life and in order to develop my argument further, it is necessary to give some indication of the scope of this vocabulary. It must include terms for Professor Ryle's "perceiving" in all its forms (although, for reasons into which I needn't go now, I should prefer to keep the older vocabulary of "images") and also terms for what Professor Ryle calls "agitations" and for what he calls "moods."

Since we must admit such a terminology, there arises the philosophical question, "In what sorts of sentences can the inner life terminology be combined with other terminologies and more especially material object terminology?" A large part of what used to be called the mind-body problem can be reduced to the enquiry, "Is it permissible to use the words 'Cause,' 'account for,' 'explain' in such mixed sentences?" Our commonsense vocabulary, which is mixed, allows such combinations. Thus, "His terror (agitation-word) caused him to stumble over the rock (material object words)." By far the most familiar type of mixed sentence, and the one I want to discuss particularly now, is of the form "I ate the chocolates because I wanted to." "Wanted" here is part of the inner life vocabulary and refers to the occurrence of imaging together with a mild agitation. The philosophical doubts as to the propriety of this terminology have been largely occasioned by the empirical fact that physical scientists have made such remarkable progress since adopting the methodological principle of always looking for physical events as the necessary and sufficient conditions of physical events. But in spite of this we all know as certainly as we ever know any proposition of this kind that an event of the inner life is sometimes at least a necessary condition of a physical event. The writing of this would not have occurred without some previous imaging on my part. This is not necessarily true of all writing, but it is true of this particular case. Now the relevance of psycho-kinesis is that it suggests not only that it is proper to use this terminology in the contexts in which we always do use it, although some philosophers have said we mustn't, but also in other and more surprising contexts. What is shown if we accept the facts is that we can cause physical events by thinking of them not only in our own bodies but elsewhere. It provides a kind of *a fortiori* argument for the obvious: "Of course we can use causal language to describe the connection between our imaginings and happenings in our own bodies, because on certain occasions we can use it to describe the connection between our imaginings and happenings in other and detached bodies."

The pattern of relevance in both telepathy and psychokinesis is the same. By finding an unexpected application for it, they recommend to us again a commonsense terminology which was in danger of being rejected in favour of one supposedly more in accordance with the demands of science.

Again, as in the case of telepathy, other philosophical questions are raised. For instance, "What is a person's 'body'?" In commonsense language, I think, that part of the criterion of a physical object being or belonging to my body is that I have some degree of direct control over it. I can make things happen to it merely by thinking of them. Suppose now that psycho-kinesis were established: should we say that the agent's body is temporarily extended, or allow him direct control over things that are not his own body or part of his own body?

These points may perhaps seem trivial. If this is all we can get for philosophy from psychical research and it is admitted that we can get the most important points elsewhere, is it worth our while to bother about it? I think that, even if this were all the relevance, it would still be worth while, because we are very apt as philosophers to forget the most obvious points. But this is not all. The full effect of psychical research on the group of problems formerly treated as the "mind-body" problem can only be known when a terminology has been worked out for scientific hypotheses about telepathy and psychokinesis. In the present paper I have not scope even to attempt this. I have made points that are perhaps trivial and obvious in order to show that there are points to be made. That the behaviouristic terminology will not suffice for the description of human life will perhaps serve as an example of a nontrivial point that can be made.

Another point that is perhaps not trivial is that the hypothesis of human survival is not meaningless, as some philosophers have claimed. This follows from the fact that we can and must have an "inner life" terminology. It then becomes possible to ask whether events describable in that terminology and assignable to me will occur after my physical death. The point can also be made very simply by considering what actually happens when we consider some of the writings of psychical researchers. After reading the accounts of cross-correspondences published by the S.P.R., we can all sit down and ask ourselves, "Does this constitute evidence for human survival or not?" And, if so, we must know what we mean by "human survival."

There is one final point of great importance to be made about the relevance of psychical research to the philosophical enquiry concerning the relationships of different terminologies to each other, but before I make it, I want to say something about the one phenomenon of psychical research on the "mental" side which might suggest revisions of terminology that would not be suggested in any other way. I refer to what is generally known as "precognition." It seems very appropriate that I should mention it since it was when we last met at Bristol that Professor Price and Professor Broad discussed some very startling revisions of terminology in this connection. I have also a personal reason for mentioning it, since it was the experience in very early life of having what would most naturally be interpreted as precognitive dreams that has led me to have a receptive or at any rate open-minded attitude towards the phenomena of psychical research.

In connection with this phenomenon I think it is very necessary for the philosopher to step in as critic and point out in the first place that "precognition" is never strictly "fore-knowledge" and rarely even "fore-belief," but is better described as "fore-imaging," and secondly that a great many cases seem to allow of alternative interpretations, *i.e.,* as telepathy or clairvoyance. This is the case with my own dreams, for example. Nevertheless there does remain a hard core of cases which must either be labelled "fore-imaging" or relegated to the inexplicable by being labelled "coincidence.""It is in order to cover these cases that it is said that we must radically revise the logic of the terms "cause" and "time." I have no such radical revisions to offer and I hope that they may be avoided. At present the phenomenon serves only the useful function of reminding us that there is still very much that eludes the descriptive and explanatory net.

It will also serve to introduce a further point. It is quite common among writers on psychical research after discussing precognition, to refer to the nothingness of time and allude to religious mysticism. This seems to me wholly irrelevant and I think it is part of the philosopher's job to point out that it is so. In other words it is a philosophical task to assign human enquiries to their proper type and point out their affinities. For historical reasons psychical research has been much "mixed up" with religion, but it seems to me that its affinities are with the empirical sciences, not with theology or religion. And this, whether right or wrong, is a philosophical remark.

My last point is a general remark about the relevance of psychical research to philosophy. We have seen that in two instances the consideration of psychical research would lead us back from scientific to commonsense terminology. This is what we should expect if I was right in what I said about the nature of psychical research at the beginning. Psychical research covers just those facts which are left out by science and can therefore be described only in commonsense terminology. Here we find the crucial difference between commonsense and scientific terminology. Commonsense terminology is in its nature indefinitely extensible, so that anything that occurs can be described in it. Scientific terminologies on the other hand have been carefully devised for the description of certain fields of experience and are constantly subject to philosophical criticism so that they have a rigid structure which prevents them being used in the description of other fields. There is a point at which any given scientific terminologies break down. Psychical research reveals the points where all scientific terminologies break down. This doesn't mean, as some philosophers seemed inclined to suggest now, that we should turn back to commonsense and rest happy there. Commonsense terminology has the defects of its virtues. Anything can be said in it, but a good many things can only be said badly. For example the few technical terms of psychical research which are an extension of commonsense without benefit of philosophical criticism are mostly very bad and misleading. But this doesn't mean again that we must drop commonsense and try to describe everything in some existing scientific terminology (the thesis of the physicalists). There are many sciences instead of one just because one terminology is not adequate to describe everything. The moral is that we must try to devise a terminology which has the merits of both scientific and commonsense terminologies in being both universal in its application and precise. From this point of view it seems that psychical research is not only relevant to philosophy but should constitute one of its main fields of interest, as revealing just those points at which all current terminologies need revision.

NOTES

1. *See* W. J. Crawford. *The Reality of Psychic Phenomena.*
2. *See Matter, Mind and Measuring* p. 120. [*Sic*; presumably *Matter, Mind, and Meaning*—Ed.]
3. Journal S.P.R., Vol. 32. Quoted by Tyrrell. *Personality of Man*, pp. 65-66.
4. Loc. cit.
5. *Philosophy*, 1938, pp. 426-7.
6. See *Matter, Mind and Meaning.*
7. Eq. the coin of M. de Ch., Quoted by Tyrrell, pp. 81-2.

II. ——*BY* R. ROBINSON.

Mrs. Kneale deals mainly with philosophy considered as linguistic analysis, and as the beneficiary, not the critic, of psychical research. Within this field, her conclusion is preliminarily stated as being that psychical research "calls attention in an extremely forcible manner to the fact that the terminologies devised by common sense and science are not in all respects adequate for the description and explanation of all known empirical facts." The final statement of her conclusion is as follows:

> Psychical research reveals the points where all scientific terminologies break down. This doesn't mean . . . that we should turn back to common sense and rest happy there. . . . We must try to devise a terminology which has the merits of both scientific and commonsense terminologies in being both universal in its application and precise. From this point of view it seems that psychical research is not only relevant to philosophy, but should

constitute one of its main fields of interest, as revealing just those points at which all current terminologies need revision.

I urge that this conclusion is both an exaggeration of the facts and also unjustified by the premises that Mrs. Kneale brings in support of it.

That it is an exaggeration of the facts may be urged as follows: "Just those points at which *all* current terminologies need revision?" "The points where *all* scientific terminologies break down?" These words surely must imply that a mineralogist could make an advance in mineralogy by studying the journals of the Society for Psychical Research, which, however, is not so.

The points at which present scientific terminologies break down are surely for the most part at present unknown. For, as soon as an inadequacy of terminology becomes known, the scientists set about repairing it, either through their Committees on Nomenclature or in some more radical way. Mrs. Kneale therefore appears to be suggesting that inadequacies which have not yet been realized by the scientists concerned would be realized by them if they studied books like Mr. Tyrrell's *The Personality of Man;* but is this probable? Take the science with which you are best acquainted, and try to make an improvement in its language on the basis of Mr. Tyrrell's book.

In the course of her concluding paragraph, Mrs. Kneale remarks that scientific terminologies "have a rigid structure which prevents them being used in the description of other fields," and there is a faint suggestion that she regards this rigidity as causing the breakdowns which, as she holds, psychical research reveals. I am unable to interpret this, and should welcome some examples of this rigidity. All that her sentences suggest to me at present is such irrelevant facts as that geological words like "Jurassic" and "Devonian" are no use to a physiologist trying to describe the kidneys.

Now for the proposition that Mrs. Kneale's conclusion is not justified by the premises that she brings in support of it. These premises fall into two groups, concerning (*a*) the physical and (*b*) the mental phenomena of psychical research.

Concerning the physical phenomena, *i.e.,* poltergeists and pseudopods, Mrs. Kneale appears to make four principal points:

(*a*1) Physicists have not dealt with poltergeists and pseudopods yet.

(*a*2) Poltergeists and pseudopods have not been shown to contradict the fundamental laws of physics.

(*a*3) Poltergeist phenomena and the like call for a decision on the scope of the terms "physical science" and "material object."

(*a*4) These matters are irrelevant to the question whether phenomenalism is true.

Only the third of these points has any tendency to confirm Mrs. Kneale's conclusion; for the fourth of them is a candid statement of one way in which psychical research is *not* relevant to philosophy, and the first two concern the relevance or irrelevance of psychical research not to philosophy but to physics.

With regard to (*a*2), that poltergeists, etc., have not been shown to contradict the fundamental laws of physics, Mrs. Kneale contemplates, without expressing an opinion on it, the possibility that such a contradiction may be revealed some time in the future. What would the physicists do then? Would they accept the data of the psychical researchers and alter their own propositions, or would they retain their own propositions and deny the data of the psychical researchers? If they did the latter, if, say, the Physical Society and the Society for Psychical Research contradicted each other, the layman would be confronted by a disagreement between two learned bodies, both claiming scientific responsibility. Such a spectacle has occurred before, notably in the clash between theologians and biologists in the nineteenth century. In that case the biologists won, for they completely convinced the great majority of us that they were right and the theologians were wrong. If it came to such a clash between the psychical researcher and the physicists, I should believe the physicists, and I have no doubt that most people would do the same.

The premiss, that poltergeist phenomena and the like call for some decision on the scope of the terms "physical science" and "material object," does tend to confirm Mrs. Kneale's conclusion; for at least the term "material object" is of concern to philosophy, and probably also the term "physical science." It is evident, however, that this premiss by itself is quite inadequate for the conclusion that psychical research shows the point where *all* terminologies *break down*. It follows that Mrs. Kneale's whole section on the physical phenomena of psychical research provides only very slight and inadequate support for her conclusion.

Before proceeding to her discussion of the mental phenomena, I wish to disagree with her view that poltergeists and the like call for a decision on the scope of the term "physical science." A good clue to the difference between us on this matter is given by her statement elsewhere that "psychical research is what is left over when the regular sciences have marked out their territories." I deny that sciences mark out territories, and therefore I deny that the names of sciences can be defined by reference to territories that have been marked out. What is the good of our legislating a meaning for the word "physical science?" None whatever, for the following reason. The gentlemen who are now actually and officially called physicists, when they come to decide what question they will investigate next, may be influenced in making their decision by their private curiosities, or by their private opinions as to what is important, or by the advice of their teachers, or by the salaries offered for studying some particular thing, or by some other cause; but one cause which is enormously unlikely to influence them is anybody's definition of the word "physics." Physics in the future is going to grow in various unpredictable directions, as these gentlemen make their choices; and what they do in the future is pretty sure to falsify any definition *per regiones* that we make now. And this is true of all sciences and of philosophy. The nearest thing to a safe definition of the word "philosophy," if we wish to include all that has been and will be correctly so called, is that it means the activity of Plato in his dialogues and every activity that has arisen or will arise out of that. And the nearest thing to a safe definition of "physical science" is something similar about such people as Galileo and Boyle and Newton. It is most improbable that all the activities that go under the name of "physics" are concerned with one territory which no other science is ever concerned with. This point was urged by Cook Wilson for the word "logic."

Science, that is to say, *Wissenschaft,* is a creative activity; and it is characteristic of a creative activity that one does not know what it is going to do next. Only dead sciences, sciences where the original impulse of the great founder is totally exhausted and no one follows in his footsteps any more, could be safely defined by a marking out of territories. Very likely the tendency to give such definitions has been encouraged by a tendency in some people to think of geometry as completed by Euclid and of logic as completed by Aristotle, though certainly not in Mrs. Kneale.

For this reason I think, contrary to Mrs. Kneale, that neither poltergeists nor any other events, except the actions of physicists, call upon us to alter or fix the meaning of the phrase "physical science." Poltergeists will be part of the subject-matter of physics when physicists believe in their occurrence and study them officially. Nor can I agree with her view that we cannot maintain that "physical science applies universally to all changes in material objects and that it is not concerned with poltergeist phenomena,'' because it seems to me proper to say: ''Physical science applies universally to all changes in material objects, but dances (although they are changes in material objects) are the concern of the anthropologist, not the physicist.'' Physical science applies to all material objects, but it does not exhaust them. It is not the whole story about them.

Mrs. Kneale comes much closer to what I believe the proper way of defining the names of traditional bodies of intellectual activity when she defines ''psychical research'' as ''the study of all those phenomena which are discussed by Mr. Tyrrell in his recent book, *The Personality of Man*,'' though I should prefer to say that the phrase means the activities of the Society for Psychical Research and whatever has arisen or will arise out of them.

When she adds another sort of definition of ''psychical research,'' she is less happy, in my opinion. According to this second definition, ''psychical research'' means the study of (*a*) physical happenings not explicable in terms of the laws known to common sense or science, or (*b*) the acquiring by human beings of information which they could not obtain in normal ways. Here (*a*) seems unfortunate because no event of any kind is explicable in terms of laws alone, but only in terms of laws plus previous events, while, if poltergeists are not explicable in terms of laws plus previous events, they *do* conflict with the present laws of physics, which, however, Mrs. Kneale elsewhere says is not known to be the case. Either the movements of poltergeisting objects conflict with the laws now believed by physicists, or they are explicable in terms of those laws, given suitable antecedents.

As to (*b*), the use of the distinction normal-abnormal here seems defective because the essence of what the psychical researchers tell us about their telepathy and clairvoyance and precognition and extrasensory perception is that they are the acquiring of information not by abnormal means but without any known means at all. The difference between telepathy and telegraphy is that in telegraphy you get information by making use of your eyes and the machines and officers employed by the Post Office, whereas in telepathy you just get information, without, so far as can be discovered, making use of anything at all. I admit that the psychical researchers use phrases like ''by paranormal means''; but I submit that, from their accounts of what happens, or rather from their lack of any account of what happens, they are not entitled to such phrases, or, if they are, can only use them in the same sense as the phrases "by unknown means" and "without means." No means of giving and receiving telepathic information have been produced. If they had been produced, we could all use them, and so we could all give and receive telepathic communications. The claim to telepathic powers is like a doctor who should say: "I can cure this disease, but I cannot tell *you* how to cure it, because I have no *method* of curing it; I just cure it."

We tend sometimes to think that the word "telepathy" is itself the name of the means by which this remarkable knowledge is obtained. But that is just faculty-psychology. "Quare ego facio absentem amicum in me cogitare? Quia ille habet facultatem telepathicam." "Telepathy" is just the name of the occurrence which consists, if it occurs, in giving and receiving information without any means of doing so. If there is telepathy, the following sort of conversation would be justifiable in certain circumstances:

"Mrs. X, having a very bad heart and being terrified of cats, has died of the shock caused by your suddenly putting a cat on her shoulder from behind. Didn't you know that Mrs. X was terrified of cats?"

"No, I had no means of knowing that."

"But you ought to have known it without means. You ought to have known it telepathically."

To call a coincidence a case of telepathy is not to explain it, but precisely to deny the possibility of one sort of explanation of it, namely, that sort of explanation of the coincidence of x and y which consists in saying that there was some sort of machinery or train of events by *means* of which x led to y. To say that the Piddingtons know what each other is thinking telepathically is to say that they do not know it by means of prearranged signals or sensory cues or by any means at all; and therefore it is inexplicable in terms of means. If a coincidence is a case of telepathy, the only sort of explanation it is capable of is a statement not of the means by which it happens (for there are none) but of the conditions in which such coincidences always will happen. Therefore psychical researchers ought not to say "the only reasonable explanation of this coincidence, apart from chance, is telepathy." Neither calling a coincidence chance, nor calling it telepathy, is explaining it. Calling it telepathy is denying that any indirect causal explanation is possible; and calling it chance is denying that any causal explanation at all is possible.

Similarly, I disagree with Mrs. Kneale that to label an event "fore-imaging" is to explain it; I think it is to say that there is no explanation of the fact that this man had an image of the event before it occurred. Again, the use in this connection of terms like "the mind," "the subconscious mind," and "the subliminal self," does not, in my opinion, reveal any means by which these surprising true beliefs are brought about, but is a way of expressing ignorance of any mechanism together with a belief that there is a mechanism and that it is something wonderful.

A means involves a causal sequence; the means causes the end to occur. Whenever the correct means is produced, the desired end will occur, unless prevented by the intervention of some other cause. If in the future some means is discovered to have been responsible for certain true beliefs which are now considered to be cases of telepathy, then either "telepathy" will become the name of knowledge obtained by this method, changing its meaning, or else the word "telepathy" will retain its present meaning and will no longer be applied to these beliefs. Whichever happens, many persons who now favour psychical research will lose interest in these beliefs, because they are interested only in knowledge without means, because only knowledge without means tends to prove the Platonic theory of the soul and man's survival of his bodily death. After the severe defeat administered to the Platonic theory of man in the previous century by biological science, those who were still unshakably loyal to the view that man consists of two parts one of which is immaterial and immortal, had two possibilities open to them. One was the way of fundamentalism and irrationalism, of closing one's ears to argument and blindly rejecting science. The other was to place their view of man upon a scientific basis, adopting the methods of obtaining evidence most approved by the scientists and the lawcourts, and thus to defeat the scientists by accepting science to the full, as Descartes defeated the sceptics by accepting scepticism to the full; and this is the way of psychical research. At least some psychical research is therefore, in my opinion, both religion and science. It is religion using science to prove its point.

Mrs. Kneale says, however, that psychical research is not a science, because its results are not confirmed hypotheses, but simply queer empirical facts. And she says that this follows from her definition. But what is there in her definition that prevents psychical researchers from making hypotheses about the queer coincidences they collect? Surely "the study of all of those phenomena" includes making hypotheses about them. And surely the psychical researchers do make hypotheses about them, from the obvious hypothesis, that there is some causal connection between a dream and a subsequent event which closely resembles it, to more remote hypotheses like this of Mr. Tyrrell's: "Normal perception tends to oust the supernormal and keep the field to itself. In order that the deep mental stratum which has the supernormal knowledge may use the normal motor mechanisms to get this knowledge externalized," etc. (p. 109 of *Science and Psychical Phenomena*, 1938). As far as making hypotheses goes, psychical research is a science, in intention at least.

Mrs. Kneale says that the results of psychical research are not "confirmed hypotheses"; but I think she does not mean to imply by this that psychical research is not a science because none of its hypotheses are confirmed. It seems clear from her discussion that the hypothesis that, for example, the coincidence of a man's willing a die to fall six up and its doing so is due to some causal relation between the two, is in her opinion sufficiently confirmed. I conclude then that her definition of psychical research does *not* entail that it is not a science; and I think that psychical research *is* a science, or at least a would-be science, in the sense of a methodical attempt to get general knowledge about the course of events by induction from particular observations.

I turn now to the second and last set of Mrs. Kneale's premises for her conclusion, those concerning the mental phenomena of psychical research. I summarize them thus:

(*b*1) *Collective hallucinations* call for some improvement of Professor Ryle's dichotomy between seeing and quote-seeing, though any really good visual hallucination (including one that had nothing telepathic about it) would do as well.

(*b*2) *Telepathy* proves that we must have a vocabulary for the inner life, and cannot manage with a purely behaviouristic vocabulary; yet we do not really need telepathy to make this point. Telepathy also raises the philosophical question: "What is the best terminology in which to formulate a scientific hypothesis about the conditions of its occurrence?"

(*b*3) *Psychokinesis* confirms and extends our habit of assuming that inner-life events can cause outer-life events, against our philosophic suspicion of this habit. It also calls for a redefinition of "my body."

(*b*4) When a terminology has been worked out for scientific hypotheses about telepathy and psychokinesis, psychical research may have a big effect on the group of problems formerly treated as the "mind-body" problem.

(*b*5) Psychical research shows that the hypothesis of human survival is not meaningless.

(*b*6) *Precognition* serves the useful function of reminding us that there is still very much that eludes the descriptive and explanatory net.

(*b*7) Psychical research is quite irrelevant to questions of "the nothingness of time" and of religious mysticism.

Would these seven points, if they were all wholly true, together constitute good evidence for Mrs. Kneale's conclusion, that "psychical research is not only relevant to philosophy but should constitute one of its main fields of interest, as revealing just those points at which all current terminologies need revision?" In my judgment the answer is definitely no. I think rather that Mrs. Kneale has damned the importance of psychical research for philosophy with faint praise.

Under *b*1 the advantage she expects can, she admits, also be secured by "any really good visual hallucination." Under *b*2 the main advantage she expects from a consideration of telepathy is, she says, one that "we do not really need telepathy to make." As to the minor advantage, that telepathy raises the philosophical question "What is the best terminology in which to formulate a scientific hypothesis about the conditions of its occurrence?," I suggest that this question is either non-existent or identical with the non-philosophical question "What are the conditions of the occurrence of telepathy?"

Under *b*3 she finds the main value of psychokinesis to philosophy to be that it confirms our habit of assuming that mental events can cause physical events—against, I suppose, the threat from parallelism and epiphenomenalism and behaviourism. I cannot think that this would be an important contribution to philosophy, since parallelism and epiphenomenalism are dead philosophies, and no *philosophical* "behaviourist," so far as I know, has denied that a physical event might be caused by a mental event. I do not think that Professor Ryle's book denies it. It merely argues that some supposed cases of a mental event causing a physical event are not cases of anything causing anything. For example, "I ate the chocolates because I wanted to" is not an account of the cause of a certain eating, but of its general nature. As to Mrs. Kneale's minor point about psychokinesis, that it calls for a redefinition of "my body," this would, no doubt, have a certain value in philosophy.

(But to digress for a moment, is not her premiss mistaken here? Does anyone think that what he means by "my body" includes his being able to make things happen to it merely by thinking of them? His thoughts have no more direct control over his hair than over his clothes; but he certainly thinks that his hair is part of his body and his clothes are not. Nor, presumably, does total paralysis change a man's opinion about which things are parts of his body. Perhaps "my body" means the body that I feel the inside of.)

Her fourth point, *b*4, is merely a hope, if my account of what she intends is correct.

Her fifth point, that psychical research shows that the hypothesis of human survival is not meaningless, serves only to suppress the exaggerations about meaninglessness that characterized the nineteen-thirties, and that only if there is anyone who has not been convinced of the significance of some metaphysical propositions in any other way and is capable of being convinced of it in this way.

Her sixth point is that precognition serves the useful function of reminding us that there is still very much that eludes the descriptive and explanatory net. I cannot help believing both that no respectable inquirer can help being reminded of this all his life anyhow, and that psychical research is an unsuitable agency for reminding anyone of it because of the current, which runs through psychical research as it does through much religion, of desiring to retain the mystery and the inexplicability.

Her seventh and last point, according to my analysis, is a rejection of one suggested relevance of psychical research to philosophy.

From this review I conclude that, even if we accept all her premises, Mrs. Kneale makes out only a thin case that philosophers should study the mental phenomena of psychical research.

Mrs. Kneale deliberately put herself at a disadvantage, and gave herself a hard task, by regarding philosophy solely as linguistic analysis. Can we take her failure (for so I think it) as adequate evidence that psychical research is unimportant to philosophy considered as linguistic analysis? Has she explored all the main possibilities of relevance here? I am inclined to think not, for she has said little about the philosophical analysis of the psychical researchers' own terms, especially "telepathy," "clairvoyance," "precognition," "psychokinesis," "extrasensory perception." I think that the study of how the psychical researchers use these inventions, and of how they use the words "psychic" and "mental," is an interesting and useful occupation which may quite properly be called "philosophy," and which frequently leads to renewed study of the philosopher's favorite subjects, knowledge and causation. For example, if it really happened, as Professor Rhine thinks he remembers it happening, that a man once guessed 25 unperceived cards right in succession, should we or should we not say that the man "knew" what the cards were? I think that I personally do not know well enough what we mean by "know" and "guess" to answer this question; and it thus provides for me a stimulus to further philosophical analysis.

For another example, what is the neologism "psychokinesis" a name for? Not, presumably, merely for the following statement about coincidences: "Sometimes a man wills dice to fall a certain way and they do so." It is a name for the following: "Sometimes a man wills dice to fall in a certain way and they do so, and their doing so is caused by his willing them to do so." This introduces the notion of cause, which seems to be also present in the ideas of telepathy and clairvoyance and extrasensory perception and perhaps also precognition. Does it fit with our ordinary conception of cause, or does it imply an alteration thereof?

Anyone who holds that causation entails regularity (whether or not it consists solely in regularity) will hold that behind the sometimes proposition, that "Sometimes a man's willing dice to fall in a certain way causes them to do so," there must be an always proposition, presumably not the obvious one that "Under conditions x a man's willing dice to fall in a certain way is always followed by their doing so," but at any rate some underlying regularity, whether obvious or remote, on which the occasional coincidences depend. And it seems that, if a man believes in psychokinesis, he should either look for the regularity or deny that causation entails regularity.

This is the kind of way in which I think that analysis of the psychical researchers' technical terms is a valuable stimulus to the philosopher in his analysis of knowledge and causation, whether or not he believes the statements which the psychical researchers construct by means of those terms. It is the same sort of stimulus, and insight into other people's thoughts, as the philosopher can find in analysing what psychoanalysts mean by "determined" and "responsible," in entire independence of the question whether to accept or reject their doctrines.

I now drop the limitation of philosophy to linguistic analysis, and consider the impact of the conclusions drawn by the psychical researchers upon the traditional topics of philosophy. I will mention only two points, first the effect upon the question of empiricism, and second the effect upon the theory of man.

The conclusions of psychical research, if accepted, seem to settle the question of empiricism. They seem to entail that empiricism is to be rejected. For empiricism seems to be the canon that we ought not to adopt any synthetic proposition except upon the evidence of our senses, whereas the belief in telepathy or clairvoyance or precognition entails that we can have good reason for believing certain synthetic propositions without any sensible evidence. The only way out of this that I see would be to define "empiricism" without reference to the senses; for the other premiss, that the psychical researchers do conclude that we can sometimes know synthetic propositions without any aid from the senses. seems quite certain. But so far I have not heard of any definition of "empiricism" without reference to the senses which did not render it a useless word. The only even plausible alternative I see is to substitute "experience" for "the senses" and say something like: empiricism is the rule that we ought not to adopt any synthetic proposition except on the basis of experience. But I am inclined to think that, if "experience" here means anything different from "the senses," the definition makes empiricism indistinguishable from rationalism.

The greatest contribution of psychical research to philosophy (or should I say "supersession of philosophy by psychical research?"), if the conclusions of some psychical researchers are true, is to another of those great questions traditionally included under the word "philosophy," from which Mrs. Kneale cut herself off by a self-denying ordinance. I refer to the choice between what may be roughly called the Platonic and the Aristotelian theories of man. According to the Platonic theory, a man is primarily something immortal and imperceptible and spiritual, which for one or more short periods is united with something mortal and perceptible and material, namely a specimen of that animal labelled "homo sapiens" by the biologists. According to the Aristotelian theory, man *is* that animal labelled "homo sapiens" by the biologists; and that animal is not linked to any immortal imperceptible twin (you see I am disregarding the famous little chapter in which Aristotle reverts to Platonism); and what we refer to as its "soul" or "mind" is the entelechy or form or higher behavior of that animal.

In my opinion the main object of many psychical researchers is to establish the Platonic view of man on the best scientific and legal evidence, and to remove the immense support which science gave to the Aristotelian view of man in the nineteenth century. The central part of their psychical research is therefore the attempt to communicate with men who are not at the time attached to any specimen of homo sapiens; and all the matters dealt with by Mrs. Kneale, the mental as well as the physical, are to them merely outliers whose main value is that they suggest the occurrence of activity with no physical basis. Consequently, the main relevance of their psychical research to philosophy is that, if you accept their conclusions, you ought in consistency to deny all Aristotelian theories of man, and, if you accept an Aristotelian theory of man, you ought to deny their conclusions.

I personally accept an Aristotelian theory of man, and deny at least their main conclusion. I find this a painful position, as the most eminent persons who have published on the subject appear to be on the other side. I have, however, no choice in the matter. I cannot help believing the Aristotelian view and disbelieving the Platonic view.

This does not mean that I think I can otherwise explain all the queer coincidences and events described in the volumes of the S.P.R. I certainly have no explanation to offer of a great many of those reports. I am usually not prepared to say whether a given report of strange events or coincidences is true or false. If it is false, I am usually not prepared to say whether it was made fraudulently or in good faith. If it is true, I am usually not prepared to say what the explanation of it is. (Nor, very often, are the psychical researchers themselves; for their so-called "explanations" of it as "telepathic" or "psychokinetic," etc., are really denials that it ever will be explained, in the sense of disclosing a mechanism.)

Is it irrational to be unable to believe the Platonic theory of man although one cannot otherwise explain all the multitudinous reports assembled by the S.P.R.? I incline to think not. I incline to think that the assertion, that every one ought to believe the Platonic theory of man unless he can otherwise explain all these reports, would be a case of the fallacy known as "the argument from ignorance," that is, in its crudest form, the argument that "p must be true because we do not know for certain that it is false."

However that may be, Mr. Tyrrell's view that what prevents my side from sharing his conclusions is their strangeness and queerness appears to me wholly mistaken. The Platonic theory of man is far more familiar to us all than the Aristotelian. We are brought up on it. And stories of telepathy and second sight and poltergeists and apparitions are abundant and inescapable. It is not possible to go to five teaparties without hearing at least one such story retailed as thoroughly authenticated; and I have been to five hundred teaparties. The emotional aura which Mr. Tyrrell's data and conclusions have for me is not strangeness and queerness but, I regret to say, boredom and banality. Mr. Tyrrell, it seems to me, is very easily amused. He quotes what he calls "a piece of dramatisation which it is difficult to believe is feigned," adding that "if it is (feigned), then the best of our dramatists may learn a good deal from the subliminal self of the ordinary person" (*The Personality of Man,* 158). This piece of monologue impresses me, however, as here and there ridiculous but otherwise a dead bore. It purports to settle the mind-body problem by information received from Professor Henry Sidgwick in his present disembodied state, in which, I suppose, the answers to philosophical problems are known. The information is that interaction is the true theory, and parallelism and epiphenomenalism are false.

The reports of the psychical researchers affect me more like clichés, or like the jokes that children bring home from school and find so good. In this way they contrast very strongly with the reports we have received in the last twenty years about what happens when communists put communists on trial, or when one piece of isotope 235 meets another piece of isotope 235. There indeed I find things strange and queer.

In accordance with this view, I deny that psychical research tells us important facts about human nature, the sort of facts that the non-theologian would expect to learn from a book entitled "The Personality of Man." Mr. Tyrrell writes: "Nothing could be more vital than that the true facts about man's nature should be known to those who teach philosophy or religion or plan the future of society" (268). This implies that psychical research has told us more important new truths about man's nature than has, say, anthropology or psychology or sociology, as pursued by Malinowski or Freud or Marx. It has not. It has told us nothing about man's nature except that he likes mysteries and likes to believe in spirits and wants to go on living. Mr. Tyrrell also maintains that a general belief in his doctrines would remove the present danger that the world may "destroy itself in an orgy of materialism" (275). It would not. Nor would it remove the much greater danger that the world may destroy itself in an orgy of spiritualism, for it is not material but spiritual vices that have produced the devastating wars of this century, not greed but pride and nationalism and the love of power over men.

If psychokinesis became a practical force, it would provide men with a new power to do evil. And this new power would be far more tempting and destructive than the atomic bomb. It would be more tempting because it would be absolutely secret and therefore secure against being brought to justice. No one could tell who had "psychomoved" the ship's chronometer to go slow and thus brought the ship on the rocks. No one could tell who had willed the neutrons to stay inside the mass and thus caused an atomic explosion below the critical size. It would be, in fact, the perfect example of that absolute power which corrupts absolutely. And the dreadful suspicion, in each of our hearts, that some acquaintance of ours had this secret power and was not to be trusted with it, would start a new witchhunt more horrible and despairing than those of the seventeenth century. In mentioning this consequence I am not adopting the common view that scientific research, or some scientific research, ought to be stopped; I am merely arguing against Mr. Tyrrell's view that his kind of research is likely to improve our morals and our happiness. Mr. Tyrrell does not, however, deal with psychokinesis in the book before us.

The disastrous secrecy of psychokinesis would, however, be avoided if at the same time telepathy became a practical force. Then we can imagine a person being accused in a court of law of having killed someone by secret psychokinesis, and the judge admitting evidence from a witness who claimed to have telepathically observed the accused committing this secret act of will. In this way telepathy might lessen the number of deaths caused by psychokinesis. Our position, however, would not be the happier for that. It would a very unhappy situation to have no secret thoughts or feelings. I suppose we should spend most of our time searching the minds of others, and learning little but that they were doing the same.

III. ——BY C. W. K. MUNDLE.

My qualifications for talking about this subject are very limited. The only branch of psychical research with which I have more than a nodding acquaintance is the experimental work on what are called "extra-sensory perception" and "psychokinesis." My arguments will be based mainly on the facts in question, and, as a result, my perspective may be somewhat unbalanced. I may, for example, fail to take sufficient account of characteristics displayed only by the spontaneous cases which psychical researchers investigate. There is however something to be said for basing our conclusions on the results of controlled experiments; for the most careful study of the reports of spontaneous cases does not enable us to answer with confidence the questions which they provoke. In this field, there seems to be no way of verifying our conjectures except by experiments in which conditions are, as far as possible, controlled and varied one at a time.

I agree with Mr. Robinson's verdict that Mrs. Kneale damns with faint praise the thesis that psychical research is relevant to philosophy. If psychical research provided only new kinds of *a fortiori* argument for obvious conclusions, it would scarcely merit the attention of philosophers. I wish to add a criticism of Mrs. Kneale's paper to those which Mr. Robinson has made.

When we ask whether psychical research is relevant to philosophy, we must be clear whether we are referring to the observational data, or to the primary hypotheses used by psychical researchers, or to the speculative theories which have been advanced in attempts to coordinate these hypotheses and render them intelligible. When Mr. Robinson criticises "the conclusions" of psychical researchers he seems usually to be referring to their hypotheses or theories. Mrs. Kneale on the other hand sets out to consider the facts. She is not, however, in my opinion, sufficiently careful in disentangling observational data from hypotheses, and in attending to the difference between describing the facts and explaining them. This has repercussions on what are, to my mind, the two most striking claims made in her paper:

(i) The conclusion, reached in her last paragraph, that "psychical research reveals the points where all scientific terminologies break down." They break down, according to Mrs. Kneale, because they cannot be used to *describe* the facts in question. (Throughout this passage Mrs. Kneale speaks as if the only function of a terminology is description.) My comments are:

(*a*) that many of the facts in question can be described in a scientific terminology. The results of experiments in guessing cards and "willing" dice can be, and usually are, expressed in statistical formulae or graphs; and if this is not a scientific terminology, what is?

(*b*) What Mrs. Kneale is (presumably) referring to when she speaks of "the breakdown of scientific terminologies" is the fact that the data in question cannot be *explained* in ways which conform with the laws and postulates accepted by the established sciences. I shall discuss this issue in due course.

(ii) Her conclusion that telepathy "establishes beyond any doubt that in order to say all there is to say about persons we must have a vocabulary for the inner as well as the outer life. . . . [that] we cannot manage with a purely behaviouristic terminology." I would agree with Mrs. Kneale that the behaviouristic viewpoint is for many purposes inadequate, but I consider it a mistake to use the data of psychical research to try to prove this point. If we examine the facts which have been generally regarded as evidence of telepathy, we find that they can be described in behaviouristic terminology, and indeed that they ought to be so described if we are to avoid begging questions about their explanation. In the typical card-guessing experiment, the role of the so-called percipient is to write down a series of symbols representing one or other of five alternative card-faces. What constitutes the experimenter's data is the percipient's overt behaviour and the written record produced thereby. In experiments of this type, percipients have rarely been asked to introspect, and, when they were asked to do this, gave little or no information about the mental process-es which accompanied their writing. When Dr. Soal wanted to find whether his subject Shackleton could distinguish which of his guesses were correct, Soal's method was one to which behaviourists could take no exception—he asked Shackleton to mark the guesses about which he felt especially confident. (It transpired that there was no significant correlation between Shackleton's confidence and his success.) If we turn to the spontaneous cases, we find that what is taken to be the product of tele-pathy is often a private experience, e.g., a dream or a private hallucination. However, little or no weight is attached by psychical researchers to the report of such a case, unless the private experience has issued, without much delay, in some overt action which can be confirmed by witnesses or by documents. It is unnecessary to provoke the behaviourists by saying, as Mrs. Kneale does, that they cannot even *describe* the facts in question. The practice of psychical researchers indicates that they accept as evidence only what behaviourists can acknowledge as hard facts. The real problems arise not in describing the facts but in trying to explain them: and to be fair, we must admit that it is not only behaviourists who find this difficult.

It is a commonplace that the expressions "extra-sensory perception," "supernormal cognition" and the like are open to criticism. They may be used simply to refer to certain facts, in which case they are technical terms whose literal meaning is to be ignored; or they may be used to refer to a certain hypothesis for explaining the facts. We need however to be able to refer to the observational data without begging (or seeming to beg) questions about their explanation. For this purpose I propose to follow the suggestion made by Dr. Thouless of replacing the above expressions by the term "psi-phenomena." As Thouless said, when he made this proposal, it would be pedantic to object to a terminology as misleading unless it in fact misleads. It seems to me, however, that the terminology in question has misled Mr. Robinson. I can, at any rate, think of no other explanation for several of the statements he makes; for example, when he says that if telepathy occurs we would sometimes be justified in telling a person that he "ought to have known" a fact by telepathy: and again, when he argues that the conclusions of psychical researchers seem to entail (and, Mr. Robinson apparently thinks, really do entail) that empiricism is to be rejected. This last argument is of sufficient importance to philosophers to deserve a more careful discussion than Mr. Robinson gives to it. It would be, to say the least, surprising, if empiricism could be refuted by means of empirically ascertained facts.

One of the premises of Mr. Robinson's argument is a certain definition of "empiricism": for the other premise we are offered two alternatives:

(i) "the belief in telepathy or clairvoyance or precognition entails that we can have good reason for believing certain synthetic propositions without any sensible evidence,"

(ii) "that psychical researchers do conclude that we can sometimes know synthetic propositions without any aid from the senses, seems quite certain."

Neither of these statements appears to be justified. Statement (ii) does not express the deliberate view of the more critical psychical researchers. Consider what Rhine says[2] about the typical subject who is successful in "ESP" or "PK" experiments—"He is unaware when and how either occurs. He does not know if they have occurred and has no reliable conviction of success or failure; *he has to find out through sensory perception when psi-abilities have functioned*" (my italics). Of course psychical researchers are not always consistent in their statements—there is at least one passage in *The Reach of the Mind* where Rhine uses the sort of language which Mr. Robinson attributes to psychical researchers, namely, when Rhine says "we have found that there is a capacity for acquiring knowledge that transcends the sensory functions" (p. 164). All this shows however is that psychical researchers as well as others are liable to be misled (or to speak as if they were) by terms like "extra-sensory perception."

Statement (i) is not, like statement (ii), an assertion about the conclusions of psychical researchers, so presumably Mr. Robinson considers it is warranted by the facts. If so he is surely mistaken. Consider for example Dr. Soal's experiments with Shackleton. Dr. Soal's conclusion that Shackleton's results exhibited precognitive telepathy does not entail that anyone has now, or had at the time of the experiments, "good reason for believing certain synthetic propostions without any sensible evidence." It is true that, in the course of the experiments, Shackleton and equally the experimenters had reason to believe it probable that, in the next run of twenty-five guesses, seven or eight would be correct against a chance-expectation of five—but this belief would have been based on ordinary inductive inference from past observations.

It is open to question whether, as Mr. Robinson claims, "empiricism" need be defined by reference to "the senses." Some would wish to define "empiricism" in terms of a version of the Verification Principle, and this may be formulated without reference to "the senses." But I know of no version of the Verification Principle which would make it impossible to attach a meaning to the statement that telepathy or clairvoyance occurs. The facts are compatible with empiricism, unless we decide to define "empiricism" so as to exclude the possibility of a person *responding appropriately* to events which are not communicated to him by his senses. But to adopt such a definition in the face of the observational data supplied by psychical researchers would be to display a perversely unempirical frame of mind!

I feel bound to make some comments on the somewhat provocative passage with which Mr. Robinson ends his paper—the passage which he introduces by suggesting that the conclusions of some psychical researchers might be described as the "supercession of philosophy by psychical research." When Mr. Robinson speaks in this context of the "conclusions" of psychical researchers, it is not clear to me whether he is referring to (*a*) the speculations of people like Mr. Tyrrell who have attempted to give a synoptic account of the normal and the "supernormal" facts: or (*b*) the hypothesis of survival. If he is referring to (*a*), I should agree that the speculative writings of psychical researchers like Myers, Tyrrell and Carington contain much that is, by the standards of professional philosophers, loosely expressed and wildly conjectural. But this has no bearing on the relevance of psychical research to philosophy. We do not (fortunately) judge the relevance to philosophy of Physics or Psychoanalysis by the wilder statements made by Jeans or Freud. Regarding (*b*), the hypothesis that some constituent of a human being survives bodily death is entertained by many psychical researchers as a possible explanation (and is accepted by some as the simplest explanation) of a set of facts which have not been discussed in this symposium. It would be frivolous to criticize these views without surveying the relevant facts—unless we maintained (as Mr. Robinson does not) that this hypothesis is meaningless. I shall assume without argument that theories about human personality are an important part of philosophy, and that the hypothesis of survival is relevant to such theories. (I should agree with Mr. Robinson that the data of other sciences, e.g. abnormal psychology and sociology, may be more relevant to such theories.) But why should Mr. Robinson suggest (if this was his intention) that if the hypothesis of survival could be confirmed this would involve the supercession of philosophy? Most of the problems which philosophers discuss would be unaffected.

Mr. Robinson makes statements about the motivation of psychical researchers which appear to me misleading and, in any case, irrelevant. He says for example "the central part of their psychical research is therefore an attempt to communicate with men who are not at the time attached to any specimen of homo sapiens, and all the matters dealt with by Mrs. Kneale, the mental as well as the physical, are to them mere outliers." But anyone who cares to survey the contents of the SPR Proceedings for, say, the last fifteen years can see that by far the greater part of their research has been on the subjects which Mr. Robinson says are to them mere outliers. And it is widely recognized by psychical researchers that the advances in their knowledge about psi-phenomena have made it much more difficult to confirm the survival hypothesis. For many, and perhaps all, mediumistic utterances which purport to originate from deceased persons may be attributed to psi-phenomena involving only embodied persons. Surely Mr. Robinson's description of psychical research as "religion using science to prove its point" is a deliberate caricature! My own impression is that most psychical researchers treat survival as a scientific hypothesis toward which their emotional reactions (whether pro or con) are irrelevant. But even if Mr. Robinson's account of the motivation of psychical researchers had been correct, would this have been relevant to the subject of our symposium? Surely not—*unless* it were suggested that their desire to prove survival had led them to be careless or dishonest in reporting experiments and collecting other evidence. If this is what Mr. Robinson meant, he should have said so.

Mr. Robinson is however correct in implying that many psychical researchers regard psi-phenomena as having some positive bearing on the tenability of the hypothesis of survival. I think he obscures the nature of the alleged connection when he depicts it as being merely an "argument from ignorance." What many psychical researchers (and some philosophers, including Professor Broad) have maintained is that psi-phenomena dispose of Epiphenomenalism. If so, this would obviously be relevant to the tenability of the Platonic (or Cartesian or Christian) theory of man, since one of the main difficulties encountered by such a theory is the support given to Epiphenomenalism by the discoveries of physiologists and biologists. We should not, I suggest, dismiss this question as Mr. Robinson does, on the grounds that Epiphenomenalism is a "dead philosophy." When a theory is accepted, as I think this one is, by a majority of educated people, it is inappropriate to call it "dead," merely because few professional philosophers at present take it seriously. I am however very doubtful whether it is possible to refute Epiphenomenalism by means of psi-phenomena. Those who have thought this possible seem to have been assuming that telepathy involves a direct causal transaction between mental events in different persons. The occurrence of telepathy would then entail at least that some mental events are not wholly determined by physical events. I think this argument is inconclusive because the observational data do not warrant the premise that telepathy, so defined, ever occurs. It seems impossible to discover whether, in cases of ostensible telepathy, the response of the percipient is influenced by an event in the *mind*, or by an event in the *brain* of the so-called agent. If the latter were true, the transactions would be cases of clairvoyance, according to the usual definition of this term; and this interpretation of the facts would be compatible with the tenet of Epiphenomenalism that each of the proximate differential conditions of each mental event is a cerebral event. If my argument here is defective, I expect that Professor Broad will expose my error.

If psi-phenomena have no positive bearing on the possibility of survival, this will make them less interesting to spiritualists, but it should not detract from their interest to philosophers and scientists. I must protest against Mr. Robinson's verdict that psychical research "has told us nothing about man's nature except that he likes mysteries and likes to believe in spirits and wants to go on living." Psi-phenomena constitute transactions of an apparently unique kind between human beings and their environment. Psychical research has shown that many people to a slight extent and a few people to a marked extent possess faculties which according to orthodox scientists are impossible. For the last seventy years, almost all scientists who have not examined the evidence (i.e. almost all scientists) have dismissed the facts as being impossible. It seems important to try to diagnose the reasons for this attitude. I think Mrs. Kneale underestimates the sharpness of the conflict when she says that she sees no reason to believe that "to accept the genuineness of the physical phenomena of psychical research would be to deny what is already established in physics."

Would any physicist agree that PK is compatible with what is thought to be established in physics? Most physicists would, I think, be inclined to take it as certain that a person's volition cannot be a *proximate* differential condition of physical events occurring at a distance from that person's body; and they would feel some (understandable) horror at the suggestion that this happens, since it appears to open the door to the return of some primitive superstitions. I shall later discuss another, more philosophically interesting, reason for the scientists' attitude to psi-phenomena. First I wish to discuss briefly the ways in which psychical researchers classify and label psi-phenomena. This may appear to be a digression, but it seems to me a necessary preliminary to discussing the subject of our symposium.

The terminology used by psychical researchers is not as confused as is suggested by Mr. Robinson's reference to "their telepathy and clairvoyance *and* precognition *and* extra-sensory perception" (my italics). The distinction they make between "telepathy" and "clairvoyance" hinges on whether the event to which a subject responds is mental or physical: their distinction between cases (of telepathy *or* clairvoyance) which are "precognitive" and those which are not depends on whether or not the event to which a subject responds occurs later than his response: and "extra-sensory perception" is a generic name for telepathy and clairvoyance, whether precognitive or not. It is a long-established tradition for the above phenomena to be classed as *mental,* whereas other phenomena, e.g. PK- and poltergeist-phenomena, are classed as *physical.* I suggested earlier that we use the term "psi-phenomena" to refer to all of the so-called mental phenomena. I wish now to go further and apply the term "psi-phenomena" also to any well-evidenced physical phenomena. (So far as I know, PK is the only kind of physical phenomenon which is evidenced by a substantial number of controlled experiments. Many psychical researchers are not convinced by the anecdotal evidence of poltergeist-phenomena). There are several reasons for extending the meaning of "psi-phenomena" in this way. Rhine has pointed out that there are many features shared by the results of experiments in card-guessing and those in "willing" dice, e.g., in respect of the effect of drugs on the subject, and of the distribution of hits within runs. A more fundamental reason for this recommendation is that, in so far as our purpose is merely to classify the facts on the basis of observable differences, the traditional mental-physical dichotomy is open to criticism. Why, for example, should we classify clairvoyance along with telepathy as being mental? This has been done, I suppose, because both have usually been interpreted as being *cognitive*, whereas the so-called physical phenomena have not. But this difference is not an *observable* one. In PK- as well as in telepathy- or clairvoyance-phenomena, we are dealing with pairs of events (or pairs of series of events) between which there holds a resemblance which cannot be attributed to chance. If our classification is to be based on the observable differences between the character of the events which stand in such relations, it would be more appropriate to adopt as the criterion for classification the distinction between human and nonhuman events, rather than the distinction between mental and physical events. (By "human event" I mean any event which occurs in a human being, whether mental or physical, private or overt.) The corresponding division of psi-phenomena would be:

(1) those which involved supernormal[3] relations between a human event or series of human events and a non-human event or series of non-human events,

(2) those which involve supernormal relations between different human events, or series thereof. (Notice that the different human events need not occur in different persons. Dunne's precognitive dreams apparently involved supernormal relations between different events in Dunne.)

If we adopted this method of classification, then most of the cases which are now attributed to clairvoyance (as well as most cases attributed to PK and poltergeists)[4] would belong to class (1): and class (2) would include all cases which are now attributed to telepathy—and perhaps more besides, e.g. the exercise of PK-influence on the body of another person, *if* this ever happens. I mention this alternative classification not because I think it has any intrinsic merit, but to emphasize that we need not be dominated by the traditional mental-physical dichotomy, and because I hope to show that the philosophical interest of psi-phenomena does not depend on our method of classifying them. I am not urging psychical researchers or others to jettison forthwith the familiar terms "telepathy," "clairvoyance" and "PK," but I want to emphasize that these terms refer to hypotheses. Whether or not these hypotheses are the most appropriate ones will be determined by future experiments.

It is obviously important that the primary hypotheses used by psychical researchers should be defined as clearly as possible. A serious ambiguity is found in the use of the terms "telepathy" and "clairvoyance": the hypotheses in question are conceived sometimes purely in terms of cognitive relations, sometimes purely in terms of causal relations, sometimes perhaps in terms of both. Thus "telepathy" may mean either—

(i) a person (A) *directly apprehending* a mental event (X) (where X may occur in another person at any date, or in A at a later date); or

(ii) A's behavior or experience being *causally influenced* supernormally by a mental event X.

Two versions of the clairvoyance hypothesis may likewise be obtained.

Those who accept the Verification Principle will regard these two versions as equivalent. If however we acknowledge what Price calls "acquaintance" and what Broad calls "prehension" as a relation which is not wholly analyzable in terms of causation, we could and should regard the causal and the cognitive versions as being distinct hypotheses. The view that cognitive relations are *sui generis* is not at present popular among philosophers, and I find it difficult to make up my mind on this issue. I shall, until further notice, use "telepathy" and "clairvoyance" to refer to the causal versions. But even when we use the causal versions we are going beyond the facts—otherwise, of course, we would not be using hypotheses. Some people might take it to be tautological to say that, when a pair of events (or a pair of series of events) resemble each other to an extent not attributable to chance, they are causally connected. I believe that "causal connection" is sometimes used by psychologists and biologists in a sense in which extra-chance correspondence between events (or characteristics) is taken as *constituting* causal connection, rather than as being evidence for some causal law, *qua* uniformity. In treating the causal versions of telepathy and clairvoyance as hypotheses, I am assuming that there are uniformities governing these phenomena; that, whether or not they are too complex to be discovered, there are, for example conditions in which a person would be 100 per cent successful in guessing cards. (My assumption may of course be false. It may be that the only laws governing psi-phenomena would have to be stated in terms of degrees of probability lying *between* 0 and 1.)

I wish now to mention a reason why, in estimating the relevance of psychical research to philosophy, we should at present concentrate on the facts rather than on the familiar hypotheses. There has been, and still is, much controversy between psychical researchers as to how many different primary hypotheses must be invoked in order to account for the facts. One controversial issue, which has been well aired, is whether all cases of ostensible clairvoyance can be explained away in terms of precognitive (or retrocognitive) telepathy or, conversely, whether all cases of ostensible telepathy can be explained away in terms of precognitive (or retrocognitive) clairvoyance.[5] I have recently discussed another problem of the same type, concerning the difficulties in experimentally isolating PK and precognition.[6] The issues are too technical to discuss here. Though they may not be worth much, I shall mention my own opinions: I am not certain that it is possible in principle to obtain unambiguous experimental evidence for *each* of the four hypotheses mentioned above, and I am not fully convinced that this has yet been done for any *one* of them. Until the experts are more or less unanimous as to what hypotheses are irreducible, others should be cautious about assuming the truth of any one of these. (By "experts" I mean persons sufficiently familiar with the facts and experimental methods—this is not of course a closed circle.) I suggest then, that in estimating the relevance of psychical research to philosophy we should concentrate on the features which are common or peculiar to psi-phenomena. This policy cuts us off from many of the more interesting aspects of physical research, but it may be wise at this stage to base our conclusions on what is most certain.

I wish first to discuss a feature common and peculiar to psi-phenomena—namely that they appear to violate what may be called "the principle of the spatio-temporal continuity of causal chains." The fact that this feature is shared by the so-called mental and the so-called physical[7] phenomena is a further reason for grouping these together under the label "psi-phenomena." It is this feature which, in my opinion, constitutes the best reason for describing psi-phenomena as "supernormal" (or "paranormal"). I should define "supernormal causal relations" as causal relations, which hold between events separated by a spatio-temporal gap, and which are not mediated by any continuous chain of events. And it is, I think, this feature of psi-phenomena which is the root of the prevailing attitude of scientists towards the facts.

The weight commonly attached to this principle of continuity may be illustrated by considering Russell's recent discussion of "The Postulates of Scientific Inference." When Russell is giving his summary of his five postulates,[8] he says "each of these postulates asserts that something happens often, but not necessarily always." His description of each of the other postulates is consistent with this statement, but this is not true of his description of the third postulate—"this postulate is concerned to deny 'action at a distance' and to assert that when there is a causal connection between two events which are not contiguous, there *must* be intermediate links in the causal chain such that each is contiguous to the next, or (alternatively) such that there is a process which is continuous in the mathematical sense." Russell seems to be treating this principle as universal and necessary. Even if his use of "must" was a slip, it would still be an illuminating one. In any case, most scientists' seem confident that this principle is universal and necessary, and their conviction has been powerfully reinforced by Einstein's success in reconciling the theory of gravitation with this principle. However, there is no evidence for, and there are strong reasons against the view that this principle applies to psi-phenomena. The issue at stake is whether it is possible to explain psi-phenomena by invoking a new kind of physical field or radiation. This question has been discussed *ad nauseum*, but as the issue is a fundamental one, I shall discuss it briefly.

There is no doubt that either precognition or clairvoyance occurs, i.e., that some human events are influenced, in a way that is not understood, either by later events or by contemporary nonhuman events. A radiation theory must account for at least one of these alternatives. I shall assume that no one will invoke a physical radiation which travels backwards through time! Consider then the clairvoyance-phenomena to which a radiation theory would have to be applied: e.g. the cases in which a subject has got significant scores in guessing the order of a pack of cards, which order was not revealed to the senses of any person until a record of the subject's previously completed guesses were compared with it. (Most of the "ESP" experiments done at Duke University in the 1930's were of this type.) Variations in the experimental conditions have established the irrelevance of—(a) the angle of the pack of cards relative to the subject; (b) the distance between the subject and the cards; (c) the objects (e.g. buildings and mountains) which absorb all the known radiations which might be supposed to do the job. How could we reconcile these facts with what is known or believed about the transmission of physical energy? Points (b) and (c) could only be accommodated by adopting a weird *ad hoc* hypothesis, namely that human bodies are the only material objects which are affected by the hypothetical radiation; that all other material objects are, so to speak, "transparent" to it, i.e., do not absorb or dissipate any of its energy. And there are other difficulties equally serious, for example, in accounting for the "selectivity" of the subject. Cards are not the only kinds of material object to which clairvoyant responses occur—we should have to suppose that all material objects emit the radiations in question. A radiation theory can give us no answer to the question—why does the subject respond to the radiation emanating from a certain object say 200 miles away, rather than to any of the others which are impinging on him? There is also the problem as to how different physical characteristics of the radiation could be translated (or interpreted) by the subject in terms of the different sensible characteristics of the object from which they emanate. [10] If we consider them collectively, the difficulties involved in trying to reconcile the facts with Russell's third postulate seem to be overwhelming.

I shall now discuss a feature which is peculiar, though not common, to psi-phenomena—I refer to what is sometimes called "temporal displacement." Russell's fourth postulate ("of the common causal origin of similar structures ranged about a centre") has here an interesting, and to Russell, I imagine, unexpected application. In his use of this postulate, Russell is taking a certain complex relational property as providing both a criterion of causal connection and a criterion of the direction of causal influence: the property in question being *spatial or spatio-temporal clustering around a central event of a set of (structurally) similar events.* As instances of this property Russell mentions the sounds occurring in the vicinity of each wireless receiver which is tuned to a given wavelength, and again, the sounds heard by each person who is within earshot of an explosion. In such a case there occurs a family of similar events (processes), which are "ranged about a central region," and we can find criteria for discovering the causal source, which is assumed to be an event (process) in the central region. The criterion to which Russell pays most attention is spatio-temporal clustering, i.e., the fact that the time when each corresponding event occurs differs from a certain time by a period proportional to its distance from the central region. But this is not our only criterion for discovering the central region. We also find a spatial clustering in respect of loudness, i.e., *ceteris paribus,* the loudness decreases in proportion to (the square of) the distance from the central region.

Now consider the results of Whately Carington's experiments "in the paranormal cognition of drawings."[11] Carington carried out a series of experiments, each of which lasted for a ten-day period. On each of the ten evenings Carington made and displayed in his study a different drawing. The objects drawn were selected by him, by a random method, immediately before they were drawn. A group of subjects scattered throughout Britain, America and Holland attempted on each of these evenings to reproduce the drawing simultaneously displayed in Carington's study. Carington noticed a marked tendency for subjects to score hits on the drawings used as targets in the current experiment oftener than they did on those used in earlier and later experiments, and he devised methods for measuring this tendency. The surprising feature revealed by his analysis of the results was that to a striking extent the hits were clustered, more or less symmetrically, around the occasion of display. To simplify exposition, let us consider the temporal distribution of the hits made on a single target-drawing.[12] Carington's results indicate that the number of different persons who were reproducing the target-drawing increased steadily during the days before its selection and display, and declined gradually during the days following its display.

We find in Carington's data what Russell has called "a group of similar events ranged about a center," but here the clustering is not spatial or spatio-temporal, but is purely temporal.[13] I suggest that this property—purely temporal clustering around a central event of a set of similar events—should be accepted as a criterion of causal connection. If this is agreed, notice that Carington's results also provide us with a criterion of the direction of causal influence, and one which is independent of the common-sense criterion (namely that this influence is always from earlier to later events). In our earlier examples of the *spatial* clustering of similar events, one criterion of the direction of causal influence was the regular dwindling of a measurable characteristic (loudness) as the distance increases, in any direction, from the central region. In Carington's results we find a regular dwindling in the number of hits as the temporal distance increases, in *either* direction, from the central period (i.e. the period when the target-drawing is selected, produced and displayed). Are we not driven to conclude that events which occurred during the central period were the causal source of similar events which had happened earlier, viz., the production of (some of) the extra-chance hits?

If one adopted Mrs. Kneale's aim of showing that psychical research "suggests modifications of terminology," one could use the above discussion for this purpose. There are some verbal changes which are called for by psi-phenomena and by nothing else; for example, that "causal connection" should not be defined, as it often has been, so as to make spatio-temporal contiguity part of its meaning: that "cause" and "effect" should not be defined so as to render analytic the statement "a cause precedes its effects." We might go on to suggest that we should not use ". . . is happening" in its commonly accepted sense as equivalent to ". . . is coming into existence;" for it appears to be sometimes the case that an event is causally influenced by an event which has not yet happened, and it seems self-contradictory to speak of an event being "causally influenced by something which has not yet come into existence." But to present our conclusions as verbal recommendations would be to conceal their importance. The problems at stake are not primarily linguistic, even if their solution does call for some revised definitions. We cannot, for example, define "to happen" as meaning something other than "to come into existence," without committing ourselves to a very peculiar theory about time and change: and in questioning the universal application of Russell's third postulate, we are challenging a system of beliefs and expectations which are deeply engrained in scientific common-sense.

If I ended my paper at this point, I would be shelving one of the central issues that I have raised, namely whether, or in what sense, it is possible to explain psi-phenomena. Despite my doubts as to whether I can say anything useful, I am going to hazard some tentative remarks on this subject. In stating the problem, I shall use Reichenbach's term "interphenomena" to refer to all the entities or processes which are postulated by science, or taken for granted by common-sense, to correlate or explain observational data. The only kinds of interphenomena which the physical sciences acknowledge[14] are either chains of spatio-temporally contiguous events, or modifications in the spatial structure of material objects. (Many physicists, of course, regard the latter as analysable in terms of the former.) The common view that psi-phenomena are unintelligible seems to be due to the apparent impossibility of explaining the facts in terms of physical interphenomena, together with the difficulty of conceiving any other kinds of interphenomena which would perform the required functions. I propose to bypass questions concerning the ontological status of the scientists' interphenomena, or the logical status of the statements they make about them. (Surely the philosopher's duty to science is not confined to, even if it includes, pronouncing that its interphenomena are "logical constructions.")

It seems to me that there are two distinct aims which the scientists' interphenomena are designed to fulfill:

(1) to achieve what may be called correlation; meaning by this the exhibiting of the largest possible number of apparently diverse phenomena as instances of the smallest possible number of the simplest possible laws,

(2) to render intelligible the interdependence of different events.

Scientists are (professionally) primarily interested in the first aim. I suggest that it is one of the philosophers' duties to discuss whether interphenomena fulfil the second aim. Positivist philosophers (and scientists) would have us believe that the second aim is identical with the first. It seems to me however that the second aim, whether or not it can be fulfilled, is certainly, *as an aim*, distinct from the first. I think it is true to say

(*a*) that it is a psychological necessity for us to postulate interphenomena for the second purpose,

(*b*) that no new science has ever made appreciable progress in fulfilling the first purpose, until it has been furnished with suitable concepts of interphenomena. For example, whether or not there exist any
entities corresponding to "magnetic lines of force," this concept was
indispensable to the thinking which guided Faraday's experiments
and Maxwell's calculations, and hence to the development of modern
physics. (When correlation is far advanced and laws have been formulated as functional equations, the interphenomena employed en route
can be ignored. But notice that some scientists are interested in interphenomena for the second purpose as well as the first—thus some
contemporary physicists regard it as a virtue of Einstein's General
Theory that it renders gravitation-phenomena intelligible.)

One thing we should not do is to adopt definitions which beg the
question whether interphenomena which are appropriate for psychical
research can be or will be conceived. Mr Robinson seems to have done
this, e.g., when he says that calling a coincidence "telepathy" is denying
that any indirect causal explanation is possible. Apart from begging an
important question, such a definition does not conform to the usage of
psychical researchers, who have made many attempts to conceive
appropriate interphenomena. I shall conclude this paper by discussing
briefly and sketchily some of the lines along which such attempts have
been made.

Since physical interphenomena will not fill the bill, psychical
researchers have naturally explored the possibility of invoking mental
interphenomena. Many psychical researchers have invoked a Common
Unconscious (mind). It is often not clear how this is supposed to help, but
one comparatively clear view is that "Common Unconscious" refers to a
medium in which traces (engrams), produced by events occurring in the
mind of one person, may be retained and may later influence events in
other minds. (The facts which have seemed to require this theory are
mainly the achievements of "mediums" in giving information which had
been possessed only by persons then deceased.) On this interpretation,
the theory of a common unconscious seems to be an attempt to deal with
telepathy along the same lines as many psychologists (e.g., Stout) have
dealt with normal memory. The more critical of those who have
entertained this theory have recognized that they have no right to describe

the interpersonal trace-bearing medium as being mental in nature. I suspect that the motive underlying this suggestion has been a desire to render psi-phenomena intelligible, by reconciling them with the principle of continuity of causal chains. The guiding thought has presumably been that, since we cannot invoke causal chains which are continuous in the spatio-temporal sense, we should postulate causal chains which are continuous in some other sense. I am doubtful whether the resulting suggestion helps to make psi-phenomena intelligible. Can we attach any empirical meaning to the notion of a continuous causal chain, if not in terms of spatio-temporal continuity? (I say *"empirical* meaning" to rule out the sort of continuity which occurs in mathematical progressions: this seems to me irrelevant.) Perhaps we can do this in the case of mental processes belonging to the same person (e.g. unconscious desires), but what sort of nonphysical causal chain can be supposed to link mental events belonging to different persons? It would be more economical to suppose that, when telepathic transactions between different people occur, an event in one person is a *proximate* cause of the behaviour or experience of another person. If we said this we would be assimilating telepathy to "mnemic causation" as this was conceived by Russell in *Analysis of Mind* (chapter 4). But is such a causal transaction intelligible?

These questions about the continuity of causal chains may be avoidable, if we interpret psi-phenomena in terms of cognitive relations instead of causal relations: may be avoidable, *if* we assume that cognitive relations possess a characteristic whch they seem to possess. Let us adopt the phenomenological viewpoint. Consider situations in which one is remembering a past event. On such an occasion I seem to myself to be directly acquainted with something which is remote in space and/or in time. If I am asked to describe my experience, I may, through habit, start talking about "(mental) images." But, as Mr. Woozley has recently argued,[15] this habit is a perhaps misleading product of philosophising. The facts do not, I think, exclude the realist theory that, in remembering, a person is directly acquainted with some remote events, which constitute the "materials" of his memory-beliefs. If cognitive relations really possess the characteristics of *spanning spatio-temporal gaps*, it is on this account that it is plausible to attribute psi-phenomena to cognitive relations, and hence to regard them as being mental.[16] If we were to adopt such a theory, we should have to say that the cognitions (prehensions) which are invoked to explain psi-phenomena are themselves, in most cases, uncognised—they would thus be interphenomena even from the viewpoint of the subject. There are several reasons for saying this:

(*a*) In the card-guessing experiments, as we have seen, subjects seem to be unable to distinguish which of their guesses are successful; and few subjects report the occurrence of any "imagery" accompanying their writing.

(*b*) It is a common feature of spontaneous cases of telepathy that the subject's experience symbolises the agent's experience in an indirect or distorted manner.

That the facts are attributable to cognitions which are usually, or always, subliminal (unconscious) seems to be the theory most commonly accepted by psychical researchers to explain telepathy and clairvoyance. This theory is often associated with Freudian concepts of inhibiting mechanisms which determine whether and when and in what way conscious events will be influenced by subliminal cognitions. Such a theory has little cash value for the experimenter. (It may have some, in guiding investigation as to which psychological conditions in the subject are conducive to success.) However, this theory is presumably designed to fulfil the scientists' second aim—to render psi-phenomena intelligible— and to do this by finding analogies between them and more familiar facts, by interpreting them in terms of more familiar concepts. I am inclined to think this theory does contribute something to this purpose.

I know of only one theory which is at all comprehensive and which is still an empirical hypothesis in the Positivists' sense. This is Carington's "Association Theory of Telepathy," which may be described loosely by saying that associations formed in a normal way in one mind may be operative in other minds; or more precisely by saying that if two objects K and O become associated for one person, this increases the probability that *any* person who thinks of K will then think of O. This theory does have some cash-value for the experimenter,[17] and it does enable us to correlate some apparently diverse phenomena.[18] It does not take us far enough, for it does not seem applicable to PK or clairvoyance: and though it may reconcile some people to psi-phenomena by subsuming them under a familiar law (or label), it may antagonise psychologists who regard the Association theory as outmoded. In any case, being an empirical hypothesis, it leaves the philosophical problems unresolved. Even if we accept Carington's theory as a working hypothesis, we can (and I think must) still ask how associations formed by one person can influence other people in the conditions in question. We have still the philosophical problem of rendering the hypothesis intelligible.

Carington's theory is compatible with interpreting psi-phenomena in terms of either causal or cognitive relations on the lines described earlier. It suggests however a possibility not previously mentioned, namely that some of the constituents of different minds are not merely alike, but are numerically identical. This notion provides one, possibly intelligible, answer to the question—how can your associating K and O tend to make me think of O when I think of K? This is *one* way of interpreting "common unconscious," and it has been entertained by some psychical researchers. I feel strongly inclined to dismiss this notion as nonsensical; but I do not think we are entitled to do this merely because our *verbal* conventions debar us from speaking of "two minds owning the same experience." (We may in any case be forced to revise this convention, if, as Russell has suggested, physiologists learn to make a nerve connecting my brain to your aching tooth.) I mention this notion to illustrate how psychical researchers are driven to entertain possibilities which are so shocking to common-sense that many people conclude that they belong to the lunatic fringe. I feel confident that philosophers will not subscribe to this verdict, if they attend to the facts which psychical researchers are trying to explain and to the scientific postulates which seem to be violated.

Regarding the question which is the subject of this symposium, I must leave it to you to decide whether the discussion of the issues I have raised is a proper and important task for philosophers. We could leave such tasks to be performed by scientists, but, whether or not science would suffer, philosophy would surely lose by this policy.

NOTES

1. *SPR Proc.*, Vol. XLVII, Part 167, pp. 77-8.
2. *The Reach of the Mind*, p. 156.
3. I shall later define my use of "supernormal."
4. There might be poltergeist-phenomena which did not belong to either class, but most alleged poltergeist-phenomena can be placed in class (1) because they were reported as occurring only in the vicinity of a particular person—usually a badly adjusted adolescent.
5. A recent discussion of this issue is to be found in *SPR Proc.*, Vol. XLVIII, Part 172. See also Dr. Soal's Myers Lecture *The Experimental Situation in Psychical Research*, Sections 34-40, giving a preliminary report of experiments which appear to exclude clairvoyance.
6. *SPR Proc.*, Vol. XLIX, Part 178.
7. I ignore stories about pseudopods.
8. *Human Knowledge*, Part VI, Ch. IX.
9. This is not true of some exponents of the Quantum Theory. But is this relevant? The events between which supernormal relations hold are not "microscopic."
10. Professor Broad formulated the extremely unplausible *ad hoc* hypotheses, which would have to be invoked to solve this problem, in his Presidential address to the SPR—*SPR Proc.*, Vol. XLIII, Part 142.

11. *SPR Proc.*, Vol. XLVI, Part 162.

12. Actually Carington did not find this regular curve in the temporal distribution of hits made on *each* target-drawing. The regular curve emerged when the results were aggregated.

13. Carington found that the spatial relations between himself and the subjects were irrelevant, e.g., the best results were obtained by subjects in America.

14. I am ignoring Quantum Mechanics. I am not qualified to discuss what its exponents mean by "waves of probability" (or "wavicles"). If such expressions were interpreted as referring to interphenomena, they would not be interphenomena of either of the kinds I have mentioned. I suspect, however, that "waves of probability" is just a short-hand device for referring to certain characteristics of the observational data.

15. A. D. Woozley. *Theory of Knowledge.* Ch. 3.

16. PK, if it is confirmed as an independent hypothesis, could not be thus explained.

17. One illustration of this is provided by Carington who re-examined the results of some earlier experiments to find whether they conformed to the sublaws of the Association theory (Recency and Frequency) and found some striking confirmation, *vide* his *Telepathy*, Ch. VI.

18. It can be applied to hauntings and "psychometry" (object-reading) as well as to "straight" telepathy.

C. D. Broad

Review of Kneale, Robinson, and Mundle Symposium

If I may say so with respect, I think that there are two things in Mrs. Kneale's paper which diminish its value as an introduction to the Symposium. One is that she thought it desirable to argue her case on the assumption that philosophy consists of linguistic analysis. The other is that she has given an ostensive definition of "psychical research" by reference to Mr. Tyrrell's book, *The Personality of Man.* As regards the former, I can only say that I seldom find it illuminating to discuss philosophical questions in purely linguistic terms. It seems to me often to involve translating fairly straightforward and simply expressible questions into a contorted and pedantic terminology, with the risk of omitting factors which are relevant and introducing others which are contingent and irrelevant because they depend on the linguistic usages of particular races and cultures. As regards the latter, it is well to bear in mind that Mr. Tyrrell, beside having made valuable contributions to experimental and theoretical psychical research, is an enthusiastic amateur philosopher, and that he also strongly believes that a general recognition of the established results of psychical research would have far-reaching good effects. This latter personal conviction of Mr. Tyrrell's seems to have acted as a red herring to Mr. Robinson and led him to conclude his paper with a discussion of the effects for good or ill which would probably follow if

Reprinted from *The Journal of Parapsychology*, volume 15 (1951), pp. 216-223, by permission of the editors.

telepathy, clairvoyance, and psychokinesis were not merely accepted as facts but became applicable in practice on a large scale. These speculations seem to me to be completely irrelevant to the subject of our Symposium. I doubt whether they are particularly relevant even to Mr. Tyrrell's enthusiasms; for what he was concerned with was the practical effects of the change in general opinion about the nature of man which he thought would follow on the general acceptance of the results of psychical research. It is obviously possible that the effects of that change of opinion might be predominantly good, while the effects of the widespread practical application of the powers by the general recognition of which the change had been brought about, might be predominantly bad.

Apart from the ostensive definition of "psychical research" by reference to Mr. Tyrrell's book, Mrs. Kneale makes two statements about the contents of that subject. One is that all the phenomena dealt with by it are "abnormal" in one or other of the following two ways. They are either (1) *physical* happenings of a sort not explicable in terms of the laws known to common sense or science, or (2) the acquiring by human beings of *information* which they could not obtain in normal ways. The other statement is that psychical research is what is left over when the regular sciences have marked out their territories. Both these statements are negative; but the former at least tries to state a negative property common and peculiar to psi phenomena, while the latter merely delimits the subject by exclusion from the territories of other named subjects. The latter seems to me wholly unsatisfactory. The territories of the various sciences are not definitely fixed, and I should have thought that much that falls outside the present territories of all of them forms no part of the subject matter of psychical research. Let us therefore concentrate our attention on the former criterion, namely, that of "abnormality."

Mrs. Kneale does not develop this theme further; but Mr. Robinson makes some remarks about it, which I will now consider. Taking first the case of physical phenomena, he says that if the data of the psychical researchers and the laws accepted by the physicists were to conflict, the problem would be like the conflict between the theologians and the biologists in the nineteenth century. I cannot see the least resemblance between the two. What we should have is a conflict between the results of certain carefully conducted and controlled experiments (for example, on dice-throwing) and generalizations about the agents and laws involved in the motions of material objects, based on a vast amount of other empirical evidence, direct and indirect, positive and negative.

C. D. BROAD

In connection with the phrase "acquiring information by abnormal means," he distinguishes between "by means which are not normal" and "without any means at all," and asserts that the latter is what the phrase signifies or ought to signify in the mouths of psychical researchers. In this connection Mr. Robinson contrasts telepathy with telegraphy, and says that "if means had been produced," in the former case, "we could all use them." Now there seems to be an ambiguity here in the word "means." One sense of it is a series of events, intermediate in time and perhaps also in space, between one event and another correlated event, so interrelated that we could call the former a "causal *ancestor*" of the latter but not the *immediate* cause of it. This seems to be what Mr. Robinson has in mind when he says that to call a coincidence "telepathic" is "to deny that any *indirect* causal explanation is possible." Another sense of "means" is something that a person can do or something that he can use in a certain way in order to secure or to facilitate the attainment of some end which he desires. This seems to be what Mr. Robinson has in mind when he talks of a means as "having been produced" in the case of telegraphy, and its not having been produced in that of telepathy.

It is evident that the two senses of "means" are different, and that there is no close connection between them. Suppose, for example, that giving the telepathic agent a certain drug and making certain hypnotic suggestions to the telepathic percipient were found to increase very greatly the rate of scoring in an experiment. Then administering this drug and making this kind of hypnotic suggestion would be a "means" to bringing about telepathy, in the second sense of "means," whether or not the causal relation between an experience in the agent and the correlated experience in the percipient were direct or mediated. Conversely, telepathy might take place through "means," in the sense of a causally intermediate chain of events, and yet we might be utterly without "means" of producing it at will or facilitating it.

The actual position at present may, I think, be fairly summed up in the following three propositions. (1) Most, though by no means all, competent students of psychical research consider that the detailed empirical facts make it almost impossible to hold that, *if* there be causal mediation in the case of telepathy and clairvoyance, it is of any of the kinds *familiar in physics*. (2) There is no consensus of opinion *for or against* the view that these processes are causally mediated *in some other way*. (3) Many of the best experimenters have actively sought and continue to seek for practical means of inducing or facilitating telepathic and

112

clairvoyant powers; but so far little, if anything, has been accomplished in this direction.

It seems to me that much the most important contribution in this Symposium to elucidating the notion of "abnormality" in reference to psi phenomena has been made by Mr. Mundle. He says that what is peculiar and common to such phenomena is that prima facie they involve causal relations between "events separated by a spatio-temporal gap and not mediated by any continuous chain of events," and he suggests, rightly in my opinion, that this is at the root of the discomfort which scientists feel in the presence of such phenomena. He notes another feature which is peculiar to some psi phenomena, though not common to all of them. This is the temporal clustering of certain events, which must be regarded as effects, about a certain event, which must be regarded as their common causal source, and the fact that some of the effect-events in such clusters *precede* the event which is their causal source.

Now I think that these features are special instances of a more general peculiarity of psi phenomena which may be taken as their distinguishing mark. And I think that it is because of this general peculiarity that psi phenomena should be of certain special interest to philosophers. The point is this. There are certain limiting principles which we unhesitatingly take for granted as the framework within which all our practical activities and our scientific theories are confined. Some of these seem self-evident. Others are so overwhelmingly supported by all the empirical facts which fall within the range of ordinary experience and the scientific elaborations of it (including under this heading orthodox psychology) that it hardly enters our heads to question them. I will call them Basic Limiting Principles. In a recent article in *Philosophy* (Oct., 1949) I stated and discussed eight of these, classified under the four heads of General Principles of Causation, Limitations on the Action of Mind on Matter, Dependence of Mind on Brain, and Limitations on Ways of Acquiring Knowledge. Psychical research is concerned with any alleged event which seems prima facie to conflict with one or more of these basic limiting principles. An event may be very abnormal indeed, for example, the arithmetical feats of calculating boys or the sensory hyperaesthesia displayed by some persons under hypnosis. But, provided that it seems possible to account for it within the framework of the basic limiting principles, even though we may have to postulate hitherto unrecognized laws or agents or both in order to do so, it does not concern psychical research.

C. D. BROAD

Now, if philosophy is what philosophers have always done, these basic limiting principles are of great concern to it, in a sense in which the particular laws and hypotheses of the various sciences are not. And, if psychical research establishes conclusively the existence of facts which conflict with one or more of those principles, it must be highly relevant to philosophy. As I, for my part, accept the antecedents of both these conditional propositions, I hold that psychical research *is* highly relevant to philosophy.

I will conclude my remarks by considering a few points of detail in the contributions to the Symposium.

(1) I am much puzzled by Mr. Robinson's remark that, if telepathy or clairvoyance or precognition were established, this would suffice to refute empiricism. In the first place, he defines "empiricism" in such a way that it would certainly be false quite independently of the results of psychical research. For he says that it is of the essence of empiricism that "we ought not to accept any synthetic proposition except upon the evidence of our senses." But surely everyone accepts, and rightly accepts, some synthetic propositions on the evidence of personal memory and others on the evidence of introspection. And surely neither memory nor introspection is sensation or sense perception. Secondly, I had always supposed that empiricism was the doctrine that the evidence for all synthetic *universal* propositions is inductive and that the ultimate origin of all our *concepts* is acquaintance with particular instances. Now the information which is alleged to be acquired paranormally is about *singular* facts, not about universal propositions. And it is not alleged that any of our *concepts* are derived from paranormally received data.

(2) I wish to make some comments on certain things which Mr. Robinson says about the possible relevance of psychical research to what he calls the "Aristotelian" and the "Platonic" theories of the nature of the human individual. By the former theory I understand him to mean the doctrine that the cognitive, conative, and affective dispositions and actions and passions of an individual are essentially functions of his ordinary visible and tangible living organism. By the latter I understand him to mean that these dispositions, actions, and passions, or at any rate the more specifically human of them, are functions of something which is existentially independent of a man's present organism, and is only temporarily connected with the latter, though greatly influenced by it during the period of their interconnection.

Now I understand Mr. Robinson to hold that, if the results of psychical research were accepted, the Aristotelian view would have to be rejected in favor of the Platonic. It seems to me that this assertion is plausible only if it refers to those phenomena which seem prima facie to suggest the posthumous existence and activity of certain human individuals. And even here it is plausible only on the assumption (which is a matter of acute controversy among experts in psychical research) that these phenomena cannot be accounted for by telepathy, clairvoyance, precognition, and unconscious dramatization on the basis of data so obtained, on the part of persons still alive in the flesh. If the Aristotelian view is consistent with all the facts of normal and abnormal (as distinct from paranormal) human psychology, I do not see why it could not be stretched to cover telepathy, clairvoyance, precognition and psychokinesis. Every one of these might have a material basis in certain activities of certain parts of the living human brain and nervous system. On the other hand, even if we were compelled by certain facts established by psychical research to accept some kind of survival of bodily death in the case of some human individuals, it is not at all clear that we should be tied down to the Platonic theory as I understand it. There are all kinds of alternatives, ranging from the full-blown survival of the individual soul animating an organism which is not normally visible or tangible, to the mere temporary persistence of some poor disintegrated fragment of the deceased individual's personality. These alternatives would have to be weighed in the light of a detailed study of the relevant facts. One of the ways in which psychical research is relevant to philosophy is that certain of its data enforce the desirability of considering other alternatives beside the Platonic and the Aristotelian views of the nature of the human individual and suggest alternatives which may be worth exploring.

It is in connection with this question that Mr. Robinson makes the remark that, if the results which psychical researchers claim to have established were accepted, philosophy would be *superseded* by psychical research. Taking this remark in its context, I assume that it must refer, not to philosophy as a whole, but to that part of it which is concerned with the nature of the human individual. Apart from this limitation it seems nonsensical. Even with this limitation the remark seems to me to be a gross exaggeration. The utmost that I could admit is that certain views on this subject, which had previously been *mere* philosophical speculations, would then gain some support from concrete empirical facts. Mr. Robinson's final remark that in any case he "cannot help believing the Aristotelian view and disbelieving the Platonic view" is a frank confession of invincible prejudice, which is of interest as a detail in his intellectual biography but is not otherwise germane to the subject under discussion.

(3) The last point which I will consider is the suggestion made by Mr. Robinson that philosophers might be usefully occupied in analyzing the terms "telepathy," "clairvoyance," "precognition," and others which are used in psychical research. This is accepted by Mr. Mundle, and I do not suppose that Mrs. Kneale would have any objection to it. I heartily agree, on one condition. That is that any philosopher who undertakes this task should prepare himself by a careful study of the relevant literature, as he would certainly do before venturing to analyze and criticize the terminology of any other special science. For these questions have been and are being vigorously discussed by psychical researchers, some of whom at least have had some philosophical training, and a good deal of analysis and clarification has been accomplished. If this condition is not fulfilled, and if philosophers rush in and pontificate *de haut en bas* on the strength of having hastily skimmed one or two popular books on psychical research they will probably incur and will certainly deserve the accusation of trying to teach their grandmothers to suck eggs.

NOTES

1. [See above, pp. 43-63—Ed.]

J. B. Rhine

The Science of Nonphysical Nature

Out of his sensory experience and its rational derivatives man has developed a general concept known as the physical universe. And out of the relationships that have been found to exist within this observed and inferred universe have emerged the recognized physical sciences and the physical bases of the other sciences. While from time to time there have been offered hypotheses of nonphysical factors in living organisms, none of these has ever become orthodox, either in biology or psychology. There are, therefore, no conventionally recognized nonphysical operations in the natural world, and, according to prevailing thought, any occurrence not fundamentally reducible to physical process would have either to be ignored or classed as supernatural (though such a category, too, is unacceptable in the sciences). Thus, even though many individual scientists have reservations on the point, nature has, in the sciences, come to be effectively synonymous with the physical universe.

There has been only one small branch of inquiry to make a scientific attack on the question of nonphysical causation in nature. This branch of inquiry logically is a division of psychological study and is known today as *parapsychology* (and by various other names such as psychical research, metapsychics, psychic science, etc.). Its problem-domain includes those natural occurrences (now called *psi* phenomena) which do not submit to

Reprinted from *The Journal of Philosophy*, volume 51 (1954), pp. 801-810, by permission of the author and editors.

classification as physical events. In more descriptive terms, parapsychology deals with the experiences and behavior of living organisms that fail to show regular relationships with time, space, mass, and other criteria of physicality.

Parapsychology began with the study of spontaneous psi (or psychic) experiences such as are fairly common throughout the world. These experiences appear to defy interpretation in terms of conventional principles. The more familiar of these were of cognitive nature, instances in which information was supplied to the person concerned, knowledge which he could not have acquired by way of the recognized sensory and rational channels. There were in such cases no adequate intermediating physical stimuli for interception by the sense organs. These spontaneous experiences, which had been familiar throughout the history of mankind, came to be identified as instances of *telepathy* if they seemed to involve a transfer of thought or feeling from one person to another, and *clairvoyance* if there appeared to be an awareness of an objective event not present to the senses.

Such occurrences became of special interest during the latter half of the Nineteenth Century when the pressure of mechanistic thinking deriving from the rapid advancement of the physical sciences challenged the spiritual concept of man. An effort was made at first to collect and study the spontaneous experiences themselves, as evidence of an extrasensory mode of perception, but this attempt gave way in time to experimental research into the problems suggested. Early experiments based on these claims of extrasensory perception (ESP) were generally exploratory in character. They did not, as was eventually recognized, distinguish adequately between the two forms, telepathy and clairvoyance. Naturally, there was to begin with no very clear concept of the basic characteristics of parapsychological phenomena; that is, what common features would identify them. The field had not yet acquired general outlines. But these exploratory tests sustained interest and stimulated further research. Criticism and discussion followed and led in time to the refinement of the test procedures.

By the second quarter of the present century, however, the development of methods had produced a crucial order of tests for extrasensory perception. The occurrence of ESP had, by the mid-thirties, been tested under conditions that, even today, have not been seriously questioned. In the most definitive experiment conducted up to that time the best subject tested for ESP was able to identify the order of cards from shuffled packs located in another building, from 100 to 250 yards away, with a success of approximately 30 percent in a series of 1850 trials, tests in which the expectation on a theory of chance was but 20 percent. Since the theoretical probability of so great a result in such a series was of the order of 10^{-24}, it may be assumed that an effective relationship between subject and object had been demonstrated. In view of the distance involved and also other precautions against sensory cues, only an extra-sensory mode of perception could have produced the results. With recurrent patterning from one pack of cards to the other eliminated, both by the shuffling and by the use of several decks of cards, rational inference on the part of the subject could not be considered as a reasonable alternative to ESP. With the provisions for independent recording (in duplicate) and even double surveillance during one section of the experiment, the hypothesis of error, whether deliberate or unconscious, was rendered improbable.

In the twenty years that have followed publication of these data many other series of experiments have been made by other investigators in the same and in other laboratories, some of them with even more elaborate precautions and more extensive design than the work described. Researches have also been conducted to distinguish between the types of ESP known as telepathy and clairvoyance. Both types of effects have been experimentally demonstrated, although in the case of telepathy it is not possible to say what the fundamental nature of the sender's operation is that constitutes the target. The mystery of the essential thought-brain relation for the present limits the investigation of the question of telepathy beyond this point.

If, as most serious scientific students who have followed the research developments will readily concede, the occurrence of ESP has been established, it will be allowable now to proceed to consider its challenge to physical explanation. In other words, assuming that extrasensory perception occurs, we may ask if it is extra-physical.

The very spontaneous experiences from which the experiments took their cue offered a challenge to physics in the first place. One of the most obvious features of these experiences is that two persons are as likely to have a telepathic experience when they are separated by thousands of miles as they are when only a short distance apart. In spontaneous experiences of clairvoyance, too, the distant scene is as likely to be perceived as that which is nearby. Moreover, a number of the exploratory tests of ESP, prior to the one described above, had involved considerable distances measured in miles, some of them even comparisons of different distances. The results failed to suggest any relationship of success in ESP to the proximity of the subject to the object.

The subject participating in the distance experiment mentioned above, in which 30 percent success was obtained at 100 to 250 yards, had, over a long series of previous tests, averaged approximately 32 percent successes with the target cards within a few feet of him. There was nothing, therefore, in the test results to indicate any lawful relationship whatever between distance and scoring rate. In the other experiments that involve distance, while it cannot be said that a nicely designed study, exhausting all possibilities, has ever yet been made, the results have been the same—there is no reliable relation indicated.

No hypothesis of a physical relationship in ESP has ever arisen from the research results. The spontaneous cases had given no suggestion of any effect of distance and the experimental evidence confirmed the impression. And yet, as a matter of course, there have been many types of conditions from which such an hypothesis could have emerged had the evidence suggested it. There have been many different barriers imposed incidentally in the experimental conditions, barriers such as walls, buildings, mountains, and thousands of miles of atmosphere. Also, the target objects have been presented at various angles. In most cases these objects were cards. They have been located in various positions, in some instances with the back of the card toward the subject, in other cases in such a position that only an edge would be turned in the direction of the subject. In addition, for any theory of radiation there is the difficulty of discriminating between numerous objects in close proximity. For example, in many ESP tests the problem involves the attempt to identify cards packed in a box in which all twenty-five are less than a quarter of an inch thick. This proximity would obviously become a limiting condition for a physical hypothesis. But in spite of all the varieties of physical conditions under which ESP tests have been conducted, the results have consistently been such that no hypothesis of a physical relationship has been suggested.

One of the most striking features of the spontaneous experiences of ESP is the fact that they are almost as likely to involve future events as contemporaneous ones. A dream of disaster occurring to a loved one may precede the tragic event itself or may merely precede the arrival of the news coming from the scene, which may be half way around the world. This suggestion that precognitive ESP might occur was reduced to experimental test following the definitive stage of ESP experiments mentioned above, and, so far as experimental comparisons have gone, the same relationship has been found as in the spontaneous cases; that is to say, time has not been found to be a limiting condition in the functioning of ESP. It is no handicap to ESP to be directed toward a target order of cards that is to be set up at a designated future time, as compared with a present order. This experimental result follows logically enough, not only from the spontaneous psi experiments but also from the results of the distance tests; it would be difficult to conceive of time as limiting a function that is independent of space. At least it will be difficult until science discovers an instance of time change involving no spatial change.

It would be too large an undertaking to recount here the steps through which the methods for testing precognitive ESP have progressed or to appraise the adequacy of the experimental design to meet the alternative hypotheses. As is natural in unfinished investigation, there still are those who have different degrees of confidence in the adequacy of the experiments thus far completed to establish a conclusive case for precognition. If, as now appears to many to be a reasonable conclusion, the case for precognitive ESP *has* been established, it will not be disputed that it is a radical development for psychology and for science in general. It introduces either an alternative to causation or a mode of causation independent of the time order.

* * *

Recoiling, however, as it naturally does from concepts it was more or less trained to reject, the educated mind demands a more developed rationale than mere statistical data on such a question as the actuality of ESP. This attitude has been frankly expressed by a number of scientific men. It is now happily possible to go far toward meeting this very human requirement and to offer a rationally cemented foundation of fact that is moderately extensive.

I have already referred to the consistency with which the various types of psi investigations have shown the same lack of a regular relation to physical conditions. This consistency extends into all the various areas of the research field, and these are too extensive to be effectively handled in a paper of this length.

Another of the tests of this lawfulness is the fact that it has been possible to use the standard scientific approach of hypothesis, prediction, and experimental verification to investigate psi. For example, on the strength of the distance tests of ESP it was possible to predict the results of the pre-cognition tests. Again, it was inferred that if the law of reaction applied in ESP there should be some reaction upon the object (e.g., the card) when a cognitive perception of it occurred to the subject. This led to the designing of delicate tests of the direct influence of the subject upon the object, tests of psychokinesis (PK) based on the throwing of dice. After about twenty years of investigation the position may safely be taken that such a direct psychokinetic effect has been demonstrated and independently confirmed.

The overall relationship of these operations between subject and object, with ESP on the cognitive side and PK on the kinetic, indicates a reversible psychophysical interaction between subject and object, one that does not involve the sensorimotor system of the individual. In ESP the essential similarities observed between the conditions affecting telepathy, clairvoyance, and precognition seem to indicate that the various forms of ESP at least go back to one common perceptual function.

As psychological information concerning these various ESP effects accumulates it adds greatly to the rational understanding of the difficulties that have been encountered in the research. For example, when eventually it was recognized that psi is unconscious in all its types, it brought greater understanding of the puzzling effects encountered than had any other single discovery. Immediately the difficulties that had been found in controlling the capacity were more understandable. The peculiar experimental effects obtained, of which there had been many, fell at once into a more reasonable relationship. There was, for example, the well-known fact that sometimes a subject would score consistently below the chance average. This was for long a baffling occurrence, but psychologically such a performance on an unconscious level became understandable enough. The regular decline in the scoring rate which the subject had been found to show as he proceeded through his test run or other unit was at least partially clarified by the recognition of the unconsciousness of psi. Curious displacement effects and other distortions (preferential patterning, consistent missing, and the like) were no longer the puzzles they had been.

But the most recent extension of the rational network of psi relationships is that involving the investigation of psi in other animals, now that it has been established in man. Fifteen or more years ago the definite decision was taken to push the search for personality correlates of psi capacity. Surely, it was argued, some people have more of it than others. Quick identification of high-scoring subjects would revolutionize the investigation of the elusive capacity. A wide range of selective methods were utilized and much seining and sifting was done. Differences in performance were actually found and some significant correlations obtained, but more and more as the studies progressed it became apparent that the results were not revealing a tie-up of the extent of native psi capacity with the trait measured; instead, a relation to the more superficial quality of adaptability to the test situation was being demonstrated. Some of these correlates associated with scoring rate were even of transient nature as, for example, the subject's attitude of belief or skepticism toward ESP.

All this investigation was important; for one thing, it provided still more evidence of the occurrence of psi. But it was not leading the investigator to any group of subjects that had a monopoly on psi capacity or even a special amount of the gift. By the time the survey had extended to a considerable extent over the various classifications of abnormality and subnormality and into some of the racial subdivisions, it finally became evident that psi must be a capacity that, in evolutionary origin, antedated man himself. In order to check on this hypothesis it was necessary to look for psi in animals. Although this excursion into species other than man is a new and recent one, it has already brought up sufficient evidence to necessitate continuance and at least to permit the conclusion that man is, indeed, not the only species in possession of psi functions.

It is an important fact that two parallel lines of study are possible in parapsychology, based on the one hand on the comparative analysis of large collections of spontaneous psychic experiences, rich in suggestions for investigation, and, on the other, the experimental findings of the Laboratory on which the conclusions are more definitely based. The opportunity for checking findings from one to the other in these two very different lines of empirical study provides a special advantage and an exceptional quality of reassurance. Very little has been found thus far by the one that has not also been encountered in the other, except effects observed in the spontaneous material that cannot yet be brought to laboratory test.

And, finally, there are certain very general rational considerations that favor parapsychology as against the physicalistic philosophy that constitutes the main bar to its acceptance. First, as I have already stated, investigations of ESP arose from the need to explain actual reports of human experiences of types that have run persistently through all recorded cultures and that, essentially in the same patterns, still recur in our most sophisticated centers of human society today. No such basis in human experience can be claimed for any version of physicalism. Second, this concept of a nonphysical function in personality runs as a fundamental belief throughout the history of the social institutions of man, most conspicuously those dealing with his religious life. The only culture remotely approximating a physicalistic philosophy of man is that of communism. Whatever rational support, then, may rightly be derived from the argument of long enduring social utility is against the philosophy that is opposed to psi.

While so brief a sketch of the growing rationale of the psi discoveries omits whole sections of data and relationships, it may serve to show that parapsychology at least is now past the point where its body of knowledge was composed of scattered, isolated, disconnected chunks of statistical findings. It now makes a great deal of sense.

* * *

It may more appropriately be the work of others than the parapsychologists to attempt a larger rational setting for psi in the scheme of knowledge. Any suggestions of this setting that may be made by the investigator as he proceeds are, of course, subject to the most careful reviewing. But they may serve the purpose of stimulating discussion on points that might otherwise be allowed to go undeveloped. It is always safe, at least, to raise questions.

For example, is it not the part of wisdom to try to fit the psi functions as far as possible into the familiar concept of causation even though the serial order of cause-effect relations as known from the physical world would not apply to precognition? One knows at least where the difficulty of squaring the new with the old is localized in such an approach, and in such a problem area one needs to take short and cautious steps.

Likewise, might not the same logic that has produced the concepts of the various energies involved in physical theory profitably be followed to the point of suggesting that a psi energy by hypothesized? It is true, there is not much use in setting up hypotheses unless they can be brought around to empirical test; but some initial thought is necessary to discover if this step is feasible.

It is no great jump from the broad concept of energy as it now prevails in physical theory over to the notion of a special state of energy that is not interceptible by any of the sense organs. Certain physical energies are already in that category. Psi energy would, of course, have to be a kind that does not regularly relate to time, space, and mass as do the better known forms of energy, but there is discussion among theoretical physicists of exceptions to this relationship in the operation of types of energies that are already recognized. For the most part physicists themselves do not balk at the notion of a state of energy operating out of the currently familiar framework of concepts. After all, the effects, the signs of "work being done," are there. It was for this that the concepts of the energies were invented.

Whatever it may be that is causing these psi manifestations has naturally to be a convertible sort of influence; for example, in PK the effect has to register in the motion of the target object (e.g., the falling die). In ESP the transition into consciousness, whatever the nature of that operation is, and from consciousness into a verbal or manual response, involves more interconversions, changes that are still for the most part unsolved mysteries in both psychology and physiology. It adds little burden to the rational mind, therefore, to recognize that the energy of psi has to be convertible to other forms in order to be detected as an occurrence in nature.

It may be tentatively proposed, then, that back of the phenomena of psi must exist an energy that interoperates with and interconverts to those other energetic states already familiar to physics. Psi energy is imperceptible by the sense organs and does not in any way yet discovered regularly function within the framework of time and space and mass, and yet does lawfully operate with intelligent purpose within the personality of the organism, though on an unconscious level. It probably belongs to the early evolutionary equipment of the organism and represents a more primitive relation between the organism and the environment. Possibly it antedates the sensorimotor system (which, of course, interacts with known energy forms and produces specific modalities of perception and behavior for the most part conscious, at least in man).

* * *

The key significance of the psi function lies, of course, in the fact that it can be measured and otherwise studied with respect to the criteria of physicality and demonstrated to depart from those criteria. Much of the rest of personality and the life functions of animals, is, on this point, ambiguous and elusive and throughout the history of science has allowed completely opposite interpretations to prevail. Psi phenomena alone bring the issue into focus and allow a decision to be reached as to whether or not the organism possesses extraphysical powers. The investigation of psi has thus provided a scientific way of dealing with the question of the nature of man with respect to the physical world.

Without a reliable answer to this question of man's nature, it is not possible to solve intelligently the most important problems confronting mankind. To appreciate the importance of this issue of the bearing of physicalism on human life, it is necessary only to consider the consequences of a strict application of a thoroughly mechanistic theory of man.

The most far-reaching and revolting consequence lies in what would happen to volitional or mental freedom. Under a mechanistic determinism the cherished voluntarism of the individual would be nothing but idle fancy. Without the exercise of some freedom from physical law, the concepts of character, responsibility, moral judgment, and democracy would not survive critical analysis. The concept of a spiritual order, either in the individual or beyond him, would have no logical place whatever. In fact, little of the entire value system under which human society has developed would survive the establishment of a thoroughgoing philosophy of physicalism.

If the importance of the psi investigations is of this general order, it is urgent then not to lose the essential focus upon its principal advantage, the method of inquiry itself. It is always and perhaps unavoidably the case that new inquiries tend to generate excessive disputation over terms, interpretations, and significances. In the psi researches reviewed above there is not enough either of essential novelty or of anything approaching finality to justify taking a strongly formulated stand and holding out for any important decision at this particular point. Rather, the merit lies in the possibilities opened up: Parapsychology has verified by relatively improved methods some old claims of powers that transcend the properties of material systems. How much more can be found out about the properties of these nonphysical operations? What more can be done with them and about them? What kind of a universe must it be that combines them and the physical world? One sees no end to questions, following one upon another. There is no time to lose over unessential issues and fruitless niceties.

One single well-established fact of parapsychology is enough to trigger such a program. Over against the iron wall of physical determinism one unmistakable sign of another order of reality is enough to justify a full-scale inquiry, a concentrated campaign of investigation to see what kind of world there is that could produce such a manifestation. Traces and faint signs have time and again in the history of discovery betokened the presence of hidden systems of reality.

Science still "moves but slowly, slowly, creeping on from point to point" as it did in Tennyson's day. But those who are most familiar with the halting, handicapped way in which radical scientific advances have been made in the past will understand the difficulties and delays. They will appreciate, too, the timely challenge the psi researchers make to a philosophy of man that, over most of the world, across national and even ideological boundaries, dominates the scientific thinking of today. Tomorrow that philosophy may, unless challenged and effectively refuted, curtain the entire range of thought for mankind everywhere.

C. J. Ducasse

The Philosophical Importance of "Psychic Phenomena"

In the title of this paper, the words "Psychic Phenomena" are put between quotation marks to indicate disclaim of any intention to beg the reality of the diverse queer kinds of occurrences that have variously been termed "psychic," "metapsychic," "parapsychological," "paranormal," or more briefly, "Psi" phenomena. The contention implicit in the paper's title is only that the many reports of phenomena of the kinds in view are philosophically important no matter whether the phenomena really occurred as reported, or not.

If they did *not* so occur, then the specificity and numerousness of the reports, and the fact that some of the witnesses, and some of the persons who accepted their reports, have been people of high intelligence and integrity, is exceedingly interesting from the standpoint of the psychology of perception, of delusion, illusion or hallucination, of credulity and credibility and of testimony. Whereas, if some of the phenomena *did* really occur as reported, they are equally important from the standpoint then of the psychology of *in*credulity and *in*credibility—or, more comprehensively, of orthodox adverse prejudice, such as widely exists among persons having the modern western educated outlook towards reports of psychic phenomena. In this connection, a recent book, *The Nature of Prejudice,* by the Harvard psychologist, Prof. G. W. Allport, is not only good reading, but can be also very salutary reading if the insight one gains from it into the

Reprinted from *The Journal of Philosophy*, volume 51 (1954), pp. 810-823, by permission of the editors and Professor Ducasse's literary executor.

determinants of prejudice does not cause one to suppose oneself *eo ipso* free from this malady.

But if some of the phenomena *did* really occur as reported, then there is another reason why they are of great philosophical and scientific importance. It is that those phenomena sharply clash with, and therefore call for revision of, certain tacit assumptions which Prof. C.D. Broad, in his recent book, *Religion, Philosophy, and Psychical Research* (p. 7), has termed "basic limiting principles" of ordinary thought; that is, principles "we unhesitatingly take for granted as the framework within which all our practical activities and our scientific theories are confined."[1]

For example, one of the most basic among those limiting principles is that an event cannot cause anything before it has actually occurred; and a phenomenon which would clash with this principle would be, not the inferring, but the *ostensible perceiving,* as for instance in a dream or vision, of an as yet future event of some out-of-the-ordinary kind one had no reason to expect. For then the dream or vision would, paradoxically, be a present effect of an as yet future cause.

The important philosophical problems regarding causality, time, perception, and memory, which a real instance of such so-called precognition would raise, are discussed by Prof. Broad with his customary acuteness, thoroughness, and orderliness, in a paper entitled "The Philosophical Implications of Foreknowledge,"[2] which deserves very careful study. It appeared in Supplementary Volume XVI of the Proceedings of the Aristotelian Society. A discussion of the paper by Prof. H. H. Price follows it, and is itself then commented upon by Prof. Broad.

The interest of the paper, however, is made the greater by the fact that some evidence, both experimental and other, today exists that events—of which precognition is one—sometimes really occur that clash thus radically with one or another of the basic limiting principles of present scientific and common-sense thinking. Moreover, that evidence is both much stronger and more abundant than persons who have not looked it up commonly suspect. Hence the need is correspondingly acute either to explain away the evidence, or else to formulate some conception of Nature capable of including and of uniting both all the facts which the natural sciences have discovered, and the rarer paradoxical and seemingly anarchistic facts with which the parapsychology laboratories and societies for psychical research have concerned themselves, but which scientists and philosophers have so far largely been content either to ignore or to declare impossible on *a priori* grounds.

Moreover, if as I believe in common with Profs. Broad and Price among other philosophers familiar with the evidence, it is in some cases too strong to be explained away, then, as Prof. Price pointed out in a recent address, philosophers ought to take a hand in devising the needed new conceptual framework; as they did when, in the 17th century, a similar need resulted from the new facts which were then being discovered. I am therefore very glad that the Program Committee[3] decided to have a symposium on this general subject and especially that the committee invited Prof. Rhine to contribute the first paper; for, as the British philosopher, Antony Flew, remarks in his recent book, *A New Approach to Psychical Research* (p. 85), Rhine's first book, *Extra-Sensory Perception,* published in 1934, is a great landmark, which has given "enormous impetus to experiment, particularly of the 'quantitative' type," in this field. There is no doubt that the energy and resourcefulness which for many years Rhine has given to these studies and to the promotion of them will assure him a permanent and high place in the history of the subject.

I have wanted thus to make clear my high regard for Prof. Rhine and my appreciation of the importance of his work because of the criticisms of some of his views which I shall have to make in what follows. Before I turn to them, however, there are two points of terminology which seem to me to call for a few words.

The first concerns the use of such words as "psychical," "psychic," "metapsychic," or "parapsychological," to designate the various kinds of phenomena in view. These terms are appropriate enough to refer to so-called extrasensory perception—that is, to telepathy, clairvoyance, or precognition—and to psychokinesis; but certain other equally queer kinds of phenomena, some of which I shall mention later, seem *prima facie* describable as paraphysical or parabiological, rather than as parapsychological, psychic, or metapsychic. For this reason, it seems to me that the word "paranormal," which begs no questions as to the nature of the operative forces, is preferable when a term broad enough to cover all the diverse kinds of phenomena in view is desired.

The other remark to be made concerns the expression "extrasensory perception." By this time, of course, this name is pretty well established and need not be misleading. But the fact nevertheless is that, because it is somewhat of a misdescription of some of the experiences it designates, it has led some psychologists to believe that it designates nothing real. The word Perception has a variety of usages in ordinary language, but in psychology and epistemology it is usually employed to designate a particular one of the processes by which *knowledge*, properly so called, is gained; and knowing does not consist simply in having or believing an idea which happens to be true, but in believing it because one has evidence that it is true. For instance, if a card—say the ace of spades—is lying face up on the table, *and I look at it*, then *I know*, or more specifically *perceive*, that it is the ace of spades. But if it is lying face down and I guess, or dream, that it is the ace of spades, my guess or dream, although happening to be true, does not constitute knowledge, or more specifically perception, at all. True guesses or visions would have title to the name of perception and of knowledge only if, in their case, the guesser's or dreamer's experience contained some feature—whether sensory or extrasensory—that were a more or less *reliable sign* that the guess or dream is true. But a study by Louisa E. Rhine of more than 3000 spontaneous "precognitive" and "contemporaneous cognitive" experiences, published in the June 1954 issue of the *Journal of Parapsychology,* shows that, in a large percentage of them, no feeling of conviction distinguished the true ones from the false. And, in experimental guesses, it is only very seldom that the correct ones feel any different from the incorrect. Thus, the great majority of so-called extrasensory perceptions are not perceptions at all in the ordinary sense of the term. This, however, should not be permitted to blind one to the real problem, which is to account for the fact that, in for instance certain long and carefully controlled series of guesses, the correct guesses (or with some guessers the incorrect ones) are significantly more numerous than chance would allow for, and moreover, consistently assume certain distinctive patterns.

From these remarks on terminology, I now turn directly to the contents of Prof. Rhine's paper. The basic contentions of the first part of it, as I understand them, are that extrasensory perception (ESP) and psychokinesis (PK) have now been experimentally proved to be facts, and that the kind of energy involved in the occurrence of these phenomena has been shown by relevant tests, so far as these have gone, to be unaffected by differences that would affect any known form of physical energy—differences, for example, of distance, of time, of spatial orientation of target cards, or of intervening material obstacles.

That all this is true is likely to be pretty evident, I believe, to anyone who takes the trouble to familiarize himself with the records and who approaches them with an open mind.

The fact that those differences do not affect the phenomena entails, Rhine contends, that in these some non-physical kind of energy operates, which, however, he regards not at all as supernatural, but as perfectly natural in the sense that its operations, like those of physical energy, conform to fixed laws; which, by experimentation scientifically conducted, we may hope to discover eventually.

Certain comments now suggest themselves. The first concerns the term "physical"—and therefore also its contradictory, "non-physical"—employed in the statement of that contention.

Prof. Rhine does not formally define the adjective, "physical," but from what he says at various places it would seem that he intends to use it comprehensively as referring not only to the entities and processes studied by physics, but also to those studied by chemistry and the other physical sciences, and also to those which the biological sciences investigate. That is, he apparently uses "physical" in the broad sense in which it means "material" ; and, by "physicalism," he means "materialism" rather than what logical positivists nowadays mean by "physicalism."

Now, as Lindsay and Margenau remark in their *Foundations of Physics* (p. 2), "the physicist has been striving for years to attach a clear meaning to the term *matter,* and undoubtedly we have reason to believe that the concept means much more to us today than to the physicists of fifty years ago." In the modern analysis of it, however, conceptions of space and time enter which are different from those of classical physics (p. 59 and ff.). And the atoms, *ex hypothesi* indivisible, which were once believed to be the ultimate constituents of matter, are now known to be more or less complex systems of electrons and protons, not to mention the neutrons, mesons, and other entities of present-day theoretical physics.

The question which these developments thrust upon us, and which is pivotal in the present connection, therefore is, In just what sense are all these atomic and sub-atomic entities and processes *material?* The answer, of course, is that they are so simply in the sense that, although they are not directly perceptible at all, nevertheless they are held to be *constituents* of the publicly perceptible objects—such as stones, water, wood, animal bodies, and so on—which are what the expression "the material world" basically denotes.

But now the question arises whether the presently known subatomic constituents of matter are themselves *ultimate* in the sense of absolutely simple. Will they not perhaps one of these days be in turn analyzed into more nearly elementary constituents? If this should occur, it is safe to say that the latter will have some properties **different from those of** the subatomic entities; just as these have some properties different from those of atoms; atoms in turn, properties different from those of molecules; and molecules, properties different from those of molar masses; for this is the general kind of fact to which the name of Emergence has been given.

Now, certain of the properties of those yet to be discovered but theoretically possible sub-sub-atomic constituents of matter might well turn out to be such as could account for ESP and PK. Even then, however, these constituents and their properties would have the very same title to be called material as have atoms or electrons and their properties; namely, those too, like these, would be constituents of the perceptually public things which the expression "material objects" basically denotes.

We might then, of course—perhaps because of the extreme peculiarity of some of the properties of those sub-sub-atomic entities,—elect to say that, although they are still material for the reason stated, yet they are not "physically" material—reserving thus the qualification "physical" for those levels of material complexity which, however different from one another, nevertheless have to time and space the relations presently described by physics; and qualifying by some other adjective, such perhaps as "psychical" or "paraphysical," those levels of material minuteness at which this ceases to be true.

It is perhaps superfluous to add in this connection that energy well might on special occasions pass from one to the other of those two levels of materiality—the "physical" and the "non-physical"—without, as Prof. Broad has shown, any violation of the principle of the conservation of energy (*The Mind and Its Place in Nature,* pp. 103 ff.) which anyway, as Prof. M. T. Keeton pointed out in the July 1941 issue of *Philosophy of Science,* is not the statement of an empirical fact, but only a defining postulate for the notion of "an isolated physical system."

That matter may have sub-sub-atomic constituents, and that these might have properties capable of accounting for ESP and PK is of course at present pure speculation. I introduce it only to make clear that reality of these and of other kinds of paranormal phenomena would not in principle require abandonment of a materialistic conception of the universe—a type of conception which, of course, has been marvelously fertile—but would only call for a materialism liberal enough to include a level of materiality still more tenuous then the presently recognized sub-atomic one.

This remark now leads me to comment on Prof. Rhine's contention that a thoroughgoing materialistic determinism would entail that man could have no "volitional or mental freedom," and that "little of the entire value system under which human society has developed would survive."

This seems to me a completely unwarranted inference, which rests on nothing more solid than failure to distinguish between the axiological and the ontological senses of the term "materialism," or "physicalism"; and similarly of the term "spirit," or "spiritual." The materialism of the natural sciences is ontological, and materialism in the axiological sense is not in the least entailed by it. Rather, if ontological materialism is true, what follows is that even the noblest artistic, ethical, and spiritual achievements of man then were potentialities somehow latent in the particular kinds of matter of which human beings consist. For those achievements are facts of historical record, which would not in the least be obliterated or made less noble by the other fact, if it be a fact, that man has been all along a wholly material being. Moreover, since man, even if wholly material, *did* somehow manage to create those noble values, there would be no reason why he could not go on adding to them in the future.

As regards human freedom, on the other hand, the fact that, under the circumstances existing at this moment, I am free to raise my arm if I will, but am not similarly free to fly through the air like a bird even if I will—this fact remains a fact no matter whether the "volitions" concerned be molecular events in the matter of the brain, or be events of a non-material but in some sense "psychic," "mental," or "spiritual" nature. Moreover, irrespective of whether those volitions were material or nonmaterial events, they had causes sufficient to determine their occurrence—or else they were affairs of pure objective chance, which is something very different from freedom.

The idea that on the one hand freedom of choice, and on the other determinism (in the sense that even volitions have causes), are incompatible is very widespread but quite erroneous. What is incompatible with freedom is not causation as such, but *compulsion,* and causation is compulsion only in cases where what one is caused to will to do is something he *dislikes*; for instance, handing his money to a holdup man who threatens to shoot. But when on the contrary keen appetite causes a person to decide to eat and he *likes* what he eats, he is then correctly said to have decided to eat and to be eating, not under compulsion but *freely*. Furthermore, if, as Prof. Rhine's paper apparently but unwarrantedly assumes, determinism inherently constituted compulsion and hence were incompatible with freedom, then this would be so quite irrespective of whether the determining causes happened to be material or non-material. A psychological robot would be just as much a robot as would a physical one; and the two of them together inside one skin, causally interacting with one another, would be a fancier kind of robot, but still only a robot.

Freedom of action, or lack of it, is simply a matter of the efficacy or inefficacy, of a volition to its particular aim. This efficacy or inefficacy is in each case an empirical fact, wholly independent of whether volitions are material events or non-material; and quite independent also of the fact that volitions, like all other events material or mental, themselves have causes of one kind or another, as well as effects.

Lastly, with regard to human responsibility: As soon as moral responsibility is distinguished from historical and from legal responsibility, it becomes evident that without determinism there would be no moral responsibility. For if a person's present volitions were not determined, for example by such causes as memories of praise or blame, of reward or punishment, and of other sorts of consequences of past voluntary acts, and by enticements or threats held out to him relating to similar future voluntary acts, then that person would be termed not morally free but morally irresponsible. This, of course, is the case with infants, idiots, or the insane; and is exactly what we mean when we say that they "do not know what they are doing," or "do not know the difference between right and wrong," and hence are not morally responsible.

The upshot of these various remarks is then that even if, as Prof. Rhine quite plausibly contends, paranormal phenomena do depend on a non-physical form of energy, this dependence has no bearing at all either on moral responsibility or on the validity of human values; or on the question of human freedom, which is simple enough when theological preoccupations are left out of it and the few essential distinctions are made; and which, as made clear above, is a semantical question and hence one to which laboratory experiments have no relevance. I therefore much regret that Prof. Rhine should have elected to rest the case for the importance of Psi phenomena on the implications for human freedom, responsibility, and values, which he believes them to have; but which, if the preceding critique is sound, they do not really have at all. Their true importance, I submit, is of the kinds—scientific and philosophical—which I mentioned at the outset.

There is, however, another sort of importance which certain paranormal phenomena might conceivably have—those, namely, which purport to be evidence of survival of the "spirit" of a person who has died. If it should be concluded that these particular phenomena do prove that the human personality has certain constituents which, even if material, are non-physical in a sense which entailed that death of the human body does not destroy them, then this would establish "survival" *of them.* But, as pointed out by

Prof. Broad, in *The Mind and Its Place in Nature,* when setting forth his hypothesis of such a surviving "psychic factor," the question would remain as to whether, without its being associated with a living human body, that "psychic factor" could nevertheless still function as an active and experiencing mind or personality. Moreover, even if it still did so function, the fact of its being then discarnate would not entail that its discarnate life is any more moral, beautiful, or intelligent, or has a larger measure of freedom, than was the case during its incarnate life. In this connection, a lecture entitled "Survival and the Idea of Another World," delivered in London a couple of years ago by Prof. Price, is exceedingly interesting and well worth looking up in the Proceedings of the Society for Psychical Research (January 1953). And further, even if there is in man a "psychic factor," *and* it survives bodily death, *and* it then still constitutes an actively living mind so that there is a genuine "life" after death—even then, knowledge of this would provide motivation (additional to the earthly motivations) for moral or generous conduct on earth only if one had reason to believe that that future life is one where the many injustices of earth are redressed. But the mere fact of its being a discarnate, "spirit" life would constitute no reason why, in that life, injustices might not go on occurring as merrily as on earth.

The next comment I wish to make concerns the scientific value on the one hand of experimental, and on the other of spontaneous, paranormal phenomena. Prof. Rhine holds, I believe, that the latter cannot establish anything, but can only suggest experiments; and that only these, when confirmed under well-controlled conditions, can establish the reality of the kind of phenomenon concerned. Now, I submit that earthquakes, hurricanes, eclipses of the sun and moon, or the fall of aerolites, are phenomena over the conditions of which we have not the slightest control; and yet that their occurrence is completely established. Hence the criterion which Prof. Rhine lays down defines not the scientific meaning of "established," but only of the narrower expression "experimentally established."

Of course, for discovery of the conditions on which a given kind of phenomenon depends, experimentation under controlled conditions is highly desirable and often indispensable. But as the examples cited make evident, such control is not indispensable for the purpose of establishing that a given sort of phenomenon *has actually occurred.* Moreover, it is the *reality* of a paradoxical phenomenon—that is, *its having actually occurred*—which establishes the existence of otherwise unsuspected ranges of possibilities; and which, even before these are explored, condemns as provincial any conception of Nature which has no room for that phenomenon.

This leads me now to consider some reports of a spontaneous paranormal phenomenon which illustrates the philosophically important point just made. Moreover, it manifests the greater richness of content which spontaneous phenomena usually have as compared with experimental ones. Another reason for considering it is that the nature and strength of the evidence on record for its occurrence is likely to be something of a surprise to philosophers who have not looked it up. And lastly, the difficulty of explaining away that evidence at all plausibly makes especially pointed the questions I mentioned at the outset concerning the psychology of credulity and incredulity, as contrasted with the logic of rational belief and disbelief.

The phenomenon I refer to is that of levitation; that is, the rising and floating in the air of a human body or heavy inanimate object without action of any of the forces known to physicists. What levitation is reported to be like in the concrete may be gathered from a statement—which I cite for its picturesqueness rather than its evidentiality—made by the Princess Pema Chöki Namgyal of Sikkim to the explorer Fosco Maraini. He quotes it on page 55 of his recent book, *Secret Tibet*. Her statement, which was about her uncle, reads as follows: "Yes. He did what you would call exercises in levitation. I used to take him in a little rice. He would be motionless in mid-air. Every day he rose a little higher. In the end he rose so high that I found if difficult to hand the rice up to him. I was a little girl, and I had to stand on tip-toe. There are certain things you don't forget!"

At least seventy saints or mystics have been reported to have levitated, but where such persons are concerned the testimony is suspect on the ground of religious bias. Yet in a few cases, such as that of the levitations of St. Joseph of Coppertino, the reports are so definite, the witnesses so numerous and some of them so eminent, and their initial biases so diverse, that to dismiss thus *a priori* what they attest is far from easy when one has acquainted oneself with their statements. (See, for instance, Dr. E. J. Dingwall's *Some Human Oddities*, pp. 9-37 and 162-171.)

But there are other and more recent reports of levitations, of persons who are neither saints nor mystics, but are only so-called "mediums"—a term which was originally intended to mean an intermediary between the living and spirits of the dead; which in the popular mind today connotes little else than charlatanry; but which in psychical research means simply a person in whose presence paranormal phenomena occur with some frequency and on whose presence their occurrence somehow depends. A good deal of evidence exists that there are a few such persons, and that, even if some of the phenomena of some of them have been consciously or unconsciously fraudulent, nevertheless certain others were genuinely paranormal. One of the most famous mediums on record was D. D. Home, of whom many readers of these lines probably have heard, and whose levitations during the second half of the 19th century were testified to by numerous distinguished witnesses. Among these was the eminent chemist and physicist, Sir William Crookes, and his testimony is so circumstantial and positive that a sample of it is worth citing *verbatim*.

In an article published in the *Quarterly Journal of Science* for January 1874, Crookes first states that the occurrences now about to be mentioned "have taken place *in my own house, in the light, and with only private friends present* besides the medium." He then writes: "On three separate occasions have I seen [Home] raised completely from the floor of the room. Once sitting in an easy chair, once kneeling on his chair and once standing up. On each occasion I had full opportunity of watching the occurrence as it was taking place." Again, in Volume VI of the *Journal of the Society for Psychical Research,* Crookes states in 1894 that sometimes Home and his chair, with his feet tucked up on the seat and his hands held up in full view of all present, rose off the ground; and Crookes adds: "On such an occasion I have got down and seen and felt that all four legs were off the ground at the same time, Home's feet being on the chair. Less frequently the levitating power was extended to those sitting next to him. Once my wife was thus raised off the ground in her chair." Another levitation of Home, which like these occurred in Crooke's own house, is described by him in the same report in the following words: "He rose 18 inches off the ground, and I passed my hands under his feet, round him, and over his head when he was in the air" (pp. 341-342).

An independent account of levitations in the presence of Home is contained in a letter of 1856 from the Earl of Crawford to his sister-in-law. It is presented and its evidentiality minutely dissected by the anthropologist, Dr. E. J. Dingwall, in an article, "Psychological Problems Arising from a Report of Telekinesis," in the February 1953 issue of the *British Journal of Psychology.* Dingwall concludes that neither the hypothesis of fraud nor that of collective hallucination is capable of explaining the facts described by Lord Crawford.

I shall add only two more citations, out of many available. The first is from the testimony of Sir William Barrett, Fellow of the Royal Society, who for many years was Professor of Experimental Physics in the Royal

College of Science for Ireland. In a book published in 1918 (*On the Threshold of the Unseen,* pp. 47-48), he states that in December 1915 he had been invited by Dr. W. J. Crawford (not Lord Crawford mentioned above), who was lecturer on Mechanical Engineering at the Queens University in Belfast, to attend a meeting of a small circle consisting of the family of a 17-year old girl, Kathleen Goligher, who worked in a local factory and with whom Dr. Crawford had been experimenting. Her mediumship, I may say, seems to have conspicuously degenerated after several years, and perhaps fraud then to have entered. But Mr. Whately Smith, who noticed this after having observed her first in 1916 and later in 1920, stresses in Volume 30 of the SPR Proceedings that no way had ever been suggested in which it would have been possible to produce fraudulently the levitations of 1915 and 1916, such as were witnessed by himself, by Barrett, and scores of times by Crawford.

Barrett, at the place mentioned, states that he and Crawford sat outside the small family circle; and that "the room was illuminated with a bright gas flame burning in a lantern, with a large red glass window, on the mantelpiece. The room was small and as our eyes got accustomed to the light we could see all the sitters clearly. They sat around a small table with hands joined together, but no one touching the table." After describing some of the first phenomena which occurred, he goes on: "Then the table began to rise from the floor some 18 inches and remained so suspended and quite level. I was allowed to go up to the table and saw clearly no one was touching it, a clear space separating the sitters from the table. I tried to press the table down, and though I exerted all my strength could not do so; then I climbed up on the table and sat on it, my feet off the floor, when I was swayed to and fro and finally tipped off. The table of its own accord now turned upside down, no one touching it, and I tried to lift it off the ground, but it could not be stirred, it appeared screwed down to the floor. At my request all the sitters' clasped hands had been kept raised above their heads, and I could see that no one was touching the table;—when I desisted from trying to lift the inverted table from the floor, it righted itself again of its own accord, no one helping it." Crawford himself, on pages 63-64 of his own book, *The Reality of Psychic Phenomena* (1919), similarly writes that one evening in his own house with the same circle, a table weighing sixteen pounds was levitated many times, and that, during one of these levitations, while "the surface of the table was nearly shoulder-high in the air, I entered the circle and pressed down with my hands on the top of the table. Although I exerted all my strength,

I could not depress the table to the floor. A friend who is over six feet in height then leaned over the circle and helped me to press downwards, when our combined efforts exerted to the limit just caused it to touch the floor" (pp. 63-64).

Now, do I believe that these various levitations really occurred as reported? This, of course, is a merely biographical question and as such unimportant. Nevertheless, I shall answer it by confessing to a slight case of dissociated personality! My habit-begotten and habit-bound, adversely prejudiced, conservatively practical self finds levitation as hard to believe as probably does any reader of the preceding citations. On the other hand, my rational, philosophically open-minded, scientifically inquisitive self notices several things.

One is that the experimental demonstrations of telekinesis by statistical treatment of long series of carefully controlled and recorded dice-castings, made in Rhine's Laboratory and elsewhere, immediately decrease the antecedent improbability of levitation, although I must say that if I were told—let us suppose by the chairman of our Program Committee, Prof. Farber—that, in his own dining room and in good light, he had seen Prof. Rhine rise eighteen inches in the air, and that, as Crookes did with Home, he passed his hand under, above and around Rhine and found nothing, then such a report would be to me even more convincing both psychologically and rationally than are the reports of the results of the dice-casting experiments. And I have no reason to suppose that Crookes was a less competent observer, or less truthful, than Prof. Farber would be.

Secondly, although this would be a contemporary report, whereas those of Crookes and the others are old, the fact is that the age of a piece of circumstantially stated, intelligent, and sincere testimony has no logical bearing on its force unless the testimony was biased by beliefs commonly held in the days of the witness but since proved to be groundless or false; or unless some normal explanation of the events judged by him to have been paranormal has since been discovered. But neither of these sources of weakness exists in the testimony quoted.

Thirdly, assertions of antecedent improbability always rest on the tacit but often in fact false assumption that the operative factors are the same in a presented case as they were in superficially similar past cases. For example, the antecedent improbability of the things an expert conjurer does on the stage is extremely high if one takes as antecedent evidence what merely an ordinary person, under ordinary instead of staged conditions, can do. The same is true of what geniuses, or so-called arithmetical prodigies, can do as compared with what ordinary men can do. And that a man *is* a genius or a calculating prodigy is shown by what he *does do, not* the reality of what he does by his being a genius or prodigy. This holds equally as regards a medium and his levitations or other paranormal phenomena. The crucial question is therefore not whether paranormal levitations are frequent, or happen to ordinary people, but whether they ever actually have occurred. If even only once, this is enough to show that some force as yet not understood by us exists.

Thus, the philosophically open-minded, critically rational part of the dissociated personality to which I have confessed finds, as standing in the way of acceptance of the clear cut testimony quoted, little else than the naive tacit assumption that if the knowledge possessed by physicists as of December 1954 cannot explain levitation, then levitation is impossible!

NOTES

1. [See Broad's essay, pp. 43-63 above.—Ed.]
2. [See below, pp. 287-312.—Ed.]
3. [of The American Philosophical Association.—Ed.]

Section II

The Argument from the Possibility of Fraud

George R. Price

Science and the Supernatural

Believers in psychic phenomena—such as telepathy, clairvoyance, precognition, and psychokinesis—appear to have won a decisive victory and virtually silenced opposition. Many other times during the past century such victory has seemed close, as evidence for the supernatural has been produced that has been found convincing by some of the world's leading scientists. But always on previous occasions, other investigators have made criticisms or conducted new tests, thereby demonstrating flaws in the evidence. What is unique about the present is that, during the last fifteen years, scarcely a single scientific paper has appeared attacking the work of the parapsychologists.

This victory is the result of an impressive amount of careful experimentation and intelligent argumentation. The best of the card-guessing experiments of Rhine and Soal show enormous odds against chance occurrence, while possibility of sensory clues is often eliminated by placing cards and percipient in separate buildings far apart. Dozens of experimenters have obtained positive results in ESP experiments, and the mathematical procedures have been approved by leading statisticians.[1]

I suspect that most scientists who have studied the work of Rhine (especially as it is presented in *Extra-Sensory Perception After Sixty Years,*[2]) and Soal (described in *Modern Experiments in Telepathy,*[3]) have found it necessary to accept their findings. Concerning the latter book, a

Reprinted from *Science* 122 (1955) No. 3165, pp. 359-367, by permission of the editor.

reviewer[4] has written: "If scientists will read it carefully, the 'ESP controversy' will be ended." Against all this evidence, almost the only defense remaining to the skeptical scientist is ignorance, ignorance concerning the work itself and concerning its implications. The typical scientist contents himself with retaining in his memory some criticism that at most applies to a small fraction of the published studies. But these findings (which challenge our very concepts of space and time) are—if valid—of enormous importance, both philosophically and practically, so they ought not to be ignored.

PRACTICAL APPLICATIONS FOR EXTRASENSORY PERCEPTION

A common belief concerning ESP experimentation is that the results are interesting but are of small importance because of the great inaccuracy of perception. For example, Boring[5] writes in a discussion of Soal's work: "You see a 'brilliant' performance in telepathy is not so very striking after all. It is only 7 out of 25 instead of 5 out of 25. When people ask why these able percipients do not get rich by telepathing directors' meetings and playing the stock market with their superior knowledge, they do not know how small an advantage the best available telepathy of the modern age provides."

But card guessing by ESP, inaccurate though it is, nevertheless is a communication system by which information is transmitted. In the terminology of Shannon's "Mathematical theory of communication,"[6] it is a case of a *discrete communication channel with noise,* "noise" representing whatever it is that causes errors. Information theory is unequivocal in showing that any system that has a finite capacity for transmitting information can (if we employ proper coding) transmit with any degree of accuracy we may desire—say, as accurately as by telegraph, or more accurately—although it may take a long time to transmit a small amount of information with high accuracy.

In an ESP experiment where 6 hits are made in a run of 25, the channel capacity is about 0.0069 bits per trial; while 7 hits corresponds to 0.026 bits per trial, or 0.66 bits for a run of 25 trials.[7] This means that (if each trial takes only a few seconds) information can be transmitted at a rate of several bits per hour and as accurately as by telegraph. Thus this appears to be a solution to problem No. 449 of the National Inventors Council, which involves "the development of a revolutionary new method of transmitting intelligence." Since ESP is independent of distance and requires no equipment (except possibly a watch for synchronization), it should be a most convenient means for transmitting information from an espionage agent in the Soviet Union directly to Washington or London.

Soal considers that there must be a selected human "sender" to aid in transmitting information, in addition to a selected percipient; but Rhine believes that a good percipient can perceive by clairvoyance in the absence of any sender as well as receive telepathically from virtually any person. Therefore, according to the findings of either Rhine or Soal, the suggestion made in the preceding paragraph is a fully practical one; but if Rhine's work is valid, then there are additional applications of enormously greater importance. In particular, while Soal has evidence that ESP may penetrate a few seconds into the future, Rhine has performed experiments of considerable ingenuity that show (in his opinion) that information concerning ESP cards can be received from as far as 10 days in the future.[8,9,10,11]

The general means for transmitting information accurately over a noisy channel is to send messages of high *redundancy*; that is, the information is repeated over and over again (in properly coded form) within the message. But events of great importance may be thought of as messages of high redundancy. Thus a nuclear bomb explosion would tell its story with enormous redundancy in terms of each of the hundreds of buildings destroyed and of the thousands of people killed (in excess of normal mortality). This suggests that ESP can be used for such purposes as accurate forecasting of a major catastrophe—assuming that Rhine's findings are valid. And this will be especially true if it is possible to use many percipients working simultaneously to increase accuracy.

Let us design a procedure to give a ten-day warning of a nuclear bomb explosion. ESP card designs are used, to make conditions closely similar to those Rhine employed in his precognition experiments. Cards are prepared that will react to the thermal flash of a nuclear explosion, so that the initial design will be bleached and a second design will develop. The cards are placed inside cameras with open shutters, surrounding a likely target area and directed upon various portions of the area. The cards are guarded and their symbols are kept secret. Each day several thousand selected percipients try to guess card symbols ten days ahead. Guesses are analyzed in terms of each of the two possible correct symbols for each card.

If card symbols have been properly randomized, then, in the absence of ESP there will be no statistically significant pattern in the relationship between guesses and possible correct symbols. Thus, it will be virtually impossible to have a false alarm if ESP is not operating. Therefore, there will be a strong presumption that there should be prompt evacuation, if some day, for cards corresponding to some contiguous area, guesses show a statistically significant relationship to the symbols-to-be-developed, while for the surrounding area there is a similar relationship involving the initial symbols.

Does this suggestion seem absurd? No. If information theory and Rhine's conclusions are both valid, this is a practical suggestion of high importance. Such a warning system would be far more effective and less expensive than radar. To be sure, it is true that Rhine's evidence for precognition is not so much in the form of large numbers of correct guesses, but rather it depends on certain statistical abnormalities in the pattern of correct guesses. But in general, any relationship between cards and guesses that is so highly improbable that it constitutes evidence for ESP can be made use of for transmission of information. And even if there is only 10 percent probability that Rhine's findings are valid, it is still the clear duty of appropriate government officials to investigate this possibility promptly and thoroughly.

Furthermore, contemporaneous clairvoyance can also be put to work in many ways. For example, the arrangement of ore in a vein provides a form of redundancy plus a means of checking against guesses not based on ESP—provided that we exercise a little ingenuity in the way we set up the guessing procedure.

In short, it appears that wherever parapsychology can yield extra-chance results, we can find a way to put it to practical use.

HUME'S ARGUMENT CONCERNING MIRACLES

Now it happens that I myself believed in ESP about fifteen years ago, after reading *Extra-Sensory Perception After Sixty Years*, but I changed my mind when I became acquainted with the argument presented by David Hume in his chapter "Of Miracles" in *An Enquiry Concerning Human Understanding.*

Hume's argument runs as follows: "A miracle is a violation of the laws of nature; and as a firm and unalterable experience has established these laws, the proof against a miracle, from the very nature of the fact, is as entire as any argument from experience can possibly be imagined. . . .

no testimony is sufficient to establish a miracle, unless the testimony be of such a kind that its falsehood would be more miraculous than the fact which it endeavours to establish. . . ."

Hume illustrated as follows the spirit in which he thought his argument should be employed: "You would in vain object to me the difficulty, and almost impossibility, of deceiving the world in an affair of such consequence. . . . with the little or no advantage. . . . from so poor an artifice: all this might astonish me; but I would still reply that the knavery and folly of men are such common phenomena, that I should rather believe the most extraordinary events to arise from their concurrence, than admit of so signal a violation of the laws of nature."

And also: "Where shall we find such a number of circumstances, agreeing to the corroboration of one fact? And what have we to oppose to such a cloud of witnesses, but the absolute impossibility or miraculous nature of the events which they relate? And this, surely, in the eyes of all reasonable people, will alone be regarded as a sufficient refutation."

Long before Hume, a similar point of view was taken by the Greek writer Lucian:[12] "To defend one's mind against these follies, a man must have an adamantine faith, so that, even if he is not able to detect the precise trick by which the illusion is produced, he at any rate retains his conviction that the whole thing is a lie and an impossibility."

And Tom Paine, a little after Hume, stated the same argument succinctly:[13] ". . . is it more probable that nature should go out of her course, or that a man should tell a lie?"

IMPROBABILITY OF THE SUPERNATURAL

My opinion concerning the findings of the parapsychologists is that many of them are dependent on clerical and statistical errors and unintentional use of sensory clues, and that all extrachance results not so explicable are dependent on deliberate fraud or mildly abnormal mental conditions.

The first step in applying Hume's argument would preferably be to make a numerical estimate of the *a priori* improbability of ESP. But unfortunately, it appears that scientific philosophy has not yet developed to the point where this is possible. This is regrettable, yet we should consider that if the problem were so simple as to permit numerical calculation, then this controversy would perhaps never have arisen.

Since I cannot prove, all I can do is try to convince by showing that ESP is incompatible with current scientific theory. It is sometimes asked:

With what scientific laws does ESP conflict? But the conflict is at so fundamental a level as to be not so much with named "laws" but rather with basic principles. C. D. Broad has presented an excellent analysis showing that the psi effects are incompatible with nine "basic limiting principles" involving our fundamental concepts of space, time, and causality.[14] I accept his analysis and incorporate it as part of the present argument.

Broad's discussion is too long to summarize here, so instead I shall list several incompatibilities of psi phenomena, described in a less fundamental manner. (i) ESP penetrates the future even in situations where rational inference is powerless. (ii) ESP is apparently unattenuated by distance. (iii) Psi effects are apparently unaffected by shielding. They come from matter and interact with matter (control of dice in psychokinesis), so why do they not interact with matter in a shield? (iv) Dye patterns on cards are read in the dark: how does one detect a trace of dye without shining light on it? (v) Patterns on cards in the center of a pack are read without interference from other cards. (vi) We have found in the body no structure to associate with the alleged functions. (vii) There is no learning but, instead, a tendency toward complete loss of ability. (So far as I know, there is for this type of behavior no parallel among established mental functions.) (viii) Different investigators obtain highly different results. For example, Soal requires a telepathic sender, but Rhine finds this unnecessary.

The parapsychologists themselves have agreed almost unanimously that psi phenomena are completely incompatible with modern physics. The situation has been analyzed in detail and with excellent logic by both Rhine[15] (Also see note 10, chap. 4.) and Soal (See note 3, pp. 303-305.). And Rhine has correctly stated (See note 10, p. 94.) that "Nothing in all the history of human thought—heliocentrism, evolution, relativity—has been more truly revolutionary or radically contradictory to contemporary thought than the results of the investigation of precognitive psi."

To be sure, some scientists have argued that there may be no incompatibility. For example, see a recent paper on "Parapsychology and dualism" by Walker.[16] And Boring (See note 5.) writes: "All you have got yet for extrasensory perception is an observed difference between two frequencies, between hits and misses, and a great deal of ignorance as to what causes the difference. Ignorance does not overthrow old concepts." But it seems to me that this is equivalent to arguing: "So you have seen a man turn into a small bat and fly away, and you think that this is evidence for the existence of vampires? Nonsense. All you have got is a difference between two patterns in which photons strike the retina, and a great deal of ignorance as to what causes the difference. Ignorance is not evidence." I feel that R. H. Thouless described matters aptly when he said:[17]"I suggest that the discovery of the *psi* phenomena has brought us to a . . . . point at which we must question basic theories because they lead us to expectations contradicted by experimental results."

If, then, parapsychology and modern science are incompatible, why not reject parapsychology? We know that the alternate hypothesis, that some men lie or deceive themselves, fits quite well within the framework of science. The choice is between believing in something "truly revolutionary" and "radically contradictory to contemporary thought" and believing in the occurrence of fraud and self-delusion. Which is more reasonable?

But the parapsychologists usually reply that we should accept both science and the supernatural. Although these may not fit together within a single scheme of things, we can imagine two separate systems, each compatible within itself. Why should we not accept dualism? To answer this here, I must try to compress a complex argument into minute space. The answer is: because past experience shows that dualistic reasoning has usually been comparatively unsuccessful in making predictions concerning observable phenomena.

Experience is all we have available as a guide to the future. As Reichenbach has pointed out, even when we consider magic phenomena, we must still base our expectations on inductive reasoning from past experience.[18] From our experience we have derived certain generalizations concerning observable phenomena. (Some of these we term *laws of science,* while others are so fundamental that we rarely name them.) In addition, we are able to make other generalizations concerning these first generalizations, for an enormous amount of pertinent data has accumulated. Thus, experience shows that scientific laws often fail when they are extended to a new range of size, like atomic size, but scientific laws do not fail in association with particular people.

For example: Suppose a physics student reports that he has found the wavelength of the red cadmium line to be two millimicrons greater than the accepted value. Now we cannot in any way at all prove that there do not actually exist some human beings whose presence can cause real, experimentally verifiable changes in physical constants—just as we cannot prove that the universe will not come to an end tomorrow. But our past experience suggests that the most profitable attitude for us will be to assume that the student made an error.

In the same way, we cannot prove that psi phenomena do not occur. Maybe in the presence of a "sensitive" the basic limiting principles no longer limit. But all our experience suggests that it will be more profitable for us to assume that the old generalizations are still valid, and that the findings of the parapsychologists are to be explained on the old, familiar basis of human error.

THE ESSENCE OF MAGIC

We now imagine a new critic, who speaks to us as follows: "This is all very well, and I concede that psi phenomena appear to me most strange and improbable, but a half-century ago I would have felt the same way concerning relativity. Does not any radically new complex phenomenon appear as baffling and improbable as ESP?"

What is required is a test to separate reported findings toward which we should be narrow-minded from those toward which we should be receptive. What is the fundamental difference between the natural and the supernatural? What is the essential characteristic of magic?

Let us compare scientific and magical methods of table levitation.[19] A scientist sits in his living room and says: "Table, rise." His speech pattern is portrayed on the screen of a visible speech apparatus. Phototubes observe the pattern through masks of appropriate shapes. A switch is closed, turning on an enormous electromagnet on the floor above. This attracts an iron plate concealed within the table top, and the table rises to the ceiling.

Similarly, the magician says: "Table, rise." And the table rises. The difference is that there is no iron plate, no electromagnet, no switch, and no speech interpretation apparatus.

Now a scientist can accept the absence of the iron plate; it is conceivable that there can exist sharply localized forces attracting wooden objects. He can even accept the absence of the magnet. What he cannot accept is the absence of the speech interpretation apparatus and the switch. New forces can be fitted into a scientific scheme of things. What cannot be made to fit is the *intelligent* manner in which the force is turned on and *directed* to act upon the table.

In the scientific process, each successive detail is provided for. In the magic process, there are just the wish and the result, and all intermediate steps are omitted. The essential characteristic of magic is that phenomena occur that can most easily be explained in terms of action by invisible intelligent beings.[20] The essence of science is mechanism. The essence of magic is animism. The way of science is to build a television system and a radio-controlled robot manipulator and have the manipulator cut a pack of cards at the 12th card and hold it up to the television camera. The way of magic is to sit in a chair with eyes closed and vaguely wish to know the identity of the 12th card down in a certain pack 100 miles away; and then the answer pops into one's mind.

Suppose that some extraordinary new phenomena is reported: should we be narrow-minded or receptive? The test is to attempt to imagine a detailed mechanistic explanation. Whenever we can imagine any sort of detailed explanation without introducing incorporeal intelligences, we should be prepared to regard the phenomenon open-mindedly. For this test it is not necessary that our explanation be simple, reasonable, or usable in making predictions. For example, any nuclear physicist could postulate a score of new forces, transition rules, and such, and so produce a complete theory of the atomic nucleus. Such a theory would be scientifically worthless, yet it would still satisfy the proposed test.

But with the phenomena of parapsychology, the situation is entirely different. Suppose that we attempt to describe mechanisms. Let us start with ESP tests at a distance of 100 miles or so, and let us feel free to imagine strange, fantastic forces without limit. Assume that we have under our control an invisible observation device that we can send in any direction at the speed of light. How do we go about locating a pack of cards 100 miles away? Would we guide ourselves by landmarks—or what? And would we not have to perceive with great accuracy in order to find the target? But how can we be accurate in perception of landmarks when we are grossly inaccurate in reading the target card? And how do we go through this locating process without any consciousness of it?

The special linkage that seems to exist between a percipient and the proper target card or telepathic sender is the sort of linkage that is characteristic of magic. In Greek mythology, the life of Meleager was linked to a piece of wood, and when his mother threw it on a fire, he perished far away. Or an African witch doctor makes a clay image and buries within it nail parings and bits of hair, and when the image is destroyed a man dies in London. Or a curse is uttered, and some magic influence goes to seek a distant victim.

Next, consider the process of "reading down" through a pack of ESP cards. How do we accurately locate card No. 12? How do we tell that we are reading the pattern on the face of card 12 and not confusing it with the back of card 13? How do we detect dye molecules in the dark? Do we subject the electrons to the same transitions that they would undergo in light, or do we employ different means of analysis? And how do we analyze just the dye and not the paper? Imagine anything you wish. Feel free to invent a new topology and a dozen different types of fields. But just describe the process in detail.

For other mental processes, conscious or subconscious, we can describe (or at least imagine) successive steps. We can describe in detail the steps involved in the creation of a great poem [21] or a mathematical theory. [22] We can explain subconscious processes such as the regulation of our heartbeat. Where information is missing, we can guess. But with the supernatural, all is different.

Moreover, how does the information get into a brain? How is it converted into electrochemical changes within neurons? And suppose that translation into neural impulses is already accomplished; then how are these signals to be interpreted? Pitts and McCulloch [23] have suggested neural patterns in human brains for interpretation of visual and auditory stimuli—but can anyone describe a conceivable nerve network for interpreting the raw data of ESP?

And finally, what conceivable way is there to explain precognition?

There is no plausible way to explain these details except in terms of special intelligent agents—spirits or poltergeists or whatever one wishes to call them. The proper target card is selected by a spirit. A spirit implants information in the brain in proper electrochemical form. The ability disappears when the spirit tires of working with a particular person. In short, parapsychology, although well camouflaged with some of the paraphernalia of science, still bears in abundance the markings of magic.

To be sure, the world of magic is a lovely world. To make a silent wish—and mysteriously influence the fall of dice. To sit with closed eyes while knowledge of the future strangely floats into the mind. These possibilities have for us the charm of childhood days, when we could fall asleep on Christmas Eve and in the morning find a tree hung with presents —like some Arabian Nights adventurer who fell asleep in a hovel and awoke in an enchanted palace. But the way of science is different. To construct a building, each brick and board must be fitted into place by human beings—not by jinn who answer the rubbing of a lamp. If our soldering is careless, our circuit will certainly be noisy; and if we make our seals poorly, our vacuum system will assuredly leak—and no incantation will help.

FRAUD AND ERROR

Following the publication in 1935 of Rhine's first book,[24] numerous papers appeared in American psychological journals pointing out possibilities of clerical errors and sensory clues and criticizing the statistical methods. These criticisms have been reviewed in detail by Pratt *et al.* (See note 2.). Later attacks of this sort were made by Nabours,[25] Skinner,[26] Rawcliffe,[27] Brown,[28] and—most recently and authoritatively—by Soal himself (See note 3.).

I believe that many of these criticisms were justified, but I am also completely convinced that some of Rhine's work and most of Soal's can be accounted for by no conceivable combination of such explanations.

What about fraud?

The parapsychologists speak of that possibility with utmost scorn: "We have done all that we can when the critic has nothing left to allege except that the investigator is in the trick. But when he has nothing else to allege he will allege that."[29] The hypothesis of "extensive and collusory fraud has yet to be responsibly suggested."[30] "The notion of such wholesale conspiracy would be to most students more fantastic than the ESP hypothesis" (See note 2, p. 166.).

Surprisingly, it is not only believers who are reluctant to imagine fraud, but virtually all skeptics as well will prefer almost any other type of explanation. It would be tedious for me to cite statistics to show that "the knavery and folly of men" are indeed "common phenomena," for everyone is aware of this—in an intellectual way. But when we try to imagine knavery and folly in connection with a particular individual, we encounter a surprising emotional blockage, and the possibility seems unreasonable. And thus we find skeptics searching for every other conceivable sort of explanation—proposing absurd systems of involuntary whispering, or indulging in the metaphysical acrobatics of arguing that ESP cannot occur because it involves a "negative hypothesis"—while the one explanation that is simplest and most in accord with everyday experience is dismissed as inconceivable. It is almost as though we give this answer to Paine: "We detest the thought that nature would go out of her course, but we will believe that or anything else rather than believe that a man would tell a lie."

It is particularly difficult for us to conceive of dishonesty in any situation where fraud would have to be complex and daring. For example, most people find it easier to imagine that some assistant may have occasionally cheated in an ESP experiment, than to suppose that a chief investigator could have deliberately designed an entire investigation fraudulently. Similarly, in the field of the "confidence game," the victim might be capable of suspecting one or two of his new "friends" as crooks, except that he cannot imagine that the entire stock exchange or gambling club to which they introduce him is an artifice, with the manager, employees, and even the patrons all "in the trick."

A good antidote against our curious mixture of credulity and incredulity is to become acquainted with some of the elaborate deceits of the past. Books that describe fraudulent production of supernatural phenomena have been written by Houdini,[31] Podmore,[32] Dunninger, (See note 19.), Jastrow, (See note 12.), and Rawcliffe (See note 27.). Confidence games involving expert understanding of the psychology of credulity are described by MacDonald.[33] And MacDougall[34] discusses the history and psychology of hoaxing.

There is a literature on the supernatural, just as there is a literature of chemistry and physics, and the scientist who ignores this literature and depends on his pure reasoning powers in evaluating reports of psychic phenomena is at a disadvantage. A little acquaintance with the careful studies of men like Podmore and Houdini will give one a broader point of view and a clearer understanding by which to evaluate modern parapsychology. For example, the man who knows that the Davenport brothers employed as many as ten confederates in a single seance (See note 31, p. 23.) should not think it unreasonable when I presently suggest that I would want seven or eight confederates in order to imitate 170 Soal sittings. And the reader who finds that he cannot conceive of the possibility that any leading modern parapsychologist could be fraudulent should compare his attitude with certain earlier judgments concerning the honesty of mediums. Consider for example, Houdini's report that Arthur Conan Doyle told him that "he did not believe any of 'the nice old lady mediums' would do anything wrong and it was just as unlikely for some old gentleman, innocent as a child unborn, to resort to trickery" (See note 31, p. 142.). Or consider William Crooke's opinion of Daniel Home:[35] "To those who knew him Home was one of the most lovable of men, and his perfect genuineness and uprightness were beyond suspicion. . . ." (Home was the most brilliant and successful of all mediums, and his patrons included the rulers of France and Russia. He could elongate his body by eleven inches, levitate himself and float around seance rooms near the ceiling, and perform numerous other miracles.)

History shows numerous men of great intelligence victimized by the simplest and most transparent trickery. Therefore, it is wisdom on our part to be aware that the rules by which we actually protect ourselves against dishonesty are little more than rules-of-thumb telling what to do in particular situations ("Don't gamble with strangers." "Know your endorser." "Always have a lawyer read the contract."), while our general principles for detection of dishonesty are mostly prejudices with little value. The courts, as a result of vast experience and utter necessity, have worked out a moderately satisfactory system of rules of evidence; but the psychological theorizing by which in daily life we judge innocence or guilt is valueless when it is applied to the work of a clever deceiver.

There is a certain stereotype of appearance and behavior that we associate with honesty, and a second stereotype that we associate with dishonesty—and successful swindlers are wise enough to imitate the former stereotype. "O what a goodly outside falsehood hath!" And so it is folly for us to survey the actions of a brilliant man and say: "This looks honest. If he were a charlatan, he would have done thus and so." Let us remember that those who seek to deceive us possibly are smarter than we are and probably have had more practice in simulating honesty than we have had in detecting dishonesty.

The wise procedure, when we seek to evaluate probability of fraud, is to try to ignore all vague, psychological criteria and base our reasoning (i) on such evidence as would impress a court and (ii) on purely statistical considerations. And here we must recognize that we usually make a certain gross statistical error. When we consider the possibility of fraud, almost invariably we think of particular individuals and ask ourselves whether it is possible that this particular man, this Professor X, could be dishonest. The probability seems small. But the procedure is incorrect. The correct procedure is to consider that we very likely would not have heard of Professor X at all except for his psychic findings. Accordingly, the probability of interest to us is the probability of there having been anywhere in the world, among its more than two billion inhabitants, a few people with the desire and the ability artfully to produce false evidence for the supernatural.

HAS THERE BEEN A SATISFACTORY TEST?

What is needed is one completely convincing experiment—just one experiment that does not have to be accepted simply on a basis of faith in human honesty. We should require evidence of such nature that it would convince us even if we knew that the chief experimenter was a stage conjurer or a confidence man. Has there been any single ESP experiment that would stand up if it were examined from this point of view?

Had I but space enough, I would analyze here all the major experiments of all the major investigators. But I do not have. I might select Rhine's work for discussion, but it apparently has not impressed critics nearly so much as Soal's. In fact, there are some indications that it has not impressed Soal himself very much.[36,37] But Soal's own work has been found convincing by eminent men of great intelligence. G. Evelyn Hutchinson[38] wrote concerning the Shackleton experiments that "they appear to be the most carefully conducted investigations of the kind ever to have been made," and that "Soal's work was conducted with every precaution that it was possible to devise." C. D. Broad wrote:[39] "There was already a considerable mass of quite good experimental evidence for telepathy, e.g. in the work of Dr. Rhine and his colleagues at Duke University, but Dr. Soal's results are outstanding.... The precautions taken to prevent deliberate fraud or the unwitting conveyance of information by normal means are described in great detail, and seem to be absolutely watertight."

So in the next two sections, I shall describe and analyze Soal's experiments. But I hope that readers will not search in these sections for psychological clues with which to bolster skepticism or belief. For example, one may note that Soal was originally himself a partial skeptic and from this conclude that he must be honest. Or conversely, one can reason: "The fact that for the Stewart series Soal altered the position of the screen aperture, raising it to eye level, suggests that he arranged conditions so that he could observe cards reflected in eyeglasses." But the wise course is to try to avoid such ethereal speculations. At best they may be treated as hunches to guide detectives but not as evidence to be presented in court. Such trivia would hardly be considered in a trial of a pickpocket, so they should not be offered as evidence for deciding profound cosmological questions.

This is the type of testimony that impresses a court:[40] "On April 17, 1910, at a seance given by Eusapia Paladino in New York City at the home of Professor H.G. Lord, I crawled under some chairs and lay with my face on the floor within eight inches of the leg of the table at the left side of the medium, and a foot came from underneath the dress of the medium and placed the toe underneath the left leg of the table, and pressing upward, gave it a little chuck into the air." Since I know of no evidence of this nature showing that Soal did or did not cheat, all that I am trying to do in the next two sections is to demonstrate that Soal *could* have cheated if he

158

wanted to, and that therefore we should demand better evidence than his before we believe in the supernatural.

SOAL'S EXPERIMENTS

In his early work as a psychic investigator, Soal published excellent papers reporting negative findings and showed himself to be a meticulous and ingenious experimenter, expert at uncovering trickery.[41] Then, allegedly, in 1939 he recalculated some old data and found that two people he had tested unsuccessfully for contemporaneous telepathy had actually been making highly significant precognitive scores.[42] These were Basil Shackleton and Mrs. Gloria Stewart. Shackleton was then studied in forty sittings dating from January 1941 to April 1943.[43] Mrs. Stewart was investigated from August 1945 to January 1950, in 130 sittings.[44] (Also see notes 3, pp. 199-337; and 37, pp. 34-56.)

The complex experimental procedure devised by Soal is most conveniently described as a cryptographic process (although Soal himself does not employ this terminology). An original number sequence of fifty terms (randomly selected from the digits 1 to 5) is enciphered by use of a *key* to yield a letter sequence. The latter is transmitted telepathically to a percipient, who records his guesses. This received letter sequence is deciphered by use of the key to yield a second number sequence, which is compared with the original. The cipher system is simple, one-digit substitution, and the key is a permutation of the letters E G L P Z (or other symbols). The total process is illustrated in Table 1, as it might occur with the following key:

1 2 3 4 5

L P Z G E

The steps in the process are carried out by (i) the "EA" (the *E*xperimenter associated with the *A*gent), who shows the original sequence, one digit at a time, to (ii) the *Agent,* who performs the enciphering and then telepathically transmits to (iii) the *Percipient.* At the close of a sitting, all received sequences are deciphered and then scored for "hits," as is shown in column VI, which indicates postcognitive ("-2" and "-1"), contemporaneous ("0"), and precognitive ("$+1$" and "$+2$") hits.

The EA and Agent sit on opposite sides of a small table, separated by a screen with a 3-inch square aperture. (The center of the aperture was 13 inches above the table top in the Shackleton sittings and 18 inches above the table in the Stewart sittings.) Resting in a rectangular box on the table on the Agent's side is a row of five *code cards* bearing animal pictures or initial letters (for example, Elephant, Giraffe, Lion, Pelican, Zebra). The open face of the box is toward the Agent, so that the code cards are shielded from the EA and others. The Percipient is in another room.

In a typical experiment, at each trial, the EA displays at the aperture the digit indicated by a random number list (column II), and then he calls out to the Percipient the serial number of the trial (column I). Then the Agent briefly raises and glances at the code card in the indicated position, and the Percipient writes his guess. For example, at trial No. 8 in Table 1, the EA displayed the digit 2 at the aperture and called out "eight." The Agent then raised the card in position 2 (second from the left) and glanced at the picture of a pelican. The Percipient wrote down the letter *G,* which was a "+1" precognitive hit.

I	II	III	IV	V	VI
			Received		
Trial number	Original sequence	Enciphered sequence	sequence (guesses)	Deciphered sequence	Type of "hit"
1	3	Z	G	4	
2	5	E	E	5	0
3	1	L	E	5	−1, +2
4	4	G	P	2	
5	5	E	L	1	−2, +1
6	1	L	Z	3	
7	2	P	P	2	0, +1
8	2	P	G	4	+1
9	4	G	Z	3	+1
10	3	Z	P	2	−2

Table 1. An example of the transformations involved in a typical telepathy experiment of the Soal type.

Sittings were usually composed of 8 runs of 50 trials. At "normal" rate of calling, each trial required between 2 and 3 seconds. At the start of each run, the Agent or an observer shuffled and arranged the code cards out of sight of the EA, thereby changing the key. After each 50 trials, the code-card order was recorded. Following the last run, the Percipient's guesses were deciphered by the appropriate key, and hits were counted.

There were a number of variations. In most experiments the original sequence was taken from a list provided by Soal, but occasionally lists were computed by outsiders and were given directly to the EA at the start of the experiment. At a few sittings the number sequence was generated by the EA during the run by drawing colored counters from a bag or bowl. Usually the sitting was in the Percipient's home, but occasionally other locations were employed; and in six sittings Mrs. Stewart made her guesses in Antwerp, with Agents in London.

In the Shackleton series, almost all the extrachance results were produced with either "R. E." or "J. Al." as Agent. With the former, most successes were "+1" precognitive hits. In 5367 "+1" trials at "normal" rate of calling with R. E. as Agent, Shackleton scored 1540 "+1" hits, for a mean of 13.77 per run of 50 trials.[45] Usually, with J. Al. as Agent, both pre- and postcognitive guesses yielded more than 13 hits per run; hits were ordinarily "−1" and "+1," but changed to "−2" and "+2" when the calling rate was doubled. Thirty-one sittings yielded extrachance results, and at all of these both Soal and Shackleton were present, plus at least one of the following: Mrs. Goldney, J. Al., and R. E. In addition, at 23 of the 31, one or more additional persons were present. Usually these took the roles of EP (*E*xperimenter watching the *P*ercipient) or EA, or watched the Agent; but two worked successfully as Agents.

In the Stewart series, 30 persons were tested as Agents, and 15 were successful. Total score for 37,100 trials by standard procedure was 9410 "0" hits, for a mean score of 12.68 hits per run of 50. In these experiments, Soal usually took the role of EA. The usual procedure was for the agent to shuffle the cards and then arrange them face up and stare at them for 30 seconds. Then they were turned over, and during the run the Agent tapped the indicated card on the back instead of lifting it. The cards usually bore initial letters about 2 inches high instead of animal pictures.[46]

ANALYSIS OF SOAL'S WORK

Before I continue, it should be clearly understood that I am not here stating that Soal or any of his associates was guilty of deliberate fraud. All that I want to do is show that fraud was easily possible.

I do not claim that I know how Soal cheated if he did cheat, but if I were myself to attempt to duplicate his results, this is how I would proceed. First of all, I would seek a few collaborators, preferably people with good memories. The more collaborators I had, the easier it would be to perform the experiments, but the greater would be the risk of disclosure. Weighing these two considerations together, I'd want four confederates to imitate the Shackleton experiments. For imitating the Stewart series, I'd probably want three or four—although it is impossible to be certain, because the Stewart sittings have not been reported in much detail. In recruiting, I would appeal not to desire for fame or material gain but to the noblest motives, arguing that much good to humanity could result from a small deception designed to strengthen religious belief.

The next step would be to devise procedures. Like a competent medium, I would want several alternatives available, so that any skeptic who suspected one procedure could be confronted by a repetition performed under conditions making the suspected procedure impossible. One main group of procedures would involve matching a prepared random number sequence to a letter or number sequence previously memorized or written out by the Percipient. At about 90 percent of my sittings, the original sequences would be taken from lists provided by me. Here are a few of the possibilities:

Procedure 1. The Percipient and the Agent are "in the trick." The Agent arranges the code cards as previously directed by me, and the Percipient writes down a memorized sequence or takes a list from a drawer if no outsider is watching him. (This would be a preferred procedure in most experiments except when an outsider determined the order of the code cards. It could succeed with outsiders as EA and EP.)

Procedure 2. The Percipient and the Agent (or the EA or an observer) are "in the trick." The code card order is determined by an outsider. The Agent (or the EA or an observer) notes this order, classifies it into 1 of 6 groups, and signals the group number to the Percipient before or after the run. Only 2.6 bits of information are needed to designate a choice of 1 out of 6. For example, the Agent glances at the backs of the cards and then says: "Ready." "All ready." "Yes, I'm ready." "Yes, ready."—And so forth.[47] The Percipient then takes from a drawer the designated guess sheet, which is already filled out in his hand writing.[48] (If the Agent is an outsider, the EA or an observer can note the card order when it is recorded at the end of the run and signal it in the conversation then.)

Procedure 3. The Percipient and the Agent are "in the trick." The Agent notes the card order and signals it (6.9 bits for the 120 possible permutations) before the start of the run. The Percipient has memorized a number sequence, and he uses the card order to encipher each number mentally. (This can work with outsiders watching both the Agent and the Percipient and shuffling the code cards; or if the Agent is an outsider, the signaling can be done by an observer who shuffles the cards.)

Next consider some of the procedures that could be used even when the number sequence was not known to me in advance:

Procedure 4. The Percipient and the Agent are "in the trick." They have copied or memorized the same lists of letter symbols. During the run the Agent records (concealed by the box) the numbers corresponding (precognitively) to the letters that he knows the Percipient is guessing, and at the end he rearranges the code cards to give the desired degree of success. For example, with a record like that shown in Fig. 1, the Agent could see that card arrangement LEGZP will yield a large number of hits. (This procedure would be particularly useful when the EA was an outsider.)

	1	2	3	4	5
E	II	IIII	II	II	I
G	II		III	II	IIII
L	III	III	II	I	I
P		II	II	I	III
Z	II	II	I	III	

Fig. 1. Type of record to be kept by an Agent employing procedure 4 for simulating telepathy. If the number sequence "12345" is replaced by the letter sequence "LEGZP," it will be seen that arranging the code cards in this order will result in 16 "hits."

Procedure 5. The Percipient and the EA are "in the trick." The EA learns the order of the code cards and signals information to the Percipient during the run. The Percipient has memorized a random sequence of letter symbols. The EA, in calling out the serial numbers, slightly alters his voice or timing a few times during each run (5 times per 50 trials to give 14 hits). Ordinarily the Percipient is to guess at random, but at each signal he writes down the next letter on the memorized sequence. (I would use this method particularly in experiments when an outsider who wore glasses served as Agent. Then the preferred experimental arrangement would be that in which the cards are turned face up for 30 seconds, the screen aperture would be located as it was in the Stewart sittings, and the lighting would be so arranged that the EA could see the cards by reflection in the Agent's glasses.)

Procedure 6. The Percipient plus the EA, the *Recorder,* or the Agent are "in the trick." In runs where the number sequence is generated by counters, I would have the EA draw counters of the needed color at particular points, or the Recorder could keep false records of counters drawn. And in some experiments, procedures, 1, 4, or 5 could be used.

The procedures that could give the highest degree of success, and that thus would be chosen when I wanted simultaneous "-1" and "+1" or "-2" and "+2" successes, are procedures 1 and 3. Any of the others would be more than adequate for scores of 12.68 hits per run of 50, or 13.77 hits in 48 trials. For long-distance experiments, procedures 1 and 4 would work. Or I could employ procedure 2 by telephoning the Percipient after the sitting to tell him which lists to mail in.

Many other procedures are possible. The six chosen for description were selected as samples of what can be done by simple means. Mental abilities required are similar to those needed for playing bridge competently, except that some collaborators would need a little memory training. Use of special apparatus or of collaborators with the abilities of a good stage conjurer would open up numerous new possibilities. Thus it should be clear that Soal's work was *not* conducted "with every precaution that it was possible to devise." The work would have been enormously more nearly fraudproof if Soal, instead of employing his highly complex arrangement, had simply had many different Agents "send" directly from lists prepared by outsiders and given directly to the Agent at the start of each run. And the examples to be given presently will show what precautions can be devised if one really wants to devise precautions.

WHY HAS THERE BEEN NO SATISFACTORY TEST?

Both Soal and Rhine have demonstrated ESP before intelligent "open-minded" outside observers, but what is needed is something that can be demonstrated to the most hostile, pig-headed, and skeptical of critics. Why has there been no such demonstration? Because when onlookers are hostile, "sensitives" allegedly lose their paranormal abilities. This excuse is an old one, long employed by spiritualist mediums, but contemporary parapsychology has modernized it with a touch of poetry. Thus Rhine asks (see note 15, p. 246.): "Would you expect, if we had a young poet here, that we could send him up to your university to write some poems for you while your committee sat staring fixedly at him to see that he did not slip them from one of his pockets?" And Soal argues (See note 3, pp. 51f.): "But one would not expect even a poet to produce a good poem if he were surrounded by people who, he felt, viewed his activities with half-concealed scorn or humorous contempt. The best he could do would be to churn out a few passable verses from which the informing spirit of poetry would be absent."

There are two replies to this excuse. The first is that it is false. It appears plausible to us because nowadays we tend to regard poets as rather erratic, neurotic beings. But in other periods, when it was expected of every educated man that he be able to write competent poetry, such reasoning would not have seemed convincing. Of course there are poets who require solitude for work, just as there are bridge players who are upset by kibitzers; but one would hardly imagine, say, Sidney or Raleigh or Byron suddenly starting to write like Edgar Guest because people were staring at him.

Poetic creation, as analyzed by John Livingston Lowes in his monumental study of Coleridge (See note 21.), is strikingly similar to mathematical creation, as described by Jacques Hadamard in his brilliant little book on *The Psychology of Invention in the Mathematical Field* (See note 22.). We expect a young mathematician to be able to do creative mathematical thinking before a hostile examining committee, and a poet or any other kind of thinker can do as well. Rhine writes (See note 9, p. 141.): "All the fickleness and skittishness of ESP and PK will find their counterparts in the fine arts, in the realm of the Muses." But this is not correct. There is no established human ability whatsoever that shows the fickleness of ESP.

Such is the first reply to the excuse of Rhine and Soal. And the second reply is that it is perfectly possible to set up fraudproof tests permitting "sensitives" to work anywhere they wish, completely alone or with whatever company they desire, and yet with the experiments subject to the most searching scrutiny at all essential points.

In other days, numerous "sensitives" willingly demonstrated their marvels before critical examining committees. In the 1870's, Daniel Home submitted to painstaking investigation by William Crookes. In the 1880's, a number of mediums appeared before the Seybert Commission of the University of Pennsylvania. Later, the British and American Societies for Psychical Research continued the type of investigations that had been started by the Seybert Commission. And from about 1880 to 1910, the great Eusapia Palladino made a specialty of holding seances before committees of scientists.

But a change came. Although scientists were often easily fooled, conjurers proved to be able foes of mediums. Houdini devoted the last years of his life to exposing mediums, and then this work was continued by Dunninger, who for many years defended the *Science and Invention* awards of $21,000 for physical spirit manifestations that he could not duplicate by scientific means.[49] So effective has such work been that now-adays we hear very little of the olden wonders like materializations or elongations, levitations or transportations. Such tricks are too risky, too easily exposed by skeptics with flashlights. Instead, today we are expected to marvel at vague statistical effects, minutiae that a conjurer would scorn to imitate on a stage. So little is claimed, and this little is demonstrated only to such restricted audiences and under such carefully controlled conditions and with so many excuses for failure available that it is quite difficult to prove that the little is actually nothing. Yet this can be done, I think.

DESIGN OF A SATISFACTORY TEST

As scientists, what sort of evidence for ESP should we demand? This sort: one test of such nature that fraud or error would seem to us as improbable as the supernatural. Let us somewhat arbitrarily think of a committee of 12 and design tests such that the presence of a single honest man on the "jury" will ensure validity of the test, even if the other 11 members should cooperate in fraud either to prove or disprove occurrence of psi phenomena. Assume that the committee includes two experimental psychologists, two experimental physicists, one statistician, and three conjurers or other experts on trickery—all prominent men and all strongly hostile toward parapsychology, with that "adamantine faith" that Lucian recommended.[50] Then probably most scientists would have confidence in the committee and would be prepared to believe in psi phenomena in pre-ference to believing that the entire committee was dishonest or deluded. In addition, so that results would be acceptable to parapsychologists, the chairman of the committee should be a person with a record of successes in psi experimentation, for it is claimed by West[51] and Soal (See note 3, pp. 388f.) that the personality of the chief experimenter may in some psychic manner determine success or failure in a psychic experiment.

To test Rhine's "sensitives," the simplest procedure is to prepare sealed packages of cards and mail them to Duke University to be examined by clairvoyants at any time and place they select, and then have them mailed back along with records of guesses. In preparing the packages, cards would be shuffled automatically by a series of machines and placed within opaque containers in such manner that no one could possibly have seen any card from the beginning of the shuffling. A good procedure for insuring against opening would be to place each set of cards in a small metal container, weld on a cover, and take photomicrographs of the weld—for it is probably impossible to counterfeit microscopic details. When the cards were returned, first the seals would be checked, and then packages would be cut open and cards fanned out by machine, with the jury watching and with a motion-picture camera recording everything.

For the type of findings made by Soal, the simplest and most fraudproof type of test would make use of the precognitive ability that Shackleton allegedly showed most of the time and that Mrs. Stewart allegedly showed for a brief time. With precognition, the only safe-guards needed are that the "message" be generated in a way not subject to ordinary human control or prediction, and that guesses be recorded before the message is displayed. Imagine a radioactive sample of high activity, plus a scintillation counter with ring-of-five scaling circuit and indicator lamps corresponding to Soal's five animal symbols. An accurate timing circuit turns off the counter at set intervals. The circuitry is wired in such open fashion that inspection is easy. The apparatus is battery-powered and is placed in a shielded case, with nothing penetrating through the shield except windows to show the indicators. The percipient and the tele-pathic sender can be wherever in the world they wish, together or far apart, in the same room with the apparatus or across the ocean from it, alone or with whatever company they want. The guesses of the percipient (transmitted via radio or cable, if necessary) are indicated in some visible form, and a single motion-picture camera records both guesses and sub-sequent "calls" of the number generator.

It is also simple to test psychokinetic control of dice. While a mo-tion-picture camera records everything, one or more dice are placed at the top of a chute or in a throwing machine. Then a ring-of-six random number generator tells the psychic controller what number to wish for, and a few seconds later the dice are automatically released. The psychic controller can be in the same room, or anywhere in the world where tele-phone or radio can reach him.

For testing contemporaneous telepathy, symbols to be transmitted should be controlled by a random number generator, and the percipient could be anywhere in the world except close to the sender. However, it is exceedingly difficult to guard against all known communication means, especially since only a few bits of information need be transmitted per twenty-five trials in order to give extrachance results. For example, the sender might signal to a member of the committee by means of slight motions of his body, and the committee member could use a pocket radio transmitter to relay the information. I have worked out several procedures that appear to be reasonably fraudproof, but the required precautions are quite elaborate, and I am not sure that others cannot think of much simpler procedures, so I prefer not to take the space to describe my ideas here. No doubt clairvoyance, precognitive telepathy, and psychokinesis should be examined first, since it is so easy to test them. Then—if anyone is still interested in the question—contemporaneous telepathy can be tested.

Even now in 1955, paranormal findings continue to be published in England [52] and America, [53] so it is reasonable for us to expect that both the British Society for Psychical Research and the Duke University Parapsychology Laboratory will gladly offer "sensitives" to be tested.

CONCLUSION

What sort of reply will the parapsychologists make to these criticisms? I have read answers they have made to others, and on that basis I might expect some of the following.

1) "Some interesting suggestions for further demonstrations of ESP have recently been made, but we consider that ESP was demonstrated beyond any reasonable doubt many years ago, and it is a waste of time to keep proving the same thing over and over again. However, there is much need for additional workers in the field, so we hope that Price will try his suggestions himself."

2) "Standards of experimentation in psi research are already far higher than those in most fields of science, so it is absurd to seek further improvement. Science would have made little progress if every chemistry and physics experiment had had to be performed before witnesses and with numerous other precautions."

3) "A foolish attack has recently been made by an incompetent man who, to the best of our belief, has never published a single experiment in the field of parapsychology." [54]

4) "Unfortunately, I can furnish no one right at present for demonstrating ESP. However, I proved everything conclusively, with odds against chance of 10^{237} to 1, back in 19—."

But the only answer that will impress me is an adequate experiment. Not 1000 experiments with 10 million trials and by 100 separate investigators giving total odds against chance of 10^{1000} to 1—but just one good experiment. And until such a demonstration has been provided, I hope that my fellow-scientists will similarly withhold belief.[55]

NOTES

1. See, for example, the press release by B. H. Camp, president of the Institute of Mathematical Statistics, quoted in the *New York Herald Tribune,* 16 Jan. 1938, sect. II-IV, p. 6.

2. J. G. Pratt, J. B. Rhine, B. M. Smith, C. E. Stuart, J. A. Greenwood, *Extra-Sensory Perception after Sixty Years* (Holt, New York, 1940).

3. S. G. Soal and F. Bateman, *Modern Experiments in Telepathy* (Yale Univ. Press, New Haven, Conn., 1954). I cite this book as "Soal," rather than as "Soal and Bateman," since large portions of it are taken almost unchanged from papers by Soal alone or by Soal and Goldney.

4. R. A. McConnell, *J. Parapsychol.* 18, 245 (1954).

5. E. G. Boring, *Am. Scientist* 43, 108 (1955).

6. C. E. Shannon, *Bell System Tech. J.* 27, 379-423, 623-656 (1948).

7. Channel capacity is given by:
$$\text{Bits/trial} = \log_2 5 + (N/25)\log_2 (N/25) +$$
$$4[(25 - N)/100]\log_2 [(25 - N)/100]$$
where N is the mean number of "hits" per 25 trials ($N \geq 5$). (This formula applies strictly only to cases where in each trial there is equal probability of selecting any of the five symbols; thus it applies strictly to most of Soal's work but will be slightly in error for most of Rhine's work.)

8. J. B. Rhine, *J. Parapsychol.* 6, 111 (1942); 9, 264 (1945).

9. ————, *The Reach of the Mind* (Sloane, New York, 1947), pp. 73-75.

10. ————, *The New World of the Mind* (Sloane, New York, 1953),pp. 94ff.

11. B. M. Humphrey and J. B. Rhine, *J. Parapsychol.* 6, 190 (1942).

12. Quoted by J. Jastrow in *Wish and Wisdom* (Appleton-Century, New York, 1935), p. 25.

13. T. Paine, *Age of Reason*; the quotation comes a few pages before the end of part I.

14. C. D. Broad, *Philosophy* 24, 291 (1949).

15. J. B. Rhine, *New Frontiers of the Mind* (Farrar and Rinehart, New York, 1937), chap. 12.

16. R. Walker, *Sci. Monthly* 79, 1 (1954).

17. Quoted in reference 3, p. 357.

18. H. Reichenbach, *The Theory of Probability* (Univ. of California Press, Berkeley, 1949), p. 476.

19. I refer here to genuine magic, not the deceptions of mediums and stage conjurers. Five methods of table levitation employed by mediums are disclosed by J. Dunninger in *Inside the Medium's Cabinet* (David Kemp, New York, 1935).

20. I am using *magic* in a particular sense, defining it in terms of what *can* be explained in a certain way—without regard to how those who attempt to practice it actually do try to explain it. Actions that overtly resemble magic ceremonies and yet are based on mechanistic reasoning (like much of alchemy), I would call not magic but gropings toward science.

21. J. L. Lowes, *The Road to Xanadu* (Houghton Mifflin, Boston, 1927).

22. J. Hadamard, *The Psychology of Invention in the Mathematical Field* (Princeton Univ. Press, Princeton, N.J., 1945).

23. W. Pitts and W. S. McCulloch, *Bull. Math. Biophys.* 9, 127 (1947).

24. J. B. Rhine, *Extra-Sensory Perception* (Humphries, Boston, 1935).

25. R. K. Nabours, *Philosophy of Science* 10, 191 (1943).

26. B. F. Skinner, *Am. Scientist* 36, 456, 482 ff. (1948).

27. D. H. Rawcliffe, *The Psychology of the Occult* (Ridgway, London, 1952). I think that most of Rawcliffe's ideas are correct, but that his explanation of Soal's work in terms of involuntary whispering is implausible.

28. G. S. Brown, *Nature* 172, 154 (1953). I think that Brown's criticism has been adequately refuted by Soal in reference 3.

29. H. Sidgwick, *Proc. Soc. Psychical Research* 1, 7 (1882).

30. W. W. Carington, *ibid.* 46, 265 (1940).

31. H. Houdini, *A Magician Among the Spirits* (Harper, New York, 1924).

32. F. Podmore, *Modern Spiritualism* (Methuen, London, 2 vols., 1902); *The Newer Spiritualism* (Holt, New York, 1911).

33. J. C. R. MacDonald, *Crime Is a Business* (Stanford Univ. Press, Stanford, Calif., 1939).

34. C. D. MacDougall, *Hoaxes* (Macmillan, New York, 1940).

35. W. Crookes, *J. Soc. Psychical Research* 6, 341 (1894). Dissenting opinions concerning Home have been written by Podmore (32), Houdini, and R. Browning. Houdini (31, p. 49) states that "His active career, his various escapades, and the direct cause of his death all indicate that he lived the life of a hypocrite of the deepest dye." (Houdini does not name the cause of Home's death, although he does quote this sentence from Madame Blavatsky's *Key to Theosophy*: "This Calvin of Spiritualism suffered for years from a terrible spinal disease, brought on through his intercourse with the 'spirits,' and died a perfect wreck.") And Browning, in "Mr. Sludge, 'the Medium,' " gives this picture of Home: "Now, don't sir! Don't expose me! Just this once!/ This was the first and only time, I'll swear,—/Look at me,—see, I kneel,—the only time,/I swear, I ever cheated,—yes, by the soul/Of Her who hears—(your sainted mother, sir!)/All, except this last accident, was truth—"

36. S. G. Soal, *Proc. Soc. Psychical Research* 50, 67 (1953), especially pp. 84, 94.

37. ———, *The Experimental Situation in Psychical Research* (Society for Psychical Research, London, 1947), pp. 25 f.

38. G. E. Hutchinson, *Am. Scientist* 36, 291 (1948).

39. C. D. Broad, *Philosophy* 19, 261 (1944).

40. Paraphrased from a report by J. F. Rinn, published by J. Jastrow in *Collier's Weekly* 45, No. 8, 21 (14 May 1910).

41. S. G. Soal, *Proc. Soc. Psychical Research* 40, 165 (1932); *J. Soc. Psychical Research* 30, 55 (1937); *Preliminary Studies of a Vaudeville Telepathist* (Univ. of London Council for Psychical Investigation, London, Bull. III, 1937).

42. ———, *Proc. Soc. Psychical Research* 46, 152 (1940).

43. ——— and K. M. Goldney, *ibid.* 47, 21 (1943).

44. F. Bateman and S. G. Soal, *J. Soc. Psychical Research* 35, 257 (1950); S. G. Soal and F. Bateman, *J. Parapsychol.* 14, 168 (1950).

45. Since there was a pause at the middle of each run, and pre-and postcognitive hits occurring across this gap were not scored, there were 48 "+1" trials per run of 50.

46. This description of Soal's experiments omits details not relevant to my argument. For example, I have said nothing concerning precautions taken against tampering with the records. Therefore, readers previously unfamiliar with Soal's work should be cautious in deciding that they have found a flaw in it.

47. Houdini states: "Regarding the possibility of using codes and cues before others without being detected I can say positively that it is not only possible but simple and practical" (reference 31, p. 259). And Soal in several different places discusses auditory codes and other signaling means: for example, in reference 3, pp. 104, 117.

48. A variety of ways are available for setting up such a system. In one of these, 22 prepared guess sheets can suffice for a sitting of 8 runs, and simple, short-cut methods are available for quickly preparing the lists of guesses.

49. Of the $21,000, $1000 was offered by *Science and Invention* magazine, $10,000 by Dunninger, and $10,000 by the same J. F. Rinn who observed Palladino's footwork at close range. Further details are given in reference 19, and in J. Dunninger, *Houdini's Spirit Exposés from Houdini's Own Manuscripts, Records and Photographs* (Experimenter Publ., New York, 1928). Of course, no medium ever won the $21,000. No doubt, if any one of them had been clever enough to devise a trick that Dunninger could not duplicate, that person would not have been a medium, for he would probably have preferred to make an honest living as a conjurer.

50. Strong hostility toward supernaturalism is desirable as a safeguard, even though it is not absolutely essential. To be sure, Houdini had strong yearning to find evidence for the supernatural, and yet he was a most effective exposer of psychic fraud, but such a combina-

tion is exceedingly rare.

51. D. J. West, *J. Soc. Psychical Research* 37, 323 (1954).

52. G. W. Fisk and D. J. West, *ibid.* 38, 1 (1955).

53. G. L. Mangan, *J. Parapsychol.* 19, 35 (1955); H. Forwald, *ibid.* 19, 45 (1955).

54. Soal (36), in replying to criticism by Rawcliffe (27), writes: "All Mr. Rawcliffe's knowledge is derived from books; to the best of our belief he has never in his life published a single experiment in the field of parapsychology." Also, Soal writes (*3*, pp. 23 f.); "It would be interesting to meet the psychiatrist or psychologist who has pursued every page of the 49 volumes of the *Proceedings* of the Society for Psychical Research, and who remains a complete skeptic." It would be interesting indeed.

55. For reading early drafts of this paper and making numerous helpful suggestions, I am greatly indebted to Herbert Feigl, Bernard Gelbaum, Gerhard Kalisch, Leo Marx, Paul Meehl, and Michael Scriven, all of the University of Minnesota, and to Claude Shannon of Bell Telephone Laboratories. However, this must not be taken as implying that these men or the Department of Medicine, University of Minnesota, necessarily endorse my views.

S. G. Soal

On "Science and the Super-natural"

I have read with some amazement the article "Science and the Supernatural."[1] In this paper George Price suggests fraudulent collusion between the chief experimenter (presumably myself) and a number of highly respectable people as an explanation of the significant results obtained in the card-guessing work carried out with Basil Shackleton and Gloria Stewart reported by F. Bateman and myself.[2] Moreover, Price makes these suggestions without being able to produce the least fragment of factual evidence that any such fraudulent malpractice ever took place. It is, I think, safe to say that no English scientific journal would have published such a diatribe of unsupported conjecture. *Nature,* the leading English scientific weekly, has nothing but praise for our work, in a recent book review.[3]

Price begins by saying that "In his early work as a psychic investigator, Soal published excellent papers reporting negative findings and showed himself to be a meticulous and ingenious experimenter, expert at uncovering trickery." But every competent critic has admitted that the Shackleton experiments, for instance, were on a higher level of technical efficiency than any of the earlier 1934-39 card-guessing experiments. In the earlier work, for example, the guesser and sender were in the same room separated only by a screen, whereas elaborate precautions were taken in the later work to eliminate all sensory cues. Apparently Price

Reprinted from *Science* 123 (1956) No. 3184, pp. 9-11, by permission of the editor and Mrs. S. G. Soal.

considers the early experiments to be "excellent" merely because they produced only negative findings. In much the same way critics hostile to extrasensory perception pronounced Coover's[4] very defective experiments to be "a notable example of painstaking, thorough research and exact treatment of numerical data."[5] There is little doubt that if Coover had obtained positive results of high significance his experimental methods would have been described in far less flattering terms.

It is very significant and somewhat comforting to learn that Price admits that "most of Soal's work" cannot be accounted for by any combination of statistical artifact and sensory leakage. He is convinced, for instance, of the inadequacy of Rawcliffe's theory of "double whispering" in disposing of the Shackleton results[6] or of Spencer Brown's suggestion[7] that the extrachance scores are due to nonrandomness in the target series or to defects in probability theory (See note 2.).

He is therefore driven, as a last resort, to suggest that the experimenters have deliberately organized fraudulent techniques that have been successfully practiced in the case of Mrs. Stewart over a period of four years without detection by the numerous academic people who have taken part in the experiments. In taking this attitude Price would appear to be trading on the prejudice and hostility that a majority of American scientists bear toward the subject of telepathy. In England the attitude of scientific men and philosophers is far more tolerant and open-minded, and such an attack as that of Price would be considered grossly unfair unless he could produce actual evidence that cheating had taken place.

Price has suggested several methods by which the experiments could have been faked. I propose to examine these suggestions in some detail.

In at least three of the procedures described the Agent or sender and the Percipient (as well as EA, the chief Experimenter) are in the trick. The Agent, sitting behind the screen arranges the five animal cards in an order that has been decided beforehand by EA. Or in another variation the Agent lays out the cards in any order and communicates this order to EA on the other side of the screen by means of some code concealed in a phrase such as "I am now ready." EA then communicates this order (or certain partial constituents of it) to the Percipient in the next room by means of a code contained in some commonplace phrase or by means of inflections of his voice, and so forth. The Percipient who is in collusion with EA has previously memorized certain numbers chosen by EA from certain key positions of his list of random numbers. As EA calls aloud the serial numbers of the twenty-five guesses, the Percipient decodes the numbers in the key positions into the corresponding initials of the animals' names.

Price goes to great length in devising variations on this theme, but they all depend on the Agent being in collusion with the chief Experimenter or with the Percipient. Now four of the Agents with whom Mrs. Stewart was highly successful were lecturers of high academic standing at Queen Mary College in the University of London. Two were senior lecturers and the other two were mathematicians who had done distinguished creative work. A fifth Agent who was brilliantly successful over a long period was a senior civil servant, in fact an assistant director of mathematical examinations in the Civil Service. Now is it plausible to suppose that I, as chief Experimenter, could persuade any of these men to enter into a stupid and pointless collusion to fake the experiments over a period of years? What had any of them to gain from such deplorable conduct? If I had gone to any of them and suggested (as Price recommends) that in a good cause a little deception would do no harm, I know quite plainly that the result would have been a first-class scandal in university circles. These men had no burning desire to prove extrasensory perception and no religious axes to grind. They had everything to lose by besmirching their academic reputations. Their only motive was scientific curiosity. It is idle, therefore, for Price to assume that these five Agents would consent to arrange the cards at the bidding of myself or deliberately to communicate the code either to me or to the Percipient, Mrs. Stewart. Certainly, one might find obscure people with no conscience who would, if they were paid for doing it, assist in faking an experiment, but not in the ranks of University of London lecturers.

If then, these Agents were not in the trick, how did EA get hold of the code in order to communicate it to Mrs. Stewart? Since in many such experiments another academic man was sitting by Mrs. Stewart handing her numbered record sheets to fill in one by one, it would be clearly too late for her to receive the code *after* her fifty guesses had been completed. Nor could she draw prepared lists of guesses from a drawer, since there was no accessible drawer at the table where she sat, and even if there had been one her every movement was under observation by the academic man sitting beside her. EA might, of course, *ask* the Agent innocently for the order of the code at the commencement of each run of fifty guesses, but all thirty Agents would swear emphatically that no such thing ever happened and that during a run EA never left his own side of the screen. Moreover, asking for the code would excite immediate suspicion. Price has made the suggestion that EA, looking through the hole in the screen, might see the reflection of the five cards in the Agent's spectacles. But with the lighting of the room as it was and the position of the hole and the size of the box, it can easily be verified that such a thing would be impossible. I have always been on guard against reflections in card experiments, and since the main object of my setup was to insure that EA who gave the signals to Shackleton or Mrs. Stewart should have no knowledge of what card the Agent was looking at, I naturally took special precautions to see that reflections in spectacles, window panes, and so forth, were impossible. I am ready to demonstrate to anyone that the spectacle theory is an erroneous one under our particular conditions.

If then the Agent is not in the trick, it would appear to be impossible for the code to have been communicated to Mrs. Stewart until she had recorded her guesses. I could cite large numbers of highly successful experiments in which both the Agent and the person who sat with Mrs. Stewart were people of academic standing. Let me give only two examples.

At sitting No. 52 on 23 April 1948, Louise Morgan (See note 2, p. 225.) a well-known journalist on the staff of the *News Chronicle*, visited us for the first time and took part as Agent. Brendel of Queen Mary College sat by Mrs. Stewart for the whole time while she was making her guesses. The checking of scores was done by Brendel, watched by Morgan and R. A. M. Kearney, a mathematician. Mrs. Stewart made a score of 109 hits in 400 guesses. This gives an excess over chance expectation of more than 3.5 standard deviations. Now no one will suggest that I could be such a fool as to attempt a collusion with Morgan. If I had done so I should have seen my name in letters of infamy in next morning's *News Chronicle.*

And here is an experiment in pure telepathy (See note 2, pp. 252-253.) in which Rozelaar of Queen Mary College was the Agent. In this case no actual cards were used, but the Agent imagined a code to be printed on five blank pieces of paper and did not divulge it until Mrs. Stewart's guess sheet was safely in the hands of Bateman (assistant director of examinations to the Civil Service Commission) who sat by Mrs. Stewart. In 200 trials she obtained 60 hits—the equivalent of 3.5 standard deviations. Here there was no question of EA (myself) reading the code in Rozelaar's glasses. (Actually at the time he did not wear spectacles). And as I have said it would be absurd to suppose that a senior lecturer of the University of London would lower himself to assist in faking an experiment. Rozelaar had no connection whatever with any psychical organization. The guesses were decoded by Bateman and checked by Mrs. Hales (a highly respectable professional pianist), and Rozelaar himself checked me as I called aloud Mrs. Stewart's guesses.

I could multiply examples of experiments of this kind. Moreover, Mrs. Stewart was successful with fifteen Agents out of thirty that were tried. Price's assumption of collusion between myself and fellow-lecturers at the University of London has no basis in reality and is a fantastic product of his own imagination. Many people would consider such a hypothesis to be more improbable than the existence of telepathy itself, for which there is a vast amount of spontaneous evidence of good quality quite apart from card-guessing. Indeed in formulating his themes of collusion, Price has not taken sufficiently into account the high quality of the personnel connected with these experiments. Nor has he any acquaintance with the mentalities of the Percipients themselves. No one, for instance, who knew Shackleton would credit him with the ability to memorize accurately certain random numbers located in varying key positions in as many as 12 or 16 columns and, in addition, to transpose these numbers into code letters at the rate of one every 2 seconds. I should experience the greatest difficulty in performing such a task myself, even at the normal rate of calling, and at the rapid rate of a call every second I should find the thing impossible. With an observer watching every movement, I should be unable to pull from my pocket any lists with which to refresh my memory. And to have to carry out such a nerve-racking performance week after week would be intolerable.

Then again the reproduction of the many subtle position effects described in Chapter XIX of *Modern Experiments in Telepathy* would be very difficult to fake.

In certain of the Shackleton experiments the lists of random numbers were prepared by Wassermann, a mathematical physicist, and I had no opportunity to see them until the experiment was over. Most people in England who know Wassermann would have little doubt about the sort of reaction that would be induced in him by a request to assist in faking an experiment!

Price evidently thinks that extrasensory perception should be established once for all by an absolutely fraudproof, cast-iron experiment. The late F. C. S. Schiller, the Oxford philosopher, used to argue that such a hope was illusory. Even if such an experiment were feasible, we should find that, as the years passed and the experiment faded into history, fresh doubts would begin to be raised about the reliability of the experimenters or the possibilities of collusion.

Another experiment would then be necessary, and the arguments would begin all over again. On this question I am in agreement with Schiller, and I favor a quite different method of approach.

The main obstacle to the acceptance of parapsychological phenomena is the apparent rarity of the people who can produce them under even reasonable conditions of control. Now this rarity I believe to be apparent rather than real. We do not know the signs by which to distinguish these exceptional card-guessers and so we waste time and effort in testing the wrong kind of people. There is increasing reason to believe that we shall not discover them in university populations and that it is a waste of time to experiment with students. But experience of the last few months has indicated that it is among the less sophisticated types that we should pursue our search—especially among children living in rural communities or in backward countries.

I think there is little doubt that with an increasing number of such high-scoring subjects much of the prejudice of ordinary scientific workers will disappear. When more and more competent Experimenters report on cases of high-scoring subjects, the hypothesis of collusion will become as extinct as the dodo. While it is, in the last resort, possible to suggest that two or three Experimenters have faked their results, this will not be possible when scores of competent investigators produce their reports on similar cases. I suggest to Price, therefore, that efforts should be directed toward the discovery of the personality characteristics of these people who make averages of 8 or 10 hits per 25 over considerable periods, the sort of communities in which they may be successfully found, and so on. In other words we should aim at repeatability by more and more investigators.

NOTES

1. G. R. Price, *Science* 122, 359 (1955).

2. S. G. Soal and F. Bateman, *Modern Experiments in Telepathy* (Yale Univ. Press, New Haven, Conn., 1954).

3. E. J. Dingwall, review of *Modern Experiments in Telepathy* by S. G. Soal and F. Bateman, in *Nature* 175, 741 (1955).

4. J. E. Coover, *Experiments in Psychical Research* (Stanford Univ. Press, Stanford, Calif., 1917).

5. C. E. Kellogg, *Sci. Monthly* 45, 331 (1937).

6. D. H. Rawcliffe, *The Psychology of the Occult* (Ridgway, London, 1952).

7. G. S. Brown, *Nature* 172, 154 (1953).

J. B. Rhine

Comments on "Science and the Supernatural"

CREDIT SIDE

Strange though it may seem, the publication of the George Price paper, "Science and the Supernatural," is, on the whole, a good event for parapsychology. It is not merely that it is better to be attacked than it is to be ignored. According to the ways of American science, a revolutionary finding has to be cuffed and kicked through the entrance in order to gain admittance. When unorthodox issues are concerned, only critical articles, and the rougher the better, are likely to be accepted by the scientific periodicals. In fact, one can easily fancy (as some readers have) that Price deliberately undertook to sell parapsychology to American science by disguising a really informative article as a slanderous critique, with charges so utterly exaggerated that they would not be believed even by skeptics of ESP. At any rate, as a way to get a lot of instruction on parapsychology into *Science,* it worked as well as if it had been planted.

It is also of value to parapsychology to have Price portray so vividly the potential importance of psi abilities. He has even more clearly appreciated the great potential applications of ESP than have many of the workers in the field. It is true that he has overlooked the limitation owing to the unconscious level on which this elusive function operates; but if (as is not unreasonable to expect) that limitation can be overcome through

Reprinted from *Science* 123 (1956) No. 3184, pp. 11-14, by permission of the author and editor.

future investigation, his picture of the utility of psi will be entirely realistic.

Again, credit goes to Price for his coverage of the older criticisms of the psi research. Although they have been answered many times in the literature of parapsychology by others, Price has summed up the case rather well—so well, in fact, that but for the philosophical blockage from which he reveals he suffers, he sees nothing to prevent the acceptance of ESP. It is true that, rather than to question the mechanistic philosophy that he recognizes is at issue, he oddly professes to believe that all parapsychologists are liars and montebanks; but such a wild charge, even if Price really intended it to apply to the dozens of university and other scientists involved, is not likely to be taken seriously. On the other hand, his effective answers to the earlier criticisms of ESP work will and should carry weight with them. In a word, he has himself rounded out a fair case for ESP for all but the utter cynics who can accept his fantastic suspicion of a vicious conspiracy among academic research workers and a monstrous half-century-long hoax.

Finally, and best of all, comes the point that most concerns Price himself. He has focused more neatly than any other reviewer the deadly, menacing sting of the psi research findings. It is of great importance, indeed, for parapsychology to have the point of this issue brought out sharply and clearly in the pages of *Science* itself! I myself, in a voice scarcely audible in conventional science, have been shouting from the housetops the very same issue that Price has drawn. It is the head-on collision between the facts of parapsychology and the prevailing physicalistic theory of man (or call it mechanism as he does, or materialism, or physical monism, or whatnot). The fact is that this philosophy, on the one hand, and these experimental facts, on the other hand, directly contradict each other in an inescapable, horn-locking manner. Walker [1] and Boring, [2] among others, while they have sparingly admitted in recent publications that there are some experimental results in parapsychology that have to be dealt with, have failed to see the lethal blow that these research results give to the belief in physicalism that both authors espouse. They hold out, rather, for some future, more elastic, physicalistic concept that may eventually account for these puzzling findings of today.

Ignoring his language, I prefer Price's forthright demand for the balancing of the books right now. He, even more than any other critical reviewer, gives indication of having felt the force of the evidence for ESP. When he turns then—albeit a bit too emotionally—and says that, according to the current concept of nature, ESP is impossible and therefore the parapsychologists must all be fakers, he at least draws the issue where it can be squarely met. The answer of the parapsychologist is: "Yes, either the present mechanistic theory of man *is* wrong—that is, fundamentally incomplete—or, of course, the parapsychologists *are* all utterly mistaken." *One* of these opponents is wrong; take it, now, from the pages of *Science!* This recognition of the issue gives point to the findings of parapsychology in a way none can easily miss.

MECHANISTIC ASSUMPTION VERSUS EXPERIMENTAL FACTS: THE SETTING

Need I ask now—above all, in *Science*—what a scientist should do when a metaphysical doctrine such as this mechanistic philosophy of man is contradicted by a set of experimental results? It is surely part of one's elementary training that one proceeds as Newton, Darwin, Pasteur, and others have exemplified in all the sciences of nature. Generally speaking, the scientist concentrates on the reexamination and confirmation of his facts until, if they bear up under these demands, the opposing belief itself gives way and a modified philosophy of nature develops—one that accommodates itself fully to the new discoveries. If, on the other hand, errors are found, they are specifically exposed and that ends the matter; but, as Price himself has explained, the better ESP work has not been successfully attacked on that score.

It may make the facts of the psi investigations more understandable to retrace from the beginning, at least in outline, the course over which the inquiries in parapsychology have progressed.[3] (We might also watch for any magic or supernaturalism along the way!) It is a course typical of the introductory history of any natural science. The investigations first arose, as in most other sciences, because of spontaneous natural occurrences. In this case, certain puzzling and unclassified human experiences started the whole inquiry. These experiences suggested that there might be a way of communication by the mere transference of thought; this was eventually called telepathy. Such communication had not appeared to be very reliable, however, and hence its possibility was neglected as unimportant until a stage in Western culture had been reached at which circumstances gave it increased importance. This new significance had nothing to do with practical utilization and, accordingly, a high order of reliability was not important.

Rather, it was its bearing on the theory of man that brought telepathy to the attention of science. When, in the latter half of the nineteenth century, materialism severely challenged the traditional spiritual view of man, there were those who thought that the claims of telepathy ought to be looked into because they suggested that a transfer of thought could occur between persons without physical intermediation. Such an operation was taken as mind-to-mind contact transcending the scope of physical explanation. It seemed, therefore, to constitute a challenge to the claim of materialism as a complete theory of human life. Hence it was the very issue that upset Price that led to the rise of parapsychology in the first place.

Eventually—by the 1870s and 1880s—experiments in telepathy were conducted and reports of them got into print. These were criticized and in due time new ones with methods modified to meet the objections were carried out. These in turn were published and received criticism, and so the cycle of all exploratory science progressed. It was not, however, until the second and third decades of the present century that the study of telepathy and extrasensory perception in general began to gain a foothold in university laboratories. But with more concentrated studies in the 1930s and 1940s, finally the professions most concerned were more or less compelled to take notice of the researches in ESP. National organizations of psychologists, statisticians, biologists, and certain medical groups in Europe and America held symposia for the appraisal of the results and claims of parapsychology. The case for ESP not only stood the test, but even more, its status gradually improved. Today, even if the only criterion were Price's type of article, it would be safe to say that ESP is making its way. Parapsychology now occupies an officially recognized place in a half dozen or more leading universities of the world, ranging from fellowships to professorships and from lectures to laboratories.

WHAT EVIDENCE HAS MECHANISM?

If, then, it was to refute the mechanistic philosophy that parapsychology arose, it is not enough for the inquirer to consider only the evidence of psi. He needs also to ask: How strong a case has been made for the philosophy that opposes it? What evidence is there for a belief in the complete dominion of physical law over man and nature? As a universal law, this claim has never had *any* truly experimental confirmation whatsoever. How in the nature of things could it have? Actually, this whole mechanistic business means only that in those areas of nature in which most of the scientists of the world have been working—the various physical sciences—physical theory *has* been adequate. Naturally. Consequently, mechanism just grew like Topsy and became a habit of mind, a way of looking at the universe. It has even proved successful in dealing with the surface problems of the fields of biology. In the more physiological areas of psychology, too, it has had great success. But to establish that this physicalistic interpretation applies to the whole of nature and that there are no other kinds of principles in the universe would call for a complete understanding of nature. Of course, we have nothing like that, as everyone well knows. As I have said, mechanism is just a habit of mind.

Even one single well-established exception would disqualify a philosophy that is assumed to be an explanation of the entire universe. In particular, any thoroughly physicalistic theory is completely defenseless against such an exceptional case as parapsychology, by its very nature, represents. Recalling, too, that the biological and psychological sciences are still far—and exceedingly far—from explaining most of the basic functions of life and mind, reminds the student of how far present knowledge still is from the final authoritative and incontestably complete view of nature that these hardshell mechanists take for granted. When anyone gives to such a belief the almost dogmatic finality that Price apparently does, it suggests that the doctrine has taken the place of a security-giving theology and is playing more than a scientific role in his life.

NATURALISTIC APPROACH OF PARAPSYCHOLOGY

Unlike the opposing philosophy of physicalism, the position of parapsychology rests wholly on experimental evidence. These psi phenomena are empirically observed biological effects; they are, more specifically, verified psychological occurrences and they have been strictly and objectively demonstrated to be a part of the natural functions of the individual. Moreover, they are lawful and, as research has revealed their conditions and properties, they make sense against the larger background of human and animal life. In fact, the ESP results warn the scientist that again the boundaries of knowledge have been drawn too close and that once more they will have to be extended. Over and over in the past, that has been the way in which the scientific map of the universe has developed.

It is because it *does* fall well outside the present boundary of conventional science that ESP is a challenge to the science of today. Its advantage is that it is an operation of the personality—the only one thus far known—that can, in a controlled experimental manner, be shown to operate with a certain independence of the physical order of nature. Thus it becomes a sort of key to a farther zone of reality that is identified with that least understood of the natural divisions, personality.

In showing effects independent of the time-space criteria of physical nature, the psi function requires the inference of an underlying energetic operation—one that is neither intercepted by the physical end-organs of the sensory system nor limited by the physical conditions that affect the more familiar energies. Yet, as the discoveries in psychokinesis have shown, this inferred mental energy, if we may call it that, is convertible into a measurable kinetic operation. Moreover, a lawful and rationally consistent picture is emerging bit by bit from exploratory studies now going on. The results are proving to be organizable and their relationships are proving to be logically coherent. Nonphysical though psi appears to be as judged by the familiar criteria of space and time, it is, nonetheless, a natural function of the normal personality, a part of the living organism and as much a part of the process system of nature as anything already in the books. Its properties, as far as they are known, have been studied by the standards and methodology of natural science in general. No favors have been asked and no concessions are needed that are not claimed by general psychology or genetics or nuclear physics or any other branch of research.

The extraordinarily hidden character of the operation of psi, however, has made its practical utilization difficult. It has also made its scientific demonstration a tedious and long-drawn-out affair. The elusive character of this deeply unconscious function of the personality still gives serious trouble in the research laboratory, as the literature amply recognizes. In fact, unless and until psi ability can be made subject to conscious control, or a device for releasing it on the unconscious level can be developed, it is hard now to see how to bring it to the fruition of ready application that Price outlined. But in any case, no claims are made in advance. The same deeply buried character of the psi function suggests, along with other indications, that psi ability has had an early evolutionary origin. Moreover, a vast storehouse of animal behavior—for example, homing—has been found lying recorded but unexplained since the days of Darwin; this behavior suggests a rich field of possible psi manifestation and application.

The brief outline I have given of what has been done in the investigation of ESP and in the interpretation of the results has been presented in order to "naturalize" it for readers who may have misconceived the whole field as an unrealistic, occult business. It can be seen, however, that except for the fact that parapsychology has turned up a type of phenomena strange to the conventional sciences, the course of development of this branch of science has followed that of a typical naturalistic and objective inquiry. The new facts themselves actually fit well enough into the systematized knowledge already familiar. The clash—and there *is* an unmistakable one—is only with the wholly theoretical philosophy of materialism. There, however, the conflict is complete and inescapable. That, of course, is what makes the findings of parapsychology controversial. It is also what makes the findings of parapsychology revolutionary.

PRICE'S OBJECTIVE

This is, I trust, my last reply to criticisms of ESP—the last of a twenty-year series—for Price has evidently "thrown the book." As he well indicates, however, there was nothing much left to say against the evidence of ESP when he took over; nothing, that is, but a few last resort name-callings, and now he has used up that reserve. On this level of discourse, he may have the last word for whatever it is worth to history. Some readers of Price's article, however, who are not familiar with parapsychology, may incline to take his objective too seriously. For them I have a few remarks.

Actually, his article appears to me rather more like an *act* than a genuine earnest critique. Take, for example, the charge of fraud—one that would ordinarily be a matter of dead seriousness. It is fairly obvious, I think, from the record alone that Price did not really believe what he tossed off without pretense of proof. Had he honestly believed there was fraud, the same impulse that led him to write this article would almost certainly have impelled him to dig up some tangible evidence concerning at least one parapsychologist. Such investigations have actually been made more than once in the past by persons who sincerely wanted to know.

Again, the experimental proposal Price flung at the parapsychologists looks just as much like a pose as the character-knifing act. After first declaring ESP philosophically so completely impossible as to justify his wholesale suspicions of fraud, he then proceeded to demand that the parapsychologists nevertheless conduct a fantastic new experiment of his designing—one that would, he implies, convince him if it gave positive results. The latter sounds open-minded, does it not? All he needs is evidence and the impossible would be possible. Price is either confused or else, as I think, he is proposing this experiment with his tongue in his cheek. Or does it matter? Certainly not so far as it concerns the values I have credited to the publication of this paper.

There were such challenges as Price's in the 1930s. The now classic Pratt and Woodruff [4] experiment in ESP was carried out to meet one that was made jointly by seven American psychologists. Pratt and Woodruff exceeded the precautionary standards submitted and their experiment was successful too; but the net effect on the seven psychologists was that it merely silenced them; it did not convince them. S. G. Soal, who was especially singled out for suspicion by Price, was himself at one time one of the leading challengers of the Duke experiments. His own negative results from years of work proved, however, on reanalysis, to contain significant evidence of ESP, and the conversion of Soal from critic to colleague stopped a lot of criticism of ESP in the 1940s. Knowing all this as he must, Price can hardly be entirely serious in his talk of conspiracy in the Soal experiments and his demand for a so-called fraud-proof experiment.

Perhaps it is enough to suggest rather that ESP has now approached the status of "big game" and one may not need to search for any other purpose than that of the hunter's impulse to bring it down. Whatever the motive, the value of the publication of Price's article in *Science* stands out well above any other consideration whatever, and it would be a mistake to overlook this outstanding service to parapsychology in the consideration of minor defects. The designing of the experiments for that field can perhaps be left to those with more experience. But it took Price, whether trophy-hunter or sincere scientist, to get nine pages on parapsychology into a lead article in *Science*, with the crucial challenge of that field sticking out like a sore thumb.

AMERICAN WAY OF SCIENCE?

This final point is not made on behalf of parapsychology but is beamed at science in general. It is something that I have culled from my prolonged participation in what has probably been one of science's fiercest controversies. Naturally, I have had to wait to mention it for the time when parapsychology was safely through its ordeal. Has that time come? Price could hardly have kicked a *dead* horse (or even a very sick one) through nine full pages of the world's leading scientific periodical.

American science, I am convinced, badly needs a forum—a journal that is open to new work, however radical its implications, without the usual practice of waiting for a savage attack to make it admissible. It is, of course, what might be called the forum attitude that is lacking. Yet it will be freely recognized by all that fair and unhampered presentation of revolutionary ideas and discoveries is especially vital to the continued advancement of inquiry. The national interest itself obviously requires the active cultivation of unrestricted investigation. It seems likely that the well-known lag of American science (omitting technology) behind European contributions in the more fundamental researches of the last fifty years (for example, in psychology and physics) is due entirely to this one distinct difference, this greater inhospitality to novel and unconventional claims that prevails in the United States.

Through the anxious years coming up, man's fitness to survive what already hangs over his head may easily depend on how well and how fast his scientists can think. But who knows what this thinking is worth until it is known—until it is made readily available in the forum, the symposium, and the periodical? It is time, and it is urgent, to borrow from the engineers their successful practice of reaching out for, instead of fending off, novel claims and unorthodox discoveries, of clarifying their status promptly and in general encouraging the creative turn of mind—and to extend this practice to areas beyond that of gadgetry and invention, areas that have to do with the understanding of man and the guiding values of life.

In this last section I have been attempting to say that Price's article is perhaps more revealing with regard to the need in American science for a more tolerant attitude than it is of the status of the struggling young science of parapsychology on which it has made a curious, bludgeoning attack. Parapsychology can now take care of itself, I think, but what about American science?

NOTES

1. R. Walker, *Sci. Monthly* 79, 1 (1954).
2. E. G. Boring, *Am. Scientist* 43, 109 (1955).
3. I will furnish, on request, a reading list to those who may wish to go over the course more fully.
4. J. G. Pratt and J. L. Woodruff, *J. Parapsychol.* 3, 121 (1939).

Paul E. Meehl & Michael Scriven

Compatibility of Science and ESP

As two of the people whose comments on an early draft of George Price's article on "Science and the Supernatural" he acknowledged in a footnote, we should like to clarify our position by presenting the following remarks.

Price's argument stands or falls on two hypotheses, only the first of which he appears to defend. They are (i) that extrasensory perception (ESP) is incompatible with modern science and (ii) that modern science is complete and correct.

If ESP is *not* incompatible with modern science, then the Humean skeptic has no opportunity to insist on believing modern science rather than the reports about ESP. If modern science is *not* believed to be complete or correct, then the skeptic is hardly justified in issuing a priori allegations of fraud about experimenters even when they claim that they have discovered a new phenomenon that requires reconsideration of the accepted theories.

In our view, both of Price's hypotheses are untenable. Whatever one may think about the comprehensiveness and finality of modern physics, it would surely be rash to insist that we can reject out of hand any claims of revolutionary discoveries in the field of psychology. Price is in exactly the position of a man who might have insisted that Michelson and Morley were liars because the evidence for the physical theory of that time was

Reprinted from *Science* 123 (1956) No. 3184, pp. 14-15, by permission of the authors and the editor.

stronger than that for the veracity of these experimenters. The list of those who have insisted on the impossibility of fundamental changes in the current physical theory of their time is a rather sorry one. Moreover, unhappy though Price's position would be if this were his only commitment, he cannot even claim that specifiable laws of physics are violated; it is only certain philosophical characteristics of such laws that are said to be absent from those governing the new phenomena.

It is true that Price attempted to give a specific account of the incompatibilities between ESP and modern science, rather than relying on Broad's philosophical analysis, but here the somewhat superficial nature of Price's considerations becomes clear. Of his eight charges, seven are unjustified.

1) He claims that ESP is "unattenuated by distance" and hence is incompatible with modern science. But, as is pointed out in several of the books he refers to, since we have no knowledge of the minimum effective signal strength for extrasensory perception, the original signal may well be enormously attenuated by distance and still function at long range.

2) He says that ESP is "apparently unaffected by shielding." But shielding may well have an effect: the evidence shows only that the kind of shielding appropriate to electromagnetic radiation is ineffectual; since detectors indicate that no such radiation reaches the percipient from the agent, this is scarcely surprising.

3) He says "Dye patterns . . . are read in the dark; how does one detect a trace of dye without shining a light on it?" The two most obvious answers would be by chemical analysis and physical study of the impression (which is usually different for different colors).

4) "Patterns on cards in the center of a pack are read without interference from other cards." The word *read* is hardly justified in view of the statistical nature of the results; however, this phenomenon is always used by parapsychologists as evidence against a simple radiation theory, which it is. But no simple radiation theory can explain the Pauli principle and one can no more refute it by saying "How could one electron possibly know what the others are doing?" than one can refute the ESP experiments by saying "How could one possibly read a card from the middle of the pack without interference from those next to it?" These questions are couched in prejudical terms.

5) "We have found in the body no structure to associate with the alleged functions." Even if true, this hardly differentiates it from a good many other *known* functions; and among eminent neurophysiologists,

J. C. Eccles is one who has denied Price's premise [originally in *Nature* 168 (1951)].

6) "There is no learning but, instead, a tendency toward complete loss of ability" a characteristic which Price believes has "no parallel among established mental functions." Now it would be reasonable to expect, in a series of experiments intended to show that learning does not occur, some *trial-by-trial* differential reinforcement procedure. Mere continuation, with encouragement or condemnation after *runs of many trials* can hardly provide a conclusive proof of the absence of learning in a complex situation. We ourselves know of *no* experiments in which this condition has been met and which show *absence* of learning; certainly one could not claim that this absence was established. Furthermore, *even if it had been established,* it would be very dangerous to assert that there is "no parallel among established mental functions." In the psychophysiological field particularly, there are several candidates. Finally, *even if it had been established and there were no parallel among mental functions,* there would be no essential difficulty in comparing it with one of the many familiar performances that exhibit no learning in adults—for example, reflex behavior.

7) "Different investigators obtain highly different results." This is the most distressingly irresponsible comment of all. ESP is a capacity like any other human capacity such as memory, in that it varies in strength and characteristics from individual to individual and in the one individual from one set of circumstances to another. The sense in which Rhine and Soal (Price's example of "different investigators") have obtained "highly different results" is when they have been dealing with different subjects or markedly different circumstances—for example, different agents; and exactly the same would be true of an investigation of, for example, stenographers' speed in taking dictation or extreme color blindness.

There remains only statistical precognition, which is certainly not susceptible to the types of explanation currently appropriate in physics: but then it is not a phenomenon in physics. Even if it were, it is difficult to see why Price thinks that we properly accommodated our thought to the distressing and counterintuitive idea that the earth is rotating whereas we should not accept precognition. His test for distinguishing new phenomena from magic is hopeless from the start ("The test is to attempt to imagine a detailed mechanistic explanation") because (i) it is of the essence of the scientific method that one should have means for establishing the facts *whether or not* one has already conceived an explanation and (ii) it would have thrown out the Heisenberg uncertainty principle and action across a vacuum—that is, nuclear physics and the whole of electricity and magnetism—along with ESP.

Finally, Price's "ideal experiments" are only Rube Goldberg versions of the standard tests plus a skeptical jury. The mechanical contrivances would be welcome if only parapsychologists could afford them, and the jury is obviously superfluous because, according to Price's own test, we should rather believe that they lie than that the experiments succeed. However, in our experience, skeptics who are prepared to devote some time and hard work to the necessary preliminary study and experimenting are welcome in the laboratories at Duke and London. Without the training, one might as well have (as Price would say) twelve clergymen as judges at a cardsharps' convention.

The allegations of fraud are as helpful or as pointless here as they were when they were made of Freud and Galileo by the academics and others who honestly believed that they *must* be mistaken. They are irresponsible because Price has not made any attempt to verify them (as he admits), despite the unpleasantness they will cause, and because it has been obvious since the origin of science that any experimental results, witnessed by no matter how many people, *may* be fraudulent.

P. W. Bridgman

Probability, Logic, and ESP

The recent article by G. R. Price in *Science* [122, 359 (26 Aug. 1955)] entitled "Science and the Supernatural" directs renewed attention to a situation that doubtless has given many people, including myself, a feeling of discomfort, to say the least. My own attitude was expressible in a paraphrase of Price's quotation from Hume to the effect that he would be unwilling to accept such phenomena as those claimed for extrasensory perception (ESP) unless he could be convinced that their genuineness would be less miraculous than the occurrence of fraud somewhere.

My own attitude did not seize on the possibility of fraud, although it seems to me that Hume's position is irrefutable; it seized, rather, on the way in which contemporary arguments for ESP depend on considerations of probability. I felt somewhat vaguely that I would rather think that my understanding of probability is faulty than believe in the genuineness of ESP. My scruples against the use of probability arguments had nothing to do with the details of the calculation of the enormous numbers that represent the odds against the scores obtained in ESP tests. I was willing to take the word of the many technically competent persons involved that the grinding of the machinery by which these numbers were obtained had been according to Hoyle. My scruples went much deeper and were concerned with the logic of the application of probability concepts to concrete events.

Reprinted from *Science* 123 (1956) No. 3184, pp. 15-17, by permission of the editor.

It has long been apparent that there is something "funny" about the probability situation. Probability rigorously applies to no concrete happening. If we calculate that the chance of throwing a 6 with a die is one-sixth, and throw the die and obtain a 6, there is no method whatever by which it may be shown that the chance "actually" was one-sixth. Yet the phenomena to which the probability calculations justifying ESP are applied are concrete actual happenings, many of them a matter of record in black and white.

My old feeling that the logical situation should be further explored was fortified by a recent occurrence that is the immediate occasion for this note. I was reading in *Science* [122, 471 (9 Sept. 1955)] a review of the recently published collection of 1 million random numbers, when it burst on me in a flash of illumination that random numbers cannot be published. For a set of random numbers is a set in which it is impossible to predict any subsequent number from the preceding numbers, or in which there is no connection between the different numbers. But the subsequent numbers may be predicted, if the set is published, merely by reading the published list, and all the numbers of the set are connected by being written together on paper. A list of numbers *obtained* by a random *process* might perhaps be published if we could answer the question, What is it that makes any specific process random? The list itself cannot give the answer, because, given only the list, the process by which the list was obtained cannot be reproduced; there are an infinite number of ways of generating any finite list.

Randomness is an ephemeral thing, having meaning only during the activity of generating the numbers, and passing into limbo with the consummation of the process. And its ephemeral meaning was a meaning only in a certain universe of operations—we could see no way of predicting the next number in terms of operations drawn from our repertoire. The repertoire was to a certain extent arbitrary, dictated to a large extent by our purposes of the moment. These purposes might, for example, dictate that we focus our attention on those aspects of the situation that can be expressed in mathematical language of an acceptable degree of simplicity. I suspect that the prospective users of the list of 1 million random numbers have in mind only such mathematical purposes and limitations, and that any remarks made here will not affect in the slightest degree the value of the list for them or diminish its sales.

The paradox inherent in the application of a probability calculation to any concrete situation is well brought out by a comment of Bertrand

Russell, who remarked that we encounter a miracle every time we read the license number of a passing automobile. For if we had calculated the chance that we would see that particular number, the chances would have been millions to one against it. In what respect is the situation here different from that presented by a better-than-chance score in an ESP experiment? a score for which we may suppose that our preliminary calculation of the chances gave the same expectation value as the automobile number. The occurrence of the automobile number does not jar us, and we continue to put it down to chance despite the odds against it, whereas the ESP result does jar us, and we say that it could not have been chance.

There are several features here that demand comment. In the first place, we have to justify ourselves in not regarding the automobile number as a miracle. This justification we offer rather easily, although it might be difficult to give a logically rigorous defense of our justification. We might, for example, offer in justification a consideration of the distribution of the chance of occurrence of all possible numbers. Within limits, the chance for the occurrence of any one number is the same as that for any other—there is no heaping up of probabilities in favor of any one number or range of numbers. We could not have *expected* the particular number to turn up, but on the other hand, we are not *surprised* when it does. We reflect that *some* number *had* to occur, and we let it go at that and think no more of it unless we are prodded. If we are prodded to tell exactly what we mean when we say "this past event was chance," we admit that there is no property inherent in the event by which we can verify that it actually was chance, and we seek for the meaning elsewhere.

We may seek the meaning of "was chance" in what we do about it. Now the paradoxical thing is that when we say "was chance" we do nothing about it—we have come to the end. The reason that we have come to the end is that consistency with our position forbids that we attempt to go further. If we went ahead and sought for an explanation or any sort of rational involvement, we would be stultifying our conclusion that the result was chance. For instance, if after seeing the automobile number and noting the state of issue, we begin to reflect on the relative number of registrations in the different states, we have abandoned our position that the event was a chance event. As long as we remain consistent and do nothing, we are safe, despite the fact that we have effectively changed our definition of chance when we pass from anticipation of an event to viewing its occurrence in the past. In fact, the operational meaning of "this *was* chance" involves our resolution to handle the situation just by doing nothing. And it is our resolution to do nothing that protects us from the logical punishment to which we would normally be subject for changing our definition.

These considerations, I think, make it particularly clear that the locus of chance is in ourselves, with strong involvements of "expectation" and "surprise," and that there is little that is "objective" about it.

Consider now the situation presented by the ESP scores. Unlike the automobile situation, there is here an enormous heaping up of probability in the neighborhood of a particular score (5 out of 25 for the conventional testing cards). We could not expect a score for which the adverse odds were millions to one, and we *are* surprised when it turns up. We cannot now say with the same cogency as before "there *had* to be *some* score," but instead we draw the conclusion that the result could not have been chance.

We have to ask what we mean when we say "this event was *not* chance." Since we have already made an attempt to tell what we mean when we say "this event *was* chance," we might be tempted to think that our new question is trivial and that its answer is implied in the answer we have already given. I think, however, and this is perhaps the crux of this note, that this is by no means the case. "Was chance" and "was not chance" are not simply related to each other as two terms in traditional Aristotelian logic, subject to the rule of the excluded middle. Because what we do to give meaning to "was not chance" is not simply or obviously determined by what we do to give meaning to "was chance." Whether there is any necessary connection in logic between the meaning of these two expressions is by no means apparent. That they are connected in use is another matter. If the advocates of ESP were content to say "All I mean when I say 'the event was not chance' is that the event was not expected and surprised me," I think we could have no quarrel. But it would be almost humanly impossible to stop with such a simple statement, and the advocates of ESP have shown their humanity by not stopping, but have gone ahead and envisaged all sorts of consequences, consequences that would usually be implied in an Aristotelian, excluded middle, system. Thus we can imagine them saying "Chance events are subject to no formulatable regularity—the events of ESP are nonchance; therefore they are subject to some regularity," with the usual additional implication that we are in the presence of a new unknown faculty of the mind. It seems to me that the only justification for drawing such a conclusion in a non-Aristotelian system is to be found in the actual exhibition of some sort of pertinent regularity, and this, as far as I know, has not been done.

There is a deep-seated difference between the way in which positive and negative probability arguments are fruitfully applied in practice to concrete situations, to which we have seen that the concept of probability does not rigorously apply at all. If the situation is a positive one, which we can characterize by saying "here we have the play of chance," then we can draw fruitful conclusions from the mere statement, without going further. This is shown by countless examples, as in the tables of a life insurance company, or the kinetic theory of gases, or the theory of the atomic nucleus with its calculation of the best construction for a hydrogen bomb by the Monte Carlo method. But if the situation is a negative one, characterized by saying "here we do *not* have the play of chance," we have something radically different. Here we *are* compelled to go further, and fruitful application is not achieved until we succeed in exhibiting the regularity that we suspect. The detective who says "It was not chance that five murders were committed by the same technique" has said nothing until he exhibits the man who committed the five murders. Wanting the ratification of exhibition, the statement of nonchance is merely an invitation, or an incentive, if you feel that way, to further investigation. ESP, with its statement of nonchance, but with its utter failure to exhibit any regularities or to perform a single repeatable experiment, is the only instance of which I am aware in which a serious claim has been made that nonchance should be capitalized simply because it is nonchance.

The situation covered by the word *probability* is a desperately complex situation, mostly of our own making and in our own minds, with a fragile and fleeting dependence on time, and never coherently connected with concrete "objective" events. I personally can now see so much here that needs to be thrashed out and clarified that I am unwilling to accept the genuineness of any phenomenon that leans as heavily as does ESP on probability arguments.

George R. Price

Where Is the Definitive Experiment?

Since I have already stated at some length my views on psychic phenomena,[1] I am reluctant to engage in continued arguments that can in no way settle the basic issue. As I wrote in the concluding paragraph of my paper, "the only answer that will impress me is an adequate experiment." Nevertheless, some brief comments on the statements by Soal, Rhine, Meehl and Scriven, and Bridgman are in order.

THE BASIC ISSUE

The most important portion of "Science and the Supernatural" was the section suggesting new experiments. My two colleagues at the University of Minnesota, Meehl and Scriven, are incorrect in stating that my argument "stands or falls on two hypotheses . . . (i) that extrasensory perception (ESP) is incompatible with modern science and (ii) that modern science is complete and correct." My argument stands or falls on the two hypotheses that (i) previous demonstrations of psi phenomena have not been convincing to most scientists and (ii) that it is possible to perform convincing experiments meeting all objections that parapsychologists have made to previous suggestions for public demonstrations.

The most significant points that the reader should notice about the

Reprinted from *Science* 123 (1956) No. 3184, pp. 17-18, by permission of the editor.

present correspondence are (i) that neither Rhine nor Soal has in any way criticized my proposed tests as unfair or technically faulty, and yet (ii) both of them reject these suggestions. Why?

Soal rejects the suggestions on the grounds that the results would be only temporarily convincing. However, if skeptics were even temporarily convinced, then numerous additional experimenters would begin investigating parapsychology and evidence could continue to accumulate.

Rhine rejects the suggestions on the grounds that a similar challenge issued by seven psychologists[2] was successfully met in the past, yet the results convinced none of the seven. But this is not correct. Angier *et al.* wrote as follows: "It must be emphasized that in no program is it possible, in advance . . . to cover all precautions. . . .It is necessary, therefore, that there be the most competent possible supervision, as indicated in Section IX below." Section IX read:

"The experiment should, throughout, be under the direction and control of two or more psychologists who are regarded by members of the profession generally as competent in the experimental field. One of these superintendents must be on duty during every work period, and have actual oversight of the conduct of the tests.

"In view of the present situation, and the need of a definitive experiment, it is highly desirable that the experiment be set up under the superintendence of three psychologists, each from a different university."

The Pratt and Woodruff experiment[3] did not meet the conditions of Section IX.

Meehl and Scriven criticize the proposed tests on the grounds that "the jury is obviously superfluous because, according to Price's own test, we should rather believe that they lie than that the experiments succeed." I cannot follow this argument at all. If people would believe the entire jury of twelve to be dishonest in preference to believing in psi phenomena, then logically Meehl and Scriven should recommend a much larger jury, instead of calling the jury superfluous.

Meehl and Scriven also state, "The mechanical contrivances would be welcome if only the parapsychologists could afford them. . . ." I cannot agree with this. The fact is that mechanical contrivances do not seem to be welcome to most parapsychologists. For example, in 1948, while Soal was still successfully experimenting with Mrs. Stewart, B. F. Skinner suggested that he use simple recording devices and other mechanical aids.[4] Far from following these excellent suggestions, Soal contented himself with writing—as he describes it—"a calm, but perfectly devasting reply."[5] Secondly, I am quite sure that money can be raised for the sort of demonstrations that I suggested. If parapsychologists have special difficulty in raising money for their ordinary research, it is probably because of the peculiar rules of their game. It would similarly be difficult to raise funds for development of a uranium mine that never shipped any ore and that could be seen only by a special group of initiates.

Are there any crucial defects in my proposed tests? I can see possibilities for minor improvements—for example, using an inaccurate rather than an accurate timing circuit in the random number generator and letting the examining committee consist of seven parapsychologists and eight skeptics since a seven to eight ratio would appear fairer than the one to two ratio I previously proposed. But nobody has yet pointed out to me any important defect. To be sure, Rhine calls my proposals "fantastic" and Meehl and Scriven use the expression "Rube Goldberg." But what do such terms mean? If any of these men or anyone else has specific criticisms or suggestions for improvements, it would be kind of them to make the suggestions known.

In addition, I hope that some properly qualified person will volunteer to take charge of planning and arranging a definitive test, in the event that the parapsychologists change their minds and offer to participate in one. I would think that, primarily, such a person should be a scientist of high reputation; and it would be desirable (though it is not essential) that he be one who has in the past taken a public stand against parapsychology.

MISCELLANEOUS POINTS

For Bridgman's views I have the utmost respect, especially because his writings have played a major role in the shaping of my own scientific philosophy. Nevertheless, I do not feel that his present probability arguments provide an escape from the dilemma of believing in extrasensory perception or in fraud. In a great deal of this work, Soal had his subjects alternate between telepathy and clairvoyance, and he found "extra-chance" results for the former only. In one run the Agent would know the identities of the five code cards (telepathy); in the next run he would not know their identities (clairvoyance). The clairvoyance runs consistently gave results in accordance with what standard probability theory predicts, and the telepathy runs gave quite different results. I do not see how this can possibly be explained on the grounds that there may be some basic flaw in our concept of probability.

It is interesting that most of Rhine's communication is devoted to stressing the incompatibilities between science and psi phenomena, while the Meehl and Scriven letter is largely devoted to arguing that there is no incompatibility. Of course I am on Rhine's side in this matter and must resist the temptation to reply to Meehl and Scriven. It does not seem proper for me to use up more space in *Science* arguing a matter in which I am strongly in agreement with Rhine and Soal.

Soal has made a number of errors in describing my suggested procedures for cheating. For example, it is not correct that my procedures "all depend on the Agent being in collusion with the chief Experimenter or with the Percipient." The Agent was not necessarily "in the trick" in my Procedures 2, 5, and 6. For imitating the Stewart series, with its 15 successful Agents, I would employ mainly Procedures 5 and 2. To imitate the experiments in the Shackleton series in which Wassermann prepared the random number lists, I would employ Procedure 4 where possible, and a variation of Procedure 5 if the Agent was being watched too closely to permit use of Procedure 4. Therefore, most of Soal's discussion of the honesty of this or that person is irrelevant. If Soal did cheat, it probably was not by procedures requiring intentional cooperation from Rozelaar, Wassermann, or the four Agents from Queen Mary College.

Soal submitted a virtually identical statement to the *Newsletter* of the Parapsychology Foundation, and this statement, together with a more detailed reply from me, has already been published.[6]

Rhine is in error in thinking that I "believe that all parapsychologists are liars and montebanks" or that I charged that "a hundred or more research scientists . .. [had indulged] in a gigantic hoax involving the hiring of confederates and such."[7] Outside of Soal's work, I do not believe that we are confronted with many experiments so excellent that we are forced to choose between ESP and fraud. But there are a few such cases.

Rhine, Soal, and Meehl and Scriven all complain that it was improper of me to discuss the possibility of fraud. Naturally I did this with considerable reluctance, but it was absolutely essential that this question be treated frankly in order to settle things one way or the other.

Rhine complains that I did not dig up "some tangible evidence [of fraud] concerning at least one parapsychologist." Now, of course, when it comes to phenomena so gross as to be apparent without statistical tests, there is available all sorts of evidence of fraud. For example, according to the March—April, 1955 *Newsletter* of the Parapsychology Foundation, the Society for Psychical Research, London, will shortly publish a 70,000-word report showing that the late Harry Price, one-time honorary secretary of the University of London Council for Psychical Investigation and author of *The Most Haunted House in England,* himself faked some of the evidence for the haunting of Borley Rectory. But in connection with phenomena so subtle as to be detectable only by statistical tests, my feeling was that it would be quite difficult to prove in 1955 that *A* had whispered something to *B* in 1945.

Soal complains that I wrote "a diatribe of unsupported conjecture." But I did not. My conjectures that parapsychologists might be capable of fraud were supported by the eminent authority Soal himself:[8]

"There is unfortunately among American investigators an atmosphere of showmanship which has created in the minds of British scholars a deep distrust. British scientists for instance are not favourably impressed by Rhine's discovery of a telepathic horse (or was it a precognitive clairvoyant pony?), by the sudden vanishing of Dr. Reiss' phantom percipient into the blue of the Middle West, by the perfect scores of 25 cards correct in 25 successive guesses alleged to have been made by Pearce and the child Lilian, by the card-guessing feats of Pearce while sitting in a motor car and similar marvels.

"Such things simply do not happen in England, or if occasionally they appear to happen they are quickly exposed as frauds or conjuring tricks. In America they are not exposed; they are proclaimed genuine with a blare of trumpets."

CONCLUSION

Rhine has stated that publication of my paper is "on the whole, a good event for parapsychology." It would be wiser for him to see it not as a good event but as a good opportunity. This challenge has presented him with the opportunity to achieve at one stroke the scientific recognition for which he has been struggling for almost thirty years. But if he and Soal continue to evade the challenge, then publication of the paper will prove to have been a very bad event indeed for parapsychology.

NOTES

1. G.R. Price, *Science* 122. 359 (1955).
2. R. P. Angier *et al. J. Parapsychol.* 3.29 (1939).
3. J. G. Pratt and J. L. Woodruff, *ibid.* 3, 121 (1939).
4. B. F. Skinner, *Am. Scientist* 36. 456. 482 (1948).

5. S. G. Soal, *Proc. Soc. Psychical Research* 50, 67 (1953).

6. The September—October 1955 issue (vol. 2. No. 5) of the *Newsletter of the Parapsychology Foundation* (500 Fifth Ave., New York 36, N.Y.) contains statements by J. B. Rhine, S. G. Soal, G. R. Price, and D. Wolfle.

7. Statement by J. B. Rhine, quoted by R. K. Plumb, *New York Times,* 27 August 1955, p. 1.

8. S. G. Soal, *The Experimental Situation in Psychical Research* (Society for Psychical Research, London, 1947), p. 26.

J. B. Rhine

The Experiment Should Fit the Hypothesis

The trouble with Price's experiment is that it is based on an unwarranted assumption about ESP. He says in effect that if ESP really operated in the researches reported, it ought to register its effects dependably in his proposed test. He assumes that such a result would *have* to follow. Therefore failure would be fatal to the hypothesis of ESP, while success would (to him at least) acceptably prove the case.

Unfortunately, ESP is not like that. No parapsychologist has ever claimed that the capacity could be made to function on demand as Price assumes. ESP is still an elusive, uncertain capacity, one that may give high scores one day and chance scores the next; it may persist in consistently missing its target or even hitting the neighboring one. The elusiveness is attributable to the fact that the ability, although voluntary, operates very largely on an unconscious level.[1]

The same mistake was made by Price in his earlier discussion of the practical application of ESP; he overlooked the fact that ESP is not a push-button effect to be turned off and on at will, as a chemistry test might be. In fact, one could easily believe science fiction has been one source of Price's conception of ESP. He has fancied a kind of repeatability and applicability that as yet simply does not exist. It is premature to expect them in such a difficult field.

Reprinted from *Science* 123 (1956) No. 3184, p. 19, by permission of the author and editor.

As far as the mere physical conditions of the proposed test are concerned, however, I see nothing wrong in principle. The test would not involve anything essentially new. Physical barriers such as the proposed metal containers are not obstructive to the capacity. Certain psychological conditions are, of course, essential—conditions such as adequate motivation on the part of the subject who is participating, confidence in his ability to work under the conditions, and freedom from distraction. But such conditions could probably be provided, and, for some subjects at least, proper adaptation to the test conditions could probably be managed in the course of time. If this adaptation were the only difficulty and there were adequate reasons for the test, the procedure could be accepted and used, although, of course, with the same unpredictability of results that attends all ESP tests. As it is, with a false premise concerning the nature of the ESP process, Price made his test unacceptable by giving it an implication of a finality that it could not possibly have.

Price is, in effect, dictating terms to nature rather than to the parapsychologists. Until someone claims to have exerted enough control over ESP to bring it reliably into operation on demand, such a test case or showdown as he suggests is, as I have said, fantastic. The point is that negative results would prove nothing at all. Until (if ever) ESP becomes controllable enough to warrant such a crucial test case, it would not be worth while going to all the build-up and expense that the proposed experiment would involve.

The principal aim of Price's proposed experiment is to exclude fraud. But he needs only to remember that science has, in the very nature of its procedure, protected itself against such weaknesses as that. When any revolutionary claim such as ESP is reported, the cautious scientist will naturally suspend judgment until an independent confirmation has been produced. On a very challenging issue a second or even a third supporting research is needed. The extreme skeptic may, of course, keep on suspending decision as long as he wishes. But when, as in the case of ESP, researches continue to come in, adding confirmation upon confirmation, decade after decade, from investigators in all sorts of professional and academic stations, only those who are extremely biased would cling to a theory of wholesale deception.

The spontaneous, uncontrollable nature of ESP naturally bothers us all, parapsychologists as well as skeptics. But many other erratic, fugitive effects can be found in nature, more especially in the mental sciences, but even in biology and physics. And they are no less "natural" than the more reliable ones, for all man's inability to reproduce them at will. Control is usually just a question of further understanding of the phenomena concerned. In the case of ESP, lack of control is likely to be nothing that more and better researches will not correct.

In the meantime, scientists who open-mindedly wish to satisfy themselves about ESP have two main lines of action open. The preferable way would be to ascertain the essential precautions and psychological conditions that are already known and to conduct an exploratory ESP experiment, as many others have already done. Parapsychology owes much of its evidence and most of its eminent supporters to just such exploratory investigations.

The other way is, of course, the one more generally followed in science. It begins with the critical appraisal of the research literature of the field. This literature is vastly more extensive and important than the few names given by Price indicate. Indeed, all the work reported by Soal and myself (the two "exhibits" that Price used) could be set entirely aside without seriously weakening the case for ESP or even involving the very best controlled experiments.[2] During the last twenty years there have been scores of researches reported (mostly in the *Journal of Parapsychology*) that have adequately met a standard of requirements of safeguarding (even against fraud) well above that of science in general. Let anyone who is able and willing critically review the evidence for ESP to show cause, if he can, why and wherein these most qualified investigations should not be taken seriously! The *Journal of Parapsychology* will be open, as always, to the publication of such reviews.

Price has, I repeat, done parapsychology much good, as, for example, in neatly showing the fallacy of Bridgman's type of criticism. His crusading against evildoing in ESP only serves to make his blows against its critics more effective. It even helps to unbar the portals of respected periodicals. If this is the way a research field has to be opened up to broader scientific attention here in the United States, we in parapsychology must be willing to pay the price and be grateful for the net gain.

Meanwhile, then, the scientist can determine by the usual methods how far it is safe to credit the ESP reports.

NOTES

1. J. B. Rhine, *J. Parapsychol.* 10, 162 (1946).
2. J. G. Pratt and J. L. Woodruff, *J. Parapaychol.* 3, 121 (1939).

Section III

Conceptual Issues in Parapsychology

Antony Flew

Describing and Explaining

The Master said: In language, perspicuity is everything.—The Analects of Confucius

The man who cannot occasionally imagine events and conditions of existence that are contrary to the causal principle as he knows it will never enrich his science by the addition of a new idea.—Max Planck

Almost all the terms in which the phenomena of psychical research are popularly described and discussed are radically unsatisfactory. Most obviously this is true of the 'mind' terminology affected by Rhine in his popular books. "The thread of continuity," he writes, "is the bold attempt to trace as much as we can see of the outer bounds of the human mind in the universe" (*The Reach of the Mind,* Faber 1948, p. 50: the U.S. edition, with different paging, is also found in the U.K.). Accounts of research are spiced with references to the mind; its powers, frontiers, and manifestations; to its unknown, delicate and subtle capacities: and the results are interpreted accordingly as striking hammer blows for "spiritual values" in the battle against "materialism." He deplores "the traditional disinclination to bring science to the aid of our value system" (*Telepathy and Human Personality,* S.P.R., 1950, pamphlet, p. 36).

Picturesque expression is no doubt appropriate in popular books: but

Originally published as Chapter IX in Antony Flew, *A New Approach to Psychical Research* (London: C. A. Watts & Co., 1953). Revised for this publication.

unfortunately Rhine—as others have done before him—misconstrues the logic of this 'mind' terminology. What that means is this: when, sententiously, we talk of the triumph of Mind over Matter, such impressive expressions can always be replaced, with a loss of pomposity but a gain in precision, by workaday statements about how people do the most amazing things in spite of all handicaps of disease, disability, and poverty. Mind-Matter and Mind-Body idioms suggest that people consist of a sort of Webb partnership—a corporeal Sidney mated to an incorporeal Beatrice. But picturesque idioms must not be taken literally. To do so is to misunderstand their logic.

This is what Rhine and others seem to have done. Taking the word 'mind' to refer to some object, some sort of not-brain, he assumes that minds and brains can significantly be said to interact. He tries to interpret his results in terms of this interaction. Not surprisingly it is found to be mysterious: "Science cannot explain what the human mind really is and how it works with the brain" (*The Reach of the Mind,* p. 11). This is to make a mystery out of a muddle. 'Mind' is not that sort of word at all. He complains that the student "finds . . . in modern psychology . . . very little on the mind as a distinct reality. Instead he studies 'behaviour' and its relations to brain fields and pathways" (*ibid.,* p. 13). But this does not convict psychologists of shirking the study of the mind: studying certain human capacities, feelings, and performances is what is meant by studying the mind. 'Mind talk' is an alternative description of the same phenomena: it does not help to explain those phenomena; nor does it record the occurrence of further phenomena. Rhine starts a chapter on "The Reach of the Mind in Space" by remarking: "Experiences suggesting that the mind can transcend space are plentiful." He continues: "The spontaneous awareness of distant events, of which no knowledge could be acquired through recognized channels, is reported fairly frequently." He then describes ESP work in which subjects scored significantly when widely separated from the target cards. But these phenomena are not *evidence for* further ghost phenomena taking place, as it were, offstage. They are part of what is *meant by* this talk of the reach of the mind in space (*ibid.,* Ch. V).

Again he complains that among psychologists "Even the word 'mind' as used by the layman, meaning something different from the brain, is no longer in good standing" (*ibid.,* p. 13). But though the word 'mind' is no synonym for 'brains,' and though 'brains' refers to visible, tangible objects; these two premises do not together entail that the word 'mind' refers to invisible, intangible objects. This would follow only on the Wonderland assumption that all significant nouns—'temper' and 'muchness' included —refer to objects. Psychologists tend to avoid mind idioms precisely because these do generate such mystifications and muddles. As Professor Ryle puts it, " 'Mind' and 'Matter' are echoes from the hustings of philosophy, and prejudice the solutions of all problems posed in terms of them" (*The Physical Basis of Mind,* ed. P. Laslett, Blackwell's, 1950, p. 79).

These are faults primarily in the popular presentation of the work. But Rhine's books have been very widely read, and this 'mind' talk does generate an unfortunate atmosphere of uplift *cum* mystification that intensifies the suspicions with which the hard-headed and sceptical naturally approach such revolutionary claims. More serious is the fact that the researchers themselves have inherited a curious polyglot terminology suggestive of half a dozen incompatible and unwanted explanatory models.

Thought-transference implies that there is some transaction, some transference, between the agent and the subject: this might be a suitable way of describing what may be going on, but it goes far beyond a description of what is actually observed in, or what we are at present justified in inferring from, the experiments. *Clairvoyance* and *extra-sensory perception* suggest that we are dealing with an esoteric or a wayward species of perception: and so naturally we are inclined to go on to ask the sort of questions, to demand the sort of explanations, which would be appropriate if this were the case. But ESP guessing is so different from the operation of what we might call—to borrow a term from the stage—the legitimate senses, that it should not be thought of as a species of perception at all. It is ludicrously unreliable:[1] whatever should we think of eyes which gave results better than guesswork only two or three times out of every twenty-five? It does not seem to be localized in any organ. It does not provide any experience which he who lacks the faculty can never have. Most important, when we see or hear—if it is genuine seeing or hearing and not "seeing" or "hearing" (in snigger or in genuflexion quotes)—there is something present to be seen and heard: and so an explanation is looked for and found in terms of some mechanical process. But with precognitive ESP the analogy of perception breaks down even here. For—to use an Irishism —the target thus extra-sensorily perceived is not yet there to be perceived.

The solemn neologism *precognition*, and its much less fashionable brother *retrocognition,* both imply that what is involved is a species of knowledge. This is precisely not the case. For if ever a subject has or could have reasons to know the value of the card which is the target of his guess, then that guess is by that token disqualified. The experiment is not then a proper ESP test. The "guess" is not a guess at all. Whether consciously or unconsciously the subject has cheated, and the experimenter has been incompetent. To talk of precognition, or even of cognition, in connection with ESP is misleading also because it suggests that the subjects know, at the time of guessing and before the score is checked, which guesses are the hits. But in dealing with the Soal and Goldney work on Basil Shackleton we must notice the fact that no relation of any kind could be discerned between the correctness of guesses and the confidence the subject had in them: while a similar fact was noted earlier as constituting one of the main difficulties in the way of investigating a possible "precognitive" factor in dreams.

Finally *telepathy* itself has drawbacks. It suggests to most people the model of wireless telegraphy (*cf.* Upton Sinclair's title *Mental Radio*). This is certainly not appropriate, for the moment we try to fit it to the facts we have to start adding complications and making excuses. For instance: all radiative effects have an intensity proportionate to the distance from source, whereas nothing like this has been observed with ESP. Again: the "precognitive" ESP effect surely rules out decisively all possibility of explanation in terms of radiation; mediumistic talk of "the vibrations," and so on is simply empty mystification. The term *telepathy* has also encouraged controversies as to whether success under particular conditions was "really produced by telepathy or by clairvoyance" and whether "both telepathy and clairvoyance really occur." The questions both of fact and of meaning involved have become inordinately tortuous and intricate since the establishment of precognitive effects. For it has looked as if all cases of apparent clairvoyance (no agent) might be alternatively described as cases of precognitive telepathy directed towards the person who later checked the scores (an unconscious agent); while all cases of apparent telepathy might likewise be alternatively described in terms of clairvoyance, precognitive, or otherwise. Though these controversies provide fascinating material for philosophers, their value to the parapsychologists is more doubtful. For, even if different experimental meanings can be given to each of the alternatives, there seems little reason to think that the question involved is as important as the controversy has made it seem, since most subjects seem to be able to score equally well (or badly) whether there is or is not an agent (though Soal's crack subjects provide an important exception).

If we insist on the analogies implied by any of these terms, philosophical perplexities will arise at the points of breakdown. Thus there is trouble if you apply the perception model. Mr. J. W. Dunne would describe his apparently precognitive dreams as cases of "observing the future": by valid inference from this mis-description he deduced that the future must somehow be present; and this encouraged him to develop his logical extravaganza, the Serial Theory of Time.[2]

Again, similar trouble may be provoked by the use of the term 'precognition.' Rhine wonders "how precognition fits in with volitional freedom," and this seems "a profound mystery indeed" (*Telepathy and Human Personality,* p. 32). But, in the first place, there is nothing essentially paranormal about foretelling the future as such: what is paranormal is successful prediction without reasons or reasoning. Astronomers, by observing and calculating, can predict eclipses enormously more successfully than any ESP subject has ever been able to guess cards. And, in the second place, there is not in any case any necessary and general incompatibility between predictability and freedom in human conduct. Again and again we correctly predict, we can even properly claim to *know*, such things as that David will marry Jean, and that they will choose to have a family, when there is no question of any compulsion on either of them. The opposite of 'free' is not 'predictable' but 'compulsory.' The opposite of 'predictable' is 'unpredictable,' not 'free.' To act of one's own free will is not necessarily, or even often, to act unpredictably, but to act without constraint. We can foresee many weddings which will not be shotgun weddings and many conceptions which will not be unpremeditated. Thus even if precognitive ESP were, which it is not, a species of knowing, it would still not have the slightest tendency to show that people never act of their own free will. To think of it in this way is asking for philosophical trouble.

What we need, therefore, is a new terminology which does not imply more than we want to imply, which is theoretically neutral, and which is not gratuitously provocative of philosophical perplexity. In the present state of our ignorance that means a terminology with the absolute minimum of implications. To cover what had been called ESP (telepathic or clairvoyant, precognitive or retrocognitive or what have you) Thouless and Wiesner have suggested "ψ(read, psi)—phenomena." This suggestion is now generally followed by students, though they do still sometimes speak of "ψ-*processes.*" This overlooks that part of the point of the innovation was, as Thouless said, "the wish to outlaw the traditional controversies [telepathy versus clairvoyance, etc.] and to replace them by the experimentally soluble problem of what are the necessary or sufficient conditions of psi success". They thus gratuitously commit themselves to saying that *process* is involved. All we know is that ψ *correlations* occur. This is certainly a different, and perhaps a crucially different, matter. After the publication of the first PK papers, Thouless and Wiesner suggested that the meaning of their term should be extended to include PK. This move committed them, of course, to one implication, that ESP and PK were associated. But this was intentional; and Rhine and his colleagues have accepted the hypothesis involved. This extension also has been generally accepted. But not yet their further suggestion that psi-phenomena be subdivided into $\psi\gamma$ (read, psi-gamma: replacing "ESP") and $\psi\kappa$ (read psi-kappa: replacing "PK"). It might be as well to introduce a further series of letters for distinguishing non-committally between "precognitive," "retrocognitive," and simultaneous effects. Perhaps the letters M (for minus, replacing "retrocognitive"), S (for simultaneous), and P (for plus, replacing "precognitive") would serve the purpose. They would be easier both to pronounce and to remember than a further batch of Greek letters.[3]

It may seem to many readers that we have laboured these points. But there is the world of difference between, on the one hand, securing a more or less unthinking assent to the proposition that all the traditional terminology suggests unsuitable explanatory models and provokes unnecessary philosophical perplexity and, on the other hand, showing why and how this is the case; so that the points bite deep into the understanding. Full understanding is most important. *First*, because, as it is neither possible nor convenient to outlaw the old vocabulary altogether; we need to possess its antidote. *Second,* because without it we shall be inclined to use even the new terms without properly dissociating them from the old ideas which they were designed to expel. *Third,* because it will also suggest, what is the case, that any and every system of classification must commit its users to *some* judgments as to what distinctions can and should be made; but once it is realized that this principle will apply, to some extent, even to classification by non-committal letters, we can guard against the attendant dangers of unconscious prejudice here. *Fourth,* because unless we really work ourselves free of the old and familiar conceptions which we naturally try to impose upon these psi-phenomena, inevitably we shall fail to realize their radically peculiar characteristics. We thus make it more difficult to form the new notions required for dealing with them.

We can now begin to bring out some of these characteristics and to say something about forming new notions. *First,* notice that the present concept of psi-gamma is essentially statistical. For—at least in the present state of our ignorance—there is no way to distinguish in any *single* case between a guess which just happens to be right and a correct guess in which a paranormal factor is operating. We cannot tell which guesses belong to the five which one would expect to get right by the law of averages, and which belong to the other one or two and a bit which have caused all the excitement. Or rather, that is a misleading way of putting it: it is not that we cannot *as a matter of fact* thus divide sheep from goats; but that *no meaning has been given* to this distinction. This is because 'psi-gamma' can—at present at least—be defined only as "the factor which gives rise to significant deviations from mean chance expectation *in a series of guesses.*" If we use the term to mean more than this, then the results so far recorded have not established the existence of psi-gamma. If 'psi-gamma' is to entail any reference to the putative unknown means or mechanism by which significant correlations are achieved, then there are no sufficient grounds for believing that psi-gamma genuinely occurs. For though conjurer's means and mechanism can produce similar *bogus* effects, we have no reason to suppose *genuine* runs are produced by any means or mechanism; and every reason to suppose the contrary. With appropriate alterations something similar surely applies even to the spontaneous phenomena. It would make no sense to speak of psi-gamma in connection with any *single* item of correspondence between a putatively paranormal dream, hunch, vision, hallucination, or what not, and what had happened, was happening, or was to happen. (Or, alternatively, we could give it sense in terms of some theory about psi-gamma. But that would commit us to going far beyond our evidence—as of course one must in proposing a hypothesis—or even against it.) Once again it is not just that any single correspondence might *as a matter of fact* be a matter of chance, but that—without committing ourselves either to unwarranted hypotheses or to the positively erroneous assumption that "the psychic always knows"—we can *give no meaning to the question* whether it is or is not. Still more paradoxically, until and unless success is achieved in "willing" deflections to instruments, and so long as the dice-and-statistics methods hold the field, the same things will apply, again with appropriate alterations, with psi-kappa. To put the essence of this difficult but vital matter another way: even granted that the precautions taken against cheating were watertight, and that the sums are all correct; still we cannot say that even the most significant results prove ESP etc., if by 'ESP' we mean any more than *significant correlations. Anything* beyond this, however justifiable, is hypothesis and interpretation. 'ESP' and its brother terms are often used to imply more: but it is only in the austerest sense of the term that the present writer is prepared to concede that the ESP effect has been demonstrated. Even 'significant' must be interpreted as a purely statistical term: not committing us to saying that causal connections will *necessarily* be found, but only that they are worth seeking.

The *second* point is an expansion of a hint given above. At any rate in the case of psi-gamma perhaps we ought to give up asking, "How (by what means) do subjects make significant scores?" For all normal[4] means and mechanisms and rational procedures have been ruled out by definition: if a performance can be sufficiently explained along these lines, then it is not a case calling for talk of psi-gamma. And the possibility of explanation in terms of some hitherto unknown means or mechanism has surely now, by the experimental facts, been ruled out most decisively by the occurrence of P psi-gamma. For any form of radiation or suchlike involved here would have to move backwards in time, to travel

> one day
> In a relative way
> And arrive on the preceding night.

This sort of argument must not be made to carry very much weight. For fundamentally it depends on maintaining our present conceptions of time and of what is to count as a means or mechanism; and either or both of these conceptions may have to be revised before we can come to terms with the psi-phenomena. But the argument is sufficient to suggest that short of some drastic development of the meaning of 'means' this question may be an improper one. If so we must be

> most duly sober,
> To give a plain no answer to no question
> (Michael Roberts, *Orion Marches,* Faber, 1939, p. 21).

This brings us to the *third* point. For it suggests what is the fundamental reason why scientists, and others sharing their professional beliefs and attitudes, have been and, but to a diminishing extent, still are inclined to dismiss out of hand all evidence for the reality of psi-phenomena. Compare the passionate protest of the great Helmholtz: "Neither the testimony of all the Fellows of the Royal Society, nor even the evidence of my own senses could lead me to believe in the transmission of thoughts from one person to another, independently of the recognized channels of sensation" (quoted by M. Polanyi in *The Logic of Liberty,* Routledge, 1951). It is certainly not that the evidence has been—still less that it is now—so much weaker than the evidence for any of the other things which we find no difficulty in believing: in religion, in politics, or even in science. Nor yet that scientists are stubbornly unwilling to give up some particular theory. Something much more important is involved than any particular theory, however fundamental, or any single factual generalization, however well established. But it is something extremely difficult to state clearly and satisfactorily. A psychologist, Mrs. Knight, writing in *Science News* (No. 18, Penguin Books, 1950, p. 9), confessed:

> The facts revealed are so odd, so apparently chaotic, in a sense so trivial and yet so difficult to organize within the accepted scientific framework, that an acute intellectual discomfort is the feeling they chiefly arouse.

The use of the expression "scientific framework" is significant. Others would talk of "scientific beliefs" (M. Polanyi) or perhaps of "absolute presuppositions" (R. G. Collingwood). But all these terms are names rather for a cluster of philosophical problems than for solutions of any of these problems.

Crudely, it can be put like this: The occurrence of psi-phenomena is apparently incompatible with certain of the fundamental beliefs and disbeliefs shared by scientists, and not only by scientists. These are beliefs both about the sorts of things which do and do not happen, and about the kinds of explanation which can be found to cover them. Consider first what might be an analogous though much more alarming case. Suppose that evidence were to be found suggesting that one or several of the animal species at present rated as higher (including perhaps *homo sapiens*) had not in fact evolved from any lower species; but had simply appeared in the geological record millions of years too soon. If this evidence just could not be explained away, if human skeletons kept on turning up in coal-seams or other still earlier strata in which they had no business to be; and if the same sort of thing happened with the fossils of one or two other higher species, then the framework of biological science would collapse.[5] Beyond even the wide boundaries of biology these discoveries would throw doubt on the general presumption of continuous development which is so vital a part of all scientific pictures of the universe. For those of us for whom science has driven the gorgons and the harpies out of the world, and revealed or imposed a new order—uncapricious, impersonal, and majestic —upon the chaos of experience, the suggestion is a nightmare.

Then, to bring out something of the difference between a scientific sort of explanation and one non-scientific sort, consider such a people as the Azande (cf. *Witchcraft, Oracles, and Magic among the Azande,* by E. E. Evans-Pritchard, O.U.P., 1937) whose world is permeated by witchcraft, the workings of which are revealed only and entirely by the operations of *benge* an oracle poison. Their ideas of what questions it is possible and proper to ask, of what requires explanation, and of what counts as an adequate explanation, are utterly different from those of scientifically educated people; and immeasurably inferior to them. Different also are those—if this is not too near the bone—of the people who seem to insist that every event must have (not merely a cause but also) a motive: and hence complain that scientists only tell them *how,* and never *why.* (Of course there are other forces behind this insistence: for example the demand that the ways of God or Nature should be justified.)

Now psi-gamma offends four times over. First: it apparently conflicts with our scientific belief that human behavior will only be determined from outside the organism by or *via* physical stimuli acting directly upon it. This belief is fundamental both for psychology and for everyday affairs. Security forces act on it when they protect secrets by preventing unauthorized people from seeing or from being told what is going on, or from seeing or hearing anything from which the secret could be inferred. They take it that no one can *just acquire* information without at any stage any mediating stimulation of his sense-organs.

Second: psi-gamma ($\psi\gamma$) seems to involve action-at-a-distance. Traditionally scientists have abhorred the notion of action-at-a-distance and have insisted on explanations involving spatio-temporal continuity: one thing can affect another only if there is a continuous chain of (physical) events between the two. If there ever seems to be a gap—between the fire and the warmed hand, between the lamp and the lighted page—they postulate and search for the connecting links. Thus gravitational attraction offered perennial scandal, until this was satisfactorily hushed up by talk of *gravitational fields*—"an incidental conception which is" as Einstein himself confessed, "indeed a somewhat arbitrary one." $S\psi\gamma$("simultaneous ESP") apparently may have to be accepted as a case of action at a distance: because as we showed earlier in this chapter, experimental findings seem to have ruled out anything we could call waves or rays, means or mechanism, involved in a transmission of information between agent and subject.

Third: $\psi\gamma$ seems to involve, temporally as well as spatially, action-at-a-distance; and that both backwards and forwards in time. In M (or P)$\psi\gamma$ (retrocognition or precognition) the subject gets his significant scores when guessing *after* (or *before*) the target series ceases to be (or becomes) available. This clashes with another scientific (and commonsense) belief: that where (as in reciting a piece of verbiage learnt by heart) some remotely past event (in this case the learning of our rigmarole) is a precondition of a present performance (inasmuch as we could not recite what we had never learnt), nevertheless there must also be connecting links between the past (partial) cause and its present effects. We seek changes in the brain caused by the original learning process; lasting changes which ensure that afterwards, suitably stimulated, we recite our piece. But, for all the looking, up to the present no such changes (called prematurely "memory traces" or "engrams") have actually been located. This led Bertrand Russell to suggest his notion of *mnemic causation*, "in which the proximate cause consists not merely of a present event, but of this together with a past event" (*Analysis of Mind*, Allen and Unwin, 1921, p. 85: the index under this head is seriously deficient, for all the important references to this Ch. IV are omitted). It was only a suggestion: made possible because there was, and still is, "so far as I am aware, no good evidence that every difference between the knowledge possessed by A and that possessed by B is paralleled by some difference in their brains" (p. 91); but not actually adopted by Russell, because he thought it best "as a working hypothesis" to maintain the belief "based upon analogies, and general scientific maxims" that the evidence postulated will in due course be found (pp. 92 and 91).

Fourth: most scandalous of all, P$\psi\gamma$ seems to conflict with our scientific (and common-sense) assurance that what will happen later cannot affect what happens now: except perhaps in a very Pickwickian sense, as one might say that people with courage, foresight, and goodwill were influenced by the Second German War even before it began; while knowing very well that what *really* affected them was their then present knowledge that Germany would soon launch that war.

The notion of *cause* is involved in all four cases, to a greater or lesser extent: least perhaps in the *determination* of the first; more in the *action* at a distance of the second and third; most in the *affecting* and *influencing* of the fourth. And, as we shall proceed to argue, it makes for a perhaps dangerously misleading misdescription. But a word first about the scientific belief aspect. Psi-gamma does offend. Yet it does occur. So it would be undignified and ultimately futile for us to imitate the ostrich confronted by the giraffe: which protested into the sand, "Impossible!" "It is clear," said Aristotle, "that things which have happened are possible: for if they were impossible, they would not have happened." If previously we believed psi-gamma was impossible: we shall just have to revise our ideas about what sort of place the universe is.

The key word here should be 'revise': there is no need and no excuse to react by abandoning wholesale positions already won by science and all our scientific principles. We must concede what occurs: but not that—as in *Hellzapoppin'*—"anything may happen and it probably will." For apart from the anomalous set of very weak effects constituted by these excessively rare and elusive correlations, everything else is just as it was before. Once the correlations are admitted as exceptions to the various general principles against which they offend there seems to be no reason why most sciences (scientists) should be upset further—at least until and unless either such correlations become very much more common or parallel phenomena are found in other fields. Of course $\psi\gamma$ is an untidy anomaly. Of course one hopes that it will in time be fitted into some scheme of scientific theory and prediction. But even suppose it cannot be, that $\psi\gamma$ remains an anomaly, this will mean only that in this respect, too, the universe is not quite as we might have wished. Perhaps we tend to be spoilt by our constant success in formulating natural laws: to think that it is somehow *necessary* that the universe *must, everywhere,*[6] present regularities making such formulation possible; whereas the fact that it does—so far as we know—do so is actually an enormous piece of contingent good fortune. $\psi\gamma$ can jolt our complacency.

It is upsetting also in apparently forcing us to admit two new species of action-at-a-distance; one spatial (to go alongside gravity); and one temporal (to which mnemic phenomena alone possibly offer a parallel). Again we must not panic: we must not abandon the so-called Postulate of Spatio-Temporal Continuity, properly construed. For this should be taken: as an invaluable *heuristic maxim,* remaining sound in spite of our occasional failures (as here) to find what it bids us seek; not as a mistaken *fundamental presupposition,* now disproved by the discovery of these exceptions, and due to bring down in collapse the whole structure of natural science supposedly at present founded upon it. As an heuristic maxim this so-called postulate has been justified a thousand times by successes in discovery. Furthermore we must recognize that it is only by a generous but reckless and undeliberate stretch of their meaning that these dynamic *causal* notions, such as *action, affecting,* and so on, can be applied to such at present non-repeatable and essentially statistical phenomena as the ψ correlations. For though it certainly sounds queer to refuse to say that the target series in a significant run *influences* the guessing, it is strictly inaccurate to say that it does; for that "the same cause must produce the same effect" is part of the meaning of 'cause' while the ψ effects are neither detectable in single cases (only in a *series* of guesses) nor in the strict sense repeatable (an experimenter duplicating the stated conditions of someone else's experiment cannot rely on repeating his results).

$\psi\gamma$ is disturbing, too, because we may have to revise or add to our basic explanatory concepts to accommodate it. This brings us to our *fourth* main point in the series on peculiarities of the notion of ψ and on forming ideas to cope with it. Confronted by $P\psi\gamma$ (precognition), Mrs. Knight was distressed by the "apparent implication that causation can work backwards in time" (*loc. cit.,* p. 13). It *is* a shock: Rhine said that even in parapsychology it acted as would the discovery in chemistry of a "universal solvent." Yet surely this is the wrong way of describing the situation: no phenomena whatever could have this implication; that the cause must be prior to the effect is not a matter of fact, a generalization which though confirmed in innumerable instances, might nevertheless, through the discovery of exceptions, one day have to be qualified or abandoned. It is a logical truism, an analytic proposition, the truth of which depends entirely upon the meaning of the terms 'cause' and 'effect.' To use an Irishism again, the effect can never precede the cause: because if it does then it's the cause and not the effect.

Someone might impatiently concede "the current meanings of 'cause' and 'effect' make it tautological to say that a cause must be prior to its effect," but insist "to leave the matter there would be to ignore what constitutes the problem, i.e., the fact that in precognitive phenomena the nature of the earlier event seems to be causally dependent on that of the later event, rather than the contrary" (C. W. K. Mundle in the *Journal of Parapsychology,* Vol. XVI, p. 265). Certainly things should not be left there. But this way of restating the issue is again misleading and in the same sense as our accounts of the offences against scientific belief (p. 216). It suggests that $P\psi\gamma$ reveals a new type of cause, operating backwards. Whereas what we have is something subtly but importantly different: facts which cannot apparently be handled in terms of 'cause' and 'effect,' in their current meanings; suggesting a need to change these (to revise these concepts). This subtle difference is important. When and only when it is grasped can we see that we have freedom to choose whether and how we reshape the concept or 'cause' (change the meaning of the word). We do not have so to change it that, in our new meaning, it makes sense to talk of future causes having present effects: *and to leave the concept (and all the others which are logically linked with it) otherwise unaltered.* To do this—as, unconsciously, do those who fail to see the point now being laboured—is to invite paradox and philosophical perplexity. Again we do not *have* to make the rash stretch involved in applying causal notions to ψ correlations. But if we do we *must* be alert to the fact that we have *stretched* the meaning of the word; and therefore changed its implications. To overlook this is to invite needless perplexity.

Mundle himself argues that P$\psi\gamma$ is "relevant to the free-will problem in a way which normal prediction is not." Because "in order to explain precognitions it seems necessary to suppose that they are due to . . . causal influence by, future events. But in order to enter into such relationships the future events would have to be in some sense actual before they happen." This leads to a paradoxical "theory of time apparently implied by precognition" which he admits, not surprisingly, "I am extremely reluctant to accept" (*loc. cit.,* p. 264).[7]

All this is unnecessary. Granting that it is now contradictory to say that something is caused by something "in no sense actual," and granting that P $\psi\gamma$ makes us decide to change the (or introduce a new) meaning of 'cause': so that *in the new sense of the word* it is not contradictory to say that some event which has not yet occurred causes an event which is occurring now. Still there is no reason why—if only we see this as a matter of conceptual innovation and not, directly, of empirical discovery—we should not during the same renovation also alter our concept (the meaning of 'cause') so that the (?) further contradiction about actuality also becomes, *in the new sense of 'cause',* no longer a contradiction. The trouble comes from using a concept 'cause' which has perhaps not been sufficiently adapted to cope with psi: without noticing that it has been adapted at all.

Russell's suggestion of *mnemic causation* (see p. 217) shows how we might adopt the concept of 'cause' or introduce a new but closely analogous notion: we might invent *psi causation,* in which what we should call the proximate cause would be "not merely a present event, but . . . this together with a past event," *or a future event.* Mundle himself once made an interesting suggestion (*Proceedings of the Aristotelian Society,* Supp. Vol. XXIV, pp. 223-5). One criterion both of causal connection and of the direction of causal influence is provided by the fact that often a set of similar events clusters around another different and preceding event, which may then be counted as their common cause. The dropping of the stone is counted as the common cause of all the surrouding ripples spreading out across the still surface of the pond. With our present conception of cause, using the word 'cause' as we do now, the criterion applies only to spatial or spatio-temporal clustering: the effects have to occur around the cause or around *and* soon *after* it. But Carington found that hits on the target drawing were made irrespective of the distance at which his subjects made their drawings: but that hits on, say, Wednesday's target clustered round Wednesday in time, before and after; scores on Tuesday and Thursday being equally good, and both much better than those made on Monday and Friday, which were also about as good as one another (see Chapter VIII). [Not reprinted here.—Ed.] This is an example of a *purely temporal* clustering. Mundle suggested that we might decide to accept such temporal clustering as a new criterion both of causal connection and of the direction of causal influence; the event which was central in time (in the Carington example, the display of the target drawing) being counted as the cause of the temporally surrounding effects. To accept this would be to revise our conception of 'cause' (to change the use of the word).

We are holding no brief for either of these particular suggestions, partly because it would be premature, but mainly for another reason, already stressed above. The concepts of ψ (both γ and κ) are at present statistical (see p. 213): and neither suggestion takes account of this. Perhaps the only laws which can be fitted to them will themselves be statistical (laws, that is, about what happens in x per cent of cases). This is not scandalous. For most physicists—and physicists seem the accepted keepers of the conscience of the scientific world—are now reconciled to the idea that sometimes only statistical laws can be got. Nor is it scandalous to hint that 'cause' has limitations as an explanatory notion: the physicists again are (not merely content, but) eager to provide functional laws in the statement, but not the discovery, of which this term is not required. (A functional law is one stating that A varies in such and such a way with B, C, and D: and is usually expressed in an equation with A on one side and B, C, and D on the other; e.g. Boyle's Law $V \alpha \frac{1}{p}$, V, the volume of a gas varies inversely with one over P, the pressure of that gas—or any of the inverse square laws). However, all this at present is speculation: the answers can be found only by progress in the research. The important thing to get hold of is the idea that our concepts, our words, should be kept under control, treated as tools to be used, adapted, and added to, as and when required. Here this involves realizing: first, that we can and should adapt or add to our conceptual equipment, if necessary; second, that we can and should do this deliberately, and as is most convenient; and third, that if we do this, then we have done this, and the words in their new senses cannot carry the same implications as they did in their old senses.

A large part of what Stephen Toulmin calls "contemporary scientific mythology" is generated by a failure of laymen to realize, and of scientists and particularly philosophers to explain or perhaps to realize, that many scientific terms are familiar words used in unfamiliar ways. Hence nothing but paradox and misunderstanding can result if people draw from the words in their new senses all the inferences which would, in their old senses, follow. The possibilities of such confusion over shifts in the meaning of 'cause' are quite appalling—especially in view of the fact that it has in its present sense innumerable logical associates, e.g. 'affect,' 'influence,' 'result,' 'effect,' etc. This is certainly a reason to hope that no changes will be made, and perhaps a reason not to expect them.[8]

The *fifth* point is that if we must have a model, in terms of which to think of experimental psi-gamma and to try to make it intelligible to ourselves, then the model of guessing would be a great deal better than those of perception, communication by radio, or the fabulous offstage activities of ghostly minds, or even—if these can be called models—those of cognition (knowing) or thought-transference. This is only offered as a convenient stopgap way of thinking of the phenomena, which is not so grossly unsatisfactory as the popular alternatives. It does not even begin to provide an explanation of psi success. Nor does it offer much promise of heuristic fertility, though it does perhaps suggest a few possibly useful questions. Similarly—and again only till the progress of research suggests a better, heuristically fertile or genuinely explanatory, model—cases of spontaneous psi-gamma might be thought of as being or involving hunches.

At this point, after these meta-theoretical preliminaries, it would be gratifying if we could either report that some current theory was beginning to look plausible, or offer a new candidate of our own. Unfortunately we cannot. Two suggestions have gained attention recently: the first was Carington's theory of telepathy; the second the Shin theory put forward by Thouless and Wiesner.

The gist of the former is that minds are systems of ideas and experiences, which he calls *psychons*: that psychon-systems are not wholly insulated from one another: and that the facts of telepathy may be explained by assuming that there is interaction of psychons in different systems by the same laws of association of ideas as used to be used by Associationist psychologists in the attempt to explain the relations of ideas in any one person. Thus Carington thought that it had been vital to the success of his experiments with drawings that all subjects had been supplied with an associative link, called a *K object*, in the shape of a photograph of his study, in which he was to display the target drawings. For thus each subject would have in his psychon-system a picture idea which the agent (Carington) had in his. In Carington's psychon-system this idea was associated with that of the target picture. So, on his theory, the subjects would tend to associate their idea of his study with that of the target picture. This theory, briskly explained and developed by Carington in his book *Telepathy* (Methuen, 1945), did seem to get away to a good start by covering several of the main features of the phenomena. But it does not pretend to cover the occurrence of psi-gamma under clairvoyance conditions, still less that of psi-kappa under any conditions.

The Shin theory postulates that "in normal thinking and perceiving I am in the same sort of relation to what is going on in the sensory part of my brain and nervous system as that of the successful clairvoyant to some external event" (viz. psi-gamma), and likewise that "I control the activity of my nervous system . . . by the same means as that by which the successful psycho-kinetic subject controls the fall of the dice or other object (i.e. by psi-kappa)." Since 'I' is clearly not being used here in the ordinary sense (for my brain and my nervous system are *parts* of me, and not things with which I can be in *relations*), but to refer to postulated entities, Thouless and Wiesner borrowed the Hebrew letter ש (Shin) to refer to these entities, pointing out that they drew on a new alphabet because they now wanted to refer to entities and not processes; and they again used a letter, rather than a word like 'soul', because they did not want their term to have any associations that were not justified by experiment ("The Psi Processes in Normal and 'Paranormal' Psychology" in *Proc. S.P.R.*, Vol. XLVIII: our quotations at pp. 180 and 181). This theory was elaborated to cover all forms of psi-gamma, and psi-kappa as well (to say nothing of séance materializations, attributed to psi-epsilon).

We cannot afford space for more than a few comments. First this Shin theory is obviously, albeit tortuously, related to the mind terminology criticized earlier. The essential difference is that the former makes as clear as may be, both that we are being offered a theory and what that theory involves. The latter, though it suggests here a much more picturesque but far less precise version of the Shin theory, pretends only to describe experiments. Second, both theories represent a reaction towards older ideas. Associationism has long since died in psychology, while Shin is the "Ghost in the Machine"[9] *redivivus*. Neither theory is necessarily the worse for that. But either is thereby bound to meet from contemporary psychological and philosophical orthodoxy with a resistance to the end. Third, while Carington's theory, after a good start, meets with a lot to explain away even in the restricted part of the field which it tries to cover, the Shin theory, which has the merit of attempting a unified account of all normal and paranormal psychology, does not—until and unless these postulated entities are supplied with some putative characteristics—seem to entail any experimentally testable consequences at all. The Carington theory, for instance, is in trouble because a number of similar experiments with K-objects duly provided have been entirely negative. The Shin theory, on the other hand, might be developed to suggest that psychological conditions such as attention and effort involved in perception and normal volitional behaviour may tend to inhibit psi performances: and—at least as far as psi-gamma is concerned— there is good reason for saying that this is so. Carington's theory is already testable, even though the verdict seems to be going against it, because it commits him to saying that the various sub-laws of association (those of Recency, Repetition, etc.) will apply to telepathic association also. The Shin theory, in its present form, is not testable, precisely because it is so excessively non-committal. It is excellent to use a vocabulary of letters, defined strictly in terms of experimental observations, when the need is for caution and for freedom from positively incorrect or possibly misleading implications and suggestions. But in theory construction something quite different is wanted. A theory must go beyond the observations preferably without contradicting any of them and imply further and fairly definite experimentally testable consequences if it is to do its job as a scientific theory.

The Association and the Shin theories are both commendably unorthodox. Any theory which is to explain psi will have to be. They deserve more attention than we can afford to give them. But a strong case can be made for saying that the research situation is not yet ripe for theory construction: for reasons which have already been considered in other contexts. The evidence at so many points is still deplorably conflicting. Unexpected effects have been discovered independently by different workers, but the ideal of repeatability has still to be achieved. Even with the best subjects on the top of their form, the psi effects are very weak. Also, another point importantly though differently related to these, the concept of psi is essentially statistical. Taken together these three facts mean that the testing of hypotheses, whether by reference to already recorded results or in new experiments, tends at present to yield imprecise or conflicting answers. If indeed the only laws we shall be able to formulate here are going to be statistical, it may be that the quantity of work needed to begin to establish them will be far greater than elsewhere. So until the present situation is radically changed—either by important discoveries about the favouring and inhibiting conditions of psi, or by finding a way to distinguish between paranormal successes and chance hits singly, or by the sheer accumulation of experimental data—the theoretical prospect seems likely to remain poor.

NOTES

1. "The evening of clairvoyance on Tuesday, 4th December, at 7 p.m. has had to be cancelled owing to unforeseen circumstances" (*East Kent Times*, quoted *New Statesman*, 22/12/51).

2. See my contribution to S. Thakur (ed.) *Philosophy and Psychical Research* (London, Allen and Unwin, 1976).

3. Cf. [The names of the vitamins] "were non-committal in order that scientific ignorance should not be cloaked. Under fuller knowledge they are already being rechristened properly and chemically. Vitamin C is ascorbic acid. . . ." (Sir Charles Sherrington *Man on His Nature*, C.U.P., 1946, p. 96).

4. It has been suggested e.g. by Mr. Richard Robinson at the Aristotelian Society that *all* means are ruled out by definition. This is not how Rhine and his colleagues use the term 'ESP'. For in the book *Extra-Sensory Perception* "the Radiation theory" is discussed and dismissed, as an *explanation*, and not as one of the "negative hypotheses," such as fraud, incompetence, etc., on which ESP would be denied.

5. "To the layman the progress of our knowledge of evolution must often seem disappointingly slow. To a biologist it is more impressive for the following reason. As it develops it becomes constantly easier to name discoveries that would disprove it. . . . Today it [the discovery of a human skeleton in a coal-seam—A. F.] would disprove evolution"—J. B. S. Haldane in *The Rationalist Annual* for 1951.

6. Of course, if there were no such regularities *anywhere*, human beings presumably could not have evolved and survived. But there could have been far more irregularity than there is, or the regularities could have been far harder to detect than they are, without preventing human life. Again, if in the infancy of natural science men had not believed that there were findable regularities *everywhere*, perhaps scientists would never have been able to muster the persistent confidence to look for and find the regularities which can be found. But now we can afford to consider the possibilities we have been mentioning, without undermining and betraying the whole scientific quest.

7. Cf. Dunne, who was misled into his similar theory partly by misdescribing $P\psi\gamma$ as "observing events before they occur": and validly inferring from his absurd premiss the para-

doxical conclusion that the future is *really* present (*An Experiment with Time,* 3rd. ed., p. 7).

8. See Bertrand Russell "On the Notion of Cause" (in *Mysticism and Logic,* Allen and Unwin, 1917: now in Pelican Books); especially for his onslaught on those superstitious prejudices about causality still favoured by people in the tradition of Scholastic Metaphysics. Also S. E. Toulmin, *The Philosophy of Science* (Hutchinson, 1953); especially Ch. I, on language shifts, and pp. 119 ff., on "cause" as a diagnostic notion. The latter may suggest why, in spite of Russell's attempts to banish it (on the grounds: that advanced sciences, in their theory construction, have no place for it; and that, when so precisified as to be unusable, it is absurd), this notion of "cause" is and will remain indispensible in its proper sphere: the occasions of practical life, including those of the laboratory work of experimental physicists.

9. Cf. G. Ryle, *The Concept of Mind* (Hutchinson, 1949).

REFERENCES

C. W. K. Mundle: "Is Psychical Research Relevant to Philosophy?" (*Proc. Aristotelian Society*, Supp. Vol. XXIV, pp. 207 ff.).

R. H. Thouless: "The Present Position of Experimental Research into Telepathy and Related Phenomena" (*Proc. S.P.R.*, Vol. XLVII, pp. 1 ff.).

R. H. Thouless and B. Wiesner: "The Psi Processes in Normal and 'Paranormal' Psychology" (*Proc. S.P.R.*, Vol. XLVIII).

W. W. Carington: *Telepathy* (Methuen, 1945).

A. G. N. Flew (Editor): *Logic and Language,* 1st and 2nd Series (Blackwell 1951 and 1953). [See especially J. J. C. Smart on "Theory Construction"; 2nd Series, Ch. XII.]

S. E. Toulmin: *The Philosophy of Science* (Hutchinson, 1953).

Stephen E. Braude

On the Meaning of 'Paranormal'

In recent years philosophers have made a number of interesting attempts to specify criteria for a phenomenon's paranormality, with an eye to getting clear on what the proper domain of parapsychological research is. It seems to me that the time has come to examine these attempts in some detail, not only in order to analyze the respective virtues and defects of the different accounts, but also in the hope of lending order to the rather sprawling body of dialectic facing the student of parapsychology. In this paper I shall examine critically some leading accounts of paranormality and some ways of remedying their defects.

PRELIMINARIES

Most people operate with a rather vague tripartite pre-theoretic distinction between ordinary phenomena on one hand, unusual or rare phenomena on another, and finally, those phenomena which—whether or not they are rare—are regarded as downright weird, bizarre, or other-wordly. To some extent this pre-theoretic distinction matches another distinction of interest to us—namely, the not-so-pre-theoretic distinction between *normal, abnormal,* and *paranormal* phenomena. Since the customary use of the term 'paranormal' and its cognates presupposes this latter distinction, presumably no attempt to specify the domain of the paranormal is satisfactory if it fails to preserve these three rather fuzzy categories. And of course we would also expect any such attempt to clarify at least the last of these categories.

However unclear the pre-analytic normal/abnormal/paranormal distinction is, it is nevertheless sufficiently clear to permit us to evaluate proposed accounts of paranormality. We may not be able to decide whether certain borderline phenomena fall into one category rather than another, but I think we have sufficient paradigm cases for each category to lend substance to the distinction. Any account of paranormality incompatible with our classifications of these paradigm cases will, it seems, be *prima facie* unacceptable.

I think it is fair to say that there is widespread agreement that certain sorts of phenomena are paradigmatically normal. Even the most conservative and eccentric among us could agree that such phenomena as thunderstorms, sunsets, and the movements of the tides are normal phenomena. But I think we also have reasonably uncontroversial paradigm cases of abnormal phenomena. These would be, for example, certain sideshow cases (e.g., a person with two heads, or the half-man/half-woman), as well as such things as cases of microcephaly and situs inversus (a congenital condition in which the position of internal bodily organs is laterally transposed).

Moreover, the class of abnormal phenomena does not seem to be the same as the class of *unusual* or *infrequent* phenomena, although these classes may overlap. Great natural disasters, for example, like floods and earthquakes, or such predictable occurrences as solar eclipses and the passage of famous comets are unusual and infrequent, but are not typically regarded as abnormal.

Although we do have obvious paradigm cases of normal and abnormal phenomena, it would be presumptuous to say that we have clear paradigm cases of paranormal phenomena. A correct and more cautious claim would be that we have clear paradigm cases of *ostensibly* paranormal phenomena. Examples of such cases would be familiar cases of apparent ESP, psychokinesis (hereafter *PK*), hauntings, mediumistic communications, and so forth. To say that these are cases merely of ostensibly paranormal phenomena is not, of course, to deny their importance. After all, some ostensibly paranormal phenomena might be genuinely paranormal. Rather, it highlights an interesting difference between the categories of abnormal and paranormal phenomena.

No one doubts that there are abnormal phenomena. No matter how people elect to draw the line between the normal and the abnormal, nobody seriously disputes whether there is a line to be drawn. But people *do* seriously question whether there are paranormal phenomena, rather than (say) merely unusual phenomena explicable in terms of mundane or familiar processes. But whether or not the class of paranormal phenomena is empty, there is widespread agreement over what sorts of phenomena are candidates for membership in that class. What we must demand of any satisfactory account of paranormality is that it do justice to our classification of certain phenomena as *ostensibly* paranormal. We want our account of paranormality to be such that those phenomena widely regarded as ostensibly paranormal seem *prima facie* to satisfy the account.

One final preliminary point merits our attention. The terms 'abnormal' and 'paranormal' might be defined in such a way that the set of paranormal phenomena turns out to be merely a subset of the set of abnormal phenomena. On the other hand, these terms might be so defined that the sets of abnormal and paranormal phenomena turn out to be disjoint. It is important to realize that these are both legitimate options. But we do not need to decide between them in advance.

Let us now proceed to examine the leading accounts of paranormality.

PARANORMALITY AS SCIENTIFIC INEXPLICABILITY

C. J. Ducasse once offered an account of paranormality, which, in more or less disguised (and usually simplified) forms, is probably the account most often advanced by parapsychologists and laymen. This account is profoundly defective; but its mistakes are instructive.

What Ducasse proposed is as follows.

    (D1) Phenomenon *P* is paranormal = df (a) the cause of P is not that from which phenomena of that sort ordinarily result, and (b) the cause of *P* is nothing yet known to the natural sciences as capable of causing a phenomenon of that sort.

One apparent virtue of (D1), which Ducasse acknowledged, is that it allows the domain of the paranormal to change with time, as the scope of science inevitably widens. Thus phenomena at one time regarded as paranormal might later come to be regarded as either abnormal or normal. I think we can agree with Ducasse that this is a virtue of (D1). Such a shift in perspective seems to have occurred with respect to solar eclipses, hypnotism, and various electromagnetic phenomena, and presumably will happen again with respect to some phenomena now regarded as ostensibly paranormal.

It is not clear, incidentally, what Ducasse regarded as an *abnormal* phenomenon when he proposed (D1). If he had a definite view at all, it was probably something like this. Unlike paranormal phenomena, normal and abnormal phenomena are both explicable by current science, and the difference in their frequency of occurrence. As I observed in the previous differnece in their frequency of occurrence. As I observed in the previous section, however, more than this needs to be said if we are to do justice to the pre-theoretic distinction between the merely infrequent and the abnormal.

In any case, (D1) has serious defects. Let us consider clause (a) first. The motivation behind this clause, and for that matter behind Ducasse's emphasis on the *cause* of the phenomenon in question, is reasonably clear. Paranormal phenomena can presumably have *manifestations* indistinguishable from those of ordinary phenomena. Sometimes, for example, pictures just fall off walls, for a variety of humdrum reasons. At other times a magician might make the picture fall, and while the causes of the picture's falling may not be humdrum, they are nevertheless ordinary mechanical causes. Now of course a picture that is made to fall off a wall by means of PK may be observationally indistinguishable from the ordinary event or from the handiwork of the Great Randi. What would make the PK case paranormal would have to do with the cause, and not the manifestation, of the event.

But despite the reasonableness of Ducasse's emphasis on causes, clause (a) of (D1) is problematical. The problem with this clause is simply that it requires at least *two* causes for the type of phenomenon to which P belongs: that from which such phenomena ordinarily result, and that from which such phenomena paranormally result. But of course some sorts of phenomena, even if they can be produced in more than one way, may be sufficiently unprecedented to have no cause at all from which phenomena of that sort *ordinarily* result. This would presumably be true in the case of such relatively uncommon phenomena as ostensible possession and potergeist manifestations (what is the *ordinary* cause of objects flying across a room *without visible signs of agency?*). Moreover, some sorts of ostensibly paranormal phenomena (e.g., such relatively frequent psi phenomena as telepathic and clairvoyant cognition) may *not* have more than one cause, and the sole cause of such phenomena may be what inclines us to regard those phenomena as paranormal in the first place. In my view, we can best avoid these difficulties by ignoring clause (a) altogether, and regarding the second clause of (D1) as expressing the substance of Ducasse's account. That is, let us consider the following account.

(D1′) Phenomenon P is paranormal = df the cause of P is nothing yet known to the natural sciences as capable of causing a phenomenon of that sort.

But even this trimmed definition is not satisfactory, since the phrase "yet known to the natural sciences" is crucially ambiguous. Suppose that some phenomenon P is in principle causally explicable in terms of current scientific theory, but that nobody in the scientific community can figure out what the explanation is. Since such human limitations may be displayed with respect to both humdrum and exotic phenomena, this state of affairs would hardly constitute sufficient grounds for regarding P as paranormal. But it would nevertheless satisfy (D1′), when that definition is understood loosely enough—that is, when "yet known to the natural sciences" is understood to mean something like "yet known to anyone in the natural sciences." At very best, the case described is one in which we are entitled to regard P as *ostensibly* paranormal. So in order to disambiguate (D1′), and also to avoid the danger of obliterating the distinction between ostensibly and genuinely paranormal phenomena, let us recast (D1′) to exclude this sort of case. What Ducasse probably had in mind is something like:

(D1″) Phenomenon P is paranormal = df P is in fact causally inexplicable in terms of current scientific theory.

Although (D1″) avoids the difficulty just discussed, it too is seriously flawed. The history of science may be regarded as a saga in which observed anomalies periodically force the scientific community to alter or abandon prevailing theories. But even when we consider those anomalous occurrences that occasioned the most profound changes in scientific theory, we find that they were not regarded at the time as ostensibly paranormal. During the twilight of Newtonian physics, for example, scientists grappled with numerous recalcitrant phenomena that current theory simply could not handle, but that were nevertheless not regarded as sufficiently bizarre to be taken as ostensibly paranormal—for example, the anomalous advance of Mercury's perihelion, the so-called "ultraviolet catastrophe", and the negative results of the Michelson-Morley experiment. Thus it seems that the really deep error in linking paranormality merely to scientific inexplicability is that it leads to the highly counter-intuitive result that all scientific anomalies are paranormal.

To his credit, Ducasse eventually abandoned this account of paranormality in favor of one offered by C. D. Broad. Broad's definition is a decided improvement over (D1) and its revisions, but it also has serious deficiencies. Let us now turn our attention to Broad's account.

PARANORMALITY AND BASIC LIMITING PRINCIPLES

The most exhaustive presentation of Broad's view is in "The Relevance of Psychical Research to Philosophy,"[2] and it is sketched in his *Lectures on Psychical Research.*[3] To understand Broad's view, we must first master a key concept in his account—namely, the notion of a *basic limiting principle* (hereafter *BLP*).

Broad's *BLP*s are called "limiting" principles because they specify restrictions or limitations on the way things can be or can be known. And they are called "basic" because they are supposed to lie at the very foundation of our conceptual system. Broad writes, "They form the framework within which the practical life, the scientific theories, and even most of the fiction of contemporary industrial civilization are confined."[4] *BLP*s are thus not merely laws of nature. Although, according to Broad, there may be borderline cases where we cannot tell if we have a *BLP* or a natural law, in general *BLP*s are more basic to our conceptual system than laws of nature. *BLP*s are, in fact, *presupposed* by our natural laws (in a sense that will be explained below). It is because we share certain *BLP*s that our natural laws (and hence our sciences) take certain forms rather than others.

Broad's taxonomy of *BLP*s differs with his different accounts, and even in his rather thorough exposition in "The Relevance of Psychical Research to Philosophy" he does not claim to offer a complete list of *BLP*s. Rather, he gives some examples, and assumes we can extrapolate from those. In the summary of his position in the *Lectures,* Broad lists the following four *BLP*s, which he seems to regard as especially important, and which are for the most part drawn or condensed from his earlier and more extensive list.

The first *BLP* imposes limitations on the ways we can acquire knowledge of another person's thoughts or experiences.

(1) We take for granted that a person *A* cannot know what experiences another person *B* is now having or has had, except in one or another of the

following three ways. (i) By hearing and understanding sentences uttered by *B*, or reproductions of such sentences, which describe his experiences; or by reading and understanding such sentences written or dictated by *B*, or reproductions or translations of them. Or (ii) by hearing and interpreting interjections which *B* makes; by seeing and interpreting his movements, gestures, facial expressions; and so on. Or (iii) by seeing, and making inferences from, certain persistent material objects, e.g., tools, pottery, pictures, etc., which *B* has constructed or used, or copies and reproductions of such objects. (*Lectures,* p. 3)

The second *BLP* restricts how we can come to know about the future.

(2) We take for granted also that a person cannot foresee (as distinct from inferring, or being led, without explicit inference, to expect on the basis of regularities in his past experience) any event which has not yet happened. (*Lectures,* pp. 3-4)

The third *BLP* restricts how we can cause changes in the physical world.

(3) We take for granted, too, that a person cannot *directly* initiate or modify by his volition the movement of anything but certain parts of his own body. (*Lectures,* p. 4)

The fourth *BLP* concerns the dependence of mind on brain and, more specifically, survival after death.

(4) We take for granted that, when a person's body dies, the personal consciousness, which has been associated with it and expressed through it during his lifetime, either ceases altogether or, if not, ceases to be able to manifest itself in any way to those still living on earth. (*Lectures,* p. 4)

With this partial list of *BLP*s, we are in a position to consider Broad's definitions. First, Broad offers the following account of a phenomenon's abnormality.

(D2) Phenomenon *P* is abnormal =df *P* seems *prima facie* to conflict only with a well-established law of nature, but *not* with any *BLP*.

Broad observes that sometimes abnormal phenomena do not really conflict with any law of nature, but can be explained in terms of existing laws *and* certain unusual boundary conditions. On the other hand, sometimes abnormal phenomena show us that laws have exceptions, or that we need to supplement or revise our original set of laws.

Before considering what Broad says about paranormality, we should observe that this account of abnormality is not entirely satisfactory. Many phenomena widely regarded as abnormal (e.g., Siamese twins, situs inversus) are so regarded even though they do not seem *prima facie* to violate a natural law. And since we have already seen that it is not satisfactory to link a phenomenon's abnormality to its frequency of occurrence, the concept of an abnormal phenomenon thus remains somewhat obscure.

Let us not dwell on these difficulties, however. Our present concern is to see if we can find an account of paranormality that countenances as ostensibly paranormal those phenomena widely regarded as ostensibly paranormal, and that also does *not* countenance as ostensibly paranormal those phenomena regarded as merely abnormal. Given the way Broad chooses to characterize abnormality, his account of a phenomenon's paranormality is what one would expect.

> (D3) Phenomenon *P* is ostensibly paranormal =df *P* seems *prima facie* to conflict with one or more of the *BLP*s, and not merely with some well-established law of nature.

> (D4) Phenomenon *P* is genuinely paranormal =df *P* in fact conflicts with one or more of the *BLP*s.

The advantage of Broad's account over that of Ducasse is that Broad requires that paranormal phenomena run up against something more fundamental than—or at least something in addition to—the dictates of science. But Broad's account does not go deep enough; it suffers from a pernicious lack of generality or abstractness. Broad has failed to explain what, in general, a phenomenon must conflict with in order to conflict with a *BLP*. In short, Broad's account is of little value in the absence of a general characterization of a *BLP*.

We saw earlier that it is plausible to regard the domain of the paranormal as something that may change with time, as our thinking about the world becomes more sophisticated. After all, this is presumably why certain phenomena which at one time were regarded as outstandingly weird or other-worldly later came to be seen as commonplace and quite this-worldly. But if the extension of the term 'paranormal' can change with time, we need a general characterization of what a paranormal phenomenon is, no matter what epoch we are concerned with. Hypnotism, we must recall, was once regarded by the Society for Psychical

Research as a phenomenon to be investigated along with those we now call ESP, PK, etc. But it does not seem to violate any of Broad's *BLP*s. And even with respect to a particular historical epoch, it is not sufficient to offer a partial list of *BLP*s in order to explain what the domain of the paranormal is for that epoch. For one thing, Broad's *BLP*s are by no means universally shared even within our own historical epoch, and probably even among those who agree on what phenomena count as ostensibly paranormal. Many people, for example, regularly consider themselves to be in communication with the surviving spirits of dead persons, and nevertheless regard this phenomenon as belonging to a special category of phenomena, distinct from the normal and the abnormal. Their rejection of *BLP* no. (4) thus seems *compatible* with regarding such ostensible communications as paranormal. But even if the *BLP*s *were* universally shared, we would still want to know the *principle* behind a phenomenon's being properly classified as paranormal. Since Broad regards phenomena as ostensibly paranormal in virtue of their apparent conflict with something, we want to know what, in general, a phenomenon must conflict with in order to be paranormal. No *list* of *BLP*s, no matter how exhaustive, will be sufficient to indicate what a *BLP* is, especially if the items on the list can change as they do in Broad's different discussions of *BLP*s. Explaining *by example* what phenomena must conflict with in order to be paranormal is rather like explaining what serial music is by providing examples of serial compositions. The question would still remain: What makes these compositions examples of serial music? Similarly, we must still ask Broad: What makes these principles examples of *BLP*s?

It is not enough to respond by saying that paranormal phenomena are in conflict with one or more of *whatever* science presupposes and which also forms the framework for our lives and theories. After all, in science (and in life) we presuppose many more things than the sorts of things Broad lists as *BLP*s, which also form a part of our conceptual framework, and which are not even *prima facie* violated by ostensibly paranormal phenomena—for example, regulative principles like the laws of deductive logic, as well as general assumptions about such things as the viability of the hypothetico-deductive method, the general veridicality of our perceptions, or the existence of other minds, and specific assumptions about, say, the fact of our own existence.

Thus if Broad's *BLP*s are in fact things presupposed in science (and life), then it appears that only one or more members of a *subset* of the things presupposed in science (and life) needs to be violated in order for a phenomenon to be paranormal. But which subset? If we put the matter this way, we see that we need some way to characterize that subset generally.

Before moving on, we should consider briefly another troublesome aspect of Broad's account. In particular, we should consider whether it is reasonable to suppose, along with Broad, that *BLP*s are examples of things more fundamental (in some sense) than laws of nature. To put this another way, is it reasonable to suppose that *BLP*s are examples of things *presupposed* in science, or is it more reasonable to regard *BLP*s as examples of things merely implied by scientific theory? This question is important, since Broad wants to say that ostensibly paranormal phenomena seem to conflict with something more fundamental than scientific theory. But if Broad's *BLP*s are simply implied by theory, they are not more fundamental, and a phenomenon which seems *prima facie* to conflict with them is really only running up against one or more consequences of scientific laws. And in that case Broad would unwittingly be making Ducasse's mistake of tying a phenomenon's paranormality merely to its scientific inexplicability.

So the question is: do our scientific theories have the form that they have (i.e., describe the world as they do) because the *BLP*s are taken for granted from the start, *or* are the *BLP*s taken for granted because certain general physical principles or laws are assumed to be true?

As I understand him, Broad would have said that our theories take the forms they do because we already have a pre-theoretic view of the world, of which the *BLP*s form a central part. But there are two ways to understand this position, one of which is patently false, and the other of which is at least very suspicious (and not simply because the notion of a *BLP* is obscure).

(i) Broad might have been making an historical claim about idea-acquisiton. He might have been maintaining that the acceptance by a person or by society of scientific theory follows the acceptance of the *BLP*s. But this, of course, is transparently false, since the *BLP*s are by no means universally held, even among those who accept current scientific theory.

(ii) For this reason, it is likely that Broad was making a claim about what we may loosely term 'the logic of belief'—that is, a claim about the *structure* of a fully articulated world view or conceptual scheme. Broad was presumably maintaining that if we were to lay out systematically and carefully the system of beliefs comprising our total world view, the structure of this system would be such that the acceptance of the *BLP*s is a necessary condition for the acceptance of our scientific theories.

The structure of this conceptual system would apparently *not* be like that of an axiomatic system, with the *BLP*s playing a role analogous to that of an axiomatic system, with the *BLP*s playing a role analogous to that of the axioms, since the *BLP*s are presumably able to support divergent and perhaps mutually incompatible scientific theories (thus Newtonian and relativistic physics seem equally to presuppose Broad's *BLP*s. But within the articulated conceptual system, *BLP*s and scientific theories are nevertheless supposed to have clearly distinct roles. Moreover, the sense in which the role of the *BLP*s is the more fundamental would be pudiating any *BLP*s. But if we were to give up some *BLP*s, we would also have to abandon the laws or theories which rested on them; and if we were to give up all our *BLP*s, we would be forced to scuttle our entire stock of scientific theories. Furthermore, since the *BLP*s may support rival theories, in repudiating our *BLP*s, not only are we forced to abandon prevailing theories, but we must also jettison an indefinitely large supply of rival theories, which likewise presupposed the *BLP*s, and which as a result can no longer be considered legitimate alternatives to the prevailing theories. We might, for example, be able to abandon Einstein's theory of gravitation without abandoning any *BLP*s. But if we were to abandon our *BLP*s, then we would have to abandon not only Einstein's theory, but also other rival theories (e.g., Brans-Dicke) which rest on the same *BLP*s.

From this point of view, the fact that some people who accept prevailing scientific theories nevertheless repudiate one or more *BLP*s, can be explained simply. Presumably, such people fail to see the logical interrelations between the theories and the *BLP*s. They can embrace the theories and reject the *BLP*s only because they fail to realize that the former presuppose the latter.

Although this construal of Broad's position is considerably more plausible than the aforementioned historical interpretation of his view, it nevertheless rests on the mistaken belief that a conceptual scheme or framework is something with a discernible or articulable structure, a structure in which the distinction between a theory's implications and presuppositions is determinable. Granted, the distinction between presuppositions and implications of a theory *can* be made with some precision, but only relative to theories with a well-defined structure of a certain sort. We can distinguish a theory's implications from its presuppositions only when we have a theory whose constitutive statements can be systematically listed and ordered in terms of their relative importance.

Most theories in the natural sciences, however, and certainly the larger cognitive structures we call "world views" or "conceptual schemes", are too ill-defined and loose-knit for there to be a clear distinction between the theories' implications and presuppositions, or between the basic and non-basic elements of the conceptual scheme. For this reason, Broad's claim that his *BLP*s lie at the very foundation of our conceptual scheme is a difficult claim to assess. It is not clear that there is any set of beliefs which is sufficiently widely shared to deserve being considered *our* conceptual scheme, and besides, even if the *BLP*s were universally or almost universally shared, their importance relative to the rest of our beliefs is by no means clear, or the same for everyone.

PARANORMALITY AND CONSCIOUSNESS

Notwithstanding these difficulties with Broad's position, it does seem that Broad was on to something. Criteria of paranormality apparently concern something beyond mere scientific inexplicability. But what? An interesting clue may be found in a recent paper by Michael Scriven.[5] Scriven was concerned in that paper with (among other things) giving an account of what it is for a phenomenon to be "supernatural." But his use of the term 'supernatural' seems to match pretty closely the use of the term 'paranormal' among parapsychologists. So let us see to what extent Scriven's account provides us with satisfactory criteria for a phenomenon's paranormality.

Following the spirit, if not the letter, of Scriven's analysis, we can say that for a phenomenon to be paranormal, it must satisfy three conditions.

(D5) Phenomenon *P* is paranormal = df (a) *P* is inexplicable in terms of current scientific theory; (b) *P* is *so* different from those events we understand as to belong to an *order of existence* not recognized by science; (c) *P* exhibits some manifestation of consciousness, like agency or personality.

The purpose of condition (b) is to require that paranormal phenomena be *especially* unusual from the scientific point of view, and, moreover, that the respect in which they are unusual is (to use Scriven's phrases) one of *exceptional* idiosyncrasy or generic difference. These expressions, however, as well as Scriven's term 'order of existence,' are really too vague to be satisfactory. Morover, the term 'order of existence' is presumably tailored to fit Scriven's discussion of the class of *supernatural* phenomena—that is, phenomena that (as Scriven puts it) fall outside the natural *order*. But I think we can state with somewhat more precision what *we* need in clause (b) for an account of the paranormal, whether or not it is what Scriven was trying to convey.

To say that *P* is especially unusual from the point of view of science is at least to say that scientific explanations of *P* demand the use of new descriptive categories, or new concepts. But even this will not suffice, since we must sometimes develop new concepts for phenomena which, however novel they may be, are not considered especially unusual in any sense of interest to us here. This was recently the case, for example, when scientists, in developing the theory of plate tectonics to explain such things as the intense geological activity along certain continental coastlines, introduced such notions as *plate subduction*. So for a phenomenon *P* to be especially unusual in the required sense, it cannot simply be that scientific explanations of *P* demand the use of new descriptive categories or new concepts. It must be, in addition, that the employment of these new categories or concepts causes major ripples elsewhere in the conceptual pool. In order to explain *P* scientifically, we must transform or amend, in some major way, science as we know it. So perhaps condition (b) can be more satisfactorily expressed as follows.

> (b′) *P* cannot be explained scientifically without major revisions elsewhere in scientific theory.

Condition (c) of (D5) is perhaps the most interesting component of that definition. Its inclusion in (D5) is an acknowledgment that extreme strangeness is a necessary but not sufficient condition of a phenomenon's paranormality. Since the exhibiting of some manifestation of consciousness is another necessary condition, (D5) leaves open the possibility that some phenomena may be extremely strange but not paranormal. This corresponds nicely to our classification of some of the strange phenomena investigated in physics and astronomy (such as black holes and quasistellar objects).

But despite these attractive features, (D5) seems vulnerable to criticism. The three conditions of (D5) appear to specify the domain of the parapsychological, rather than that of the paranormal. Since the former is presumably a subset of the latter, it would perhaps be better to regard the first two conditions of (D5) as specifying the domain of the paranormal, and then to take condition (c) as indicating which subset of the paranormal is the parapsychological.

But this maneuver does not seem to be enough. As I observed above, the remaining conditions (a) and (b′) seem at best to be necessary but not sufficient conditions for a phenomenon's paranormality. While some phenomena which many would regard as paranormal, and which would not (presumably) exhibit any manifestation of consciousness, satisfy these conditions, other phenomena, which many would *not* want to classify as paranormal, likewise satisfy (a) and (b').

Suppose (quite plausibly) that phenomena observed in the vicinity of black holes, or phenomena connected with certain subatomic processes—or, for that matter, ordinary cases of human volition—satisfy conditions (a) and (b). Intuitively, many people would not regard such phenomena as paranormal, however intractable they may be from the point of view of science. But these same people would no doubt regard it as paranormal if a tree were to turn to stone overnight, or if it were to rain blood, or if a television set were to turn into Leonard Bernstein. Wherein lies the difference?

At this point, some may be tempted to register the following protest. The category of phenomena in which we are really interested is, in fact, that of the parapsychological. Such occurrences as trees suddenly turning to stone or its raining blood are admittedly odd, but are simply members of the class of abnormal phenomena. Abnormality, after all, is exhibited in varying degrees; some phenomena are more abnormal than others. Perhaps in some respect raining blood is more unusual than any phenomenon connected with black holes, but it is nevertheless only highly abnormal, and clearly more so than situs inversus. In fact, perhaps the category of paranormal phenomena is spurious, and the distinction we want to articulate is between normal, abnormal, and parapsychological phenomena. But in that case, our revised (D5) is what we want after all.

This line of thought is eminently reasonable, and gains in plausibility when we consider that while a tree's suddenly turning to stone might be regarded as abnormal, if the tree instead began to talk or sing, or if it began to reach out malevolently for passers-by, this would be regarded as something else again. And notice, the singing or grasping tree would presumably be exhibiting some manifestation of consciousness.

This approach to the problem, however attractive it may be from the point of view of theoretical simplicity, probably does not appease the nagging suspicion some may feel that between such phenomena as those connected with black holes (or deep scientific anomalies generally) on the one hand, and such phenomena as raining blood and trees turning to stone on the other, there is a difference worthy of categorization. Readers who do not share this suspicion, may, I suppose, stop here. But for those who do, let us consider some suggestions for improving upon (D5).[6]

SOME POSSIBLE SOLUTIONS

When we consider what might separate the exotic phenomena connected with black holes or subatomic processes (no matter how deeply scientifically anomalous) from such things as television sets turning into people or its raining blood, it is tempting to think that the difference lies in some *subjective* factor. That is, raining blood (say) would thwart our ordinary expectations about meteorological phenomena, not to mention those of which blood is a component, whereas phenomena connected with black holes conflict with none of our familiar expectations. Although members of the scientific community might have certain expectations about what they will encounter in deep space, in general the really odd phenomena investigated in astronomy violate no familiar expectations. We simply have no familiar expectations about such recondite aspects of nature. However odd black holes may be from a scientific perspective, such phenomena will at most thwart only certain specific scientific expectations. This does not mean that there could be no paranormal phenomena involving black holes. For example, if a black hole were to sing "You Are My Sunshine", then this would thwart everyone's expectations concerning the behavior of celestial objects, including those of the astrophysicist. Moreover, while some people—or even scattered groups of people—may actually expect trees to do such things as suddenly turn to stone, such expectations hardly characterize the human community generally. And it is this large community whose attitudes and expectations we are presumably concerned with.

A promising approach may thus be to add some condition to (a) and (b') of (D5) which captures this apparent subjective aspect of paranormality. Such a revised definition might look like this.

(D6) Phenomenon *P* is paranormal = df (a) *P* is inexplicable in terms of current scientific theory; (b) *P* cannot be explained scientifically without major revisions elsewhere in scientific theory; (d) *P* thwarts our familiar expectations about what sorts of things can happen to the sorts of objects involved in *P*.

The addition to (a), (b'), and (d) of condition (c) of (D5) would thus give us a definition of 'Phenomenon *P* is para*psychological*.'

Our new condition (d) perhaps captures what was most valuable in Broad's account of paranormality. Broad relied on *BLP*s not simply because he believed that paranormal phenomena violate something more fundamental than scienific theories, but apparently also because he believed that what such phenomena violate is intimately tied to general beliefs about and dispositions with respect to our familiar environment. Without trying to distill these expectations into something like a list of *BLP*s, it does seem clear that with respect to familiar objects, we do expect that they will do certain sorts of things or exhibit certain sorts of characteristics rather than others.

But it is probably a hopeless task to try to specify these expectations in a way that permits us to draw clear lines between abnormal and paranormal phenomena, especially if we want our statement of these expectations to be sufficiently general to reflect the attitudes of appropriately large portions of the human community. This inevitable fuzziness in our expectations, however, is not surprising, and would account in part for our difficulty in deciding how to classify certain phenomena. The fuzziness of condition (d), then, is not a fatal flaw in (D6). We needn't demand that an account of paranormality enable us to classify decisively any phenomenon in question. There is no reason to suppose that the concept of paranormality is that clear. We need only demand that our account of paranormality capture the criteria used to classify phenomena as paranormal, even if those criteria are less precise than we would like.

But condition (d) also makes the concept of paranormality more relativistic than I suspect some would like. We have already tentatively agreed that the domain of the paranormal may change with time. But with condition (d) it appears that the domain of the paranormal may vary even from culture to culture. For example, we could imagine primitive cultures in which the movement of tree branches in the vicinity of virgins is taken to be a kind of lascivious clutching by the tree (rather than as something resulting from the wind), and in which people expected trees to behave in this way. Lascivious tree behavior would thus not count as paranormal in such a culture, although it certainly would in ours.

I, for one, do not find this consideration particularly worrisome. The reason it seemed plausible initially to allow the domain of the paranormal to change with time had to do with the ways in which our increasing conceptual sophistication influenced our attitudes toward and resulting classifications of different phenomena. Our attitudes toward hypnotism, for example, have advanced beyond the stage when "mesmerization" was seen as something sinister. The fact that certain societies may, relative to their own degree of conceptual sophistication, classify certain phenomena differently than we do, should be no more problematical than the fact that we, at different stages in our own intellectual history, classified phenomena differently than we do now.

Moreover, the words 'normal' and 'abnormal' seem also to be relativistic in this way. In Alaska a heavy snowfall is a normal phenomenon, while in Panama it would presumably be abnormal. It is normal for there to be carnivorous fish in the rivers of Brazil, whereas this is abnormal for the rivers of Illinois. And we can imagine cultures in which public masturbation is normal behavior, although this behavior is highly abnormal in most cultures. Offhand, at least, it seems reasonable that the term 'paranormal' should exhibit a similar relativity of extension.

As reasonable as this seems, however, there is another way of looking at the matter that warrants serious attention. While it might appeal to our aesthetic sensibilities for the terms 'normal,' 'abnormal,' and 'paranormal' to be comparably relativistic, there is no reason to insist on this sort of parity. The term 'paranormal' might, in fact, have a fixed extension. We might choose to analyze the term 'paranormal' in the way the word 'miracle' has sometimes been analyzed—for example,

> (D7) Phenomenon P is paranormal $=$df P is *in principle* inexplicable (i.e., by any science).

One consequence of adopting (D7) is that if such phenomena as telepathy and PK are explained by some future science, they will turn out never to have been paranormal. They will only have been mistakenly taken to be paranormal.

From the point of view of theoretical simplicity, some may prefer (D7) to (D6). But (D7) does not seem to be a definition of the term 'paranormal' as this term is most commonly used. It seems to me that most people—including philosophers like Broad and Ducasse—have wanted to allow that phenomena which at one time count as paranormal may (or will) ultimately be explained scientifically. Moreover, if we understand the strong inexplicability in (D7) to be such that any phenomenon which is in principle inexplicable is *ipso facto* an *impossible* phenomenon (in whatever sense of 'impossible' is relevant here) presumably there can never be any genuinely paranormal phenomena. But then (D7) conflicts even more conspicuously with the most widespread use of the term 'paranormal.' We are, of course, free to legislate definitions. The issue to be confronted here is to what extent our prescriptive definitions can fly in the face of common usage. The normal/abnormal/paranormal distinction is neither wholly theoretic nor wholly pre-theoretic, and which definition of

STEPHEN E. BRAUDE

'paranormal' we choose may ultimately turn on how we intend to use the distinction. [7]

NOTES

1. "Paranormal Phenomena, Nature, and Man", *Journal of the American Society for Psychical Research*, vol. 45, no. 4 (Oct. 1951), pp. 129-149.
2. In *Religion, Philosophy, and Psychical Research* (London, 1953).
3. London, 1962.
4. *Lectures*, p. 3.
5. "Explanations of the Supernatural" in S. C. Thakur, ed., *Philosophy and Psychical Research* (London, 1976).
6. For those who care, it is at this point that I personally stop having intuitions one way or the other.
7. I would like to thank my colleagues at University of Maryland-Baltimore County for an extremely helpful critical discussion of an earlier version of this paper. I am also grateful to Fred Feldman, Michael Hooker, and Jan Ludwig for valuable comments and criticisms.

James M. O. Wheatley

Notes on Guessing

The word *guess* is commonly used in the literature of parapsychology, where its meaning and reference usually seem to be taken for granted. This is (I guess) fair enough much of the time, but on occasion—perhaps when reading the account of a telepathy experiment—one wishes for a clearer and more definite indication of the word's work than what is given. Curiosity is whetted by the preference of some authors, when they are discussing ESP, to clothe *guess* in quotation marks. For example, R. Heywood reports in a recent article that:

> . . . a partial solution to the problem of repeatable ESP was worked out by Professor J. B. Rhine. . . . one person . . . would look through a pack of cards at a given time and speed while at the same time and speed another person in a different place would "guess" its order. . . . even if every "guess" were not correct, the number of hits in proportion to the number to be expected by chance alone could be assessed statistically.[1]

Do the *guess*-enclosing quotes in such a passage express hesitancy or a more positive qualification? Are "guesses" different from guesses in important respects? While no attempt will be made here to answer these questions fully, I shall suggest a partial answer in the course of discussion. But mainly I shall be offering some thoughts on the logic of the concept as

Reprinted from the *Journal of the American Society for Psychical Research*, volume 64 (1970), pp. 286-295, by permission of the author and editor.

it is used nakedly, without quotation marks, as in the following passage, for instance:

> Most ESP tests . . . consist of long series of guesses of targets with the same probability values, such as the five common ESP symbols where the probability of a hit is always one fifth.[2]

In order to exhibit the standard meaning of the word *guess*, I shall discuss the relation of guessing to knowledge, belief, and evidence. And more specifically, I shall compare parapsychologists' use of the word with the sense intended when scientific method is said to be based on guessing and testing. For if scientific hypotheses are often guesses,[3] it seems to me that they must be guesses in the same *sense* as a subject's calls in an ESP card-guessing experiment, though scientific hypotheses and ESP calls are normally not guesses of the same *kind*. No doubt there are deviant or derivative senses of *guess*, exemplified in such colloquialisms as "Yes, I guess you're right," "I guess I'll be there," etc., but these will not occupy us. In what follows, I am basically concerned with the noun form of *guess* but sometimes, for convenience, up-shift my phraseology to utilize its verb form. Let it be understood that the latter is reducible to the former through the assumed equivalence of *to guess* with *to make a guess*. Thus, though probably the verb is historically prior, I shall proceed on an assumed logical priority of the noun.

II

First to be considered is not what the word *guess* means or connotes, but what it refers to when employed as a common noun. I believe it normally refers to (a) the uttering, orally or in writing, of a declarative sentence, or words that stand for a sentence; or (b) something that serves as such an utterance. I mean by (b), for example the behavioral response of an experimental subject who is instructed to guess such and such by pressing one of two buttons. His actual pressing of button B at time *t* is regarded as the guess that he makes at *t*. It may be wondered whether the uttering of a word, sentence, number, etc., or the pressing of a button or the pulling of a lever, is not an expression of a guess rather than the actual guess. But were we to assume this, the identification of the actual guess would be needlessly perplexing. Let us follow custom and take *guess* to denote the very response itself. Of course, one can make a guess without making it aloud or public: "Guess what card I'm looking for but don't tell me yet what your guess is" is a perfectly understandable instruction. But in a case of silent guessing we do tell ourselves in some way what we are choosing, and this telling ourselves constitutes the unrevealed guess.

The above references to a time *t* at which a guess is made serve to illustrate that a guess is not dispositional, as belief often is, but is rather occurrent. The word *belief* commonly refers to a disposition of an organism to behave in such and such ways in certain circumstances, as distinct from any particular stretch or item of behavior. Your saying "1865," in an appropriate situation, will express your belief about when Lincoln was assassinated, but your utterance is not identical with the belief, and in fact you may truly be said to believe that in 1865 Lincoln was assassinated at times when you are not contemplating Lincoln or his assassination at all. But if when I ask you when Beckett was murdered, you reply "I'm not sure," and I say "Well, guess," then if you comply by saying "Oh, I guess about 1150," this last utterance [4] of yours is not an expression of your guess—it *is* your guess. At least, it is a guess given that certain requirements, referred to below, are fulfilled. And it should be noted that when these have been set out it will be clear that the declarative sentence for which the guess-constituting utterance "I guess about 1150" stands is "Beckett was assassinated about 1150" (not: "I guess that Beckett was assassinated about 1150"). Lastly, while one might assert "I long believed that Lincoln was assassinated in 1864," one would not say "I long guessed . . . ." But I shall examine the relationship between guessing and believing in the next section.

III

Being concerned with the logic of a concept generally leads to pointing out that certain statements are entailed, and that certain other statements are not entailed, by a given statement containing the concept. Accordingly, since our purpose is to clarify the notion of guessing, it is relevant to observe that "At *t*, S guessed that *p*" entails "At *t*, S did not know whether *p*." If you know that there are 255 pingpong balls in a glass jar you cannot guess that there are 300. Here, in fact, is one of those requirements that I said must be fulfilled if your uttering "I guess about 1150" is to count as a guess as to when Beckett was murdered. The requirement is that you not know when the assassination occurred. If you do know this, or know how many balls a jar contains, you can still pretend to guess the answer in either case, but counterfeit guesses will not be considered.[5] Moreover, just as you cannot guess that "*p*" is true if you know that it is—or if you know that it is not—so you cannot guess that "*p*" is true if you are certain that it is in cases where, however, you have no right to be certain, i.e., in cases where your certitude lacks a rational basis (even if it later turns out that "*p*" is, as you irrationally believed, true). It seems that we now have a possible explanation why some writers, in referring to ESP card-guessing series, choose to put quotation marks around *guess*. Perhaps it is because subjects in such experiments sometimes do feel certain what the target is. They may think that they *know* what it is. Feeling certain, they cannot guess, and hence their calls are not really guesses at all but rather quasi-guesses—"guesses"! (I suspect that in some cases it would be better to go further: instead of *guess* in quotation marks, to use a different word altogether.) Again, "*guess*" might well be taken to designate what is apparently a guess but which may or may not be a genuine one. The quotes, as it were, would leave the possibility open.

Since guessing that *p* entails not knowing whether *p*, we may next ask whether it also entails not believing that *p*. If *believe* is taken in the strong sense, which entails that the believer is certain that such and such is the case, the answer is implicit in what I have already said. But if the word *belief* often denotes an epistemic state where doubt may exist as to the truth of the proposition believed; where one is not altogether sure that the proposition is true but is more or less inclined to think that it is, or where it seems to one quite likely to be true. In this weaker sense of belief, then, are guessing that *p* and believing that *p* logically incompatible? The question *might* tempt the reply that a proper answer depends on what sense of *guess* is intended. In one sense, this reply might continue, "S guessed that *p*" does entail that S did not believe that *p*,[6] while in another sense this entailment would not hold. For in referring to a scientist's hypothesis as a guess surely there is no intention to *deny* that the scientist is inclined to think the hypothesis true?

Granted, there is no such intention. Yet if we consider more closely the relation between guessing and evidence, a simpler alternative to the foregoing suggestion can be offered. We need not maintain that the ESP subject and the scientist are guessing in different senses. Let us try speaking in terms of a scale of evidential support for a proposition, ranging from "zero" to "conclusive": in one direction extending to conclusive evidence for a proposition "*p*," in the other to conclusive evidence for its contradictory "*-p*." Where the available evidence for a proposition is approximately balanced by the available evidence against it, it may be convenient to consider the evidence one has for (or against) it to be approximately zero. Many situations, alternatively, involve a proposition of unknown truth-value where we have no positive grounds for thinking it true, yet have some reason to believe that it is false. A case in point is given by an ESP subject who has to guess which one of five symbols is the target and guesses that it is a star. If he knows that the likelihood of the target's actually being a star is only one fifth, the proposition he guesses to be true is really not one for which he has *zero* evidence, but is rather one for whose contradictory he has *some* evidence, though it falls a good deal short of being conclusive. (If only two possible targets are involved—say white and green—then if he guesses "green," say, he is guessing the truth of a proposition for which he does, I suppose, have zero evidence.) Imagine also another sort of case: we must guess in order to select one item from a number of listed alternatives, and we find we have some evidence for one of them, not so far as we have positive grounds for thinking it the right one, but only so far as we have some reason to disbelieve that any of the others is right. This situation is familiar to those who have written aptitude or other multiple-choice tests, and suitably illustrates the desirability of so-called "educated" or "informed" guesses. Some such guesses are based on inconclusive evidence as to what is the case, some on inconclusive evidence as to what is not.

I do not propose to consider what *constitutes* conclusive evidence for a proposition or, for that matter, what constitutes just good evidence for it. With regard to the former, it has often been argued that no empirical propositions are ever conclusively evidenced or that this strength of evidence is possible only in special cases (e.g., sense-datum propositions). But these issues need not be debated here. Suffice it to say that we can have (i) no evidence for or against a proposition at all, (ii) some evidence for its truth but also approximately as much for its falsity, (iii) a balance of evidence for (or against) a proposition without yet having, in Ayer's phrase, the right to be sure, and (iv) such strong evidence as to put a proposition beyond reasonable doubt. So much, I assume, is non-controversial. And in my view it is possible both to guess about the truth of a proposition for which one has no evidence (or no balance of evidence) and to guess, in the same sense, not where one has conclusive or practically conclusive evidence for a proposition's truth or falsity, but where one can offer *some* evidence regarding its truth-value. As B. F. Skinner has put it, "A scientist may guess at the results of an experiment before the experiment is carried out . . . ," but no "prediction [is] probably ever made wholly without evidence"[7]. That the ESP subject and the scientific problem-solver are guessing in the same sense, however, does not mean that they are making guesses of the same kind. On the contrary, "zero-evidence" guesses and "some evidence" guesses will be guesses of different kinds, just as ping-pong balls and baseballs are different kinds of balls, though they are balls in the same sense.

How much evidence is consistent with guessing cannot be said with any precision. If there is enough evidence to support strong belief in the truth of a proposition, then one who appreciates this evidence cannot guess that the proposition is true. (If it is true he will *know* that it is.) But as we noted just now, one can possess evidence for propositions that, while still not negligible, is so weak as to leave room for rational doubt whether they are true. With reference to the proposed evidential scale, then, does guessing shade off into believing? It is rather suggestive to say this, but we cannot properly depict guessing as shading off into believing, because of their disparateness. Not only is there the occurrent/dispositional difference already mentioned—guessing is always occurrent, believing is mostly dispositional—but also guessing, roughly speaking, is something we *do*, believing is not, though of course it may result from something we do. Belief, like desire, is rather something that for a time gets into us, or that we acquire. Accordingly, it would be preferable to say that after such and such an amount of evidence for a proposition is at hand—the quantity and quality varying according to subject matter, context, etc.—what would have been a guess about its truth has become an expression of (rational) belief in its truth. But even this description needs to be qualified. For it applies just where belief in the strong sense is involved, where to believe is, as I have said, to be sure. If instead we consider the weaker form, where we can believe that something is the case without being certain that it is, then although we have evidence enough for believing that "*p*" is true (and none for believing that it is not), we may still guess that it is.

In these same circumstances, however, we may guess that the proposition is *false*. Let us say that if we do this, we are making an *illogical* guess, as opposed both to a *logical* guess, one made in conformity with the balance of evidence possessed, and to a *non-logical* guess, one made in zero-evidence situations. If we make an illogical guess, it may be that despite the evidence we have for believing "*p*" to be true, we just do not believe that it is; it may be that we do believe it is true, yet prefer to make an incorrect guess; or it may be that the ground rules of the guessing situation itself void any guess that would not be illogical (thus the subject guessing Zener cards is normally debarred from guessing what the target is not). So to make an illogical guess is often legitimate or justified, and perhaps unavoidable. Nevertheless, if one has sufficient evidence for believing that a certain proposition is probably true, but guesses that it is false, or makes a guess that either is or serves for an utterance of a sentence which logically implies its falsity, then he is making an illogical guess in the proposed sense. Illogical guesses in this sense should not be confused with what are commonly termed wild guesses. Illogical guesses are made by persons who, in situations where there is sufficient evidence to warrant weak-sense belief in the truth of a proposition "*p*" and insufficient evidence to warrant belief in its falsity, appreciate the available evidence for "*p*" but nevertherless guess that *q,* where the propositions "*p*" and "*q*" are mutually inconsistent. So-called wild guesses, on the other hand, are made by persons who, in such situations, fail to appreciate the available evidence for "*p*." Hence it seems likely that most guesses made by subjects in parapsychological experiments are either illogical or non-logical, depending on the experimental arrangement, rather than either logical or wild. By contrast, scientific guessing will usually be logical, though sometimes, no doubt, it is non-logical, and sometimes, alas, even wild.

IV

I have observed that a necessary condition of S's guessing that *p* is that S not know—and not believe that he knows—whether *p*. Though it is not easy to state, a further condition to be satisfied if an utterance is to qualify as a guess will now be offered. If a man in his sleep utters the sentence "I guess you're holding the queen of hearts," we cannot count his utterance as a guess, any more than we could allow that a parrot were guessing if it came out with such words. While it is hard to form precisely the requirement involved, we can venture to say that if an utterance is to be a guess, an appropriate context is always needed; certain things need to be presupposed. Specifically, for S's utterance R to count as a guess *it has to be the case that S is aware of a question* to which, as we have seen, he does not know the answer (a question like "What is the color of the card in this envelope?," for example, or "During the past decade, why did the annual suicide rate in country X rise by about the same percentage as that by which the corresponding rate in neighboring country Y fell?"). Further, S *must regard R as supplying an answer* to that question, where *answer* is not synonymous with *right answer,* but is meant in the sense that both "1865" and "1965" are answers to the question "In what year was Lincoln assassinated?"

This reference, however, to the familiar restricted sense of *answer* in which it *is* short for *right answer* invites acknowledgement of a comparable usage of the word *guess,* which is often employed in the sense of *guess correctly.* It is so used in "You'll never guess who phoned today," "I bet you can't guess how many we sold," and "Try to guess the answer." For our purposes we need not dwell on this "achievement" sense of *guess,* but it is worth noting as a reflection of its etymology, through which *guessing* is shown to be cognate with finding, grasping, and getting.[8]

An etymological sleuth might pleasurably trace the abstraction of *guessing* from the concept of grasping or getting, an abstraction that allows us to speak without self-contradiction of guessing incorrectly and without redundancy of guessing correctly. But here we shall take it for granted. In what has become standard usage, guesses can be either hits or misses, and surely in fact they are usually misses. (Let the history of ESP research attest to this.) But though guessing right is comparatively rare, guessing is still something that most people do and, it would seem, take pride in doing well. When we guess about a proposition's truth we do not endorse the proposition as we do if we claim to know it, yet an element of self-commitment is evident. That there is, as it were, a little bit of ego in our guesses is shown by the fact that one normally feels pleased when he guesses correctly, even if no reward is forthcoming: even if, it seems, the proposition whose truth he has guessed describes what is for him an unpleasant situation. To guess right is gratifying. If a guess is a shot in the dusk or the dark, then if we hit somewhere near the bull's-eye we are apt to feel it was clever of us to do so. On the other hand, a ready protection against damage to our self-esteem inheres in guessing. The self-commitment is far from complete, as it is complete in promises and claims to know. "So," we are told after having guessed and missed, "you were wrong—it wasn't what you guessed at all." But now we can typically shrug without much discomfort. "Well, it was only a guess." As Professor Ryle remarks, "To make a guess is not to give an assurance . . ."[9]

These observations, however, direct us more toward the psychology of guessing and hence beyond the scope of these notes. This is not the place to canvass the variety of motives that may lead a person to guess (a need to solve problems, a wish to win prizes or pass examinations, a desire to act as subject in an ESP test, etc.) or the different satisfactions derived from guessing right. Nor is it a time to say much about what guides and determines guessing once it has been motivated, with the result that some people are better guessers than others.[10] Yet on this latter question a brief comment does seem appropriate. It might be natural to suppose that what guides guessing is the evidence that one thinks he possesses in favor of the guess's being right. And no doubt it often is. The evidence in such cases cannot, indeed, be sufficient to certify the guess as right, but it may be adequate to justify considering the guess to be plausible or promising. Here, it will be seen, I am employing the distinction, made by N.R. Hanson in his advocacy of a logic of discovery, "between (1) reasons for accepting an hypothesis H, and (2) reasons for suggesting H in the first place. (1)," Hanson observes, "is pertinent to what makes us say H is true, (2) is pertinent to what makes us say H is plausible."[11] Normally, then, what makes one person a better guesser than another is his being more adept at sizing up that evidence which, after he makes his guess, can be adduced for its plausibility. *Why* he appreciates it more readily, or what determines him to perceive the evidence that in turn determines his guess, is another question and it lies outside both the logic of truth and the logic of plausibility. (As Hanson himself allows: "What leads to the intial formation of H—the 'click,' intuition, hunch, insight, perception, etc.—this *is* a matter of psychology.") Extralogical also is the question why a person guesses as he does in zero-evidence situations. In these, presumably, his guess is a matter of habit, conditioning, whim, aesthetic preference, or some form of ESP. Where there is no evidence, one person can be *luckier* than another (and he may be more responsive to para-normal determinants) but he cannot be *better*, in the sense of being more logical. Nor is this at variance with Polya's thesis that ability to guess can be strengthened through learning or with his insistence on the cardinal importance of *teaching* students to guess. Doubtless the thesis is sound and the insistence sensible, but surely Polya is not thinking of guessing in zero-evidence situations. What he says, indeed, is: "Ignorant and careless students are likely to come forward with 'wild' guesses. What we have to teach is . . . 'educated' 'reasonable' guessing . . . based on judicious use of inductive evidence and analogy . . ."[12] So it is possibly misleading to declare, as he does, that one of the first rules of "plausible reasoning" should be: "Let them learn guessing." Would it not be more apt, though less epigrammatic, to say instead: "Let them learn to make guesses that are as reasonable, or logical, as possible"?

My task in these notes, however, is not to traverse big questions in the psychology or the logic of discovery, but to deal with matters of a perhaps more preliminary nature. By way of informal analysis, I have thus tried to make some useful suggestions about the identity and kinds of guesses, and to help clarify the standard sense of a word that is, at least in the literature of parapsychology, a very common noun.

NOTES

1. Heywood, R. "Notes on Changing Mental Climates and Research into ESP." In J. R. Smythies (Ed.), *Science and ESP*. New York: Humanities Press, 1967, p. 56.

2. Roll, W. G., and Burdick, D. S. "Statistical Models for the Assessment of Verbal and Other ESP Responses." *Journal* A.S.P.R., Vol. 63, July, 1969, 287-302. Quotation from p. 299.

3. I do not wish to imply that all scientific hypotheses are guesses. It has become common-place to observe that a solution to a problem sometimes comes as an intuition, a vision, or a revelation where from the first the problem-solver is sure that the answer he has thus "seen" is right—at least in outline—even though it must yet be subjected to empirical test (when, of course, it may prove to be wrong despite the certainty attending its conception). In such cases, presumably, we are still dealing with hypotheses, but not with guesses.

4. The word *utterance* is ambiguous in that it refers both to a sentence that I wrote or spoke at time *t* and to my writing or speaking it at *t*. It is the latter sense that is meant when I say that an utterance may constitute a guess.

5. I note that the points of these last two sentences have also been made by Richard Taylor in a context in which they are incidental to a most interesting discussion of deliberation. In *Action and Purpose* (Englewood Cliffs, N.J.: Prentice-Hall, Inc., 1966), Taylor remarks that "speculation, inference, and even guesswork . . . all presuppose ignorance, in the absence of which they can only be shammed" (p. 174).

6. Although not that he *disbelieved* it, which he may very well have done. Consider a situation where as a guesser I am presented with five possibilities only one of which will prove to be actual—say the five represented by the symbols in a deck of Zener cards. In this situation, in the absence of evidence that would indicate which one of the five is actual, it is surely rational for me to disbelieve that the target is a star, for instance, even though I guess that it is.

7. Skinner, B. F. "Are Theories of Learning Necessary?" *Psychological Review*, Vol. 57, July, 1950, 193-216.

8. Eric Partridge, *Origins: A Short Etymological Dictionary of Modern English* (New York: Macmillan, 2nd ed., 1959) contains the following entry: "guess (v, hence n): M[iddle] E[nglish] *gessen:* perh[aps] of Scan[dinavian] origin, but prob[ably] imm[ediately] from M[edieval] D[utch] *gessen,* var[iant] *gissen:* akin, ult[imately], to O[ld] N[orse] *geta,* to get . . ." (p. 270). And on p. 253 of this work, links are traced between *get* and the notions of finding, taking, stealing, grasping, and holding.

9. Ryle, G. *Dilemmas*. London: Cambridge University Press, 1954, p. 18.

10. I believe this result is consistent, however, with Ryle's point that "[g]uessers are neither reliable nor unreliable" (9, p. 18).

11. Hanson, N. R. *Patterns of Discovery*. London: Cambridge University Press, 1958, p. 200.

12. Polya, G. *Mathematical Discovery*. New York: John Wiley & Sons, 1965. (Vol. 2.), ch. 13.

Harold W. Baldwin

Conceptualizations of Experimental Clairvoyance

The concepts used to describe and analyze a kind of phenomenon can have a major effect on the problems and solutions associated with that phenomenon. Issues that arise from the use of one set of concepts may not arise from the use of another set: and solutions that are possible when one set is used may be impossible or even inconceivable when another is used.

Both Kuhn[1] and Toulmin[2] have elaborated this theme, and Toulmin has given a good example of it: Aristotle thought that a continuously applied force was necessary to explain sustained motion. Thus, the flight of an arrow after it leaves a bow was a problem since there seemed to be no applied force sustaining its motion. Newton provided a solution to this problem by reconceptualizing the whole issue of motion, holding that it was not the sustaining but the changing of motion that needed explanation. Thus, not the flight, but the ceasing of flight, was the problem. Likewise, some of the problems and criticisms that can arise under certain conceptualizations of experimental clairvoyance can be avoided by an analysis using an alternative concept.

One of the most important of these criticisms directly confronts the most challenging aspect of experimental clairvoyance, namely, the sensory isolation of the subject from the target. Certain principles, say the critics, are fundamental to our understanding any phenomenon. If some phenomenon violating these principles is alleged to occur, then such an occurrence must be rejected and explained in more normal ways, for example, by fraud, because the principles are so much more well-founded than the

Reprinted from the *Journal of Parapsychology*, volume 40 (1976), pp. 136-144, by permission of the author and editors.

alleged phenomenon. Philosophers, such as C. D. Broad,[3] have commonly held that one of these principles is that a person cannot perceive or know something unless he can sense it, which, in turn, requires physical mediation between subject and object. It is at this point, of course, that the issue is joined, for experimental clairvoyance seems to violate this principle.

However, this criticism, which has been at the root of much controversy, is irrelevant.[4] It arises from incorrectly applying certain concepts to the phenomenon and can be avoided by an alternative conceptualization. First, an analysis of these concepts will show the difficulties which they generate as well as the error behind the argument. Then it can be seen how the problems and the error might be avoided, without at all denying or explaining away the phenomenon.

One of the most fundamental reasons this issue is spurious is that, if a knowledge or perception claim is made (e.g., to explain extrachance results or describe findings), such a claim is incorrect. This is because the conditions for correctly using these concepts are not met.

Consider knowing first. A mere claim to know is not sufficient to show that one does know. Proof must be offered, for we do not simply accept whatever someone says. Moreover, the proof must be such that others can use it to check that it does give the person the knowledge he claims. For instance, if a claim to know that the neighbors are away is doubted, it can be proved by citing, for example, a lack of response to their doorbell or telephone and the absence of their car for the past few days. Furthermore, the doubter can use this proof himself to check that it does indeed provide the knowledge claimed. However, if no proof usable by others is offered, the knowledge claim must remain merely that—a claim, for it cannot be fully validated. Finally, even if what a person states is, in fact, the case, it does not follow from this alone that he has knowledge. A person who says that the neighbors are away, when in fact they are, does not therefore know this. If he cannot support his statement, he does not have knowledge, although what he says is true. He just happens to be right.

Precisely because of these features, the concept of knowledge does not apply to clairvoyance. It would be wrong to say that the subject knows the target, for he cannot give a proof about what it is. Nor would clairvoyance do as a basis for a knowledge claim, for others cannot use it to check that the subject can on that basis properly claim knowledge. And even if what he asserts is correct, it does not follow that he knows it.

Hence, what he says amounts to just a claim.

One of the characteristics of perception is that, at least in principle, others can verify perceptual claims by seeing for themselves. Thus, if someone makes a perceptual claim and is doubted, he can invite the doubter to step over and see for himself. This feature of perception helps us to identify hallucinations, for if others cannot see one's dragon, then there is some doubt whether there is a real object there. However, in clairvoyance others cannot "step over and see for themselves." Since this characteristic of perception is lacking in clairvoyance claims, it would be incorrect to use the concept of perception with regard to such claims.

The argument has shown, then, that knowledge and perception are not concepts properly applicable to experimental clairvoyance. This means, in turn, that the previous criticism is irrelevant. For if knowledge and perception do not properly apply to clairvoyance, then clairvoyance cannot violate a fundamental principle concerning them. The a priori base for many objections is then removed. Furthermore, by not using these concepts, problems which they generate, such as accounting for a physical connection between subject and object, can be avoided. (See Flew, 1953,[5] p. 122, for related problems.)

If such concepts are inappropriate and create possibly avoidable problems, the question obviously is: What concept or concepts would be better?

In the literature there is already a term, "guessing," which if taken seriously could resolve certain problems and clarify others. It will not resolve all the theoretical problems facing experimental clairvoyance, but it may at least provide a new way of thinking about them.

In guessing there is no knowledge of the object of the guess, for if it were known, there would be no need to guess. Nor can the statement made as the guess be proved, for if it could be, there would be no need to guess. Guessing is characterized, then, by a lack of proof; a guess is a statement or claim made without sufficient information to provide proof for it. Furthermore, even if correct, the guess does not thereby become knowledge. In the absence of proof, it is not knowledge, but just a guess which happens to be correct.

Information about the object is not totally lacking when a guess is made, and the amount of information available permits a distinction between a reasonable or informed guess and a mere or simple guess. In the former case, the information is sufficient to provide a reason or basis for making one particular guess rather than another; whereas in the latter case, it is not sufficient and the guess is simply made with as much reason (or lack of it) for making one guess as another.

Consider, for instance, a horse race. The winner is guessed at just because there is no proof, and hence no knowledge, of which horse will win. The person whose horse comes in—just as much as the one whose horse doesn't—was guessing. Although his guess was correct, he could not prove that his horse would win, and thus he could not and did not know it. However, there is information available (e.g., previous records of the horses) which can make one guess better than another. One who has this information because, say, he follows the horses and bases his guess on it, will make a better guess, an informed guess, than one who lacks it. The latter person will be simply guessing.

A further, and very important, feature of any kind of guessing is that the guessing must occur in a context of knowledge and information. This context is necessary if the guess is to be appropriate. In order to be able to make an appropriate guess about which horse might win a race, the guesser must know what horses are in the race and when and where it is being run. Lacking such information, he might make up a name; but if no horse by that name were in the race, the guess would hardly be appropriate. Or suppose there were no race on a given day; it would hardly be appropriate to guess at the winner that day.

In addition, the context is necessary if the guess is to be directed. Guesses are always at or about something—one does not guess at nothing in particular. But a guesser could hardly direct his guess at something if he did not have some general information about what he was supposed to direct it *at*. The context supplies this information. If a person were asked to guess the winner of a race but *which* race was not specified, then, lacking this information, he would not have a particular something to direct his guess at and could hardly guess *at* something at all.

The object of the guess does not cause the guess, whether right or wrong, to be made. Even if the guess is correct, this does not imply that the reason it was made was due to the object or because the guesser had some knowledge of or access to the object. The guess is correct, of course, because it corresponds to a certain state of affairs, but the reason it is correct and the reason it is made are two entirely different things. The state of affairs which makes the guess correct need have no bearing on the reason the guess was made; guesses can be made for the most extraneous reasons. For instance, suppose the winner of a certain race is (correctly) guessed. A certain state of affairs—the chosen horse crossing the finish line first—is the reason the guess is correct; but the reason the guess was made could be, for instance, the number of letters in the guesser's name—something entirely unrelated to both the object of the guess and the reason it is correct.

Finally, the information which provides the context for the guess is obtainable in quite ordinary ways; for example, the guesser is told. But the guess is nonsensory, although in quite a normal way. This is simply to say that guessing is not a kind of perception and does not rely on sensory contact with the object of the guess. The guesser does not have to perceive the object or situation he is guessing at in order to obtain the information which provides the context and target for his guess, or in order to make his guess. Once he has the information providing the context, which is all he needs in order to make his guess and which he can obtain in ordinary ways, he can make his guess and can be anywhere to make it.

Suppose a person has to guess the winner of the first race at Aqueduct on a specified day. To make his guess he does not have to be at the track or see the horses. All he needs is the context of information—which he can get without being at the track—and, having that, he can do his guessing anywhere. Distance is irrelevant; he can be in New York or Bangkok.

In view of the preceding characteristics, the concept of guessing is indeed appropriate to experimental clairvoyance. A guess is not a matter of proof, and no issues about proof arise with clairvoyance calls. Indeed, it is precisely in conditions like those imposed by the experiment that one has to guess. In addition, in such conditions there are no grounds for inferring what the target most probably is. This is one of the characteristics of clairvoyance—but also of simply guessing. Calls, then, would be simple guesses. Whether right or wrong, a guess, like a call, is just that; even if correct, it is not transformed into something else, for example, an item of knowledge. It is a successful call, a correct guess, but it is still a call or guess. Furthermore, a call, like a guess, is made in a certain context of information. At the very least, the subject knows what symbols will be on the targets; sometimes he knows more (e.g., the rate of presentation). The subject obtains this kind of information normally, for it is given in the process of explaining what he must do. In addition, a call, like a guess, is directed at something, namely, its target; and indeed it must be, for, in order to permit scoring, a call must be associated with a target, its target. These features of experimental clairvoyance which show that the concept of guessing may be appropriately applied, arise from the conditions which are necessary in order to have an experiment at all. If the subject is to provide data for *this* experiment, his guesses must be appropriate to it and directed at the targets in it. If they are not, the subject might as well be writing down an arbitrary sequence of arbitrary symbols to be matched against any experiment's sequence of targets. But then the subject would not be participating in this—or any—*particular* experiment.

Given that the concept of guessing may be applied to experimental clairvoyance, there are two advantages to using it to think about the phenomenon. First, it obviates certain problems which would otherwise arise. Second, it clarifies certain problems about the phenomenon.

Since guessing is neither a kind of knowledge nor a kind of perception, an analysis in terms of guessing obviates problems, generated by the other analyses, about how the subject and target could be connected. Guessing is nonsensory, and the information which provides the context needed to make a guess is obtained in normal ways. In order to guess, no contact with the target is needed. Furthermore, analyzing calls in terms of knowledge and perception creates another difficulty. In such analyses, nonchance correct calls will be cases in which the subject knows and has contact with the object. However, since the correctness of the call does not demonstrate either knowledge or contact, these must be shown independently of its correctness. Moreover, of course, they must be shown independently of the subject's introspective report, for others besides the subject must be able to verify their occurrence. However, if calls are conceived as guesses, such problems do not arise. Nothing beyond the correctness of the guess need be shown, for a guess is just a guess, whether right or wrong. This distinction arises—nonproblematically—in the scoring, and no contact between the subject and target need be invoked to explain even a correct guess.

An analysis in terms of guessing also clarifies certain other problems. The central problem raised by experimental clairvoyance is how to explain the fact that the subject makes a greater number of correct guesses than would be expected by chance. In general, there is no problem of explaining individual correct guesses since guesses are expected to be correct sometimes just by chance and are thus not in need of explanation. However, since the extrachance number is compounded of individual correct guesses, there seems to arise a subsidiary problem of explaining why the subject makes (at least some of) these guesses.

The most immediate explanation that comes to mind is that, in making the correct guesses, the subject has some sort of guidance—knowledge or perception of the target being the sources of guidance that are most readily thought of. Such may be the correct explanation, but an analysis in terms of guessing can help to clarify some aspects of the problem. First, the difficulties associated with the use of knowledge or perception do not arise initially with the description of the experimental findings; they arise only secondarily when an explanation involving knowledge or perception is proposed. Yet such an explanation would be just one among a number of other possible explanations. Second, even assuming that guidance is a requisite factor in a satisfactory explanation, the difficulties arise only as a result of specifying knowledge or perception as the kind of guidance needed. However, these means of obtaining guidance are only two among a variety of possibilities ranging from a flip of a coin to reasoned deliberation based on knowledge. For instance, in other fields, policies and strategies provide guidance; and indeed, part of their function is to do this regardless of what state of affairs may actually develop. Furthermore, they are called successful precisely when they create a desired result more often than would occur by chance. Third, as was seen earlier, while a certain state of affairs makes a guess correct, it need have nothing to do with making the guess. Thus, an explanation for an individual correct guess, and hence the extrachance number compounded of them, does not have to refer to the target; it could be found in the reasons, whatever they might be—and they might be unrelated to the target—for making the guess. Fourth, since guesses are expected to be correct sometimes, the fact that a guess is correct does not necessarily force the inference that the guesser had to have specific knowledge of the target to make that guess. In summary, the second, third, and fourth points amount to noting that the explanation for any given correct guess, or for an extrachance number of them, does not have to lie in the target or the guesser's knowledge or perception of it. Thus, the concept of guessing can help to open new lines of theorizing.

It might be worth noting that the extrachance number of correct guesses does not have to be explained by the summation, as it were, of individual correct guesses, each one then being explained by an interaction between the guesser and the target. Quantum mechanics is a notable example of a science that has given up the goal of explaining every individual event that occurs and requiring an explanation to refer to specific interactions. The alternative approach would focus on the fact which encompasses the individual hits, namely, the extrachance number of them, rather than on the individual hits themselves. The subject's task would be conceived as the production, not of an individual correct call, but of an extrachance number of them. It would be comparatively unimportant which calls were correct and whether the subject knew which were correct as long as there was an extrachance number of them. In this approach, then, an explanation would refer to the conditions regularly connected with an extrachance number of hits rather than being concerned with how an individual correct call was obtained.

Finally, indications are that the concept of guessing fits the experimental findings. (For overviews of the findings, see, for example, J. B. Rhine, 1954,[6] or L. E. Rhine, 1971.[7]) For instance, guesses are always at or about something, and clairvoyance is always directed at something, its target. Distance does not influence guessing, which fits the lack of distance effects in clairvoyance. Indeed, the lack of distance effects might be taken as evidence supporting an analysis in terms of guessing. Moreover, if the phenomena were so analyzed, the lack of distance effects would not be a problem at all. It would be expected, for guessing is uninfluenced by distance. In addition, it would normally be expected that guessing and a person's willingness to guess would be influenced by the overall situation in which he would make his guesses. This fits findings that the experimental context, the attitude of the experimenter, and the attitude and personality of the subject influence performance.

The concept of guessing is appropriate to experimental clairvoyance. An analysis of the phenomenon in terms of guessing obviates certain problems, clarifies others, and fits the experimental results, all of which suggest its potential value. Whether in fact it will be useful can only be seen by its fruitfulness in suggesting new directions for thought, new experiments to perform, and new ways to systematize the phenomenon.

NOTES

1. Kuhn, T. S. *The structure of scientific revolutions.* Chicago: University of Chicago Press, Phoenix Books. 1962.

2. Toulmin, S. Ideals of natural order. In D. Shapere (Ed.), *Philosophical problems of natural science.* New York: Macmillan. 1965.

3. Broad, C. D. *Religion, philosophy, and psychical research.* New York: Harcourt, Brace and Co., 1953, pp. 7-26. [See also Broad's essay, pp. 43-63, this book.—Ed.]

4. For example, Price, G. R. Science and the supernatural. *Science.* 1955. 122, 359-367. [See the paper by Price, pp. 145-171, in this book.—Ed.]

5. See Flew, A. *A new approach to psychical research.* London: Watts, 1953. [See page 216.—Ed.]

6. Rhine, J. B. Rational acceptability of the case for psi. *Journal of Parapsychology,* 1954. 18, 184-194.

7. Rhine, L. E. The establishment of basic concepts and terminology in parapsychology, *Journal of Parapsychology.* 1971. 35, 34-56.

Antony Flew

Parapsychology Revisited: Laws, Miracles, and Repeatability

My long-out-of-print first book was entitled, perhaps too rashly, *A New Approach to Psychical Research* (London: C. A. Watts, 1953). When I reviewed the evidential situation at that time it seemed to me that there was too much evidence for one to dismiss. Honesty required some sort of continuing interest, even if a distant interest. On the other hand, it seemed to me then that there was no such thing as a reliably repeatable phenomenon in the area of parapsychology and that there was really almost nothing positive that could be pointed to with assurance. The really definite and decisive pieces of work seemed to be uniformly negative in their outcome.

It is most depressing to have to say that the general situation a quarter of a century later still seems to me to be very much the same. An enormous amount of further work has been done. Perhaps more has been done in this latest period than in the whole previous history of the subject. Nevertheless, there is still no reliably repeatable phenomenon, no particular solid-rock positive cases. And yet there still is clearly too much there for us to dismiss the whole business.

It is in response to this estimate of the evidential situation that I want to develop here the thesis that repeatability is essential to the idea of a natural science; the notions of repeatability and of a law of nature are

Reprinted, with revisions, from *The Humanist*, volume 36 (1976), pp. 28-30, by permission of the author and editor.

inseparably linked, while the latter is esssential to the idea of a natural science.

1. SOME FUNDAMENTAL DEFINITIONS

In order to make my meaning clear, I have to begin with explanations of various semi-technical terms. I take a *proposition* to be whatever can be asserted or denied; a proposition is what comes or can come after the word *that* in sentences like *He said that the cat was on the mat* or *He said that it was all a load of rubbish.* A *universal proposition* is one that asserts that all or any such-and-such is this or that, or that no such-and-such is this or that.

Among *universal propositions*, we have to distinguish between those that are *logically necessary* and those that are *logically contingent.* As an example of the former, take the statement of Hamlet: "There's ne'er a villain living in all Denmark but he's an arrant knave." This is a logically necessary proposition, because to deny its truth would involve the denier in self-contradiction. As an example of a *logically contingent* proposition, take this from the sociologist's Hamlet (it will be observed that this particular sociologist, like so many of his British colleagues, has difficulty in distinguishing sociology from socialism): "There's ne'er a villain living in all Denmark but he is the product of an exploitative capitalist economic order." Whether this most fashionable affirmation happens to be true or false, there certainly would be no contradiction in either asserting it or denying it. In order to know whether it is in fact true or false, we need to do or to refer to some actual study of the home background of Danish villains, whereas, in order to know that what Hamlet actually did say is both true and necessarily true, we need to refer only to the meanings of the words involved.

Within the class of *logically contingent universal propositions*, we need further to distinguish between the *nomological* and the *non-nomological.* Propositions of the former sort state what are thought to be either laws of nature or causal connections: they state that certain things in fact must happen or in fact cannot happen; although, since they are *logically contingent*, these propositions assert not that something is *logically necessary* or *logically impossible* (inconceivable) but that it is *in fact necessary* or *in fact impossible.* A *logically contingent non-nomological proposition* affirms only that this or that will in fact be accompanied or followed by this or that, with no suggestion whatever that it is necessary that this should be so or impossible that it should not be so.

To bring out both the meaning of this last distinction and the point of making it, consider a slightly amended version of the celebrated illustration introduced by the seventeenth-century Flemish occasionalist philosopher Arnold Geulinex. Suppose there are two clocks that are ideally regular in their running, but that one is a split-second faster than the other. Granted further that no one will in fact ever interfere with either of these clocks and that they are also ideal in the sense that they will never actually run down, then we can be sure that a telling of four o'clock by one will, as a matter of fact, always be followed by a telling of four o'clock by the other. This statement constitutes a *logically contingent non-nomological universal proposition.* Geulinex introduced the example in order to bring out how different is a statement of this sort of regularity from a statement of causal connection. For certainly no one would want to say that the telling of four o'clock by the fast clock causes or brings about the telling of four o'clock by the slow one. If we were to be able to say this in the present case, then we could infer that—all other things being equal—if someone were to destroy the first clock then the second clock would thereby be prevented from ever again telling the time as four o'clock. It is indeed precisely and only because we are sure that this consequent *counterfactual conditional proposition* is false that we refuse to rate the case supposed by Geulinex as a case of causal connection.

2. SOME FUNDAMENTALS OF CRITICAL HISTORY

We now put the notions explained in section 1 aside, ready for use as required, and turn to some considerations about historical method. In the *History* of Herodotus, we read that some Phoenician sailors at the time of Pharaoh Necho II (about 600 B.C.) claimed to have circumnavigated the continent of Africa. They sailed south from the Red Sea and arrived at the Mediterranean coast of Egypt nearly three years later. The interesting thing for us is their report that during the voyage the relative position of the sun shifted from the south to the north. Herodotus, recording that they said this, states that he himself does not believe what they said. He had two good reasons for disbelief: first, he knew that Phoenician, and not only Phoenician, sailors are apt to tell tall stories; and, second, he believed that he knew that what the sailors reported was physically impossible. Herodotus therefore had good reason to dismiss this story, and did in fact dismiss it.

But for us, of course, what was for Herodotus an excellent reason for incredulity is the decisive ground for believing that the Phoenicians did in fact circumnavigate Africa at this time. They could not have reported the changing relative position of the sun correctly unless they had actually made the voyage that they said they had made.

We can learn from all this something about historical method. What a historian tries to do is to reconstruct what actually happened in the past by interpreting the present detritus of the past as historical evidence. He interprets this detritus—documents, ruins, and so on—as historical evidence only and precisely by appealing to what he knows or thinks he knows about how things in fact happen in the world, what is in fact probable or improbable, and what is in fact possible or impossible. Thus Herodotus, in trying to interpret the evidence of the Phoenicians, rightly appealed to what he knew, or rather to what he thought he knew, about astronomy and geography. We, following exactly the same fundamental principles of historical reconstruction, but having the advantage over him of knowing more about astronomy and geography, reach different conclusions by fundamentally the same methods.

Now it seems to me, as it seemed to Hume two centuries ago, that there is one very important general consequence to be drawn from this understanding of the nature of historical inquiry. It is that, whether or not anything did in fact happen in the past inconsistent with what we at present believe to be a law of nature, one cannot possibly know on historical evidence that it did so happen. The reason is simply that, if something miraculous is to have occurred, the miracle is precisely something that in the light of present knowledge is thought to be impossible. It is precisely an event overriding, or an account inconsistent with, what we presently believe to be a law of nature. To the extent that we have good reasons for thinking that there are laws of nature, that there are nomological regularities or necessities in the world that rule out such-and-such ongoings, as historians we have to say that one thing we cannot know on historical grounds is that a miracle occurred. After all, what we are doing as historians is applying all we know, or think we know, to the interpretation of the evidence. Suddenly to say that in the past things were different and that miracles occurred is to abandon quite arbitrarily fundamental principles of historical inquiry. On what principles, then, could we say when a miracle had occurred and when not?

Of course, it may well happen that through some independent advances in the natural sciences our successors as historians may have to take another look at the historical evidence and conclude that what their predecessors refused to believe, because on the evidence available to them it would have had to be rated as miraculous, was entirely possible in the light of what they will then know. This is still not discovering that a genuine miracle did occur, or probably did occur. Their reason for saying that it may in fact have occurred is that they will then know, or think they know, that had it occurred it would not in fact have been miraculous.

Consider here the instructive case of the miracles alleged to have been performed by the Roman emperor Vespasian. Eighteenth-century skeptics—including Hume, the greatest of them—maintained that these stories were altogether incredible, notwithstanding that the evidence for their truth was far and away better than the evidence for any of the miracles of the New Testament. Suppose that we actually look up the accounts in Suetonius and Tacitus—something that almost no one seems ever to have done in this connection. According to Suetonius, when the Emperor was in Egypt "two labourers, one blind and the other lame, approached him, begging to be healed; apparently the god Serapis had promised them in a dream that if Vespasian would consent to spit in the blind man's eye and touch the lame man's leg with his heel, both would be cured." According to the longer account in Tacitus (in which the lame man had a withered hand), Vespasian "asked the doctors for an opinion whether blindness and atrophy of this sort were curable by human means. The doctors were eloquent about the various possibilities: the blind man's vision was not completely destroyed, and if certain impediments were removed his sight would return; the other man's limb had been dislocated, but could be put right by correct treatment . . . Anyway, if a cure were effected, the credit would go to the ruler; if it failed, the poor wretches would have to bear the ridicule."

Vespasian, who was a shrewd old soldier, did what was asked. The men were cured. In the light of what we now know, or think we know, about psychosomatic possibilities, we have to say, not that two genuine miracles occurred and that we now know this on historical grounds, but that what Hume had dismissed in the *Inquiry Concerning Human Understanding* as something that would have been miraculous and therefore did not occur in fact did occur but was not miraculous.

3. SCIENCE AND REPEATABILITY

The threads of sections 1 and 2 can now be brought together. What, we now ask, justifies us in asserting logically contingent nomological universal propositions, and what justifies us in ruling out in our historical work evidence for what would have been miraculous if it were to have occurred? It is, surely, only the fact that, given certain conditions, those universal propositions upon which we thus rely have been and still can be tested anywhere and at any time, or else that they are logical consequences of others of which this can be said. The reason for saying that such and such a thing is in fact impossible is that either we or other people have tested the nomological proposition that rules out this occurrence as being impossible; that you can too; and that its truth guarantees that certain things will necessarily and repeatably happen, given the appropriate and stated preconditions.

Compare the nomological universal proposition in this respect with the singular past-tense proposition, saying that such and such a thing did happen in the past. The only possibility of directly testing the truth of the latter was at the time that it occurred. For us, the only way of discovering whether what is said to have occurred did or did not in fact occur is to reconstruct somehow the story, now inferring what actually happened on the basis of whatever evidence is still available today. The proposition on the basis of which we rule out the ostensible miracle is one on which we have far better reason for relying than we can possibly have for relying on the singular past-tense proposition that affirms that something occurred that would have been miraculous if it did occur.

Someone may well maintain that the so-called miracle genuinely was an overriding of what elsewhere is a natural necessity, that the miracle did in fact actually happen. To this, we must reply that maybe it did happen. But what we have to insist is that we certainly cannot know, on historical evidence, that it did in fact happen.

If scientific-minded people view the evidence of psychical research with suspicion because it is not repeatable, then they are quite right. The whole object of the scientific exercise is to discover true laws, and theories that explain the truth of these laws. If the alleged phenomena are not repeatable at all, then they clearly cannot be subsumed under any natural laws, even if they do occur. Everything said before about the methods of critical history constitutes a reason for doubting, in the present state of the evidence, that paranormal phenomena have ever occurred.

But, as I said at the beginning, it does still seem to me that the evidence is too strong to be dismissed out of hand. We have a situation that in part resembles one that might have occurred, although I do not think it has ever in fact occurred, in the development of more orthodox science. Suppose that, at the time the first word of ancient Chinese eclipse observations came to the West, our Western scientists had in fact held a theory that precluded the occurrence of eclipses visible at the times and places that the ancient Chinese astronomers reported eclipses had been observed. Then, it seems to me, the evidence for the occurrence of such supposedly "impossible" eclipses would rightly have been seen to be good enough to require some rethinking by those Western astronomers. But would it have been reasonable and right for the Western astronomers simply to abandon what previously appeared to be a well-tested theory until and unless they had succeeded in developing another and better theory— a theory that was at least as successful as its predecessor in explaining whatever phenomena that predecessor did explain, a theory which at least did not preclude the possibility of the Chinese eclipses, and which at best retrodicted them? For, presumably, the old theory explained and either predicted or retrodicted various repeatable phenomena. It could scarcely be accounted a scientific theory if it did not.

Gardner Murphy

The Problem of Repeatability in Psychical Research

There are many "ways of knowing," but there are more systematic ways and less systematic ways. The more systematic ways involve the confident expectation that in well-defined situations well-defined observations can be made. The belief that Nature is orderly has grown upon us since Chaldean shepherds watched the stars and Stonehenge architects pointed their shafts at the returning sun. Among the family of the ways of knowing— the poetic, the prophetic, the mystic, the heuristic—the ways of science have grown upon us since Galileo and Harvey, since Newton and Darwin, Planck and Einstein. And in every sphere of knowledge called scientific the generalized realities, the scientific laws to which a uniform and explicit method has given rise, become the firm foundation for a society ever more insistent regarding the ultimate regularity of the events among which man must thread his way to an inscrutable future. He may indeed create chaos, but the laws of Nature thus misapplied are nevertheless laws before which he must tremble. If there is to be a benign application of science, it must depend upon discovery and utilization of the orderliness of Nature.

Now repetition is not the *only* hallmark of science. There are unique events in the history of the stars and the history of life on this planet and, of course, in the history of each of us as individual human beings. The uniqueness must be honored and its internal structure and external

Reprinted from the *Journal of the American Society for Psychical Research*, volume 65 (1971), pp. 3-16, by permission of the editor and author.

contextual relations fully understood. This, however, is largely because the systematic methods of observation which go with science permit comparison of events across different portions of the face of the earth and across various expressions of life and across the contemporary successive events which permit a recognizable lawfulness in human life in general and in the sequences which make up the individual life. Among the life sciences laws are at least as fundamental as they are in the physical sciences. In fact, the more probabilistic conceptions of nature—those which stress uncertainty and indeterminacy—belong to the hard core of science much more than they belong to the everyday reality of bio-chemistry, embryology, physiology. Not by any means would we insist that order or lawfulness is universal in the data marked and hailed as science; but as a very strong trend in the development of science as *science*, a conception of uniformity, of process, has had to be built into the very structure of methods of investigation. There are, of course, artifacts, unclassifiable events, "strays" we may call them, observations which we cannot subsume under any category. There are the "flying saucers," so to speak, of physics and chemistry as well as of the mountaintop, the Loch Ness monsters, events which have neither a home nor a rationale.

Years ago I read a charming article in the *Scientific Monthly* with the title: "Do fishes fall from the clouds in rain?" Solemnly indeed, the author traced Greco-Roman observations shown on coins, Medieval and Renaissance fantasies, right up until he showed records of hurricanes which had lifted fishes by the hundreds from the Caribbean and dropped them two hundred miles inland from the Atlantic coast, to continue their splashing in water still salty enough to let them live. The problem here is only in a small measure a problem of replication. You will notice I am not at all pleading that replication is the one inescapable tag by which a scientific kind of reality can be affirmed. I am saying that if the event is unclassifiable, then it is doubly important that it have a rational interpretation, that is, one that fits with the thought patterns of the contemporary human mind. If it has no clear rationality, its only chance of demanding scientific attention is replication. This is my first point then: the joint necessity of replication and of rationality, and the weaker the one leg on which to stand, the more important it is that the other can bear the weight to be borne. One might go as far as J. B. Conant[1] in saying that no event is ever accepted as science until it falls into an ordered and accepted system. Or we might follow T. S. Kuhn's position[2] that scientific discoveries are never accepted until an old system of ideas has long been overripe and ready to fall, and until new observations are not only intrinsically strongly and clearly heralded, but plainly offer the rational possibility of bringing in a new and orderly system. Those of you who know the field of experimental parapsychology know how very far we are from a coherent system which is ready to replace the Newtonian and the nineteenth-century types of physics. We may rail at them and say that in terms of Planck, Einstein, and Heisenberg they are all rotten ripe, ready for decay. But it will take both honest experimental replication up to the hilt and with it an ordered system of ideas before the new science has any chance of establishing itself.

The problem of replication in its broad contours relates primarily to the consistency with which certain described conditions offer observable evidence of well-defined events. And secondly, there is the matter of the consistency of individuals in maintaining their own type of performance under constant or closely comparable conditions. The former problem, the problem of consistency of results under specific conditions, is the challenge with which I think we must now deal.

Do we have in parapsychology laws comprising generalizations about the conditions under which extrasensory perception occurs—laws like the conservation of energy, or the laws of Charles and Boyle regarding pressures of gases, or laws like Einstein's $E = mc^2$? Let us take three widely quoted parapsychological laws. The first relates to motivation. It indicates, as in much of the early work of Rhine at the Duke University Parapsychology Laboratory,[3] the superiority of motivated over unmotivated conditions. Here we might include the instances in which very great motivation pushed some of the early subjects to fantastically high scoring levels, or under adverse conditions drove them to extreme subchance scoring. These are dramatic instances of lawfulness—or would be if anybody could, in fact, show that uniform application of motivation produces uniform enhancement of results. Notorious indeed are the decline curves within continuous card-calling and from one session to another, or the so-called loss of parapsychological powers evident even in big-time results like those of Martin and Stribic.[4,5] But no one can say whether increasing motivation through rewards and punishments will really work or not. It is convenient to resort to the concept of satiation or a sheer confusion in the maintenance of a favorable working attitude. Motivation is one of those things that works when it works.

The second factor, closely related to this, is that of the intensity of the affect involved in the target material, as in the experiments of Moss;[6] or another closely related matter, the intensity of the affect related to the experiment or the experimenter or the experimental partner. From Moss's data we would conclude that the affective tone of the target material itself is important; but from a comparison of different experimenters working with comparable subjects, and from the studies of subjects emotionally close to one another, as in one of Stuart's series [7] and as in the work of Soal [8] with Gloria Stewart, we become confused as to the precise role which the affect is playing. No replication experiment, so far as I know, has been attempted to see just where the affect plays its part.

From this we pass to a third factor, the factor of general attitude toward the task, so intensively explored for a quarter of a century by Schmeidler [9] with a rather striking series of successful replications, showing that those who believe in the possibility of success in clairvoyance under the experimental conditions have scores that run above chance expectation, while those contrarily disposed tend to run below chance. In an analysis by Mangan [10] it appears that not only has this factor of attitude been rather well replicated in the majority of studies by Schmeidler herself, but also in the majority of those by other experimenters. Schmeidler has herself drawn attention to the fact that attitude toward the experimenter and the experimental setting may complicate the procedure, and we are far indeed from the possibility of setting up a multivariate design in which the various attitudinal and affective factors can be combined with some confidence that a particular experiment will succeed.

One factor quite evident here when you look at the phenomena from a psychometric point of view, a point of view based on familiarity with psychological tests of all sorts, is the fact that most of the scoring levels are only slightly above chance expectation. Consequently, only a very small fraction of the variance which appears in the above-chance scores is attributable to ESP; in other words, ninety-nine per cent or more of the observed variance is due to factors other than ESP. What are the possibilities for getting a decent replication under these conditions? Only, of course, by securing very large masses of material and with heroic patience and devotion continuing year after year. Where would chemistry be if the replication of its familiar daily demonstrable effect depended upon phenomena of this sort? We may think of the Curies extracting a milligram of radium from many tons of pitchblende, but here it was possible as by a sort of distillation to increase the concentration of radium, week after week. So far, attempts to build up ESP in this way have failed. Of course, Tart [11] has told us that our model is wrong and that if we reward the subject for success we can build up a successful reinforcement schedule. We shall, however, be rewarding for the observed high scores ninety-nine per cent of whose variance is irrelevant to the issue, so that we are mostly reinforcing the wrong things. I don't say the problem is insoluble; I do say that we have not honestly and consistently faced it.

So I turn now to a fourth favorable factor which we think we have detected in the research literature; namely, the factor of a certain splitting of the mind, a dissociation or abstraction, or indeed we might at times say a concentration by which part of the mind or part of the functioning system is directly preoccupied with the task and the target, while the rest of the total living system is split off, minding its own business, having nothing to do with the target. In this way the vast array of distracting factors can be picked up, so to speak, and neutralized by those major portions of the organism which are not playing the game at all. This is, of course, a negative way of looking at a phenomenon. It may mean that most of the time we are too preoccupied with other activities to have any energies for the ESP target at all. From this point of view disinhibition or the inhibition of an inhibition, as in the Pavlov system, would be the shortest road to success. In the early days of S. P. R. experimentation in London and Cambridge, hypnosis and semi-sleeping conditions were frequently used for this purpose and of course the recurrence of the concern with altered states of consciousness may give us a battery of devices for lulling to sleep all the scattered stray energies of the hapless individual who would like to hit a distant target but is actually busy in his own intrapsychic conflicts and preoccupations.

It cannot be claimed, however, that anybody today knows how to dissociate or split a mind so as to get a consistently positive result. It must, of course, be noted that the high concentration used by Rhine and his associates (See note 3.) in the early Duke days may well have succeeded because of the morale of the laboratory group and the very considerable fear of failure. In other words, the dissociation factor was not working by itself but contaminated by the motivation factor. It is quite possible that the same high motivation without any expressed dissociation could produce the same result. Some of you will remember the name of Margaret Pegram Reeves, one of the pioneers in the Duke group. Noting her brilliant application of Lewinian "field theory" to paranormal phenomena,[12] Laura Dale and I tried to find out whether the decline curves that were being observed everywhere could be due to satiation, boredom, or something of the sort—that is, lack of motivation—or to confusion and inhibition from working with the same targets over and over again. We therefore made up an inordinate number of batches of targets so that fresh target material could be used for every call, thus eliminating the confusion factor and supposedly helping the motivation factor to work without contamination.[13] Actually we got no significant results at all. This was one of the many things which led me in those early years of work at the A.S.P.R. to doubt whether enough is known about favorable conditions to set up any replication likely to be successful while using ordinary subjects. And this pointed to the need for finding big-time subjects who could rattle off 8s, 9s, and 10s per deck with some regularity. Actually, I have never seen anything like this. I did, however, see the extraordinary case of Lillian Levine of which I will remind you here.[14] Using a two-way signaling device, she pushed a telegraph key to indicate the target in a study in which Laura Dale was acting as agent, with Ernest Taves observing. Miss Levine went on a binge and made fifteen consecutive hits which, if you do a little arithmetic, you will find is very much too high a score to expect even if every man, woman, and child in the world had a series of tries at this task. Then, as suddenly as ESP walked in, it walked out. Of course Miss Levine was asked to come back and tell her life story, take various psychological tests, etc. What we did learn from this was that during the moments of success she had seen the coils of a steam radiator take on the form of wavy lines, the corner of the table seemed to indicate a star, a design in the rug turned into the shape of a cross, etc. It was one of those cases where the external form was not too firm to allow the subjective factor to play a large part in structuring it.

However, the point which I must sadly stress in the present connection is that this not only did not repeat; it didn't even last for one working session. It is nowhere near as good as the Brugmans performance[15] which, as you will remember, lasted a number of weeks, nor as good as the Moss performance now in its third replication, nor the Schmeidler performance now in its twenty-seventh year. But it was a big-time phenomenon for all that.

Where do we stand, though, regarding those psychological laws we thought we had to start with, the laws of motivation, of intensity, and of dissociation? I think they remain benign hunches from about the time of the French and British workers of the 1880s; I do not think that we have taken them seriously and have not dignified them to a point where we can even state them in firm, clear, quantitative form, ready to be given a scientific test.

But I said that there was another approach to the problem of replication, namely, one which is conceived in individual terms. That is to say, a question of the relative standing of a person in relation to others working at a task. This is the kind of thing that would appear if we asked whether individuals maintain the same rank or even the same scoring level from one performance to another. I think it is shocking that there is almost no work of this sort to report. I can think of a few tiny little fragments, but not enough even to establish whether there is any real retest reliability at all. I do not, for example, even know whether Schmeidler's sheep contained any individuals of relatively stable superiority on retest. But considering what I said about the fact that ESP is only contributing one per cent or less to the original high scores, it is scarcely probable that the long-time work of looking for such retest reliability would pay off. It would, of course, be possible to show continuity in mediumistic performance during the lifetime of Mrs. L. E. Piper, or the big-time ESP performances of Gloria Stewart or Pavel Stepanek. This, however, is a type of reliability rather different from studying a person's relative position within a group, thus permitting personality dynamics, life history, and other factors to be consistently related to outcomes. I do not disparage the importance of individual long-range studies. I say, however, that they belong to the very important sphere of biography, and that in order to give us scientific data on the conditions under which phenomena appear we need to combine them with studies in which groups of individuals and their relative performances can be studied. There is still one other type of quantitative approach to reliability possible here, namely, the one used by Riess[16] in the case of his high-scoring subject in which internal consistency in the performances, run by run, was reported; that is, a tendency for odd-numbered components and even-numbered components of the same task to vary concomitantly is further evidence that we are not dealing with sheer flukes or so-called runs of luck.

But perhaps I have said enough to suggest to you why I think our case for replicability is today quite weak despite the brilliant thrusts into the dark that have here and there been carried out. I am going to turn now to a more positive approach in what I believe to be a feasible program for the development of true and extensive replicability of ESP research material. In a way it will be long and hard, but none of us in this field has asked for anything easy. I am going to begin by a reference to a series of studies in the general field of altered states of consciousness, particularly in reference to the observed subjective or personal world of the participating subject. Years ago this would have been called introspective data, or Titchener, fifty years ago, would call it existential. The later and more modern uses of the term existential and the term phenomenological could also be brought in if you like. Perhaps the word experential is the best of all. For I am referring now simply to getting all the possible views of the person's own experiences, both as naively given and as structured, altered, and even distorted by the attempt to describe it. I am speaking of the world of inner knowledge which has been so greatly enhanced by modern studies of yoga and Zen and most of all by those feedback techniques of Kamiya,[17] Brown,[18] Green,[19] and others in which one can directly see on a panel the course of inner activity—proprioceptive, enteroceptive, or EEG—which reflects the inner psychophysiological world. One thus learns, by anchoring the experiences on particular physiological indicators, to get more and more voluntary control and more and more systematic describability. We have, of course, the great tradition of German and American introspective psychology; the distinctions between sensations, images, and feelings, and the more subtle "determining tendencies" and the "thought elements" of the Würzburg School; the Galton studies of individuality in imagery; and then we have the area of feelings described by existentialists and phenomenologists. We encounter the problem of a mode of observation and a language appropriate to the fleeting and complex character of this inner world. We have learned much from the psychoanalysts, and other clinically-oriented students, of the world between the conscious and the unconscious, whether we call it preconscious or whatever our predilections may be. Kamiya and Brown have explicitly sought to extend and enrich and pin down so far as possible this inner world as it relates to a world of EEG and the world of the processes by which these inner phenomena play their part in the triggering of the EEG phenomenon. Exciting possibilities have been suggested, as for example the possibility that in certain parts of the EEG spectrum there may be regions specially favorable for the reception of paranormal messages. I do not know whether we are ready to leap ahead that fast, but we are certainly ready to dig in and make systematic and disciplined studies of this vastly important inner world, side by side with the psychophysiological world, which students of relaxation, students of hypnosis, students of drugs, students of peak experiences have taught us to regard with the most poetic excitement on the one hand and the most desperate seriousness on the other. Brown and Kamiya have hoped that we could vastly increase our knowledge and our objectivity in the reporting of these subjective states by pinning them to physiological changes; and we may, through a good description, proper grouping, proper developmental analysis, proper factor analysis perhaps, disentangle, regroup, reinterpret, and freshly test the series of psychophysiological states which may be relevant to the subtle paranormal processes which we need to understand. There needs to be a taxonomy of these psychological states, using natural groupings and true phenomenological categories of experience as well as true physiological units or factors. Such factors must, I suppose, ultimately agree at some level with the factors found at the psychological level. At least this much isomorphism of the maddeningly complex physiological with the maddeningly complex psychological seems to be a premise with which we must indulge ourselves for the present.

Kamiya hopes that a greatly enriched new psychology of the subjective world might result in this way. Perhaps some of our old hunches having to do with motivation, emotional intensity, dissassociation, and stable individual differences may be supported by these new studies looming on the horizon. But perhaps light will be thrown more directly upon a series of phenomena which we have not yet learned even to notice. It may well be that the more important characters in the play are still in the wings and that the whole action will change when they come upon the stage. It may be, for instance, that there are devices which we all use to keep these characters off the stage, so that not even a whisper of the reechoing footsteps far back in the wings can be heard. It may be that we shall learn by these new feedback skills where we have been driving them away; we may learn the nature of the defensive operations that have been tightening up our muscles and flattening our affects—the cut-off affects which we have handled sharply as by a cookie cutter to keep us from understanding them in their whole context. They will all begin to force their way upon the stage as we learn how to disarm our own defenses, learn how to minimize the massive forces in our society and in our own individual character which make us unwilling to confront the paranormal, even unwilling to confront the very signals by which the presence of the paranormal might be hinted. The existentialist, the psychoanalyst, the physiologist will join hands with new workers from unguessed future psychological schools to enrich our understanding of that vast system of the here-and-now which has been so unwilling to come to terms with the there, the far-away, the displaced in time which is a special preoccupation of parapsychologists.

I would especially emphasize the problem of pattern or system, the problem of interrelated aspects of our life and of the deep reciprocities between our inner life and the social world of physical and cultural ecology beyond which lies the world of energies not yet guessed, the world of cosmic relationships which unconsciously pushes up like a suboceanic volcano to break into the world of experience, whether of cosmic consciousness or of telepathy, clairvoyance and precognition, or of other functions for which we have no names. I would specially emphasize also the conception of interaction in R. A. Fisher's sense,[20] the probability that no single variable will turn out to have coercive control of the mainsprings from which the paranormal makes its entrance, but rather the more delicate problem of interactions in which major cues, as yet unguessed, may still cooperate with essential minor cues of many sorts, of which we have preliminary and fragmentary knowledge.

What a lot of work you think I am asking. Yet, look back to the physics of 1600 in which Gilbert did his experiments on magnetism, and Francis Bacon wrote about inductive methods, a world even before Harvey, and long before Newton. That world of 1600 is about where we stand with regard to any real systematic understanding of the paranormal, and the fortresses will not fall easily to the blunted shafts of today's scattered arrows, but only to the battle-axes of a very much more formidable and determined scientific effort. Even when the laws begin to line up in an orderly way, they will still, like all things biological and psychological, display staggering and bewildering individual differences which lie partly in the depths of molecular biology and genetics, and partly in unique ecological relationships between persons and certain fields as yet unguessed.

Repeatability, then, depends upon the identifiability of components and of the requisite interactions considered systematically. Very broad generalizations—for example, about relaxation and motivation—are probably just barely worthy of being mentioned again, but most of the needed work will probably be of a more specific and refined type. It is certainly clear today that the gross ESP phenomenon does not ordinarily appear just by providing large quantities of the obvious variables—motivation, emotion, relaxation, disassociation, and the rest. Challenge me if you like. Set up an experiment tomorrow using these things and get a clear-cut positive result! You know that it will not be that easy, and you know that vast numbers of unsuccessful experiments lie cluttering the desks and files of many parapsychologists. Repeating the experiments of A, B, C in the hope of getting the results M, N, O reminds me of Crumbaugh's heroic attempts,[21] with the help of two of his graduate students, to replicate the beautiful series of studies of ESP in the classroom carried out by Anderson and White.[22] Using a very adequate method and with very adequate groups, a clear confirmation was obtained in one of the Crumbaugh replications, and no results at all in the other. If this is true of our best studies, what shall we say of our ordinary studies? We will say that the data have not been analyzed in anything like sufficient detail to permit real replication. It is that for which I am pleading.

For good performances just won't replicate without the series of steps, the analytical work for which I have pleaded, both at the phenomenological and physiological level, and at the mathematical level of a careful study of factors and particularly of interactions. One experimenter with both genius and patience may replicate his or her own work, but it is very much more than this that we must demand. Outstanding today, in addition to the work which I have already mentioned, are the efforts of Ullman and Krippner.[23] But these experiments, based upon the largest personnel and upon the most extensive pilot investigations, are still very far indeed from permitting prediction as to results of the next replication study which will be carried out. The Ullman-Krippner data especially emphasize the individual factor, the replication results with particularly gifted subjects which is, of course, a strength of method in dealing with this kind of phenomena, but which will make replication in the usual routine sense doubly difficult. It will take a long time to find out whether the results are traceable to a series of working conditions or only to those conditions when interacting with particular experimenters and particular subjects whose work is being replicated.

Now of course I will agree with any critic who would interject at this point the fact that a computer of average transience (CAT) could probably comb out some slight generic factor that is usually present in successful ESP experiments. That is, one might find a way to short-cut with modern techniques the enormous mountain range of complexities which I have suggested. Let us, however, think twice about this. If it is really true that some slight effect can be teased out by a CAT, we will still have the problem of finding out what it is in the organism or in the organism-environment relations that made that particular effect appear. If we knew what particular parameter in our experimental procedure is causing this positive result, we would be more than half way to our goal, but that is exactly what we do not know. We shall have to do the hard psychophysiological work to find out and give a name to a particular aspect of our procedure, expression of which will then appear through the CAT. We might as well, indeed, be looking for such major components right now as we use sensitive equipment. In fact, the CAT will be a wonderful cane to assist us in walking, but a very poor crutch if we expect to swing along with its unaided support. It is only because elaborate procedures like those of Ullman and Krippner are available that there is any serious chance that some delicate positive factor will emerge in sufficient strength to be noted and measured. The computer will help us if we are already marching along.

But what can we do to prepare ourselves for what is needed at this juncture? What are our practical strategic possibilities? I think they are two:

The first strategy might be as follows: Just try patiently and energetically to replicate exactly whatever experiments have been most successful. Go back and do all over again the Brugmans experiment, the Estabrooks experiment, the Tyrrell and Soal experiments, the Pearce-Pratt, Carington, Schmeidler, Osis, Moss and Ullman-Krippner experiments. When you get the thing running smoothly, then drag in reluctant scientific collaborators if you can find them, saying, "If you do exactly the following in the necessary order you will get confirmatory results." Then you could go after funding on the assumption that a hard-bitten scientific collaborator who has gotten results somewhat like your own will be an active, or at least a passive, support to you with NIMH, FFRP, NSF, or any other alphabetic support to which hard-nosed investigators can appeal. This, I think, is mostly what we have been doing and the results have not been exactly spectacularly rewarding. In fact, it has been the maverick individual, not the foundations and not the federal agencies, that has had the sensitivity of ear, the far-flung imagination, or the tender heart, or some combination of all these, to support us in the pinch. Maybe it is only the maverick, spaced far out in time, that can ever be expected to support our efforts.

But there is another strategy involving three major steps: (*a*) Disentangle the fact, the ESP, the psi phenonenon, by all the phenomenological and other methods described above, getting the picture reasonably full and clear as to what the components in the successful method actually are; then replicate, bit by bit, and all the bits together, with a full, complex multivariate design to see the component and interactive aspects of the replicated successful outcome. (*b*) Then, as you replicate over and over again, disentangle some factors for specially close study, distinguishing between generic results which call for human subjects in general and on the other hand individual results which relate to the biology and ecology of a single individual who is nevertheless capable of replicated positive work month after month. (c) Then systematically separate out and also combine two or three or more factors which appear to be responsible for your success, until you get something that is intelligible as well as repeatable; that is, something which is rational in the sense that it can be conceptualized both for itself and in its relation to other scientific conceptualizable principles, something which hangs together and can be described so as to keep your colleagues informed and motivated to attempt replications from one research center to another, using not only grossly similar methods but a comparable design. What is replicable, then, in the narrow sense becomes replicable in the broader sense, not limited to particular times, places, and persons. Go after your funding for your broad support by serious scientific bodies, insofar as something has actually met the replicability test. Then, with a very, very deep breath, ask for the kinds of support that will be offered to anyone who, after this running of the marathon, this running of the gauntlet, accepts this ordeal by staff and study sections, interdisciplinary committees, editors of AAAS and APA[24] journals, official and unofficial spokesmen of the whole array of pundits, who will determine what science can and cannot allow to exist, and will be ready to acknowledge that you have reached the goal. By that time you will have gone through all the steps requisite to build a model, i.e., a general theory of parapsychology. You will have done what Conant and Kuhn asked you to do: you will have marshalled not only a brilliant little jewel of a fact which you want everybody to acknowledge, but you will have done the hard work in putting together a new system of observations and concepts in which your jewel, like any self-respecting jewel, is properly set and can shine to advantage. Replication will not come your way as a prize for ingeniously copying some new experimental technique. It won't copy, won't replicate, it won't even know itself when next you try to show it to your skeptical colleagues. Replication will come when the context of the event is well understood; and when it comes, it will be a fulfillment of a long series of immature fragmentary incomplete replications, none of which was ready to become the authentic fulfillment of our hope, until the phenomenon was so well understood that it created for itself a context in which it could live.

NOTES

1. Conant, J. B. *On Understanding Science.* New Haven: Yale University Press, 1951.
2. Kuhn, T. S. *The Structure of Scientific Revolutions.* Chicago: University of Chicago Press, 1962.
3. Rhine, J. B. *Extra-sensory Perception.* Boston: Boston Society for Psychic Research, 1934. (Rev. ed., Boston: Bruce Humphries, 1964.)
4. Martin, D. R., and Stribic, F. P. "Studies in Extrasensory Perception: I. An Analysis of 25,000 Trials." *Journal of Parapsychology,* Vol. 2, March, 1938, 23-30.
5. ———. "Studies in Extrasensory Perception: II. An Analysis of a Second Series of 25,000 Trials." *Journal of Parapsychology,* Vol. 2, December, 1938, 287-295.
6. Moss, T., and Gengerelli, J. A. "ESP Effects Generated by Affective States." *Journal of Parapsychology,* Vol. 32, June, 1968, 90-100.
7. Stuart, C. E. "GESP Experiments with the Free Response Method." *Journal of Parapsychology,* Vol. 10, March, 1946, 21-35.
8. Soal, S. G., and Bateman, F. *Modern Experiments in Telepathy.* New Haven: Yale University Press, 1953.
9. Schmeidler, G. R., and McConnell, R. A. *ESP and Personality Patterns.* New Haven: Yale University Press, 1958.
10. Mangan, G. L. "A Review of Published Research on the Relationship of Some Personality Variables to ESP Scoring Level." *Parapsychological Monographs No. 1.* New York: Parapsychology Foundation, 1958.
11. Tart, C. T. "Card Guessing Tests: Learning Paradigm or Extinction Paradigm?" *Journal* A.S.P.R., Vol. 60, January, 1966, 46-55.
12. Reeves, M. P. "A Topological Approach to Parapsychology." *Journal* A.S.P.R., Vol. 38, April, 1944, 72-82.
13. Dale, L. A., Taves, E., and Murphy, G. "Research Notes: A Short Report on a Series of Exploratory Studies." *Journal* A.S.P.R., Vol. 38, July, 1944, 160-170.
14. Taves, E., Dale, L. A., and Murphy, G. "A Further Report on the Midas Touch." *Journal* A.S.P.R., Vol. 37, July, 1943, 111-118.
15. Brugmans, H. I. F. W. "Une communication sur des expériences télépathiques au laboratoire de psychologie à Groningue faites par M. Heymans, Docteur Weinberg et Docteur H. I. F. W. Brugmans." *Le Compte Rendu Officiel du Premier Congrès International des Recherches Psychiques,* Copenhagen, 1922, 396-408.
16. Riess, B. F. "Further Data from a Case of High Scores in Card-Guessing." *Journal of Parapsychology,* Vol. 3, June, 1939, 79-84.
17. Kamiya, J. "Operant Control of the EEG Alpha Rhythm and Some of its Reported Effects on Consciousness." In C. T. Tart (Ed.), *Altered States of Consciousness.* New York: Wiley, 1969. Pp. 489-501.
18. Brown, B. B. "Recognition of Aspects of Consciousness through Association with EEG Alpha Activity Represented by a Light Signal." *Psychophysiology,* Vol. 6, January, 1970, 442-452.
19. Green, E. E., and others. "Feedback Technique for Deep Relaxation." *Psychophysiology,* Vol. 6, November, 1969, 371-377.
20. Fisher, R. A. *The Design of Experiments.* London: Oliver and Boyd, 1942.
21. Desguisne, A., Goldstone, G., and Crumbaugh, J. C. "Two Repetitions of the Anderson-White Investigation of Teacher-Pupil Attitudes and Clairvoyance Test Results." *Journal of Parapsychology,* Vol. 23, September, 1959, 196-214.
22. Anderson, M., and White, R. "A Survey of Work on ESP and Teacher-Pupil Attitudes." *Journal of Parapsychology,* Vol. 22, December, 1958, 246-268.
23. Ullman, M., and Krippner, S. "Dream Studies and Telepathy: An Experimental Approach." *Parapsychological Monographs No. 12.* New York: Parapsychology Foundation, 1970.
24. [That is, American Psychological Association.—Ed.]

Section IV

Precognition and Its Problems

C. D. Broad

The Philosophical Implications of Foreknowledge

When the Secretary asked me to introduce a philosophical discussion on a subject connected with psychical research, I felt that I had a plain duty to consent, although I would much rather have declined. As readers of my books are aware, it has always seemed to me most strange and most deplorable that the vast majority of philosophers and psychologists should utterly ignore the strong *prima facie* case that exists for the occurrence of many supernormal phenomena which, if genuine, must profoundly affect our theories of the human mind, its cognitive powers, and its relation to the human body. I could say a good deal, which might be interesting but would certainly be painful, about some of the psychological causes of this attitude; but I prefer to welcome the very evident signs of a change in it, and to congratulate the Aristotelian Society and the Mind Association on their courage in treating with the contempt that it deserves the accusation of "having gone spooky" which they will certainly incur in some circles.

I do not myself think that the evidence for alleged supernormal *physical* phenomena is good enough to make them at present worth the serious attention of philosophers. I have no doubt that at least 99 percent of them either never happened as reported or are capable of a normal explanation, which, in a great many cases, is simply that of deliberate

Reprinted from the *Proceedings of the Aristotelian Society*, Supplementary Volume 16 (1937), pp. 177-209, by courtesy of the Editor of the Aristotelian Society. Copyright 1937 the Aristotelian Society.

fraud. We may, therefore, confine our attention to alleged cases of supernormal cognition. These may be roughly classified as follows. We may divide them first into supernormal cognitions of contemporary events or of the contemporary states of things or persons, and supernormal cognitions of past or future events or the past or future states of things or persons. Under the first heading would come Clairvoyance and Telepathy. In my opinion the evidence, both experimental and non-experimental, for the occurrence of these kinds of supernormal cognition is adequate to establish a strong *prima facie* case, which philosophers and psychologists cannot ignore without challenging invidious comparisons to the ostrich. I have dealt with the philosophical implications of clairvoyance and telepathy to the best of my ability in my presidential address on *Normal Cognition, Clairvoyance, and Telepathy* to the Society for Psychical Research in May, 1935. It will be found, by anyone whom it may interest, in Vol. XLIII of the S. P. R. *Proceedings*.

Under the second heading would come such knowledge of the past as was claimed by Miss Jourdain and Miss Moberley in their book *An Adventure*, and such foreknowledge as is claimed by Mr. J. W. Dunne in his book *An Experiment with Time*. We will call these "Supernormal Postcognition" and "Supernormal Precognition," respectively. In the present paper I shall be concerned primarily with supernormal precognition, but I shall have to refer occasionally to supernormal postcognition by way of comparison.

I will begin by stating what parts of the subject I do, and what parts I do not, intend to discuss. (1) I am not going to put foward or to criticize any theory about the *modus operandi* of veridical supernormal precognition, supposing it to be possible and supposing that there is satisfactory evidence that it actually occurs. I have no theory of my own to suggest. The only theory known to me which seems worth consideration is that proposed by Mr. Dunne in his *Experiment with Time*. I have tried to restate and criticize it in an article entitled *Mr. Dunne's Theory of Time* in *Philosophy* for April, 1935. As anyone who cares to consult that article will see, I cannot accept the theory as it stands, though I think it reflects very great credit on Mr. Dunne's originality and ingenuity. (2) I am not going to state or appraise the evidence which has been produced for the occurrence of supernormal foreknowledge. So far as concerns the English evidence, this has been admirably done by Mr. H. F. Saltmarsh in his *Report on Cases of Apparent Precognition*, which will be found in Vol. XLII of the S. P. R. *Proceedings*. There is also a great deal of very impressive evidence from French sources in Dr. Osty's *La Connaissance Supranormale* and Richet's *L'Avenir et la Précognition*. I shall assume that the quantity and quality of the evidence are such as would make the hypothesis that veridical supernormal precognition occurs worth serious consideration *unless* there be some logical or metaphysical impossibility in it. No amount of empirical evidence would give the slightest probability to the hypothesis that there are squares whose diagonals are commensurate with their sides, because this supposition is known to be logically impossible. Now a great many people feel that the hypothesis of veridical supernormal precognition is in this position. (3) It is therefore very important to discover why this *a priori* objection is felt, and whether it is valid or not. This is a question for professional philosophers, like ourselves, and it is this question which I shall make the central topic of my paper.

I think that the *a priori* objection which many people feel against the very notion of veridical supernormal precognition can be dissected into at least three parts. No doubt they are closely interconnected, and no doubt the plain man does not very clearly distinguish them; but it is our business to do so. I propose to call them the "Epistemological," the "Causal" and the "Fatalistic" objections, and I will now treat them in turn.

(1) *The Epistemological Objection.* —We must begin by noticing that veridical precognition would not raise any special *a priori* difficulties if it consisted in inferring propositions about the future from general laws and from singular facts about the present or the past. It might still be supernormal in some cases. But, if so, this would only be because in some cases it might require a supernormal knowledge of general laws or of singular facts about the present or the past or because it might require supernormal powers of calculation and inference. The epistemological objection with which we are going to deal is concerned only with veridical precognition which is assumed to be non-inferential.

This being understood, the objection may be put as follows. To say that a person P had a non-inferential veridical cognition of an object O at a moment t is to say that the object O stood at the moment t in a certain relation to the person P, viz., in the relation of being cognized by P. Now an object cannot stand in any relations to anything unless and until it exists. But to say that P had a non-inferential veridical *pre*cognition of O at the moment t implies that O did not exist at t, but only began to exist at some later moment t^1. So the phrase "non-inferential veridical precognition by P of O at t" involves a plain contradiction. It implies that O stood in a certain relation to P at a time when O did not exist, and therefore could not stand in any relation to anything.

Is there anything in this objection? The first point to notice is that, if it were valid at all, it would be just as fatal to memory of events in the past as to veridical non-inferential cognition of events in the future. If it is obvious that a term which does not yet exist cannot yet stand in any relation to anything, it is equally obvious that a term which no longer exists can no longer stand in any relation to anything. But to say that I remember at t_2 an event which happened at t_1 is to say that at t_2 this event has the relational property of being cognized by me. On the other hand, since the event no longer exists at t_2, it can have no relations to anything at that time. The argument is precisely parallel in the two cases. Since memory is certainly non-inferential postcognition, and since we are not prepared to reject the possibility of veridical memory, there must be something wrong somewhere in the epistemological objection to the possibility of non-inferential veridical precognition. What is it? I will first give the solution for memory; it will then be easy to apply it to non-inferential precognition.

It is worthwhile to remark at the outset that non-inferential precognition, if it happens at all, must on any view be more like memory than like perception of contemporary events. For such precognition would agree with memory and differ from sense-perception in that the cognized object is cognized as occurring at a different date from the act of cognizing. Let us then begin by considering the nature of memory. Here, of course, we shall be confining our attention to memory in the sense of a present non-inferential cognition of certain events as having happened in the past. The word "memory" is also used to mean an acquired power to repeat or to utilize in the present something that was learned in the past, as when I say that I remember the opening lines of *Paradise Lost* or the first proposition of Euclid. Memory, in this latter sense, has obviously no close likeness to precognition.

I must begin by pointing out and removing certain tiresome verbal ambiguities. In ordinary language to say that X is remembering such and such an event implies that the event actually happened. If we believe that it did not happen, we say that X does not really remember it, but only thinks he remembers it. Yet, from a purely psychological and epistemological point of view, the experience may be exactly alike whether it be veridical or delusive. Now we want to analyse such experiences psychologically and epistemologically, without implying by the words which we use anything whatever as to whether they are veridical or delusive; for we know that some are delusive and we believe that others are veridical. Therefore we want a purely psychological term with no implications about truth or falsity. I propose to use the terms "ostensible memory" and "ostensible remembering" in this purely psychological sense. We can then distinguish two sub-classes of ostensible rememberings, viz., "veridical" and "delusive" ones. What is expressed in ordinary speech by saying that X is remembering so-and-so would therefore be expressed by us in the phrase "X is ostensibly remembering so-and-so, and this ostensible remembering is veridical." What is expressed in ordinary speech by saying that X only thinks he is remembering so-and-so would be expressed by us in the phrase "X is ostensibly remembering so-and-so, but this ostensible remembering is delusive." We must now try to analyse the experience of ostensibly remembering an event.

Such an experience contains two utterly different but intimately connected factors. In the first place, the person concerned is imaging a certain image, visual or auditory or otherwise. This image is a *contemporary* existent; and if the person who is imaging it attends to the question of its date, he has no hesitation in saying that it is present and not past. The second factor is that the experiment uncritically and automatically takes for granted that there was a certain one event in his own *past* life, of which this image is the present representative; and he automatically bases on certain qualities of his present image certain beliefs about the character and the recency of this assumed past event. These two factors may be called respectively "imaging" and "retrospectively referring."

Imaging can occur without the image being retrospectively referred. I may image a certain image, and it may be uniquely related to a certain one event in my past life in such a way that it is *in fact* the present representative of that past event; and yet I may not base upon it a belief that there was such an event. In that case I am not ostensibly remembering that past event. On the other hand, the second factor cannot occur without the first. One must be imaging an image in order to have something as a basis for retrospective reference. I propose to call any image which is *in fact* the present representative of a certain past event in the history of the person who images it a "retro-presentative" image, regardless of whether the experient does or does not retrospectively refer it.

Now the retrospective beliefs which a person bases on his awareness of a present image may, like any other beliefs, be true or false. There may or there may not have been one particular event in his past life of which this image is the present representative. And, if there was such an event, it may or may not have had the characteristics which this retro-presentative image causes him to believe that it had. If the retrospective beliefs are true, the ostensible memory is veridical; if they are false, it is delusive.

I have said that in ostensible memory we have certain retrospective beliefs "based upon" awareness of a present image and its qualities. I must now say something about this vague phrase "based upon." In the first place it does *not* mean "inferred from." Of course we have plenty of inferential beliefs about the past, and many of them are about events in our own past lives. But the very essence of ostensible memory is that it is not inferential. In any inference there must be at least one general premise and there must be a process of reasoning. Plainly there is nothing of the kind in ostensible remembering. Moreover, we could not have any inferential beliefs about the past unless we already had some non-inferential beliefs about it. For the general laws or the statistical generalizations which are used as premises in such inferences are believed only because of observations which we ostensibly remember to have made in the past. What is meant by saying that the retrospective beliefs are "based upon" awareness of a present image and its qualities is roughly as follows. These beliefs would not have occurred when and where they did if the experient had not then and there been aware of an image; and the propositions believed by him would have been different in detail if the image had been different in certain respects.

It is useful to compare the part played in ostensible memory by awareness of an image with the part played in ostensible sense-perception by awareness of a sensum, *i.e.,* by sensation. In ostensible sense-perception, whether veridical or delusive, I sense a certain sensum, visual, auditory, tactual or what not; and I automatically and uncritically base on this experience a belief that there is a certain one physical thing or event, outside me in space, which is existing or happening *now* and is manifesting itself to me by this sensation. In ostensible memory I image a certain image, and I automatically and uncritically base on this experience a belief that there *was* a certain one event in my own past life, of which this image is the present representative. The three vitally important points for us to notice are the following:—(i) Both ostensible sense-perception and ostensible memory are "immediate" experiences, in the sense that they do not involve inference. In this respect they can be contrasted respectively with my present belief that there are chairs in the next room and my present belief that England was formerly connected by land with the Continent. (ii) Both of them *seem* to the uncritical experient to be "immediate" in the further sense of being acts of *prehension* or *acquaintance*, in the one case with contemporary physical things or events, and in the other with past events in one's own life. (iii) In both cases a little philosophical reflexion on the facts of delusive ostensible sense-perception and delusive ostensible memory shows that they are not "immediate" in this sense. They do indeed involve acts of prehension as essential constituents. In ostensible sense-perception, whether veridical or delusive, the experient really is acquainted with *something,* viz., a sensum; and in ostensible memory, whether veridical or delusive, he really is acquainted with *something,* viz., an image. But what he claims to be perceiving, in the one case, is not a sensum, but a contemporary physical thing or event outside him in space; and what he claims to be remembering in the other case is not a present image, but a past event in his own life.

We are now in a position to remove the epistemological objection to memory, and to see how it arises. And, when we have done this, we shall be able to see how non-inferential precognition must be analysed if it is to escape this kind of objection. The epistemological objection to the possibility of veridical memory rests entirely on the tacit assumption that to remember an event is to have a present prehension of an event which is past. This would entail that the event, which *no longer* exists, nevertheless stands to the act of remembering, which is *now* occurring, in the direct two-term relation of prehended object to act of prehending. And this is condemned as absurd.

The answer to this objection is simply to give the right analysis and to point out how the wrong one came to seem plausible. On the right analysis *something* is prehended, viz., an image. But this is contemporary, and it is not the remembered event. Again, something is judged or believed on the basis of this prehended image. This something is a *proposition,* to the effect that there was an event of such and such a kind in the experient's past life and that the prehended image is its present representative. This proposition, like all propositions, has no date; it is not an event or a thing or a person, though it is about a person and about a past event. There is, therefore, no difficulty in the fact that it can be the object of a present act of believing. Lastly, if, and only if, the ostensible remembering is veridical, there actually *was* such an event in the experient's past life as he believes there to have been on the basis of the present image which he is now prehending. In that case, and only in that case, there *is* a relation, though a very indirect one, between this past event and the present experience of ostensibly remembering. It is this. The past event then corresponds to or accords with the present belief about his own past which the experient automatically and uncritically bases on his present image.

No doubt, the causes of the wrong analysis of ostensible memory being so prevalent are the following. In the first place, people are inclined to confine their attention to ostensible memories which are veridical, and to forget that there are plenty which are delusive and that the latter are *psychologically* indistinguishable from the former. Now the purely prehensive analysis of ostensible memory has no plausibility whatever when applied to ostensible memories which are delusive, but it seems quite plausible if one forgets about them and thinks only of those which are veridical.

Secondly, the fact that ostensible memory, like ostensible sense-perception, is "immediate," in the sense of being non-inferential, may lead people to think that it is "immediate" in the sense of being purely prehensive. And they may be confirmed in this mistake by the fact that ostensible memory really does contain a prehension as an essential factor, and that it is rather easy to overlook the other factor which is equally essential. This other factor is not a prehension of a particular existent, but is the uncritical acceptance of a proposition (true or false) about one's own past life.

Lastly, it must be noted that everyone who is not a professional philosopher tends to regard sense-perception as purely prehensive, viz., as consisting in a prehension by the percipient of some contemporary physical thing or event. It is only reflective analysis which shows that this account is much too simple to fit the facts as a whole. Now there are likenesses between ostensible memory and ostensible sense-perception, and there are striking differences between both of them and discursive or inferential cognition. Therefore there will be a strong tendency to think that memory is prehensive of past events, since sense-perception is mistakenly believed to be prehensive of contemporary physical things and events.

It remains to apply these remarks to precognition, and to remove the epistemological objection to the possibility of veridical non-inferential precognition. I shall begin, as before, by stating how I propose to use my terms. I am going to use the term "ostensible foreseeing" as equivalent to "ostensible non-inferential precognition." And I am going to use both these equivalent phrases in a purely psychological sense, just as I used the terms "ostensible memory" and "ostensible sense-perception." Then I shall distinguish between ostensible foreseeings which are veridical and those which are delusive. There is no doubt that there are ostensible foreseeings; the only question is whether any of them are veridical and whether these are too numerous and too detailed to be attributable to chance.

Now, in order to avoid the epistemological objection, we have simply to analyse ostensible foreseeing in the way in which we analysed ostensible remembering. When a person has an ostensible foreseeing the experience involves two factors. He images a certain image, which is, of course, contemporary with his act of imaging. And he automatically, uncritically, and non-inferentially bases upon his prehension of this image a belief that there *will be* an event of a certain kind, of which this image is the present representative. If his ostensible precognition is veridical, this present belief will eventually be verified by the occurrence of such an event as he believes to be going to happen. If it is delusive, the belief will be falsified by the non-occurrence of any such event in the context in which it was expected to happen. Even if the ostensible foreseeing should be veridical, there is no question of its being a present prehension of the future event which later on happens and verifies it. *Something* is prehended, but it is the present image and not the foreseen future event. Something is judged or believed, viz., a timeless proposition to the effect that there will be an event of a certain kind in a certain context and that the prehended image is its present representative.

So the purely epistemological objection to the possibility of veridical non-inferential precognition vanishes in smoke. The fact is that most people who have tried to theorize about non-inferential precognition have made needless difficulties for themselves by making two mistakes. In the first place, they have tried to assimilate it to sense-perception, when they ought to have assimilated it to memory. And, secondly, they have tacitly assumed an extremely naïve prehensive analysis, which is plausible, though mistaken, when applied to ostensible sense-perception, and is simply nonsensical when applied to ostensible remembering or ostensible foreseeing.

Before leaving this topic I must mention the following possibility. In talking of memory, I said that a person may be aware of an image, which is *in fact* retro-presentative, without at the time basing any retrospective belief on it, and therefore without ostensibly remembering the past event which it in fact represents. Suppose that this person keeps a diary, and that at some later date he is reading through one of his old diaries. Then a certain passage in the diary which he is now reading may both make him remember having had this image and give him reason to believe that it was a representative of a certain earlier event which is recorded in this passage.

Now suppose that veridical foreseeing occurs, and suppose that our analysis of ostensible foreseeing is correct. Then it is likely that there would be "pro-presentative" images on which the person who has them bases *no* prospective belief at the time, just as there are retro-presentative images on which the person who has them bases no retrospective belief at the time. Let us suppose that this happens to a person in a dream, for instance. Then at the time he does not have any experience which can properly be called "ostensibly foreseeing" a certain future event, any more than the person in my previous example had any experience which could properly be called "ostensibly remembering" a certain past event. But suppose that the dream was, for some reason, recorded or told to another person at breakfast. Later on, events may happen which give the dreamer or the friend to whom he related his dream good reason to believe that the dream was *in fact* pro-presentative of those events. Much of the evidence adduced for supernormal precognition is really evidence for the occurrence of images which were *not* prospectively referred by the experient at the time when he had them, but were shown by subsequent events to have been *in fact* pro-presentative.

It remains to notice an intermediate case which is fairly common. A person may dream that he is witnessing or taking part in certain events at a certain familiar place, and in the dream he may take those events to be present. *E.g.,* he may dream that he is watching a race at a well-known racecourse, that he is seeing a certain horse coming in first, and that he is hearing the crowd shouting a certain name. On waking he, of course, recognizes that the incidents which he has been ostensibly previewing are not contemporary, and he may recognize that the dream refers to a race in which he is interested and which he has arranged to attend next week. He therefore now refers the image of the winning horse and the shouted name to that future race-meeting. If that horse should win in that race, this will *pro tanto* be evidence in favour of the view that his dream contained images which were *in fact* pro-presentative. But it cannot be said that the *dream itself* was an instance of veridical foreseeing; for it was not an instance of ostensible *pre*cognition at all. It was an instance of ostensible sense-perception; and, in that respect, it was delusive, though subsequent reflexion on it enabled the experient to precognize a certain event correctly.

(2) *The Causal Objection.* —Suppose that, at a certain moment t_2, I remember a certain event e which happened at an earlier moment t_1 in my life. If we ask for a causal explanation of the occurrence of a memory of this particular event at this particular moment, we are given the following

answer, which we find fairly satisfactory in principle. We are told that the original experience e at t_1 set up a characteristic kind of process or a characteristic structural modification in my mind or my brain or in both; that this process has been going on, or that this structural modification has persisted, during the interval between t_1 and t_2 ; that at t_2 a certain other experience (which we may call a "reminder") occurred in me; that, for certain reasons which could often be assigned, this reminder linked up in a specially intimate way with this structural modification or with the contemporary phase of this continuous process; and that the cause of my remembering e at t_2 is the conjunction of the reminder at t_2 with the simultaneous phase of this continuous process or with the persistent structural modification initiated by my experience at t_1 . There may be a good deal of mythology in this causal explanation; but it is acceptable mythology, bearing a close analogy to certain observable facts in other departments of phenomena.

But suppose that, instead of remembering at t_2 an event which happened at an earlier moment t_1 , I veridically foresaw at t_2 an event which did not happen until a later moment t_3 . Or suppose that, even if I did not have at t_2 an experience of ostensible foreseeing, I had then an image which subsequent experience shows to have been in fact pro-presentative of a certain event at t_3 . How can we account for the occurrence of a pro-presentative image of this particular future event at this particular moment? Since the event which it pro-presents had not yet happened when the pro-presentative image occurred, it cannot yet have had any effects. It cannot yet have initiated any characteristic kind of process or structural modification in my brain or my mind. Any *past* experience of mine may have causal *descendants* in all the later stages of my history. But an experience which has not yet happened can have no causal descendants until it has happened. It may, of course, have causal *ancestors* in the earlier stages of my history. It will do so, *e.g.*, if it is the fulfilment of an intention which I had formed earlier and gradually carried out. But in most cases of veridical foreseeing, or of images which turn out to have been pro-presentative though they were not prospectively referred at the time, there is no question of the pro-presented event being brought about by a process which was already going on in the experient at the time when he had the image. No doubt the pro-presented event had then a causal ancestor *somewhere* in the universe, if the Law of Universal Causation be true. But, as a rule, this causal ancestor was completely outside the mind and the body of the experient.

So the causal objection comes to this. At the time when a certain person had an image which was pro-presentative of a certain event, that event cannot have had any causal descendants. And, in many cases, its causal ancestors lay wholly outside the experient's body and mind. How, then, could we possibly account for the occurrence in this person at this particular moment of an image which is pro-presentative of this particular future event? The pro-presented event had no causal representative, either ancestor or descendant, in the experient at the time when his pro-presentative image of it occurred.

Before considering the causal objection it is desirable to consider a little more fully the analogy between ostensible remembering and ostensible foreseeing. In my definition and analysis of "ostensible remembering" I said that the experient judges that there was a certain event *in his own past life,* of which the image which he is now having is the present representative. Now it might justly be objected that this is too narrow. We claim to remember events which are not our own experiences; thus, *e.g.,* a person who had been to King George VI's coronation would claim to remember the coronation. On the other hand, it would be contrary to English usage to claim to remember an event which was neither a past experience of one's own, *e.g.,* an attack of toothache, nor the object of a past perception of one's own. Nobody now alive could properly say that he remembers George III's coronation, because no one who is now alive witnessed that event.

Consider now the case of Miss Moberley and Miss Jourdain, the experients who wrote the book *An Adventure.* They claimed to have non-inferential veridical postcognition of certain events which happened at Versailles during the French Revolution. But they did not claim to *remember* those events; and, if they had done so, they would have been understood to be claiming to have pre-existed their present bodies, to have animated other bodies at the time of the French Revolution, and to have witnessed these events when they were happening.

I shall express this limitation, which is part of the definition of "memory," by saying that memory is veridical non-inferential postcognition which is "intra-subjectively circumscribed."

Now this is, so far, merely a question of the meanings and usages of words. But we now come to a point which is not verbal. It is this. We always assume that every normal veridical postcognition is *either* intra-subjectively circumscribed *or* is due to inference from observed present facts and general laws *or* is due to hearing reports or reading records made by other human beings. When our attention is called to an alleged case of veridical postcognition which is apparently not intra-subjectively circumscribed and yet apparently does not rest either on inference or on testimony, such as the case presented by Miss Moberley and Miss Jourdain, we feel extremely puzzled. If we accept it as veridical and as too detailed to be due to chance coincidence, we have to regard it as supernormal, and we try to bring it under our general rule in one way or another. Thus, *e.g.,* some people would try to assimilate it to memory by suggesting that the minds of these two ladies had pre-existed their present bodies, and that they had been witnesses (in bodies, which they had previously animated) of the events which they postcognized in a subsequent incarnation. Others would try to assimilate it to knowledge based on testimony by suggesting that the souls of the persons concerned in these incidents at Versailles in the eighteenth century survived and communicated telepathically with these ladies in the twentieth century. Others again would try to assimilate it to looking at an old photograph, depicting a past scene, which was taken when the scene was still present and has been preserved.

Plainly the difficulty which makes people fly to these rather far-fetched suggestions is a *causal* difficulty. If we adopt any of these suggestions, we can see, at least in outline, a continuous causal chain connecting the original events with the occurrence of the postcognition of them. On either of these theories the original events would be factors in a certain total state of affairs in the eighteenth century which is a causal ancestor of the subsequent postcognitive experience in the twentieth century. But, unless we accept one or other of these suggestions, there seems to be no continuous causal connexion between the occurrence of the postcognitive experiences and the events which are postcognized. In that case why should the images which occurred in the minds of Miss Moberley and Miss Jourdain at a certain moment have corresponded to *any* actual past event? And why should they have corresponded to the particular past event to which they did correspond, rather than to any other of the infinitely numerous events in the past history of the world which these ladies had never witnessed?

Now it is evident that we must draw a distinction among ostensible precognitions like that which I have just been drawing among ostensible postcognitions. In the first place, there will be intra-subjectively circumscribed ostensible precognitions. Here the events which are ostensibly precognized are either future experiences of the subject or are events which he will himself perceive. Secondly, there may be ostensible precognitions which are not intra-subjectively circumscribed. Here the events which are ostensibly precognized are neither experiences of the subject nor events which he will perceive.

Among events of the latter kind three sub-classes must be distinguished:—(i) Those whose occurrence will be reported to the subject or verified by his own observations and inferences *after* they have happened. (ii) Those which the subject will be able, at some *intermediate* date to anticipate with reasonable confidence by normal means from information which will by then be available to him. (iii) Those which fall under neither of these headings. Now the first and the second of these sub-classes could easily be assimilated to the class of intra-subjectively circumscribed veridical precognitions. For it might be suggested that, in these cases, what the subject primarily precognizes is the report which he will in future hear or read, or the anticipation which he will later make on the basis of data which will then be available to him.

Now only intra-subjectively circumscribed veridical precognitions, in the strictest sense, would be analogous to memories. The first sub-class of precognitions which are not intra-subjectively circumscribed would be analogous to remembering a report which one had heard or read, of an event which one had not personally witnessed. The second sub-class would be analogous to remembering an inference which one had made, to the effect that a certain event had probably happened at some earlier date. It is only the third sub-class which would be analogous to the completely anomalous kind of veridical postcognition which is alleged to have happened to Miss Moberley and Miss Jourdain. From the nature of the case most ostensible precognitions which have been shown to be veridical are either intra-subjectively circumscribed or fall into the first or the second of our two sub-classes. The following would be an instance of our third sub-class. Suppose that I have an ostensible precognition of a certain event, that I write it down without mentioning it to anyone, and that I die before it is due for fulfilment. Suppose that my executors find the prediction among my papers, and that it is subsequently fulfilled. This would fall into our third sub-class, and would be analogous to the veridical postcognition claimed by Miss Moberley and Miss Jourdain.

So far I have been pointing out analogies between ostensible postcognition and ostensible precognition. But now we must note the difference in our attitude towards the two. We have not the least *a priori* objection to the possibility of veridical memory. But our *a priori* objection to the possibility of that kind of veridical precognition which would most closely resemble memory is almost as strong as our *a priori* objection to the possibility of that kind of veridical precognition which would resemble the anomalous postcognitive experiences of Miss Moberley and Miss Jourdain. This difference in our attitude is bound up with the causal objection, as I will now show.

Even if what I veridically precognize is an experience which *I* am going to have or is an event which *I* am going to witness, there seems to be no possible causal explanation of why a certain image which I now have should correspond to *any* future event or to *this* rather than to any other of the infinitely numerous events which will happen from now onwards. The complete cause of the occurrence of a present image in my mind must be in the *past*. If this image is pro-presentative of a certain event, the event which it pro-presents is in the *future*. In the case of memory the causal explanation is in terms of a "trace," left in the subject by a past experience, and a present "reminder." The trace is the present causal descendant in him of a certain past experience of his; and the reminder is some present experience of his which stirs up this particular trace. The immediate causal condition of the ostensible memory-experience is the present excitement of *this* trace. It therefore seems intelligible that the present ostensible memory should correspond to a certain past event, viz., to that particular experience which was the causal progenitor of this particular trace. But there cannot now be in a person a "trace" of an experience which he has not yet had. And, unless there is now in him something analogous to a "trace" of a future experience, how can anything that happens to him here and now play the part which is played by a "reminder" in memory? What conceivable causal account, then, can be given of veridical non-inferential precognition, even when it is confined to the subject's own future experiences or to events which he will personally witness?

In face of this causal difficulty, which attaches equally to *all* ostensibly non-inferential veridical precognition, we tend to act as many people have acted in face of the anomalous kind of ostensibly non-inferential veridical postcognition claimed by Miss Moberley and Miss Jourdain. We tend to fall back upon one or other of the following five theories:—(i) That the subject has himself subconsciously inferred, from data which he has subconsciously noted, that a certain event will probably happen in a certain context; and that the results of this inference have emerged into consciousness in the form of an ostensibly non-inferential veridical precognition. (ii) That the subject himself has subconsciously formed an intention to bring about a certain event, and has initiated a course of action which is likely to fulfill this intention; and that the veridical precognition is a by-product in consciousness of this subconscious intention. (iii) That the occurrence of the ostensible precognition, however it may have been caused, sets up a desire for its fulfilment; and that this sets up processes, of which the subject remains unaware, which tend to bring about the ostensibly precognized event and thus to verify the precognition. (iv) That some other human being, now living on earth, has consciously or unconsciously inferred that a certain event will probably happen in a certain context, or has formed a conscious or unconscious intention of bringing it about; that knowledge of his inference or of his intention has been conveyed telepathically to the subconscious part of the subject's mind; that the information, thus subconsciously received, emerges into the subject's consciousness in the form of an ostensible non-inferential precognition that this event will happen; and that this is correct, either because the other man's inference was sound or because the other man's intention is eventually carried out. (v) This theory is the same as the fourth, except that we now substitute the phrase "some non-human person or the surviving soul of some dead man" for the phrase "some other human being, now living on earth." We may, if we like, ascribe to such minds a much greater knowledge of past and present facts and general laws and much greater powers of inference than those possessed by any human being now living on earth.

These five alternative theories are not, of course, mutually exclusive. The first three of them do not *explicitly* involve any super-normal factor. But I think it is certain that a great deal of the alleged evidence for veridical foreseeing could not be fitted into them except on the assumption that human beings have supernormal powers of perception, of inference, and of action on the external world. The fourth involves no supernormal *agents*, but it does presuppose the supernormal *process* of telepathic conveyance of information from one embodied human mind to another which may be in no obviously close relationship with it at the time. It would seem, however, that some such process as this has to be postulated in order to account for many well-attested facts of mediumship which have nothing ostensibly precognitive about them. The fifth theory involves both supernormal processes and supernormal agents, for the existence of which we have little, if any, independent evidence. It is, therefore, to be avoided if possible. Yet, if there were many well-attested cases of veridical ostensibly non-inferential precognition which could not be brought under any of the first four heads, we might be forced to accept the fifth theory as a *pis aller* in view of the causal difficulties.

All these rather fantastic theories are proposed in order to avoid the causal difficulty about veridical foreseeing. Is that difficulty genuine and insuperable? Let us consider what a person means when he says that the available evidence suffices to show that there is veridical foreseeing. Plainly he does not mean simply that in many cases a later event, which a person had no rational ground for expecting, *happens* to accord to a very high degree with an earlier experience in this person of ostensible foreseeing. He means that there is an amount of accordance between such subsequent events and ostensible foreseeings which is too great to be ascribed to "chance coincidence." He may admit that, if each case stood alone, it might be reasonable to count it as a chance coincidence. But he asserts that, when the reported cases are taken together, this view of the accordance between ostensible foreseeings and subsequent events cannot reasonably be held.

Now we are not concerned here with the truth or falsity of this opinion, but with its implications. What is implied by saying that a certain correlation between the intrinsic characteristics of x and those of y is not a "chance coincidence"? It is equivalent to saying that this correlation is due either (*a*) to x being a cause-factor in a causal ancestor of y or (*b*) to y being a cause-factor in a causal ancestor of x, or (*c*) to x and y being effect-factors in causal descendants of a common causal ancestor z. Suppose now that x is an ostensible foreseeing or an image which turns out to have been pro-presentative, and suppose that y is a subsequent event whose concordance with x is said to be "something more than a chance coincidence." Alternative (*b*) is ruled out by the self-evident general principle that an event cannot be a cause-factor until it has happened, and that it can then be a factor only in determining *later* events. We are thus left with alternatives (*a*) and (*c*). The first of these alternatives is equivalent to saying that the ostensible foreseeing or the pro-presentative image was a cause-factor in a causal ancestor of the event which subsequently verified it. The theory (iii) in our enumeration of five theories above is an instance of this alternative. The other alternative is equivalent to saying that there is a certain causal ancestor which has a series of successive causal descendants, that the ostensible foreseeing or the pro-presentative image is an effect-factor in one of the earlier of these causal descendants, and that the event which verifies it is an effect-factor in one of the later of them. Theory (ii) in our enumeration above is an instance of this alternative.

Since we are tied down to alternatives (*a*) (*b*), and (*c*) by the definition of "not being a chance coincidence," and since (*b*) is excluded by a principle about causation which appears to be self-evident, it would seem to be legitimate to infer that all possible theories about veridical ostensible foreseeing must be variations on the following four themes:—(i) That the concordance between an ostensible foreseeing or a pro-presentative image and a certain subsequent event, however detailed it may be and however numerous may be the instances of it, is merely a chance coincidence. (ii) That the precognitive experience is only ostensibly non-inferential, but really depends on inference either in the subject himself or in some other mind; and that the pro-presentative image is just a by-product which arises in the subject's mind as a result of inferring a certain conclusion about the future. (iii) That the ostensible foreseeing or the pro-presentative image is a cause-factor in a causal ancestor of the event which subsequently fulfills it. (iv) That there is a certain causal ancestor which has a series of successive causal descendants, that the ostensible foreseeing or the pro-presentative image is an effect-factor in one of the earlier of these, and that the event which subsequently verifies it is an effect-factor in one of the later of them. If this be granted, the fundamental difficulty of the subject is this. It is alleged that ostensible foreseeings have been verified by subsequent events too often and too accurately to allow us to accept the first alternative. On the other hand, many of the best cases are such that it is impossible to bring them under any of the remaining three alternatives unless we postulate additional dimensions of space or agents and causal laws which are quite unfamiliar and for which we have no independent evidence.

If I were faced with a choice between these evils, I should consider that the least of them is to postulate additional dimensions of space, provided that this will account for the facts. If I thought, as Mr. Dunne seems to do, that I should have to postulate an unending series of dimensions and then an "observer at infinity" (who would plainly have to be the last term of a series which, by hypothesis, could have no last term), I should, of course, reject this alternative as nonsensical. But it is certain that these extravagances are not needed in order to account for the possiblity of veridical ostensible foreseeing on the lines of Mr. Dunne's theory. For this purpose five, and only five, spatial dimensions are needed. The fallacy which caused Mr. Dunne to embark on his wild-goose chase after the "observer at infinity" can easily be detected and avoided. Therefore there is no *prima facie* objection to a theory which tries to explain veridical ostensible foreseeing in the way in which Mr. Dunne tries to do so. And, although I am wholly dissatisfied with Mr. Dunne's detailed explanation, as it stands, because I cannot see what would correspond in the physical and mental world to the various geometrically defined entities involved in the theory, I do think that there is at least a chance of working out a satisfactory theory on his general lines.

If this much be granted, I think it is obviously preferable to postulate a five-dimensional space rather than to pursue the other alternatives that I have enumerated. After all, nothing could be more completely contingent than the apparent fact that the space of nature has just three dimensions. As Hinton showed, there are some physical facts which would be rather neatly explained by the assumption that it has four dimensions. The assumption of a fifth dimension, in order to explain certain very odd cognitive phenomena, is internally consistent and intelligible, and we have no ground for holding it to be antecedently improbable. I do not think that this can be said of any of the other alternatives open to us.

If I were wise, I should leave the matter at this point. But I propose to "go in off the deep end" while I am about it, and to make a perfectly fantastic suggestion. I believe that this suggestion is of some interest on two grounds: (i) So far as I can see, it is the one and only way in which the prehensive analysis of ostensible foreseeing, which we rejected long ago, could possibly be made intelligible and rehabilitated. And (ii) even if we continue to reject the prehensive analysis, the suggestion would enable us to deal with the causal difficulty in a way which we have hitherto shunned as impossible.

It will be remembered that we rejected the prehensive analysis of ostensible foreseeing because it entails that an event which has not yet happened "co-exists with" the foreseeing of it, and therefore in some sense "already exists." Let us ask ourselves now whether there is any possible way of giving a meaning to such apparently nonsensical statements.

So far as I can see, the only way in which a sense could be given to such statements would be to ascribe a second dimension to time. A point which is *east* of another point may be either *north* of, or *south* of, or in the *same latitude* as the latter. Suppose that "east of" corresponds to "later than" in the only temporal dimension that we ordinarily recognize. And suppose that there were a second temporal dimension and that "later than" in this dimension corresponds to "north of" in the case of points on the earth's surface. Then an event which is "after" a certain other event, in the only temporal dimension which we ordinarily recognize, might be either "after" or "before" or "simultaneous with" this other event in the second temporal dimension which persons who accept a prehensive analysis of foreseeing would have to postulate.

Now, if we had to postulate a hitherto unsuspected second dimension of time, we should have to revise all our "axioms" about the connexion between time and causation. We might have to say that x cannot be a causal ancestor of y unless x is before y in *at least one* temporal dimension; but that x can be a causal ancestor of y, provided it is before y in *one* temporal dimension even if it be after y, in the other temporal dimension. Nothing could seem more self-evident to most people than the proposition that a material object could not get into or out of a continuous spherical shell unless a hole were made in the latter. Yet it is easy to show that this proposition is not *intrinsically* necessary, but is only a necessary consequence of the quite contingent proposition that the space of nature has but three dimensions.

It may be worth while to develop this very wild suggestion a little further. Consider any two points x and y on the earth's surface. Let us represent the proposition "x is due north of y" by the symbol xNNy; and let us use similar symbols, *mutatis mutandis,* for the other possibilities. Then there are eight possible spatial relations in which x may stand to y, viz., (1) xNNy, (2) xNEy, (3) xEEy, (4) xESy, (5) xSSy, (6) xSWy, (7) xWWy, and (8) xWNy, The corresponding relations in which y may stand to x are, of course, (i) ySSx, (ii) ySWx, (iii) yWWx, (iv) yWNx, (v) yNNx, (vi) yNEx, (vii) yEEx, and (viii) yESx. A person who could recognize the distinction of east and west but not that of north and south would lump together cases (1) and (5) and say that x and y "coincide in position" in each case. He would lump together cases (2), (3) and (4), and would say that x is "east" of y in each case; and he would lump together cases (6), (7) and (8), and would say that x is "west" of y in each case.

Now we supposed above that the temporal relation "after," in the one temporal dimension which is familiar to us, is analogous to the spatial relation "east of." And we supposed that "after," in the second temporal dimension with which we are not normally acquainted, is analogous to the spatial relation "north of." Let us denote "after" and "before," in the first temporal dimension, by A and B respectively; and let us denote "after" and "before," in the second temporal dimension, by α and β respectively. Then, in the spatial analogue, A corresponds to E, B to W, α to N, and β to S.

Suppose now that x and y are two events. If a person judges that x is *simultaneous with y*, it may be that (*a*) *x* is simultaneous with *y* in both temporal dimensions, or (*b*) *x* is simultaneous with *y* in the first and before *y* in the second, or (*c*) that *x* is simultaneous with *y* in the first and after *y* in the second. These alternatives may be symbolized respectively by $x \equiv y$, $x\beta\beta y$, and $x\alpha\alpha y$. There is no spatial analogue to (*a*); but (*b*) is analogous to xSSy, and (*c*) is analogous to xNNy. Next let us suppose that a person judges that *x* is *before y*. Then it may be that (*a*) *x* is before *y* in both dimensions, or (*b*) that *x* is before *y* in the first dimension and simultaneous with *y* in the second, or (*c*) that *x* is before *y* in the first dimension and after *y* in the second. These alternatives may be symbolized respectively by xBβy, xBBy and xBαy; and they correspond respectively to xWSy, xWWy and xWNy in the spatial analogy. Lastly, let us suppose that a person judges that *x* is *after y*. Then it may be that (*a*) *x* is after *y* in both dimensions, or (*b*) that *x* is after *y* in the first dimension and is simultaneous with *y* in the second, or (*c*) that *x* is after *y* in the first dimension and before *y* in the second. These alternatives may be symbolized respectively as xAαy, xAAy and xAβy; and they correspond respectively to xENy, xEEy and xESy in the spatial analogy.

Now let us suppose that the true rule about the connexion between causation and temporal relations is the following:—An event *x* can be a cause-factor in a causal ancestor of an event *y* if, and only if, *x* is *before y* in *at least one* of the two temporal dimensions. (The spatial analogue is that it is necessary and sufficient that *x* should be *either west or south* of *y*.) Plainly these conditions are fulfilled in the following five cases and in them only, viz., xAβy, $x\beta\beta y$, $x\beta$By, xBBy and xBαy. (These correspond to xESy, xSSy, xSWy, xWWy and xWNy, respectively, in the spatial analogy.) How would these five cases appear to a person who recognizes only the B-A dimension of time? In the first he would judge that *x* is *after y;* in the second he would judge that *x* is *simultaneous with y;* and in the remaining three he would judge that *x* is *before y*. Thus, other things being equal, the cases in which it would appear to him that a *later* event is a cause-factor in a causal ancestor of an *earlier* event would be only one-fourth as numerous as the cases in which it would appear to him that this causal relation relates an earlier event to a later one or relates two simultaneous events to each other. And it is easy to conceive of special conditions which would reduce this proportion enormously below one-fourth. This would be so if, for some reason, there is a very high negative correlation between standing in the A-relation to an event and standing in the β-relation to the same event.

There is one more point to be noticed before leaving this topic. The relations from y to x which are equivalent to the five relations from x to y enumerated above are, respectively, $y\alpha Bx$, $y\alpha\alpha x$, $yA\alpha x$, $yAAx$, and $y\beta Ax$. Let us now apply our rule about causation to these. We see that y could be a cause-factor in a causal ancestor of x in the *first* and the *fifth* and in them only. For these are the only two in which either B or β occurs. How would these two cases appear to an ordinary observer? It is plain that they would present a double paradox to him. In the first place, as we have already seen, it is possible that what appears to him as a later event may be a cause-factor in a causal ancestor of what appears to him as an earlier event. But, further, in this case x may be a cause-factor in a causal ancestor of y, whilst y may *also* be a cause-factor in a causal ancestor of x. For here x is before y in one of the temporal dimensions, whilst y is before x in the other of them.

I will now sum up about this fantastic suggestion. (i) As I have pointed out, there is nothing in the least fantastic in the hypothesis of more than three *spatial* dimensions, as in Mr. Dunne's theory. But the suggestion that *time* may have more than one dimension may be simply nonsensical. Certainly it ought not to be lightly admitted into society merely on the dubious claim to kinship with perfectly respectable hypotheses about additional spatial dimensions. (ii) I believe that some such suggestion as this is the only way to make sense of a purely prehensive analysis of veridical foreseeing and of memory. But this does not do much to recommend it to me. For I do not hanker after such an analysis of these experiences, and I think it most unlikely that any such analysis of them is correct. (iii) The main interest of the suggestion is in reference to the Causal Objection. Although the non-prehensive analysis of ostensible foreseeing does not *require* the hypothesis of a second temporal dimension in order to make it intelligible, as the prehensive analysis appears to do, yet it *could* be combined with that hypothesis if this were found desirable. Now it will be remembered that we rejected (as contrary to a self-evident principle about causation) the suggestion that the event which subsequently verifies an ostensible foreseeing or concords with a pro-presentative image might be a cause-factor in a causal ancestor of the foreseeing or of the image. We see now that, if we are prepared to swallow the hypothesis of a two-dimensional time and to relax our causal "axiom" in a certain way, we need not necessarily reject this alternative. So we must now, very tentatively, add this alternative to the list of four which we previously stated to be exhaustive.

(3) *The Fatalistic Objection.* —In order to state this objection clearly it will be necessary to define certain terms. I will begin by defining the statement that a certain event *e* was "dependent on" a certain voluntary decision *d.* It is to have the following meaning. If the person who made the decision *d* had instead chosen a different alternative, and all the other circumstances at the time had been as they in fact were, then *e* would not have happened. There is no doubt that we all believe, with regard to many events, that they are in this sense dependent on voluntary decisions.

Next, I will define the statement that a certain event *e,* which happened at t^1 in a certain place or in a certain person's mind, was "already completely predetermined" at a certain earlier moment *t.* It has the following meaning. There is a set of facts about the dispositions, the mutual relations, and the internal states at or before the moment *t* of the various substances then existing, which, together with the laws of matter and of mind, *logically entails* that an event exactly like *e* will happen after an interval $t^1 - t$ in the place or the mind in which *e* did happen.

Suppose now that *e* depends on *d,* in the sense defined, and that *d* is not completely predetermined at any moment. Then it follows that *e* is not completely predetermined at any moment *before* that at which *d* happens. Of course, *e* may still be completely predetermined at moments *after d* has happened.

Finally, the following proposition seems self-evident to many people. If an ostensible precognition occurs and is subsequently fulfilled, then, unless this is a mere chance coincidence, the event which subsequently fulfilled it must have been already completely predetermined at the time when the ostensible precognition took place.

Now in many cases an ostensible precognition or a pro-presentative image has been fulfilled by a subsequent event which was, to all appearance, dependent on a voluntary decision which took place *after* the ostensibly precognitive experience. Suppose we hold that the fulfillment was not a mere chance coincidence; and suppose we accept the proposition which many people find self-evident. Then we shall have to draw the following conclusion: Either (*a*) the event which subsequently fulfilled the precognition did *not* really depend on the voluntary decision on which it seemed to depend; or (*b*) if it did, then that voluntary decision must have been *already* completely predetermined at the time when the precognition took place. On the first alternative, the voluntary decision was quite irrelevant and ineffective as regards the event which seemed to depend on it. On the second alternative, the voluntary decision was completely predetermined some time before it took place. Now many people find it highly repugnant, both intellectually and emotionally, to admit either of these alternatives about voluntary decisions and the events which apparently depend on them. Hence they feel a strong objection to admitting the possibility of veridically precognizing events which are apparently dependent on subsequent voluntary decisions. I think that this is the essence of the Fatalistic Objection.

So far as I can see, there is nothing wrong with the reasoning. It only remains, then, to examine the premise, *i.e.* the following proposition:—"If an ostensible precognition occurs and is subsequently fulfilled, then, unless this is a mere chance coincidence, the event which subsequently fulfilled it must have been already completely predetermined at the time when the ostensible precognition took place." Is this really self-evident?

I think that it is very important to distinguish a certain pair of statements, which are rather liable to be confused with each other, and to see logical connexion or lack of connexion between them. One is the statement that "the future is already *predeterminate*"; the other is the statement that "the future is already *predetermined.*" I have explained what the latter means. What is the meaning of the former? Let c be any characteristic that can be manifested in time. Suppose that a judgment is made at any moment t to the effect that an event manifesting the characteristic c *will* happen in a certain place or in a certain mind at a certain future moment t^1. Then this judgment is *already* true or it is *already* false, as the case may be, at the time t when it is made. The actual course of future history will *show* that it *was* true or will *show* that it *was* false, as the case may be; but the judgment will not *become* true or *become* false, from being neither the one nor the other, when the moment t^1 is reached. I do not know whether this proposition is important or is a mere triviality; but, whichever it may be, it is all that is meant by saying that "the future is already predeterminate."

Now consider an event e which actually happened at a certain moment t^1 in a certain place or in the mind of a certain person. What would be meant by saying that e "was already completely predeterminate" at a certain earlier moment t? It would have the following meaning: If c be any characteristic which e manifests, then a judgment made at t to the effect that there will be a manifestation of c at t^1 in this place or in this mind would *already* have been true at t.

It is now plain that to say that an event was already *predetermined* at a certain moment and to say that it was already *predeterminate* at that moment are two entirely different statements. The former is a proposition involving the notion of causation, whilst the latter involves no such notion. There is not the least inconsistency in saying that a certain event e, which happened at t^1, was already completely predeterminate at t but was not then completely predetermined.

Now, so far as I can see, the premise on which the Fatalistic Objection depends seems to be relevant only because these two notions are not clearly distinguished. I think that the following two propositions *are* self-evident: (i) The occurrence of e at t^1 could not be *inferred with certainty* at an earlier moment t from facts about what has existed or happened at or before t unless it were already completely *predetermined* at t. (ii) An event e which did not happen until t^1 could not have been *prehended* at an earlier moment t unless it were already *predeterminate* at t. The first of these is an immediate consequence of the definitions of the terms which occur in it. The second of them is a consequence of the nature of prehension and the definition of being "predeterminate." If an event can be pre-prehended, it must in some sense co-exist with the pre-prehension of it; and the precognition must consist in knowing by acquaintance that it has such and such characteristics. This would be impossible unless it is in some sense *already* true that it has these characteristics, *i.e.,* unless it is in some sense already predeterminate. Supposing that a meaning can be given to the notion pre-prehension, it is quite clear that an event need not be completely *predetermined* at the time when it is pre-prehended. All that is necessary is that it should then be *predeterminate*.

I suspect that the premise of the Fatalistic Objection is a confused mixture of the two propositions which I have distinguished above. Now no one supposes that veridical ostensible foreseeing consists in inferring from facts about the past and the present with complete certainty that certain events will happen in the future. Hence the first of these propositions is irrelevant to the whole subject of this paper. On the other hand, the second of these propositions has nothing to do with *predetermination*, and is therefore irrelevant to the question of the determination and the causal efficacy of voluntary decisions.

Now that this confusion has been removed we can easily settle the question for ourselves. Suppose that the occurrence of e at t_3 was foreseen by A at t_1. Suppose, further, that the occurrence of e at t_3 was in fact dependent on the occurrence of a certain voluntary decision in B at an intermediate date t_2. Does this entail that the occurrence of this decision in this person at t_2 was already predetermined at t_1?

It certainly *does* entail the following proposition: If A had recognized at t_1 (as he very well might in some cases) that the occurrence of e at t_3 would be dependent on the previous occurrence of such a decision as d in B, then he could have inferred that B would make this decision at some time between t_1 and t_3. But this is *not* equivalent to, nor does it entail, the proposition that the occurrence of d in B at t_2 was already predetermined at t_1. In order to see this it is only necessary to look back at our definition of "being completely predetermined at a certain moment." In accordance with that definition the statement that the occurrence of d in B at t_2 was already completely predetermined at t_1 would have the following meaning. It would mean that there is a set of facts about the dispositions, the mutual relations, and the internal states *at or before* t_1 of the various substances *then* existing, which, together with the laws of matter and of mind, logically entails that an event which has all the characteristics of d *will* occur in B *after* an interval $t_2 - t_1$. The difference between the two propositions is now obvious. The first (which really is entailed by our original suppositions) is about the possibility of inference from factual data about the *remoter future* to factual conclusions about the *less remote future*. The second (which is not entailed by our suppositions) is about the possibility of inferring from factual data about the *present or the past* to factual conclusions about the future.

Finally, the following point is worth noticing. I can infer from events in the less remote past that Julius Caesar decided in the more remote past to cross the Rubicon. No one imagines for a moment that this fact shows that Caesar's decision to cross the Rubicon was completely predetermined at any previous date. Suppose now that an augur at Rome had foreseen those later events from which *we* infer that Caesar had decided at an earlier date to cross the Rubicon. Obviously, he could have drawn precisely the same conclusion about Caesar's *then future* decision as we draw about his *now past* decision. And, if the possibility of our making this inference from these data does not require Caesar's decision to be completely predetermined, why should the possibility of the augur's making the same inference from the same data require this?

Lewis Foster

The Causal Objection to Precognition[1]

Veridical cognition occurs in memory, anticipation and perception. A perception is ostensibly veridical when its events or data are accorded an immediate and current presence. Anticipation includes the veridical inferences of common sense and science. For instance, while repeating a successful experiment a scientist may correctly infer and visualize the result before it actually occurs. Common sense expectation, although less sophisticated than science, is also inferential. Even the occasional "spontaneous" forethought is presumed inferential in principle. There are also ostensible non-inferential veridical post-cognitions. These are our personal memories, such as today's image of yesterday's sunset.

There are other forms of veridical cognition less prevalent than these. Telepathy and clairvoyance are modes of perception, apparently discerning mental and physical phenomena without the organs of sense. Retrocognition is the apprehension of a past event, the original of which was never experienced by the subject. Such a claim is made by the Misses Moberly and Jourdain in their account of veridically perceiving the Petit Trianon at Versailles at the time of Marie Antoinette.[2] Retrocognition is not a form of memory without some hypothesis of continuity, such as transmigration of personality. Finally, there is ostensible non-inferential veridical precognition, a peculiar form of anticipation which prospectively refers to an event which has not yet occurred.

Reprinted from *The Personalist*, volume 50 (1969), pp. 473-489, by permission of the author and editor.

Its relevance to the non-existent makes precognition an interesting but difficult kind of cognition to explain. Veridical perception encounters the immediate present, that is, contemporary objects, events or sense data. Memory, being *re*-presentational by nature, can claim at least a legacy to the present. But, precognition is pro-presentational in character. A part of its data includes future events. Future events or experiences are those which have not yet occurred and consequently do not actually exist. Some people find it difficult to reconcile a veridical image with a non-existent, yet somehow fulfilling, event. They therefore judge precognition to be impossible. This denial issues out of what Professor Broad has called the "causal objection" to precognition,[3] the detail of which is discussed below.

In spite of the objections, evidence for foreknowledge progressively accumulates. It has been stimulated both by recent general interest and by the professional encouragement of The Society For Psychical Research, its American counterpart, and other like groups. Of course, students have investigated prophetic claims since Biblical times[4] but today's communications media and more enlightened attitudes have enhanced the intensity and the quality of scholarship in this area. Some researchers, H. F. Saltmarsh, Tyrrell, Tenhaeff, Chari, and L. E. Rhine, notably, have emphasized the investigation and classification of "spontaneous" type cases, while J. B. Rhine, Pratt, Schmeidler, Thouless, and others have concentrated on the discipline of scientific methodology.

Because evidence is now so overwhelming, and because so much of it is disciplined, hardly anyone is satisfied simply to dismiss foreknowledge as chance correlation. If only isolated instances were occasionally reported, chance coincidence would be the most reasonable hypothesis, but the amount of material impresses the notion that precognition involves something more than a random coincidence of occurrences. Not everyone, however, is prepared to agree with Professor Broad that this view implies a notion of causality.[5]

Our interest lies not so much in the opinions about foreknowledge as with the logical relations the term implies. In this regard, a familiarity with Professor Broad's classification of the different forms of precognition will be useful. First, there is prevision where the events which are ostensibly foreseen are either future events which will happen to the person himself or are events which he will veridically perceive. This has been called "intra-subjectively circumscribed ostensible precognition."[6] Secondly, there are ostensible precognitions which are not confined to the subject, and two classes of these ought to be distinguished. There are the occurrences which will either be reported to the person or will be verified by his own immediate or inferred experience *after* they have happened. There are also those occurrences which the person will be able to anticipate by usual means because of certain information made available to him at some intermediate date.[7]

A good example of the first type of precognition is given by Raynor Johnson. Although she had never been to Yorkshire, Mrs. Calder dreamed of a grey-stone house set in a valley there, through which ran a stream of clear, but black-looking water. Only one-half of the house was occupied, and outside the door of this half was a barrel which served as a dog-kennel. Some months after this dream, a change of positions took Professor and Mrs. Calder house-hunting in Yorkshire. They came upon and subsequently rented one-half of the house imaged in the dream. They found that the water of the stream frequently was discolored by indigo from a dyeworks nearby. About a year later there was a change of tenants in the other half of the house, and the new people arrived with a dog. They promptly placed a barrel outside the door for its kennel.[8]

The second type may be exemplified by a "psychic reading" given by Edgar Cayce on August 27, 1926.[9] While in trance, Cayce was asked about imminent weather conditions and predicted that, ". . . on or about October 15th to 20th . . . there may be expected . . . violent windstorms— two earthquakes, one occurring in California, another occurring in Japan—tidal waves following, one to the southern portion of the isles near Japan."[10] Months later, the U.S. Weather Bureau's *Monthly Weather Review* stated that October had been exceptionally stormy. There had been several tropical disturbances over the Atlantic ocean with one of record severity, creating havoc in Cuba on October 20th. On the 14th and 15th, hurricane force winds prevailed near the Kuril Islands, and in the vicinity of the Philippines, four violent typhoons were reported.[11] A U.S. Coast and Geodetic Survey report shows that an earthquake took place in California on October 22, 1926, and in Japan a series of three occurred on the 19th and 20th of the same month. However, no tidal waves, in the sense of seismic sea waves, were reported to have followed these shocks.[12]

In another reading, Cayce foresees the earthquake destruction of Los Angeles and San Francisco before the end of this century. Recent scientific investigations into the active faults in these areas have led several geologists to postulate independently a high probability of such destruction.[13] Should this prophecy be fulfilled, the verification will exemplify the third class of precognition.

In accounting for the phenomenon of prophecy, there are four theories, allowing for variations, which consistently dominate the general literature. (1) A person subconsciously decides upon and initiates a course of action very likely to be realized, and the precognized image is a conscious manifestation of the subconscious decision. (2) A subconscious inference is made about the probable occurrence of an event, and the product of the inference appears to consciousness as the precognitive image. (3) However the precognition may be caused, it sets up a subconscious desire for realization, with this desire initiating subsequent physical or mental processes, which in turn bring about the fulfilling event and verify the precognition. (4) A person subconsciously receives data by telepathy from an incarnate or discarnate mind, and these data emerge into consciousness as veridical foreknowledge.[14]

The striking feature about these accounts is not that they are more or less extravagant, but that they all assume a common requirement which each tries to satisfy in a different way. They presuppose that between an apparently non-inferential veridical precognition and the subsequent event, a cause-effect relation will obtain. A causal sequence with no unaccountable gaps is implied as a necessary condition. It is precisely the causal condition which seems to make precognition objectionable.

Suppose a person veridically precognizes at T-2 an event which does not happen until a later time T-3. Or, suppose that at T-2 he does not experience the image as precognitive, but that subsequent experience reveals it to have been in fact pro-presentative of a certain event at T-3. How shall we explain the occurrence of a pro-presentative image of a particular future event at this particular time? The event which is foreseen has not yet happened when the prospectively referring image is experienced, and it cannot yet cause any effects. It cannot yet have conditioned the person's experience by initiating any characteristic kind of process or structural modifications in his brain or in his mind or in both. On one account, at least, any of his *past* experiences may have causal *successors* in the later periods of that person's life. But an experience which has not yet happened cannot have causal successors until it happens. It *could* have causal antecedents in the earlier stages of the person's history, e.g. as the later fulfillment of an earlier intention. But, many instances of veridical precognition, or of non-prospectively referred images which later turn out pro-presentative apparently exclude the foreseen event's being a product of a process going on in the person at the time he has the image, even though it be granted that the event has causal antecedents somewhere in the world.

The argument for rejecting precognition comes to this. At the moment when a person has a pro-presentative image of a certain event, that event has not yet had any causal successors. It is impossible to explain the occurrence of a pro-presented image of this particular future event at this moment because that event has no causal agent, either antecedent or successor, in the person at the time his precognitive image occurs.[15]

What is one to think? On one side, the quantity of evidence persuades us to reject the notion that ostensible non-inferential veridical precognition results from chance coincidence, but on the other side, the causal objection seems to preclude its logical possibility. This situation apparently does not arise with veridical non-inferential memory, even when the hypothesis postulates the same constituent elements, i.e., events, images, and their causal relations. Moreover, no one would seriously suggest that memory results from chance. There is also the odd fact that virtually no one has the least *a priori* objection to the possibility of non-inferential memory, but there is still considerable *a priori* repugnance to the possibility of precognition.

These reflections pose some question about the propriety of a precognition-memory analogue, but Professor Broad thinks it provides an adequate working basis.[16] He also finds no objection inherent in a causal account of memory;[17] that the objection to precognition stems from the conditions of causality;[18] that the objection might possibly be countered by a hypothesis of two-dimensional time.[19] Supporting Professor Broad's approach through analogy, our intention is to expose the causal objection as a pseudo-problem, generated from certain inadequacies in its analogue; to show that a confusion of causality with time provokes much of the difficulty; to suggest an alternative hypothesis, which within the given frame of this whole discussion, will avoid the causal objection.

Turning to the analogy first, there are several similarities between veridical precognition and memory, but the most striking one is their occupation with non-being. Veridical perception, normal or paranormal, deals with the real world of current events. Precognition and memory, on the other hand, are modes of experiencing non-currently existing events. Memory recollects occurrences which have already happened and no longer exist, and precognition foresees occurrences which will happen but do not yet exist. That which is remembered or foreseen is representative and pro-presentative of these occurrences. Secondly, both memory and precognition assume some essential accordance between the images and the events, and the problem turns on what sort of relation this may be.

Also, both types of cognition are thought to be *intra-subjectively circum-scribed.* With memory, the term refers to the person's own image of his original experience, while in precognition, his image is of an event he is going to have. The term "ostensible" calls attention to the fact that neither pre- nor postcognition may submit to public verification. Time is another important factor of similarity. Time separates images from events in both forms of cognition although their sequential order is reverse of one another.[20] Finally, both forms of cognition seem to imply causal factors, and having already presented the implications of precognition, we turn to Professor Broad's explanation of memory.[21] Together, these sources will suffice to initiate the critical examination to follow.

Suppose that instead of foreseeing at T-2 an event which happens at a later time T-3, a person remembers an event which happened at an earlier moment T-1. The occurrence at T-1 sets up either a type of process or a structural modification in the brain or in the mind or in both, and persists during the interval between T-1 and T-2. Suppose that at T-2 a certain experience, designated a "reminder," happens to the person, and that it connects up in some special way with the structural "trace" or with the present stage of the process. The cause of the person's remembering the original event will be the conjunction of the reminder with the simultaneous stage of this continuous process or with the persistent trace set up by the person's experience at T-1. Professor Broad adds this remark: there ". . . may be a good deal of mythology in this causal explanation; but it is acceptable mythology, bearing a close analogy to certain observable facts in other departments of phenomena."[22]

What these departments are, he does not say. However, they are unlikely to disperse the metaphorical clouds which hover about this account and make much of the mythology unacceptable. Two of the more unsavory mythical characters are the *event* and the *image*, and the crucial point in the theory is when the reminder event connects with the persistent element at T-2 to cause a representation of the original event at T-1. This conjunction constitutes the immediate cause of the memory image. Accepting this account, Professor Broad naturally finds veridical precognition objectionable because of an inherent contradiction. The statement that foreknowledge consists in perceiving an *image* of a future event is contradictory by virtue of its own terms.[23]

However, the proposition is contradictory only because of Professor Broad's tacit assumptions about the nature and relation of events and images. It is curious that he does not subject these key terms to the analytical rigor for which he is famous. The context leaves no doubt, however, about his endowment of a nonsymmetrical causal relation between them: events may cause images or other events, but images are the effects of events and are in no case causal agents. Now there may be an adequate reason for this discrimination, but we are not told what it is. This omission is an unhappy one because without some justification for the limiting principles in operation, the whole question of the causal objection goes begging.

Surely, it is not intended that events and images be understood as differing in kind, e.g., the one physical and the other mental. With a radical dualism, it would be intelligible why images could not cause events, but the assumption that events cause images must also be denied, and hence, the possibility of both memory and precognition precluded.

Perhaps, metaphysical considerations are out of place and the supposition of some common characteristic or other will be sufficient for this type of explanation. Still, there are certain fundamental questions which cannot go unanswered; that is, if the account of memory is to be sufficiently de-mythologized. For example, do events have objective existence or are they the content of cognition or both? Are structural traces, processes, and images to be classified as events or as elements *in* events? Again, can images cause the occurrence of other images? Are the various modes of veridical cognition considered events, and is the conjunction of reminder and trace still another kind of event? Finally, and more concretely, why couldn't a person's memory image at T-2 of a sunset experienced at T-1 set up a structural modification or type of process which, when its trace or present stage conjoined with a certain reminder event at T-3, would cause the person to have a memory image, not of the sunset perceived at T-1 but of its memory image recollected at T-2? No one could deny that we remember previous memories without contradicting patent fact. But, if the fact is to be consistent within the trace theory framework, images must be granted causal efficacy. That allowance will be sufficient to nullify the objection to precognition because it will then be theoretically possible for pro-presented images to be causal factors in the occurrence of prospectively referred events.

Holding to the implications of "ordinary linguistic usage," three conditions are normally regarded necessary and sufficient for an image type occurrence. (1) An occurrence or a datum of experience is an image when its dependent relation on another occurrence or datum of experience is other than chance coincidence and probably causal. (2) An image and its referent resemble one another. (3) The image is temporally posterior to its referent. It is only by special license that I may truly claim to have an acquaintance who is the *image* of Senator Goldwater. Now the causal theory of memory is thought to satisfy all these conditions. The memory image occurs as the latest link in an imperceptible chain, set up originally by the event it resembles. In precognition, resemblance occurs between the foreseen event and the pro-presented image. If an imperceptible causal series is granted between the image and event, adopting, for example, the third of the four theories cited above, two of the conditions are thereby fulfilled. But, the third will be violated because the image occurs *before* the resembled event; hence, the objection that precognition is absurd.

This conclusion cannot be reached without begging the question by a one-way causal relation between events and images, based upon some presupposed substantial or qualitative distinction. An observer, unfamiliar with this bias, would argue to the contrary, that all the above conditions are satisfied in principle by both precognition and memory. In each case, one sees, and sees only, that an experiential occurrence Y happens *after* another experiential occurrence X which it resembles and on which it is probably causally dependent, chance coincidence being unlikely. In both forms of cognition, Y refers *only* to an experience which verifies by resemblance a prior experience X. If this hypothetical observer had experienced during his lifetime an equal number of precognitions and recollections, neither of these classes could in any way be claimed dominant or prior. For him, the evidence would be sufficient to postulate the causal efficacy of both image occurrences and event occurrences. In any case, they must stand or fall together in their theoretical intelligibility, and the idea of a causal objection to either precognition or memory will be absurd. This line of thought shows how the failure to elucidate the basic terms explicitly and adequately both embarrasses the trace theory and negates the relevance of the causal objection. The most serious impediment, however, to the understanding of either memory or precognition lies in the causal relation between these elements, and it is to this problem that we now turn.

From Professor Broad's discussion, the necessary and sufficient conditions of causation emerge as *contiguity* and *location*.[24] These two terms express, he believes, what are ordinarily thought to be self-evident causal principles. If X is a cause factor in a causal ancestor of Y, the first event must adjoin the second so as to admit no separation in time. If they are contiguous, either immediately or by mediation, there will be no temporal gaps. "Two events . . . are adjoined so that the end of one exactly coincides with the beginning of the other. . . ."[25] With regard to their mutual location, the condition is absolute that the cause must without exception precede the effect and the effect follow the cause. A reversal, Y occurring earlier than X, would be an example of temporal dislocation. Now suppose that X is an event at T-1 wherein a hypnotist suggests to a subject that he do a dance one hour later, and Y is the event at T-3 wherein the subject finds himself dancing. Suppose also that these events are not contiguous in time. Then, one believes it to be self-evident that Y is not caused by X directly. If X is causally related to Y, there must be a series of causes and effects to close the gap between them, and each link in the chain will be a causal successor of X and a causal antecedent of Y.

On the basis of these two causal conditions, the trace theory of memory will appear inconsistent. The immediate cause of a recollection is said to be the conjunction of the reminder with the enduring trace or the present phase of some characteristic process, and one question is whether "conjunction" covertly implies causation. In any case, the reminder must somehow structurally modify the percipient in order for the persistent brain change to be stimulated and the memory image recalled. If the event is prior to this initial modification, it will qualify as a cause factor of it but cannot therefore conjoin with it. To conjoin, both of them must be present. But if they occur concomitantly, then the simultaneity of their conjunction precludes succession and disqualifies the event as a causal antecedent. It is unimportant whether or not the reminder be considered in direct or indirect relation to the trace of the original event. What is important is the meaning of "conjunction." Unfortunately, its significance in the theory includes both the notions of simultaneity *and* succession, but these terms are mutually exclusive. Two simultaneous elements co-exist with one another at the same time: with succession, one element must exist before or after the other, but never concurrently with it.

If this embarrassment could be remedied, say, by designating "conjunction" to mean the simultaneous contiguity of the reminder either with an original trace or the trace of an original event and by asserting that their conjunction is the cause of the memory, there would still be another difficulty to face. At least, the causal conditions are now satisified since the memory image occurs after the conjunction and is contiguous with it. But, on what grounds does the conjunction cause a memory image and not merely another structural trace? What is like a structural modification but another of the same? The difficulty in this is that probably an assumption has been tacitly made that memories imaged in consciousness are different in kind from traces in the brain or electrical impulses susceptible to instrumental measurement. If this is really the case, there is no reason why the conscious image should not occur *simultaneously* with its concomitant structural modifications, and with this brand of psychophysical parallelism, the condition of temporal location will be violated again.

Should an adequate reason somehow be given to meet this condition, so that the image will occur *after* the conjunction, then we will be pushed back again into an irreconcilable causal dualism between physical and non-physical entities or occurrences. On the other hand, a denial of the above assumption will identify "memory images" with "structural traces" and provoke in turn a hopeless equivocation. It would imply, for one thing, that images could function as the causes of bodily events. All of these confusions are a detailed reflection of the mythological and obscure language of the trace theory and the argument against precognition.

The main source of these difficulties lies in a failure to distinguish the necessary and sufficient requisites for causality, described above, from the elements of time. Assuming that time, i.e., ordinary clock-type time, consists in the monitoring of change, its requirements will include the occurrence of two or more elements in direct sequence, one succeeding another which has occurred prior to it. It is obvious that the idea of an immediate sequence of moments is identical to that of causal contiguity, and the uni-directional property of time characteristic of causal location. Just as two moments of time cannot be reversed, so, an effect cannot precede its cause.

This confusion of time and causality ultimately vitiates Professor Broad's time-hypothesis reply to the causal objection to precognition,[26] but it does help to ferret into the open two conditions for causality which he has not made explicit. One of these, a necessary condition, may be called "the persistent correlation principle" and is identifiable with Hume's idea of constant conjunction. In addition to the contiguity and proper location of two or more events, the occurrence of these events must be repetitive. In other words, for a temporal relation, it is necessary and sufficient that any two events occur only once each; so long as they appear together, one after the other. In order to be causally related, it will be necessary, in addition, that the temporal conjunction of two events occur often. Probably, this condition is so obviously necessary that Professor Broad has omitted it purposely. Probably, also, he would permit a temporal series to be contiguous in principle as he has insisted a causal series may be. As in memory, for example, an unbroken but *imperceptible* causal series is postulated between the original event and its memory image or trace, so probably, a like temporal series would obtain between the last moment before sleep and the first waking one.

There is another causal condition, not so obvious, which also has to do with indirect contiguity. It figures prominently in the trace theory and the causal objection. In a situation where a certain cause and a certain effect are temporally discrete but mediated by an imperceptible series of agents and patients, some condition sufficient to discern the causality of this particular pair will be required. In terms of memory and precognition, some axiom of association must determine certain events and images to be causally related though temporally separated. With memory, for instance, by what principle does the reminder event conjoin with just *this* particular trace to cause an image of this particular past event and none other?

The answer is obvious, but not explicit, either in Professor Broad's essay or in Professor Price's commentary. In several places they refer to the amount of "accordance" between ostensible precognitions and fulfilling events.[27] Discussing the retrocognitions of Miss Moberly and Miss Jourdain, mentioned above, Professor Broad speaks of the "correspondence" between the twentieth-century images and the eighteenth-century events.[28] Also, the word "correlation" is used extensively to designate a content relation between events and images. All these terms really express the same condition, namely, a resemblance of content between events or cognitions, and the best evidence for this comes out of the statement of the objection to precognition.

In that statement, a distinction is made between the person who veridically precognizes at T-2 an event which does not happen until a later time T-3, and the person who at T-2 does not refer the data prospectively, but whose later experience shows it to have been in fact pro-presentative of a certain event at T-3. The latter person could not classify his experience as precognitive *until* the occurrence of the event at T-3. Since there is no quality to his earlier experience at T-2 which would prompt a prospective referral to a later occurrence, the only possible basis for relating this particular event with that particular cognition is the resemblance of content between them. Actually, this person's experience is not properly precognitive. It demonstrates a form of memory. At T-3, what he experiences is really a reminder event which stimulates the persistent trace of his cognition at T-2. Of course, he might then go on to draw some inference on the basis of content similarity, especially if such conjunctions should occur often.

There is hardly an objection to resemblance serving as one of the conditions sufficient for a causal relation, along with the necessary factors of contiguity, location, and persistent correlation; provided, either that this phenomenon is self-evident or that adequate reasons are given for its acceptance. But, it is not self-evident that characteristic similarity implies causality, and no hypothesis is ventured which explains, for example, how it is that the reminder event associates with one particular memory or how the present cognition is associated with a certain future event among an infinity of others. By keeping the discourse at a certain level of abstraction, the problem appears to be avoided. But in no case can one ignore that if these four factors constitute the conditions for causality, causation being differentiated from time by a regular correlation of like data, then precognition will be as acceptable as memory. The analogy between memory and precognition breaks down and provokes the causal objection only on the unwarranted hypothesis, exposed above, of a nonsymmetrical causal relation between events and images.

Even at this level of abstraction, i.e., accepting much of the mythology to which we have been exposed, a hypothesis is conceivable whereby both memory and precognition may prove acceptable and compatible. Curiously enough, the inspiration comes again from the causal objection, but the center of attention this time will be the person who ostensibly precognizes at T-2 the event which occurs at T-3. The point to note is that he prospectively refers the content of his present experience to a future occurrence. The nature of precognition, however, lies not in the mere content correlation of present and future occurrences. Its essence is epistemological and consists in *how* the experient apprehends the presentationally immediate data. Like any of the classes of veridical cognition outlined in the beginning,[29] precognition is a mode of experiential discrimination.

If a person states a claim to precognition, he means that the content of his present experience is also accompanied by or contains in itself an element of immediate judgment or inclination or emotional persuasion which prospectively refers that content to a certain future time. The person who claims a memory will distinguish the present fact of cognition from its content which he retrospectively refers to a certain time in the past. When, for example, someone finally utters the name that another person has forgotten and is trying to recall, the recognition is immediate, and it is by no overt discursive inference that the latter *re*-collects and discriminates that image from all the others. And, just as one cannot substantiate his denial of another's private claim to remember a past event, so one's claim to be foreseeing the future must also go unchallenged. This does not mean that the element of verification is totally absent from these modes of cognition. The essential idea being stressed is that our veridical cognition is partially *a priori.* While *what* we experience may indeed be empirically grounded, it is not experience that conditions us to qualify the presentationally immediate *as* past or *as* future.

It is not necessary to accept this *a priori* character of cognition in order to accept the hypothesis we are about to suggest. This account assumes the same general context and even some of the mythology implicit in the development of Professor Broad's thesis. But it proposes a way to render precognition intelligible while avoiding the causal objection to it.

Suppose we allow that a person may experience a reminder event conjoins with a certain set of traces and causes at T-2 an experience whose content is representative of a past event at T-1. He knows or believes that an event similar to the content of his experience at T-2 actually happened at T-1. Since we have no reason sufficient to explain the person's experiencing the T-2 occurrence as a reminder type instead of some other, suppose we allow another person to experience at T-2 what may be called a "provider" event. The provider effects a conjunction with a set of traces in a novel system or synthesis, causing an experience whose content is pro-presentative of a future event at T-3. He also knows or believes that an event similar to his experience at T-2 is going to happen at T-3. Now if we may assume an unbroken, but imperceptible, series of causal agents between the reminder and the representation of the past event, then we must also assume the same kind of continuity between the provider and the pro-presentation of the future event. And, if we can assume another unbroken, imperceptible causal series between the representative of the past event and the past event itself, why shouldn't we also assume the same sort of series between the pro-presentation of the future event and that event itself? Finally, if the veridical representation of the past event, e.g., today's correct image of yesterday's sunset after repeated effort, can in any way be said to verify the reminder, then in some sense, it must be said that the veridical pro-presentation of the future event, i.e., the provider, is verified by the later occurrence of the future event.

LEWIS FOSTER

NOTES

1. This topic was introduced by Professor C. D. Broad in a symposium read at the joint session of The Aristotelian Society and The Mind Association in Bristol, England. The participants in this discussion on precognition were Professor Broad and Professor H. H. Price. Cf. The Aristotelian Society, Supp. Vol. XVI, *Knowledge and Foreknowledge*, Harrison and Son, London, 1937. [For Broad's contribution, see pp. 287-312, above.—Ed.]

2. Moberly, C. E., and Jourdain, E. F., *An Adventure*, 4th edition, Faber and Faber, London, 1947.

3. Broad, C. D., "The Philosophical Implications of Foreknowledge," *Knowledge and Foreknowledge*, p. 189. [Page 296 in this collection—Ed.]

4. Zorab, George, *Bibliography of Parapsychology*, Parapsychology Foundation Inc., New York, 1957. This compilation is basically complete but now is in need of supplementation with more recent publications.

5. Broad, C. D., p. 197. [Page 303, above—Ed.] Cf. Price, H. H., "The Philosophical Implications of Precognition," *Knowledge and Foreknowledge*, pp. 226-227.

6. Broad, p. 192. [Page 299, above—Ed.]

7. *Ibid.*

8. Johnson, Raynor C., *The Imprisoned Splendor*, Harper and Row, New York, 1953, p. 151; quoted from Saltmarsh, H. F., *Foreknowledge*, G. Bell and Sons, London, 1938, pp. 64-65.

9. Edgar Cayce is recognized primarily for his medical clairvoyance, but his psychic ability was demonstrated in many areas. For a good biography, Cf., Sugrue, Thomas, *There Is A River*, Henry Holt and Co., New York, 1945.

10. Anonymous, *Earth Changes*, A.R.E. Press, Virginia Beach, Va., 1961, p. 26. The author holds a Ph.D. from a reputable American university and is Professor of Geology in another. He explains his anonymity on pages 59-61.

11. *Ibid.*, p. 27.

12. *Ibid.*, pp. 27-28.

13. *Ibid.*, pp. 35-39.

14. Broad, pp. 195-196. [Pp. 301-302 above—Ed.]

15. *Ibid.*, pp. 189-190. [Pp. 297-298—Ed.]

16. *Ibid.*, p. 180. [Page 290—Ed.]

17. *Ibid.*, p. 189. [Page 297—Ed.]

18. *Ibid.*, pp. 236-240.

19. *Ibid.*, pp. 199-204. [Pp. 305-308 above—Ed.]

20. An interesting speculation is that there may be no real difference between precognition and memory; that with regard to activity and content they are identical; that this temporal quality is the essential condition for their differentiation.

21. Broad, p. 189. [Pp. 296-297 above—Ed.]

22. *Loc. cit.*

23. *Ibid.*, pp. 194-195. [Page 301—Ed.]

24. *Ibid.*, pp. 202-203 [Page 307—Ed.]; 237-240. Professor Broad does not employ these identical terms.

25. *Ibid.*, p. 237.

26. *Ibid.*, pp. 199-204. [Pp. 305-308—Ed.]

27. *Ibid.*, p. 197 [Page 303 above—Ed.] and Price, H. H., p. 214.

28. Broad, p. 192. [Page 299 above—Ed.]

29. Cf. pp. 1-2. [Page 313 above—Ed.]

C. W. K. Mundle

Does the Concept of Precognition Make Sense?

We cannot profitably discuss the concept of precognition in isolation from the evidence, so I shall start by saying something about this, but not very much, for I have elsewhere[1] tried to evaluate the evidence, and the purpose of this paper is to focus attention on the problem of rendering the relevant facts intelligible. I shall not discuss spontaneous cases, where the information comes in the form of dreams, hallucinations or a compulsion to act in an apparently irrational manner. A collection of such cases is available in *Foreknowledge* by H. F. Saltmarsh.[2] Despite the interest of such cases, I should never be convinced by anecdotal evidence unless it were supported by experimental evidence. I shall describe briefly some experiments done in England which provide evidence for precognition.

Shortly before the last war, Whately Carington carried out a series of experiments at Cambridge.[3] What he was looking for was evidence for telepathy, not precognition. On each of ten successive evenings he hung up in his study in Cambridge an outline drawing of a familiar object which remained there from 7 P.M. till 9:30 A.M. next morning, a different drawing on each evening. Meanwhile a number of subjects, scattered throughout England, Scotland, America and Holland attempted to re-

Reprinted from the *International Journal of Parapsychology*, volume 6 (1964), pp. 179-194, by permission of the author and the Parapsychology Foundation, Inc.

produce by telepathy the drawing then hanging in his study. The matching and scoring of the results was done by a third party, and I shall not go into details. Suffice it to say that there was no significant resemblance between the drawings made by the subjects on a particular evening and the target drawing used on that same evening. There was, however, a striking tendency for the subjects' drawings to resemble the target drawings which had been used on the two previous evenings, and, to an equal extent, to resemble the target drawings which were going to be used on the next two evenings. The hits (successful drawings) showed a temporal displacement, which, Carington calculated, could be expected by chance once in about 10,000 such experiments. This seems to provide strong evidence for precognition, for Carington did not choose the subject of a drawing or make it, until just before 7 P.M. when it was displayed; and he chose the subject by a randomizing procedure which would seem to make it impossible for anyone to predict the outcome—he opened a book of mathematical tables at random, picked the last digits of the first two or three groups of numbers he saw, then turned to the corresponding page of a dictionary, and picked the first suitable word on that page. This experiment was completed in 1939.

In 1939 Dr. S. G. Soal [4,5,6] —then a lecturer in mathematics at Queen Mary College, London—had recently finished an elaborate attempt to repeat in England the type of card-guessing experiment which J. B. Rhine pioneered in America. Soal had, over a period of years, tested 160 people,but had found only chance scoring. In view of this, he had publicly expressed his scepticism about Rhine's claims. But in 1939, Carington announced the results of his experiments which I have described. Carington persuaded Soal to re-examine his records, looking for a similar effect. (Soal had scored the guesses of his 160 subjects only against the card they had been aiming at, i.e., the one the agent was looking at when the guess was made.) Soal reluctantly agreed, and, to his surprise, he found that two of his subjects tested three years earlier had been getting significant scores of the kind Carington predicted, i.e., on both the preceeding (-1) and the ensuing (+1) card position.

With each of these subjects Soal later carried out an elaborate series of experiments. With the first, Basil Shackleton, he worked for about two years. Throughout this period Shackleton got high scores of the precognitive type, scoring above the chance level on the card the agent was going to look at 2 to 3 seconds later. Usually this was the card *one* ahead (+ 1), for at the normal rate of guessing the interval between successive guesses was

2 to 3 seconds; but when the guessing was speeded up to twice this rate, Shackleton's high scoring switched to the card two ahead (+2). With the three chief agents, Shackleton made about 7,000 guesses at the normal speed and his rate of scoring on the (+1) card averaged just over 7 per run, instead of the 4.8 expected by chance. (There are only 24 opportunities per run of a (+1) hit.) The odds against chance are astronomical.

* * *

Let us turn now to the question of interpreting and explaining the kinds of facts I have described. Notice that the terms "ESP" and "precognition" are loaded with theory. They have been chosen on the assumption that the facts in question are to be assimilated to sense-perception, and that, just as sense-perception involves knowledge by acquaintance, so the psychic subject must possess knowledge by acquaintance, knowledge of objects or events not accessible to his senses. Psychical researchers have sometimes *defined* "ESP" as a kind of non-inferential knowledge. Now, this terminology is question-begging, and it is not warranted as a description of the facts. In card-guessing experiments the subjects rarely claim to have any idea as to when they are succeeding. Shackleton was an exception: he expressed confidence that he could tell in advance which of his guesses were successful. Soal tested this by getting Shackleton to mark the guesses he felt most confident in making, but it was found that these guesses were correct no more frequently than the others. Saltmarsh points out, in discussing spontaneous cases, that most precognitive experiences "are not at the time of their occurrence consciously recognized as having a reference to the future"; in other words, experiences are usually classified as precognitive only in retrospect, in the light of the later events which fulfill them. In view of such facts, we must recognize that if we define "precognition" as non-inferential knowledge of a future event, precognition is a hypothesis to explain the facts. If one accepts this hypothesis one will have to say that the knowledge in question is usually unconscious and that it spasmodically influences the subject's conscious experience or actions.

We can however avoid the language of perception and cognition. We can drop the term "ESP" and follow Dr. Thouless in using the non-committal term "psi-phenomena," and we can describe the facts in a causal terminology. We can say that the actions of the psychic subject are being influenced by, that he is responding appropriately to, events which he has not observed or inferred. Now, this seems appropriate in the case of straightforward telepathy or clairvoyance, but there is an obvious objection to describing or defining "precognition" on these lines—to saying that a person is "responding to a later event" or that his actions are "influenced or (partially) caused by a later event," for this involves the notion of causal influence operating from later to earlier events.

On the face of it there are decisive objections to each of the ways of defining "precognition" that I have mentioned. It appears self-contradictory to say that an event which has not yet happened, not yet "come into existence," could be either "an object of non-inferential knowledge" or "a cause-factor influencing what happened earlier." The latter phrase is certainly self-contradictory as the word "cause" is normally used, for it is part of the meaning of "cause" that a cause must precede its effects. Some philosophers, for instance Michael Scriven,[7] have recently shown themselves willing to revise the concept of causation in this respect. But the difficulties cannot be overcome simply by legislating that a cause may (logically) succeed its effects. For we want to understand what sort of causal explanation of the phenomena could in principle be offered. In all other fields, causal explanations involve mechanisms whereby causes bring about their effects, either by modifying the structure of a substance, or by initiating a chain of events which spans the spatio-temporal gap between cause and effect, or by a field possessed by or a force exerted by some substance. It seems impossible to *conceive* of any mechanism whereby what happens now could be acted upon by things which have not yet happened. Can we then explain the facts in question without being driven to talk of non-inferential knowledge of the future or of the causes succeeding their effects? Two escape routes seem open to us.

(1) The first I shall refer to as the *Unconscious Inference theory.* On this theory, although cases of so-called precognition appear to be non-inferential, this is not really so. The suggestion is that the psychic subject has performed an unconscious inference based on premises acquired by ESP of the non-precognitive kind. In many cases, we should have to suppose that the subject's powers of unconscious inference greatly exceed his powers of conscious inference. But we have some independent evidence for this sort of thing. Consider the so-called "calculating boys" or "arithmetical prodigies."[8] Some of these boys have never developed any ability for mathematical reasoning or analysis, and yet they were able, usually between ages of 4 and 20, to give instantly, or within a few sec-

onds, the solutions of problems like extracting the cube root or determining the logarithm of large numbers and so on; and they did this without knowing *how* they got the answers; the answers, we're told, just came into their heads without any conscious calculation. Presumably we would want to say that they must have been performing unconscious inference. Notice however that the kind of unconscious inference made by the calculating boy is deductive. The rules required to guide such inference are clear-cut and comparatively few in number. But what is precognized is some particular occurrence. The inference in this case would have to be inductive. The forecasting of a future event by rational inference requires premises of two types: (1) laws or generalizations, and (2) singular propositions; e.g., to calculate the future occurrence of an eclipse one needs to know both the laws of mechanics and singular propositions (particular facts about the position, mass and motion of the relevant bodies at a given moment). Our present theory of precognition will require us to assume that the subject can learn by ESP not only particular facts, but laws or generalizations with which he was not familiar. Here, notice, we shall be going beyond our evidence; for all that has been established experimentally is that some people can learn, by ESP, particular facts (e.g., the character of a particular card or drawing).

* * *

Our present theory could be applied to *some* cases which have been cited as precognitive. In many spontaneous cases the event precognized is the death of another person. Suppose that his death was already determined at the time of the precognition by his organic condition (e.g., the state of his heart). The precognitive experience could be explained by supposing that the subject ascertained by ESP both the nature of the incipient disease and the relevant laws of physiology, and inferred when and in what sort of circumstances the person was likely to die. To generalize, our present theory could be applied to any case in which the precognized event could in principle have been predicted by rational inference, by anyone who was fully conversant with the particular facts which obtained at the time of the precognitive experience and with the relevant laws of nature. But there are many spontaneous cases in which this condition does not *seem* to have been fulfilled, cases in which the precognized event is an accident or incident which could not have been rationally predicted—unless with the aid of laws of nature much more detailed and precise than have been established by the sciences. It seems moreover to be very difficult to apply our present theory to some of the experimental evidence.

Consider the experiments with Shackleton which employed the counters method and the rapid rate of calling. With the counters method, the order in which the agent looked at the target cards was determined in the following way. Two hundred counters, forty of each of five different colors, were mixed together in a bag or bowl. An experimenter (Mrs. Goldney) had to select a counter by touch and show it, through an aperture in a screen, to the agent. The color of this counter determined which of the five cards, lying before her in a box, the agent should lift and look at. Another experimenter (Dr. Soal) sat next to the agent, in a position in which he could not see the cards, and recorded the card-positions corresponding to the color of counters which he saw through the aperture. With this method, Shackleton made high scores on the (+2) targets. The point to be stressed is that the cards on which Shackleton was scoring high had not yet been selected at the time he made the corresponding guesses. (Note that this may not have been true of the counters experiments at the normal rate of calling; for Mrs. Goldney has recorded that she dipped each hand into the bag alternatively "and showed a counter at the screen aperture with one hand *while the other hand was already delving in the bag for the next counter*" [My italics.].)

Now, how could we try to apply our present theory to this case? We might suppose that Mrs. Goldney followed more or less fixed habits in selecting counters from different parts of the bag or bowl, and that Shackleton, by ESP, learned these habits, as well as the changing positions of the different counters. But this explanation seems to be precluded by a feature of the procedure which I have not mentioned. Before selecting each counter, Mrs. Goldney reshuffled the counters with a twist of the hand, and consciously attempted to avoid any fixed habits, by picking counters from different parts of the bag or bowl in a random manner. In these circumstances it seems scarcely credible that anyone could have calculated in advance the color of the counters which Mrs. Goldney was going to select next. If our present theory were correct, we should expect to find chance-scores when this method was first introduced, followed by a progressive improvement in the scoring-method. In fact, the scoring was high from the start and showed no improvement with practice. Thus the theory we have been considering seems extremely unplausible when we try to apply it in detail.

(2) I cannot think of any convenient label for the second type of theory.

The gist of it is this: it concedes that there is a causal connection between a so-called precognition and the corresponding later events. The suggestion is that either the precognition itself influences the later event, or that both are influenced by some other pre-existing factor. To illustrate how this theory might be applied: The simplest case would be where the memory of a dream causes a person to act in such a way as to fulfill the dream. In some cases of alleged precognition, a person dreams of the house in which he is later to live. But could we ever be sure, in such a case, that memory of the dream did not (whether consciously or not) influence the decision to buy or rent the house in question? But this does not take us very far, for no reputable psychical researcher would regard cases of this type as providing strong evidence for precognition. The evidence to which the psychical researcher would appeal are cases where the later event is an incident which involves the actions of *other* people, and which could not have been influenced by any normal means by the subject of the precognitive experience.

To make this theory work we should have to suppose that the subject exercises a mysterious influence on the actions of other people, or on physical events. But can we rule out this possibility? Telepathy involves one person influencing the thoughts or actions of another person. From the point of view of the agent telepathy is a way by which the agent influences the thoughts or actions of the subject. Moreover, I think we must here take account of the possibility of psychokinesis (PK). (Admittedly there is not nearly as much evidence for PK as there is for ESP, but there is some good evidence, especially, I think, Mr G. W. Fisk's experiments with Dr. J. Blunden.[9] Dr. Blunden made 13,600 dice-throws in her home in Devon, willing that the dice should come to rest with the target-face uppermost—but without having been told what the current target was! The target for each day's work was selected by a randomizing procedure by Fisk at his home in Surrey, 170 miles away. Dr. Blunden was not told what the targets had been until the record of her throws had been posted to Fisk and scored by him. The results which gave a rate of scoring 7½ percent higher than the chance-level, seem to require us to attribute to Dr. Blunden a combined exercise of ESP and PK.) In view of this, we might elaborate our present theory as follows: Let us suppose that a pre-cognitive experience is caused by a desire (or fear or fixed idea) in the mind of the person who has the experience, that this desire or fear persists, consciously or unconsciously, and causes the later event which seems to fulfill the precognition either by telepathic influence on other people or by psychokinetic influence on physical events.

To explain Shackleton's results in the counters experiments, we might suppose that his guesses (presumably involving wishes) exerted a psychokinetic influence on the later finger-movements of the experimenter, making the latter select a counter of the appropriate color. There are other precognition experiments, conducted by Rhine, which could be explained on our present theory by supposing that the subject's guesses exerted a psychokinetic influence on a randomizing machine (a card-shuffling machine), which was operated to determine the order of the target cards some time after the subject's guesses had been made. It does seem (logically) possible to explain all the existing evidence (and indeed all possible evidence) for precognition on our present theory, but only by making very heavy demands on our credulity. We should have to suppose that a person's thoughts, fears or wishes can exert a mysterious influence on machines and on other people's behavior, a much more extensive influence than is suggested by any of the experimental evidence for PK. We should, it seems, be re-introducing a concept of magical causation, of the sort of power that witches and medicine men have been supposed to possess— and this is something repugnant to the scientific outlook. So this theory, too, is most unplausible when we try to apply it in detail.

Notice in passing that the chief obstacle in applying either of the theories which I have outlined is the fact that the target cards are set up by a randomizing procedure after the guesses have been recorded. Scriven in the above-mentioned article treated this as an essential feature of a precognition experiment. Flew has described Scriven's stipulation as "providential" and "cunning";[10] but this is unfair, for if an experiment did not involve such a randomizing procedure, it would be comparatively easy to explain the results without postulating precognition.

* * *

Notice that if "precognition" is defined as I defined it earlier (following the usage of psychical researchers), each of the theories I have described would explain precognition *away*. On the first theory cases of so-called precognition are attributable to inferential knowledge or belief: on the second theory there is no temporally reversed causation—it is the earlier events which exert a queer influence on the later. But each of these theories involves making extravagant assumptions about men's powers— prodigious powers of inductive inference and the ability to discover laws of nature by ESP on the first theory; a magical power to influence machines and other people's actions on the second theory.

In view of this it is not surprising that some people have preferred to accept the implications of the concept of precognition as I defined it earlier in terms of non-inferential knowledge of the future, or in terms of temporally reversed causation. It has often been argued that the apparent contradiction in these definitions can be removed if, but only if, we suppose that future events are already actual or real; so that to make the occurrence of precognition intelligible we must adopt the view that the whole history of the universe co-exists, that past, present, and future events are spread out in a fourth dimension along which we, the observers, move. This theory would have to be dismissed out of hand if it had the implications which J. W. Dunne believes it has;[11] namely, that there is an infinite number of time-dimensions, and that each person comprises an infinite series of observers, a three-dimensional observer, a four-dimensional observer and so on to the alleged "observer at infinity." But it seems to me that Dunne's extravagant conclusions result from a gratuitous assumption. I shall try to diagnose his mistake.

Dunne starts by assuming that any physical object, such as my brain, is a four-dimensional entity spread out through time. It can be represented by a straight line from A (the date of my birth or a little earlier) to B (the date of my death or a little later). Any point on this line represents a three-dimensional cross-section of my brain (i.e., a momentary state of my brain). My experience of change is attributed to the fact that I, as a three-dimensional observer, move along this track through the four-dimensional world. Anything that moves must, Dunne reasons, move at a certain speed; speed means distance covered in a unit of time. But regarding the motion of the three-dimensional observer, the distances covered are stretches of the familiar time-dimension, Time 1 (T_1), so the time *taken* by such motion must be measured in units of a different time-dimension, Time 2. We must move from past to future in Time 2 (T_2). So Dunne elaborates his diagram. The line AB which represents a four-dimensional entity—the whole history in T_1 of my brain from birth to death—is pictured as moving upwards as a whole in T_2. A four-dimensional observer is now introduced, capable of apprehending, at any moment of T_2, the whole, or any part, of my history in T_1. It may, for example, while I sleep, take a peep at parts of my life which are, from the viewpoint of the three-dimensional observer, still in the future. (Thus does Dunne explain precognition.) Its movement in T_2 requires us to postulate a third time-

335

dimension with a five-dimensional observer; and so *ad infinitum.*

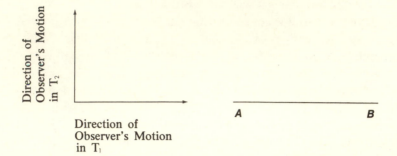

The source of Dunne's infinite regress is his assumption that the concept of motion can and must carry all of its normal implications when it is said that the conscious observer moves through time. To this, the short answer is that it is meaningless to ask how long it takes us to move from 8 P.M. to 10 P.M., or from Christmas to Easter, *if* the question implies that our motion has to be measured in units of a different time-dimension. But this answer does not dispose of the first stage of Dunne's analysis—his assumption that all events, past, present, and future, co-exist. This assumption does not commit us to more than one time-dimension, though, admittedly, time cannot then be identified with T_1 since Dunne is treating T_1 as a fourth dimension of space. When he speaks of observers moving along this dimension, he is introducing a new concept of "motion"; in *this* use, motion is a change *of* time, though not a change that *takes* time. One could say that such motion *constitutes* the passing of time, without saying that the passing of time is itself a process whose speed is variable or measurable. If we can conceive of the physical world as a four-dimensional manifold, all of whose parts co-exist (and many people besides Dunne have persuaded themselves that they can do so), this removes the apparent contradiction in talking of non-inferential acquaintance with future events.

Are there, however, any reasons, apart from the evidence for precognition, for adopting this Four-Dimensional World theory? It can be argued that this theory is rendered respectable both by modern logic and by modern physics. Professor Quine has written: "The four-dimensional view of space-time is part and parcel of modern formal logic, and in particular of the use of quantification theory in application to temporal affairs."[12] He speaks of "the denizens of space-time" as being "thing-events, four-dimensional beings." I have argued elsewhere[13] that this common interpretation of quantification theory is gratuitous; that it is due to the assumption that, when the existential quantifier is rendered "there exists an event such that . . .," "exists" is *both* timeless *and* in the present tense; and that the existential quantifier ought to be rendered "there has occurred *or* is occurring *or* will occur an event such that . . . ."

But what about physics? I am not qualified to make pronouncements, but let me pose some questions: if a physicist accepts Minkowski's model of a four-dimensional world, does this require him to think of future events as existing now, waiting for us to come across them? Could he not equally well adopt the view advocated at one time by Professor Broad[14] that the Universe is growing longer in the time-dimension? In other words, *if* the physicist wishes to represent time as an extra dimension of space, why should he not picture the passing of time as a line growing longer as the pen moves across a blank page, rather than as something moving along a line which is already drawn? And one more question, when physicists talk of time being "at right angles to" *each* of the dimensions of space, can they *really* attach any meaning to this except as a device for drawing diagrams? (I can't.)

Apart from the evidence for precognition I can see no reason to adopt the Four-Dimensional World theory. Moreover, this theory is open to what many, including myself, would consider an objection—that it would be incompatible with human freedom, in the sense in which "his choice was free" implies "he could have acted otherwise." I do *not* say that the Four-Dimensional World theory entails Determinism; for I would define Determinism as the doctrine that there are laws (whether we know them or not) such that *if* anyone knew all the laws and all the relevant facts about the present state of the world, he could *deduce* the occurrence and character of any later events. The falsity of Determinism would however be no comfort to the defender of free will if he accepts the Four-Dimensional World theory, for this implies that all future events, including his own actions, are already actual, waiting for him to come across them as he journeys through the fourth dimension! In this connection, Dunne makes a valiant attempt to have his cake and eat it. Dunne argues that a person may have a precognition at time 1 of an undesirable event (such as his own death) located at time 2, but that, as a result of his precognition, he may interfere with the course of history and prevent the fulfillment of this precognition. Just as you can alter the shape of a piece of cardboard along its whole length by bending it at one point, so according to Dunne, you can instantaneously alter future stretches of the fourth-dimensional world by a present action. But consider what this involves, on Dunne's premises. Suppose it is written in the book of history that John Brown dies in an air crash on his twentieth birthday; but a few days earlier he has a precognitive dream which leads him to cancel the air passage; and consequently he lives to a ripe old age, begets children, who beget children—he founds a dynasty of Browns. Dunne's theory implies that the decision to cancel the air passage instantaneously created, and so to speak *inserted* into the four-dimensional world, many new four-dimensional entities, including himself from age of twenty to his death, and all his descendants. To accommodate free will, Dunne is committed to the extravagant notion that a person can instantaneously create great chunks of the future part of the four-dimensional world. Dunne does not acknowledge this embarrassing implication of his theory, but perhaps he is aware of it, for when discussing this problem he sometimes slips into a different terminology, saying that what is precognized is the *probability* that so and so will happen. But if we take such statements literally Dunne has abandoned his original theory. The point of adopting the Four-Dimensional World theory was to make it logically permissible to postulate non-inferential *awareness* of future *events.* But this bold theory is being abandoned if you say that what is precognized is merely the probability of a future event; for the probability of a future event is not a future event—it's not any kind of event, but a way of referring to what we are entitled to (problematically) *infer* about the future. Thus Dunne renders his theory incoherent by trying to reconcile freedom of choice with the Four-Dimensional World theory. If one accepts the latter theory one ought to conclude that one can no more alter the future than one can alter the past.

***

I am tempted to stop here and to leave the problem in the form of an unsolved trilemma, but, for what they may be worth, I shall indicate my present views concerning the choice of an escape route. Although in discussing Dunne's theory I have not challenged the intelligibility of the Four-Dimensional World theory, I question whether it would be seriously defended by anyone who had fully worked out its implications. Those who profess to accept this theory have not, I think, done this: they continue to employ familiar words or concepts which have no place in the conceptual scheme which they profess to have adopted. They persuade themselves too easily that this theory is intelligible by means of some such pictorial image as that used by Professor Ducasse.[15] We are to picture the four-dimensional physical universe as "an endless variously mottled snake," the length of the snake representing physical time (Dunne's T_1). We are to picture this snake as crawling through our specious present (or our specious present as creeping along the snake), so that a short and continuously changing segment of the snake is, so to speak, illuminated by or to our consciousness.

To this I reply, "Very well, but if you accept this model you must accept its implications." One of these is that you must abandon *our* concept of a physical event. What *we* mean by a physical event is some *change* in the history of some physical object(s). But you, in spatializing time, are *reifying* all changes which have been and will be undergone by what we think of as physical objects; but in so doing you are dissolving *our* concept of a physical object. *We* conceive of the world as composed of three-dimensional physical things which move and change in various ways. *Your* model precludes you from saying that things like apples move or change in color or shape, for in your scheme an apple is a (four-dimensional) strand in a four-dimensional manifold. Since your model leaves no room for change in the physical world, it leaves no room for *our* concept of physical events. And since you cannot accommodate the concept of a physical event you cannot accommodate either the concept of physical causation (for we conceive causation as a relation between events). One could go further, but this should suffice to show how your theory dissolves the most fundamental concepts in terms of which men interpret their experience and describe the world. I do not say that it is *impossible* for you to reconstruct a consistent alternative conceptual scheme—this is the sort of task metaphysicians attempt to perform—but at any rate the onus is upon you to do this, and it is not enough for you to appeal to the ease with which we can picture a snake sliding along under a spotlight.

My present view is that the Four-Dimensional World theory and the other attempts to render the concept of precognition intelligible, for instance by multiplying dimensions of Time, generate such extreme paradoxes that I feel obliged to explain precognition *away* by one or other of the two methods I described earlier. No empirical evidence could ever logically *oblige* us to accept the occurrence of precognition, as the term is usually defined. One can always say, for instance, that the subject's guesses exerted a mysterious influence upon the randomizing procedure by which the targets were set up; or that the precognitive dream influenced the event which "fulfilled" it (if it was not a coincidence or the result of unconscious inference). I recognize that this position may get uncomfortable if there is strong evidence for precognition of such events as the death of a stranger, or of some disaster like an earthquake.

It boils down to the question: which of the rival interpretations of these awkward facts is the least irrational to accept? In view of the extent to which accepting the concept of precognition would violate the basic structure of our thought, I feel constrained to vote against it. Perhaps I should add, to prevent misunderstanding, that I have no objection to the continued use of the *word* "precognition" (which it is doubtless too late to erase from our vocabulary), so long as this is given an operational definition. We might define "a precognition experiment" as one in which a subject is asked to predict the outcome of randomizing procedure in circumstances which preclude the subject from inferring or controlling the outcome *by any method which we can understand.*

NOTES

1. Mundle, C. W. K.: The Experimental Evidence for PK and Precognition. *Proceedings* of the Society for Psychical Research, Vol. XLIX, 1949-52.

2. Saltmarsh, H. F.: *Foreknowledge.* London: G. Bell & Co., 1938.

3. Carington, W.: Experiments on Paranormal Cognition of Drawings. *Proceedings* of the Society for Psychical Research, Vol. XLVI, 1940-41 and Vol. XLVII, 1942-45. See also *Telepathy.* London: Methuen & Co., 1945.

4. Soal, S. G.: Fresh Light on Card-Guessing—Some New Effects. *Proceedings* of the Society for Psychical Research, Vol. XLVI, 1940-41.

5. ——— and Bateman, F.: *Modern Experiments in Telepathy.* London: Faber & Faber, 1954.

6. ——— and Goldney, K. M.: Experiments in Precognition Telepathy. *Proceedings* of the Society for Psychical Research, Vol. XLVII, 1942-45.

7. Scriven, M.: Randomness and the Causal Order. *Analysis,* Vol. 17, No. 1, 1956.

8. Myers, F. W. H.: *Human Personality.* London: Longmans, Green & Co., 1903; new edition, New York, 1954.

9. Mitchell, A. M. J. and Fisk, G. W.: The Application of Differential Scoring to PK Tests, *Journal* of the Society for Psychical Research, Vol. 37, No. 674, 1953.

10. Flew, A.: Causal Disorder Again. *Analysis,* Vol. 17, No. 4, 1957.

11. Dunne, J. W.: *An Experiment with Time.* London: A. & C. Black, 1928; revised edition, 1934. *The Serial Universe.* London: Faber & Faber, 1934.

12. Quine, W. V.: Mr. Strawson on Logical Theory. *Mind,* Vol. LXII, No. 248, 1953.

13. Mundle, C. W. K.: Broad's Views About Time, in *The Philosophy of C. D. Broad.* New York: Tudor Publishing, 1959.

14. Broad, C. D.: *Scientific Thought.* London: Routledge & Kegan Paul, 1923.

15. Ducasse, C. J.: Broad on the Relevance of Psychical Research and Philosophy, in *The Philosophy of C. D. Broad.* New York: Tudor Publishing, 1959.

Bob Brier

Mundle, Broad, Ducasse and the Precognition Problem

Of the three kinds of ESP (clairvoyance, telepathy, and precognition), precognition, or ESP of the future, seems to raise the more interesting philosophical questions. To my knowledge no philosopher has argued that either clairvoyance or telepathy is logically impossible, but the majority of philosophers who deal with parapsychological issues agree that precognition is logically impossible. In this paper I try to analyze the arguments of three such philosophers and attempt to show where they go wrong.

MUNDLE

In an article entitled "Does the Concept of Precognition Make Sense?"[1] C. W. K. Mundle comes to the conclusion that the concept does not make sense, and alternative explanations must be found. One virtue of Mundle's treatment is that he attempts to analyze what is entailed by the term "precognition" as it is normally used.

Mundle says that "precognition" and "ESP" are loaded with theory.

> They have been chosen on the assumption that the facts in question are to be assimilated to sense-perception, and that just as sense-perception involves knowledge by acquaintance, so the psychic subject must possess knowledge by acquaintance, knowledge of objects or events not accessible to his senses.

Reprinted from *Philosophy Forum*, volume 14 (1974), pp. 161-169, by permission of the author and Gordon and Breach Science Publishers Ltd.

He goes on to assert that if "precognition" is defined in terms of non-inferential knowledge of a future event "one will have to say that the knowledge in question is usually unconscious and that it spasmodically influences the subject's conscious experience or actions. (See 1, p. 182.)

Mundle seems to believe that there is something wrong with this, but never states precisely what it is. It would appear that what Mundle rejects is a fair description of the situation. In any event, Mundle prefers causal terminology. Thus, the psychic subject can be described as responding appropriately to events which he has not observed or inferred. Eventually, Mundle rejects this description also because it would involve "a cause-factor influencing what happened earlier." This, he says, is self-contradictory because part of the meaning of "cause" is that a cause must precede its effects. He supports this by saying that causal explanations involve mechanisms whereby causes modify structures of substances, initiate chains of events which span the spatiotemporal gap between causes and effects, etc. Mundle then asserts that it seems inconceivable that what occurs now could be acted upon by things which are not yet in existence. This is why Mundle rejects the possibility that precognition involves a cause coming after its effect.

To summarize Mundle's position, it may be said that he has argued that the notion of precognition does not make sense for two reasons: (1) It involves the concept of knowledge by acquaintance which would be unconscious and spasmodic, and there seems to be something wrong with this. (2) It involves the concept of a cause succeeding its effect, and there is something self-contradictory about this.

One sees nothing objectionable in the first "objection." Concerning the second, I have argued elsewhere[2] that there is no reason to believe that it is logically impossible for a cause to come after its effects. Thus, Mundle's second reason for rejecting precognition can have merely linguistic import, if it is indeed part of the meaning of "cause" that the cause precedes its effect. Thus, one might not reject precognition, but merely come up with a revised definition of "cause" or a new word to use in place of the old.

Since he has rejected precognition, Mundle is still faced with the task of explaining the facts on nonprecognitive terms. One alternative he offers is unconscious experience. That is, all ostensible precognitive experiences are the result of acquiring knowledge by nonprecognitive means and then inferring the future event in question. Mundle's second alternative involves the "precognitive experience" causing the precognized event to come true. It is not necessary to discuss either of these attempts to discredit the concept of precognition, for Mundle is correct in saying that they do not involve precognition. This paper is concerned with the logical possibility of precognition, not alternative explanations of the facts or evidence for precognition.

BROAD

A treatment of the problem somewhat similar to Mundle's is offered by Broad in a recent article, "The Notion of Precognition."[3] Broad, who has probably done more work on the concept of precognition than any other philosopher, gives what is perhaps the most thorough analysis of "precognition," or "ostensible precognition," as he calls it. Rather than defining the word "precognition," Broad chooses to define the statement "*X* was a precognition of *Y*." This definition contains five clauses. A summary of the essence of each follows:

1) *X* was either a single or sequence of human actions, and *Y* a single event or sequence of events.
2) *X* happened at *t*, and *Y* at a later moment, t_2.
3) *Y* corresponds in detail to *X* in such a way that one should say that *Y* was a fulfillment of *X*.
4) It is not a mere coincidence that *X* was followed by *Y*.
5) *Y*'s being related to *X* cannot be accounted for by either (a) *X* being a cause-factor or causal ancestor of *Y* or (b) *Y* having a common cause-factor ancestor, *W*.

The above is a fair representation of Broad's definition.

There are three points which should be made concerning Broad's analysis, two of which can be made relatively quickly. The first point is merely that for some reason Broad seems to believe that precognition is an ability only of humans. This is clear from his first clause of his definition. There is no reason for this restriction, and indeed there are many cases reported of apparent precognition in animals. Should Broad's remaining four conditions be satisfied, there is no reason that he should not accept the case as an example of precognition. This is a minor point, however.

The second point is similar to one discussed in relation to Mundle's article and involves Broad's fifth condition. Here, Broad also rules out the possibility that both the precognition and the precognized event have a common cause prior to the precognition. Once again, it must be pointed out that this is merely a linguistic point and not a logical one. Broad, like Mundle, has merely legislated what he wishes to consider as a precognitive experience. In terms of the evidence available, there seems no reason for ruling out such a possibility. Consequently, although this consideration might eventually be shown to be one of a set which suggests that it is impossible to obtain evidence for precognition as Broad defines it, it in no way suggests that the overt evidence which parapsychologists claim to have collected involves contradictions, and thus there must be some error.

The third point involves the issue which has been central in this section: Can a cause come after its effect? Broad clearly denies the possibility and asserts:

> . . . the alternative suggestion, viz., that the *fulfilling event or state of affairs* contributes to set up a chain of effects and causes which contributes to cause the *pro-referential experience*, is plainly nonsensical. For *until* the event which will answer to the present experience in such a way as to be a fulfillment of it, shall have happened, *nothing* can be caused by it. And *when* it shall have happened, anything that it may contribute to cause must be later than it. (See 3, pp. 191-192.)

Broad does not offer a demonstration for his claim, merely presents it as a self-evident truth. He does point out that, in the case of a cause coming before its effect (as in a case of past-perception, or seeing an event which is in the past, such as viewing sun-spots), the past event is connected with the present perception by a causal chain. In this chain each event is an effect of the immediate successor in the chain. According to Broad, nothing analogous is possible in the case of precognition. This is so because, until an event happens, nothing can be caused by it. The point here is not merely a linguistic one, arising from the way "cause" and "effect" are used. Rather, it is a factual point. A future event is nothing but an unrealized possibility and thus cannot influence anything. Broad goes on to claim that it is probably this fact which has caused "cause" and "effect" to be used in the way they are.

Although Broad is begging the question by asserting what is at issue, his treatment still has instructive value. This is so because he explicates how the impossibility of a cause succeeding its effect mitigates the notion of precognition. There is no condition in the definition which asserts that the precognized event must be the cause of the precognition of it. The problem arises when the fifth condition is examined for X being a precognition of Y. Here, he has ruled out X causing Y, and X and Y having a common cause prior to each. To this Broad adds the self-evident fact that Y cannot have caused X. Thus, it seems as if X and Y can in no way be causally related, and coincidence is left as the explanation for the correspondence between X and Y. This, however, is ruled out by the fourth condition in the definition which says that the relation between X and Y must not be mere chance coincidence. From what has just been stated, Broad's conclusion is not surprising: As he defines it, nothing can satisfy his definition of precognition. From what was stated earlier when considering the questions of backward causality, opposition to Broad's position is evident. His first error lies in admitting the possibility of Y causing X; this is something which he has prematurely rejected. Second, there is also the possibility of the common prior cause.

Throughout the analysis of causality, one works within the framework of the constant conjunction conception of causation. That is, A and B are said to be causally related if they are constantly conjoined. This thesis, of which Hume is the foremost proponent, has many problem areas. For example, night and day always follow each other, but is one the cause of the other? It will be noted that this statement of the thesis allows for backward causation. This is not actually the case as Hume puts it. One of his rules by which one is to judge causes and effects is that the cause must be prior to the effect.

DUCASSE

There have been many criticisms of Hume's position, but few philosophers have attempted to offer usable alternatives. In *Causation and the Types of Necessity*,[4] C. J. Ducasse attempts this. For purposes here, most of Ducasse's thesis can be ignored. He asserts that causality is a relation obtained among three terms of a perfect experiment: A, the state of affairs, and B and C, two changes in it. It will be of interest here briefly to note what Ducasse has to say about backward causation.

In discussing Russell's theory of causation, Ducasse points out that one result of what Russell says is that there is no reason to assume that a cause cannot come after its effect. Ducasse feels this is wrong and says:

"But I say that the only conclusion which is open to any English speaking, or rather English understanding reader, when he is told that an effect may well be supposed to precede its cause, is either that the assertion is staringly false, or else that in spite of appearances, it is not really expressed in English, but in some other tongue in which the words "cause" and "effect" also occur, but surely with very different meanings indeed than in English." (See 4, p. 42.)

Although Ducasse's causal theory does not specifically legislate against backward causation, Ducasse feels compelled to make the linguistic legislation against it which has been seen several times before.

It is interesting to note that Ducasse has an article which deals specifically with how his notion of causality relates to parapsychology.[5] The article is general, and does not, for the most part, deal with precognition. Rather Ducasse briefly recapitulates his triadic theory of causation and discusses determinism, psychokinesis, etc. Toward the end of the article he mentions the causal question with precognition and sketches the form his solution will take: He will try to make out that "past," "present," and "future" can be defined only with reference to psychological states and have no meaning in purely physical terms. Ducasse suggests that such a realization will help one out of the apparent paradox involved in precognition experiences suggesting a cause later than its effect. He does not give any of the details of his argument here, but presents them more fully in a later article.[6]

In this paper, Ducasse is criticizing a paper in which Broad tries to show how parapsychology is relevant to philosophy.[7] In this paper Broad discusses a wide range of topics, and Ducasse comments on each of these. This section of the discussion is limited to the precognition—causation paradox. Broad's position in the article is basically the same as in his later article in the *International Journal of Parapsychology* which was discussed earlier. He argues that it is an analytic truth that no event should have effects before it has happened. What is of interest here is that Ducasse accepts this "analytic truth" and attempts to show that it is not violated by precognition. However, some other, more vulnerable assumption must yield in the resolution of the paradox.

The basis of Ducasse's theory is that no definition of "past," "present," and "future," applied categorically, can be given in purely physical terms. Thus, physical events, apart from the psychological events which are percepts of them, are not categorically past, present, or future. Physical events are past, present, or future only conditionally—relative to other physical events. Ducasse gives a rather confusing explication of what he means here, but it may be possible to avoid analyzing this portion of his thesis. However, what he says about psychological events must be considered.

Ducasse claims that "past," "present," and "future," which apply only to psychological events, derive their meaning from a characteristic—*liveness*—which is present to different degrees in the psychological events. As an example, the hearing of the word "inductively" is presented. When the whole word is heard, liveness is that characteristic which is possessed in its maximal degree of the syllable "ly," in somewhat lower degree by "tive," etc. This is the definition for liveness.

For several reasons this "definition" is not sufficient. First, it seems as if there might be several characteristics which "ly" has in the maximal degree, "tive" to a lesser degree, etc. Here, other characteristics may be included, such as being later in time. If other characteristics are mentioned, Ducasse might reply by saying that liveness includes *all* such characteristics, but with being later in time, he cannot do this, since concepts like "present" are inseparably tied to time. But there is more wrong with the definition than just this.

Consider the psychological event of watching and being engrossed in a movie. While the viewer is attentive to the dialogue, someone whispers "inductively." It would seem as if the experience of hearing the word "inductively" has less liveness than the experience of hearing the movie dialogue, both of which are contemporaneous. This is a situation Ducasse would not want.

Still another difficulty with the definition is that "present" is defined in terms of *maximal* liveness, but no criterion for determining maximal liveness is offered. At first it seems as if it might be difficult to determine what is present. Another way of putting this is that the difference between past and present, as Ducasse makes it, is one not of quality, but of quantity. The only difference between a past and present event is that the present one has more of a certain characteristic. Because of this, there is a special difficulty in defining "future." If "present" means having the most liveness and "past," having less liveness, what is there to say about "future"? In defining "future" Ducasse says nothing positive about it; he presents a negative definition. All psychological events which are neither past nor present are future. This, too, leaves something to be desired. Before offering his example involving "inductively," Ducasse said that he could not describe the characteristic about which he was talking. This may suggest that there might be something basically wrong, or at least incomplete, about his treatment of "past," "present," and "future" as predicates of psychological events.

In summarizing his thesis, Ducasse says, " . . . psychological events can be *actually experienced* only in the order of their respective degrees of liveness, and thus of recency. . . . This entails that *the time-series of psychological events has intrinsic direction."* (See 6, p. 389.) The first point to be made here is that the connection between liveness and recency has not been established as Ducasse says it has. It seems quite possible for an earlier event to have more liveness than a later event. One remembers his last birthday more vividly (inferring this is related to liveness) than the day after it. Thus, liveness is not necessarily concurrent with recency. From this emerges a second point concerning the "intrinsic direction" of psychological events. It is conceivable that a person's experiences could exhibit an inverse relation between recency and liveness. Ducasse has given no argument against such a possibility. Thus, there seems to be no entailment that psychological events have intrinsic time direction.

It is probably evident how Ducasse uses his theory to resolve the causal paradox involved in precognition. Physical events, by themselves, do not categorically have pastness, presentness, or futureness. When a given physical event is precognized and precognition of it is a psychological event, then the physical event receives presentness, not before. Thus, there can be no problem of a nonexistent event causing something to be in the present. As soon as an event is precognized, it is present.

Aside from attacking Ducasse's method of definition, there are several approaches one can take. The following is one of the less obvious objections. An essential feature of Ducasse's scheme is that physical events, by themselves, do not have futurity. Thus, he can solve the problem of precognizing physical events. He cannot, however, handle the precognition of purely psychological events—events which would have pastness, presentness, etc., independent of the precognition of them. An example is precognitive telepathy, the precognition of someone's thoughts.

In summary, Mundle, Broad, and Ducasse all deny that precognition is a logical possibility. From the above analysis it should be clear, however, that if precognition is to be rejected as a logical possibility it will have to be on grounds other than those offered by the three philosophers discussed.

NOTES

1. C. W. K. Mundle, "Does the concept of precognition make sense?," *International Journal of Parapsychology* 6, 179-198 (1964). [Pp. 327-340, above—Ed.]

2. Bob Brier, "Is precognition logically possible?," in *Philosophical Essays in ESP*, Raymond VanOver (Ed.) (New York: Harper and Row, 1975).

3. C. D. Broad, "The notion of precognition," *International Journal of Parapsychology* 10, 165-196 (1968).

4. Curt John Ducasse, *Causation and the Types of Necessity* (New York: Dover Publications, 1969).

5. Curt John Ducasse, "Causality and parapsychology," *Journal of Parapsychology* 23, 90-96 (1959).

6. Curt John Ducasse, "Broad on the relevance of psychical research to philosophy," in *The Philosophy of C. D. Broad* (New York: Tudor Publishing Company, 1959), 375-410.

7. C. D. Broad, "The relevance of psychical research to philosophy," *Philosophy* 24, 291-309 (1949). [See pp. 43-63, above—Ed.]

Section V

Parapsychology and the Philosophy of Mind

John Beloff

Explaining the Paranormal, with Epilogue - 1977

The field of psychical research must be unique in one respect at least: no other discipline, so far as I know, has its subject-matter demarcated by exclusively negative criteria. A phenomenon is, by definition, paranormal if and only if it contravenes some fundamental and well-founded assumption of science. This alone is what makes it of interest to this Society.

Now, one would need to be almost perversely fond of mystification to sustain an interest in anything for any length of time for no other reason than that it was odd and inexplicable. Most psychical researchers, I feel sure, are drawn to their pursuit *because* they intuitively feel that these phenomena represent an important riddle about the nature of things which they want to decipher. Of course, there can be no logical guarantee that paranormal phenomena will turn out to possess anything in common beyond their negative qualifications, but there is plenty of precedent for trying to find some overall guiding principle which might embrace at least the major phenomena. In this talk I want, therefore, to discuss what such a guiding principle might be. Now, there are, on my reckoning, no more than five possibilities that are still seriously worth considering. I propose, therefore, to describe briefly each of them in turn and then weigh their respective claims on our allegiance.

The first of these basic positions which immediately confronts every

Reprinted from the *Journal of the Society for Psychical Research*, volume 42 (1963), pp. 101-114, by permission of the author and editor.

student of the psychical is the purely negative one of total disbelief. On this view there are no paranormal phenomena, there are only phenomena mistakenly believed to be paranormal. If they are of any interest this can be only to the student of human credulity and self-deception. This is the simplest and most clear-cut of my five alternatives and if we can accept it it would certainly save us a great deal of bother. We should then no longer have to explain the paranormal, instead we should simply explain it away. What, however, we shall later have to decide is whether in the face of the evidence the mental gymnastics required to sustain this position is worth the effort.

The second answer I shall discuss is much less familiar. Indeed, it seems to have had so little appeal that in most discussions of psychical research it is overlooked altogether and, yet, logically it is perfectly sound. According to this line of argument there are phenomena that are genuinely paranormal but they have absolutely no other significance. They are, in fact, the exceptions in an otherwise well-ordered universe. They occur from time to time and we may take note of the fact but nothing whatsoever follows from their existence. The laws of nature still stand, everything goes on as before, only maybe a few scientists feel chastened at the discovery that their theories have not quite the universal application which, in a more self-confident mood, they might have claimed for them.

The earliest reference I have come across to this interpretation of the paranormal as a sort of natural anomaly is in the writings of William James. In a paper he wrote in 1909 he half playfully puts forward the suggestion that perhaps the lawfulness of nature, that we had so come to take for granted, might, itself, like everything else be the product of a gradual, and still incomplete evolution. Initially there might have been nothing but absolute chaos and, conceivably, the queer goings-on that we sometimes stumble up against in psychical research may be nothing more than the vestiges of this 'primordial irrationality' as James calls it. There is not much to suggest that James himself ever took his idea very seriously but one can find an echo of it in a recent work *A New Approach to Psychical Research* by Prof. Antony Flew, the philosopher. Flew is at pains in his book to present the paranormal in as unmysterious a guise as possible without being forced to deny categorically all the evidence. Accordingly, he suggests that the phenomena are best regarded as weak anomalous effects devoid of further scientific or philosophical implications.

Both the positions we have considered so far offer reasons why *no* explanation of the paranormal is called for. My third, however, does not allow us to preserve the *status quo.* If paranormal phenomena are genuine, it asserts, so much the worse for a science which declares them to be impossible. What we must now do is to reformulate science so that they will no longer lie beyond the bounds of scientific explanation. If necessary we shall introduce new postulates into physics, bring in additional dimensions of space and time, propose new psychic fields of force, but eventually we shall arrive at a new model of the universe, a new synthesis where the distinction between normal and paranormal will no longer appear permanent and absolute. This is a point of view which is, I am sure, familiar to you all. It is one which can generally count upon a sympathetic response nowadays, especially among those who pride themselves on an enlightened and progressive outlook. The prospect of such a reconciliation between science and psychical research appears more hopeful, many now think, than it did in the early days of our Society. To the Victorians, orthodoxy in science presented a much firmer outline than it does to us. We have already witnessed a number of major revolutions in physics and this has shaken our complacency about the immutability of even the most sacred assumptions of science.

Nevertheless, if we turn to those who have actually done most to further the cause of psychical research, we shall find that, by and large, they were inspired by quite a different outlook. They did not usually think of themselves as engaged in pushing the frontier of natural science one stage further forward; they believed, on the contrary, that they were using the methods of natural science to demonstrate the existence of phenomena that testified to an entirely different order of reality: namely to a psychic or mental reality. So far from apologizing for the inexplicability of their findings from a scientific point of view they exulted in evidence which seemed to point to an aspect of human personality that did not seem to belong to the world of mere objects where physical necessitation is paramount. They combined, in fact, what might be described as a transcendental or even religious attitude to man with a wholly scientific attitude towards factual evidence, a keen appreciation of the strength of scientific materialism with a sensitivity towards its implications.

My fifth and final position is one which I hesitated to present to you. In the first place it sounds ridiculous and I am not at all sure yet whether it is even logically defensible, and, secondly, it is the brain-child of one particular individual rather than the view of a group of thinkers. However ours is a field where we cannot afford to be too 'choosy' but must gratefully accept any insight that offers the least possibility of an escape from our present perplexities. I refer, then, to the theory of meaningful coincidences or 'synchronicity' (to give it its technical though somewhat misleading designation) which was first propounded by the late C.G. Jung in a small book which came out in Zurich in 1952.[1] I may add that my hesitation seems to have been shared by its author who waited many years before finally deciding to publish.

The crux of Jung's thesis lies in this curious phrase 'meaningful coincidences'. At first glance one might well suppose that we were faced here with a plain contradiction in terms. As the word is ordinarily used a coincidence implies a purely fortuitous conjunction of two or more events of a specific sort. How, then, can a coincidence be meaningful? Well, you may point out that we can always invest any set of events with a significance of our own devising, as when, for example an artist descries a profound aesthetic significance in some purely haphazard juxtaposition of assorted objects, or when we like to attribute to destiny or providence the accidents of fortune. But this would be to misunderstand Jung, who explicitly denies that he is talking about any merely subjective significance. Synchronicity, he insists, is an objective fact about the universe, or, at any rate, is no less objective than those other fundamental categories such as space or time or causality by means of which we apprehend the external world. Indeed, there are, according to Jung, precisely four ways in which any two events may stand in relation to one another: (1) in spatial relationship (2) in temporal relationship (3) in causal relationship and finally (4) in a relationship based on what he calls an 'a-causal connecting principle' or synchronicity.

Now, if we adopt Jung's schema the interpretation of the paranormal becomes clear: paranormal events are demonstrably not based on the causal principle that appears to hold in the case of ordinary physical events, but neither are they based on some kind of para-mechanical causation such as the dualist would like us to imagine when he speaks of mind-matter interactions. The concept of causation, Jung argues, is indissolubly linked up with the transmission of energy in space and time, and it is just this that is lacking in paranormal phenomena, which can, therefore, only be manifestations of synchronicity.

I think you will recognize that we have here an idea which, however audacious and even preposterous it may appear to us educated westerners, is, in fact, of very ancient provenance. If we cast our minds back to the pre-scientific and magical past or even if we stop to consider some of the popular superstitions and occult practices in our midst, we shall be forced to admit that synchronicity has always been acknowledged implicitly by mankind even if we had to wait for Jung to give it a name. Take, for example, the many different arts of divination that one finds in almost every age and culture and which Jung, with his fantastic erudition, is able to discuss with remarkable authority. Now, a striking feature of so many of these practices is that the oracle is induced to yield its answer following the application of what we nowadays call a randomizing procedure. Jung describes some of the elaborate procedures recommended in the 'I Ching' or 'Book of Changes', that semi-magical, semi-philosophical, ancient Chinese treatise that has recently come out here in a paperback translation; but we are all familiar with the idea from such homely examples as telling fortunes from tea-leaves. Now, this random element shows that those who took such practices seriously realized perfectly well that there could be no conceivable causal connection between the disposition of the signs and the events which they portended, and nevertheless they treated it as a meaningful not a chance connection. Indeed, the whole logic of astrology, insofar as it can be said to have a logic, is the logic of synchronicity. Astrology is peculiarly repugnant to people of a rational cast of mind just because the lack of any causal connection between a man's fate and the configuration of the solar system at his birth is so glaring; but to those who think astrologically this absence of causality is no impediment. The same is true of alchemy, which was not simply a more primitive version of chemistry but was governed by the once universal belief in a natural and meaningful bond of sympathy between the external world and the world of personal private events, between what was called the macrocosm and the microcosm.

Now, Jung's point is that we would be wrong to dismiss these ancient beliefs as so much primitive rubbish. There is, he maintains, definite tendency discernible in nature for meaningful coincidences to occur in conjunction with certain psychic states of the individual. Certain emotional states, in particular, are conducive to their appearance especially those that reflect subconscious attitudes. Jung then attempts to apply his theory to the results of Rhine's ESP experiments which he does, to his own satisfaction, despite the relatively unemotional atmosphere in which such experiments are conducted.

This completes my survey of the five basic interpretations of the paranormal which it was my intention to deal with. If I may refresh your memory these were first, the sceptical interpretation, according to which the paranormal had no more significance than attaches to any other species of delusion; secondly, the theory of natural anomalies, according to which paranormal events, if they don't actually prove any rules, at any rate don't disprove them; at worst they constitute a mild nuisance to those engaged in legitimate scientific pursuits; thirdly, a view which, to give it a label, I would call scientific monism because it seeks to preserve the unity of science by accommodating the paranormal within the scope of an extended physics; fourthly, the view which is I think most aptly described as substantial dualism. And fifthly and lastly Jung's theory of synchronicity.

I do not claim that my list is, by any means, exhaustive. I have said nothing at all about any of the various supernaturalist and spiritist accounts, or about any of those other occult doctrines of an esoteric kind that still have their adherents. The fact is that I find I already have my work cut out trying to convince some of my academic colleagues that there is still a case to be made for even a relatively straightforward dualism, without my getting involved with any of these more exuberant speculations.

For the remainder of this paper I propose, with your permission, to drop the mask of the impartial expositor and attempt a critical evaluation of the rival viewpoints I have been describing. First, then, need we explain or can we explain away? Explaining away will probably always be an important part of psychical research, because we deal with matters where the sham article so often masquerades as the real thing. A great deal, as you know, has already been explained away; the question is, given a bit more time and patience, will everything in our field be eventually explained away? Here, I am afraid, there is no right or wrong answer, there is only the evidence and one's personal judgment in evaluating that evidence. It is not enough, unfortunately, to point to the excellent credentials behind some of that evidence, for, in the last resort we are all of us fallible human beings, so that even so staunch a friend of psychical research as Gardner Murphy, the American psychologist, had to confess in his latest book that he could not, "in good conscience accept the simple statement that men of integrity and good will do not deceive themselves, do not get caught in ethical traps, do not withhold data, do not give false impressions."[2] Nor is it enough to point out, what is undoubtedly the case, that most die-hard sceptics are notoriously ignorant of the evidence; there are some authorities who are both intelligent and well versed in the literature who are still not persuaded that there is anything in the alleged phenomena.

In the circumstances, therefore, I can only give you my personal opinion, and it so happens that I am convinced that there *are* paranormal phenomena. I say this, not on the basis of first-hand experience or first-hand research however, but simply because I cannot entertain the supposition that everything which has transpired since our Society was founded in 1882 is just so much smoke without even the flicker of a fire. But what will, I believe, eventually settle the issue, regardless of our personal beliefs, is whether the evidence will go on accumulating, and whether, as a result, psychical research will move towards a better understanding of the paranormal. If this does *not* happen, then sooner or later serious investigators will give up out of sheer boredom and the topic will slowly die a natural death, whatever its past history; just as many pseudo-sciences have perished already, despite whatever initial successes they may have gained. Although, like some of these pseudo-sciences, it may continue indefinitely to captivate the popular imagination. If, on the other hand, this *does* happen, then the arguments of the sceptics will soon become irrelevant and obsolete.

The great mistake which the sceptics have made, in my view, is to treat psychical research as if it were an historical issue that was at stake, like, for example, the authorship of the plays of Shakespeare. As a result, after failing to invalidate parapsychological experimentation, once for all, on some general grounds like hyperaesthesia in the subjects or recording errors on the part of experimenters or fallacious statistical analyses and so on, they have been forced into mounting a separate *ad hoc* attack against each new major investigation as it came along, even where this involved accusing reputable scientists of downright fraud. This being so, the only sensible thing to do, I would suggest, if you are a confirmed sceptic about the paranormal is to ignore it altogether. To set up as a psychical researcher with no other intention than to debunk the phenomena strikes me as about on a par with becoming a professional art critic with the intention not merely of castigating what is bad or mediocre but of proving that there never has been and never could be any such thing as good art!

But, if we agree that we cannot entirely explain away, do we still need to explain? Can we not rest content just to acknowledge these as 'wild phenomena' that defy explanation? Certainly some of the alleged facts that we are called upon to consider exhibit a degree of waywardness and absurdity which leaves us almost no option. What, for example can you make of the following incident that is recounted by the Swedish psychical researcher Dr John Björkhem in a book of his which was reviewed in the

Journal of the Society a few years ago by Professor Broad:[3]

In October 1948 a certain Swedish textile worker suffering from emaciation was admitted to the hospital at Lund, where Dr Björkhem was working as a physician. While in there the patient confided to Dr Björkhem that for some months previously he had been persistently haunted by the ghost of an elderly English gentleman. Although the patient understood very little English he had managed to gather that his ghostly visitor had during his lifetime been very active in psychical research and the name he gave was Price. Now, in point of fact, although Björkhem himself, please note, did *not* know this at the time, Harry Price had died in March of that year.

Was the patient pullling the doctor's leg? It seems most improbable. Is Björkhem pulling our leg? Again it seems most unlikely. Was Harry Price, then, really making a posthumous come-back in psychical research? And, if so, why on earth should he do so in such an incredibly devious fashion? No wonder even Prof. Broad confesses that he is baffled.

However, although this digression may illustrate the fact that one needs a sense of humour in psychical research, I do not think that an element of the absurd is by any means a necessary feature of psychical phenomena. Sometimes these phenomena make very good sense from a psychological point of view, especially if we bring to our aid a knowledge of unconscious psychology. Perhaps even the incident I mentioned, if we are to take it seriously, is not quite so lacking in rhyme or reason as may first appear. Perhaps a condition of emaciation is conducive to seeing hallucinations. Perhaps the disembodied Harry Price exploited this chance to put in an appearance. We are told that it was at Price's instigation that the patient registered at the hospital at Lund instead of in his own district, with the result that this episode came at last to the ears of Dr. Björkhem. At any rate there is plenty of evidence of purpose in this story, if that is what you demand, although it would be a strange irony of fate if ultimately Harry Price as a ghost should carry more conviction than he ever did as a ghost-hunter!

At all events, to make a policy of bewilderment is surely the worst form of defeatism. I regard this solution therefore as probably the most unsatisfactory of the five and one that should be accepted only as a last resort.

I would like next to deal with, and if possible to eliminate, the much more serious proposal put forward by Jung. Before I criticize it, I will confess that I am not without a certain sneaking sympathy for it. I say 'sneaking' advisedly, because I heartily despise superstition; and yet, if there is one irrational belief which, before I ever read Jung's book, I might, if really pressed, own up to, it is a belief in what I would call the non-randomness of runs. By this I mean that I have often been struck by the fact that, if some unusual or remarkable event occurs once, it often occurs several times more in close temporal succession, but independently on each occasion, and then never perhaps occurs again. Now I have never attached much significance to this casual observation, assuming it could really be explained on conventional lines as an allowable bunching effect, but I mention it to show that far from starting with a prejudice against Jung's theory I was quite ready to cock my ears when someone came along with the suggestion that the nature of things is such that we must revise our assumptions not only about causality but also about randomness.

Nevertheless, as I understand it, Jung is here guilty of a fallacy and it is, to be precise, the fallacy of identifying the concept of causation with what should properly be called 'mechanistic causation'. Now, in mechanics, that is to say classical mechanics, if an event A is causally connected with event B it follows that there must be an intervening chain of spatio-temporally contiguous events. Jung quite correctly points out that in ESP, information is transmitted without any such intervening chain of events, and he then concludes erroneously that causation is inapplicable to the psychic realm. Indeed, he even goes so far as to favour a Leibnizian theory of pre-established harmony to account for the normal mind-body relationship, rather than be forced into acknowledging any kind of causal interaction between mind and body. Yet the truth is that nothing in post-Humean philosophy obliges us to interpret the causal relationship in this way. Logically, an event A may be regarded as the cause of an event B provided it can be shown that an event of class A is a sufficient condition for the occurrence of an event of class B. It is immaterial whether this implies action at a distance, action across a time interval or whether A is a mental event and B a physical event. It is useless for Jung to describe such a possibility as a case of magical causality; it would still be a matter for empirical investigation whether such magical causality ever in fact occurred. And the whole evidence of the ESP work points to the fact that it *does* occur. If the concept of synchronicity implied no more than the existence of certain peculiar correspondences in nature, then one could either take it or leave it. But the whole point about the experimental method is that a deliberate attempt is made to produce certain effects. If the attempt is successful, and the possibility that the result was due to chance can be ruled out as too remote to be worth considering, then the logic of science leaves us with no option but to postulate a *causal* connection between the result and the experimental situation.

My verdict then is that, *if* Jung is right in subsuming all paranormal phenomena under the principle of synchronicity, then experimental parapsychology becomes a contradiction in terms. This seems to me a good enough reason for thinking he must be wrong. In fact, I suggest that synchronicity is a concept which has wandered by mistake into psychical research and that it belongs, if anywhere, to the field of literary criticism. In fiction meaningful coincidences abound, they are for example the basis of 'dramatic irony', but they make little sense applied to real life, unless we are going to regard our lives as preordained by a supernatural dramatist, an idea that is conspicuously absent from Jung's theorizing.

We are thus left finally with only two serious contenders: scientific monism and substantial dualism. This, as I see it, is the central issue for the philosophy of psychical research, and my final task now will be to explain where I stand on this issue. The first thing which, I think, needs to be said on this point is that, if I believed that there was any prospect at all of the kind of integration of physics and psychical research, such as the scientific monist has in mind, I would regard it as no less than an act of intellectual sabotage not to take his part. After all, ever since we abandoned the older teleological interpretation of nature every important scientific advance has come about by holding fast to the assumption that every new phenomenon, no matter how puzzling or how intractable it may at first have seemed, would eventually be comprised within the all-embracing framework of a deterministic science. What justification have we therefore for supposing that the paranormal will constitute an exception?

Now, there is one peculiarity of paranormal phenomena that tends, sometimes, to be overlooked: they almost invariably occur in connection with a human person. Now there is no a priori reason why this should be the case. One could conceive of a world in which inanimate objects took an occasional paranormal holiday during which they behaved entirely capriciously. But as it is, with the dubious exception of certain phenomena of a so-called poltergeist type and with perhaps the marginal exception of animal ESP, paranormal events are always bound up with people. Thus, whatever else they may be paranormal phenomena are always psychological phenomena and it is hardly surprising that the terms paranormal and psychical have become virtually synonymous.

The question we must ask ourselves, then, is in what way does a human being, considered as a physical phenomenon, differ from other physical phenomena? And the only answer appears to lie in the complexity of the human brain and nervous system. Accordingly, if the scientific monist is to make his case, everything will depend on how much he can squeeze out of this one critical difference.

Consider first the problem of telepathy, perhaps the best attested of all psychical phenomena. There was a time when the idea that telepathy might turn out to be some form of biological radio communication looked quite promising. This idea was further strengthened when in 1929 Berger discovered that every living brain emits a continual sequence of rhythmic fluctuations of electrical potential, and indeed Berger himself encouraged this conjecture. Today, however, I do not think that anyone, not even Soviet parapsychologists, would pin much hope on this solution. There are a number of sound technical reasons for this, but perhaps I need only mention one: the electrical activity of the brain is much too feeble to enable it to function as a transmitter. Thus, according to Dr. Grey Walter, one of the foremost authorities on electroencephalography, even the most pronounced of these brain-waves, the so called alpha rhythm, falls below 'noise level'—that is to say below the theoretical threshold for detection— a mere few millimeters from the surface of the head.

But actually the situation is much worse than this, because the evidence for other ESP phenomena such as clairvoyance or precognition can hardly be considered much inferior to the evidence for telepathy. Consequently it would be arbitrary to accept the one while rejecting the other. The possibility of explaining ESP, therefore, in terms of any hypothetical brain mechanisms or unknown forms of radiation is, to say the least, quite unrealistic. What scientific monism requires, if it is to work, is something far more radical than this: nothing less, in fact, than a new physics, a physics which can dispense entirely with the postulates of mechanistic causation.

Such a step would be revolutionary but not, we may note, wholly unprecedented. Indeed, one could point out that quantum physics long ago abandoned mechanistic causation, and in general we may observe that new physical laws and new systems of physics have arisen during the present century as a result of studying what we may call extreme states. This, at any rate, would seem to be true of relativity physics where extreme velocities are involved, it would seem to be true of the physics of fundamental particles where extremely small magnitudes are involved, to some extent it would seem to be true of low-temperature physics. Consequently it might not seem too wildly implausible to suppose that when matter reaches a certain critical stage of complexity—and we must not forget that functionally speaking the human brain ranks as by far the most complex structure in nature—a new set of physical effects might, under certain conditions, become observable and that these effects would account for the so-called paranormal phenomena.

Now it would be foolish, after all that has happened, to rule out any future development in science as unthinkable, merely on account of its novelty. Nevertheless we must preserve a sense of perspective and not let ourselves be completely carried away. The development of such a 'physics of complex systems', as I have hinted at as a minimal programme for scientific monism, would be a stupendous undertaking, one that would far outclass any previous revolution in our conceptions of the physical world. For one cannot simply create a new physics by introducing certain verbal formulations, one has got to give it a rigorous mathematical structure which one can then use to make precise verifiable predictions. And finally one has still to show how conventional physics can be derived from it as a special case. Now, if your thinking takes you in this direction, I am the last person who would wish to disillusion you. However, if you are at all inclined to talk glibly about a new synthesis, or a new unified cosmology, I would beg you to remember that nothing short of these demands can possibly foot the bill.

In view of these considerations I hope that none of you will denounce me as a reactionary mystagogue if I declare that I would prefer to put my money on a horse of a very different colour. The fact is I can see no future in the attempt to force the paranormal into the conceptual framework of systematic science. To me, on the contrary, the whole significance of psychical research, the very core of its positive content, lies in what it can tell us about mind as an autonomous principle in nature. It has become a cliché among a certain school of modern philosophers and psychologists to insist that the human person is *of necessity* a mind-body unity and is inconceivable in any other sense. I am afraid I cannot accept this as an ultimate truth about reality. Man in his natural state *is* such a unity, and it is the single psycho-physical organism that forms the subject-matter of psychology; but there are, I believe, methods by which we can hope to isolate the psychic component in man, and it is just *this* that parapsychology, as an experimental science, is concerned to do. In support of my view I would remind you that a mere century ago it was still thought that the atom was the indissoluble unit of matter, indeed the very origin of the word pointed to its indivisibility. And yet today, while it still remains true that matter insofar as ordinary chemistry is concerned has an atomic constitution, we have learned to live with nuclear physics as well as with electronics. Paranormal phenomena I maintain mark the boundary conditions beyond which we can no longer treat the individual as a psycho-physical atom; just as, to pursue the analogy, radioactivity in the heavy metals marks the boundary conditions beyond which it is no longer possible to treat matter along conventional chemical lines.

I do not agree with those who regard such an approach as a betrayal of science. I have no wish to interfere with the work of a physiologically oriented psychologist like Prof. Hebb who takes his stand on an automaton theory of mind. On the contrary I consider that the only way in which we can arrive at a better understanding of psychical phenomena is by finding out how far behaviour can be explained in purely mechanistic terms. Neurophysiological psychology is the obverse of the parapsycholog-ical medal. Nevertheless for many scientists and philosophers of science the very concept of explanation has become identified with explanation as understood in the exact sciences, where a phenomenon is said to have been *explained* only when it can be deduced from some general theory together with a set of specified initial conditions. In this sense, admittedly, I am asking you to abandon the attempt to explain the paranormal. But I would remind you that there is another weaker sense of explanation, which has a very respectable basis in common usage, and that it may be of more relevance to our purpose.

In this sense to explain something means essentially to conceive of it, not as an isolated fact, but in terms of some broader perspective. This is what we mean for example when we talk of a critic trying to explain some new movement in the arts or of an historian who is trying to explain some controversial historical episode. In this sense, too, we are forever trying to explain one another's behaviour, meaning by this not of course deducing it from a general theory as a scientist would try to do, but trying to make it intelligible to ourselves in the light of our practical knowledge of our fellow men, as a biographer or novelist would try to do. Now, when we come to the paranormal our first task should be to see if we can make the phenom-ena intelligible in straightforward human terms. Our second task, I sug-gest, is to try to make the fact of paranormality, as such, intelligible in re-lation to our philosophical presuppositions. And on this latter point only some form of substantial dualism can, I believe, meet this requirement.

This, then is my conclusion. I do not claim for it any originality; on the contrary, I would be content to think it would have gained the approval of the founding fathers of our Society, of men like Myers or Sidgwick.

NOTES

1. C. G. Jung & W. Pauli *Naturerklärung und Psyche* Verlag. Zurich. 1952. It was reviewed in this Journal 37. No. 673. 1953. 26-35. An English translation has since appeared under the title *The Interpretation of Nature and the Psyche*. Routledge & Kegan Paul. 1955.
2. Gardner Murphy *The Challenge of Psychical Research*. Harper. New York. 1961. p. 284.
3. John Björkhem *Det Ockulta Problemet*. Lindblads Förlag. Uppsala 1951. It was reviewed in this Journal 37. No. 673. 1953. 35-38. A German translation has since appeared under the title *Die Verborgene Kraft*. Olten. 1954.

EPILOGUE 1977

Evidence for the paranormal has continued to accumulate over the intervening years and parapsychology has expanded in a number of surprising ways. The intellectual climate of the late '70s, moreover, is very different from that which prevailed in the early '60s and in a sense that should favour a more tolerant attitude towards unorthodox beliefs. Nevertheless, the five basic positions that I described in the aforegoing article still stand, none so far has yielded to any other. Consider, first, the sceptical position. It remains just as difficult for a parapsychologist to get a paper accepted by *Science* or by *Nature* in 1977 as it was in 1963. It is not that the referees can point to specific weaknesses in the design or execution of the experiment in question, it is simply that they are not willing to accept the results at their face-value. The fact is that parapsychology has so far failed to pass the standard test that is applied to any controversial new finding in science, namely that it should survive independent attempts at corroboration. My own experience has taught me how hard it is to replicate another's claims in this field. Hence, until the problem of repeatability is solved, the sceptical option remains a valid one. For, in science, personal authority is never sufficient, nobody's integrity is beyond suspicion, indeed certain tragic exposures, both inside and outside parapsychology, in recent years have served to remind us of this harsh fact.

On the other hand, if scepticism is optional it is by no means mandatory. One can even say, today, that, with the introduction of automated test procedures and with the tightening up of experimental controls that is now characteristic of the better evidence, scepticism can only be sustained by assuming experimenter fraud on an alarming scale. The time is past when one could dismiss the evidence by pointing to possible methodological weaknesses or to possible contamination from experimental or statistical artefacts.

Let us turn next to the second of my five positions which aimed not so much to explain away the phenomena as to insist that no explanation, be it physicalist or mentalist, was even in principle conceivable. Supporters of this position invite us to regard psi phenomena as pure anomalies, as the undigested gobbets in the cosmic pudding. I am tempted to call this option 'Flewism' in honour of Antony Flew who is still its most eloquent and forceful exponent. Its appeal is mainly to a certain type of common sense philosopher of the Anglo-American school who is deeply suspicious of anything that savours of occultism or mystery-mongering but, at the same time, is anxious to demonstrate his empirical commitment to the facts. It is a view, however, which has found support even among parapsychologists. Thus we find no less an authority than Alan Gauld suggesting that it may be fallacious to think of ESP as representing any kind of cognitive act or information-gathering process. Instead, "the knowledge concerned," he suggests, "is, from the point of view of our everyday notion of how we acquire factual information, totally anomalous, the knowledge is not 'acquired,' the information does not 'arrive.' The knowledge, so to speak, 'happens'." [1] This, of course, is the purest Flewism.

My third position, based on the principle of Synchronicity, implies, no less than my second position, an acausal interpretation of psi phenomena but it also carries certain positive implications about the kind of universe in which paranormal events can occur. Originally I introduced this approach somewhat apologetically as being the wayward brain-child of Jung. As things have turned out, however, it has more than held its own and, latterly, has received a powerful boost from the pen of Arthur Koestler. [2] Koestler, it seems, was attracted to the idea not from studying the works of Jung but from writing the biography of Paul Kammerer. [3] Rather than invoking the collective unconscious Koestler invokes the critique of randomness which G. Spencer-Brown was the first to discuss in a parapsychological context. Essentially, however, whether we come to the idea via Jung or via Koestler the critical question which it raises is whether there can be such a thing as a 'meaningful coincidence' in the sense of a conjunction of events that is not just a chance occurrence which happens to produce important consequences for those involved? In a recent paper where I have discussed this question at length [4] I argued that such a concept is defensible but only if we adopt an appropriate cosmology to go with it. Even then it is of dubious value when applied to experimental parapsychology which, by definition, implies causation. The type of cause may be very different from that which has become paradigmatic for science as when an effect is propagated through space and time but, logically, it is still a case of cause and effect. If, therefore, synchronicity is worth defending at all it would be as an independent feature of the world, not as an explanation of psi. For example, if the astonishing evidence which Michel Gauquelin has been mustering in support of certain astrological type hypotheses is vindicated we would almost require something like a synchronicity principle to make sense of it. [5]

We come finally to my two last positions which I still consider the most important contenders: scientific monism, on the one hand, and

368

mind-matter interactionism on the other. One development that has occurred during the intervening period is, perhaps, a closer rapprochement between these two fundamentally antithetical options. Although a few scientists taking up a last-ditch stand are still hoping that the problem of the paranormal can be made to yield to a conventional physical interpretation—for example by having recourse to the idea of the psi information being carried by extremely low-frequency electromagnetic radiation—the prospect of this providing an adequate solution is becoming increasingly unreal and one, at least, of its foremost proponents, the mathematician John Taylor, has already publicly admitted that it cannot be salvaged.[6] Much the most promising approach at the present time, so far as the scientific monist is concerned, is one that derives from a particular interpretation of quantum physics. The link with quantum physics arises from the peculiar status which the observer occupies in modern as opposed to classical physics in the determination of a quantum event. Walker, whose theories in this connection have attracted more attention than any other, treats such concepts as 'consciousness' and 'will' as the hidden variables of the quantum mechanical process.[7] Both Walker and Schmidt[8] stress the significance of feedback in a parapsychological experiment, the idea being that it is at this point that the psi event, the ESP or PK, is triggered by dint of activating the subject/observer conceived as a psi-source.

An encouraging sign in the parapsychology of the '70s is the number of physicists who are active in research either as experimenters or as theorists. For this we have to thank primarily the resurgence of strong, i.e. directly observable, PK effects. As in the early days of physical mediumship, such phenomena inevitably attract physicists with an adventurous cast of mind. In this respect Uri Geller, whatever else may be said about him, has played a key role. Paranormal metal bending, an entirely novel manifestation of PK, has invaded the laboratory and already, in the work of John Hasted, has been exploited to good effect.[9] Whatever the ultimate answer may prove to be one can only welcome these bold attempts to probe the modus operandi of psi as it engages with the real world.

And yet there is a crucial difference whether the psi source is thought of as a function of a brain state or as a function of a non-physical entity or mind interacting with the brain. I have argued elsewhere[10] that our best hope of making sense of the paranormal is to start from the assumption that normal sensorimotor behaviour is just a special case of mind-matter interaction, namely the case in which mind extracts information from the brain in the form of a conscious percept or feeds information into the brain allowing intentional action to ensue. Thus normally, because our biological evolution decreed it so, we function as unitary psychophysical entities. However, in special circumstances, and it is the peculiar task of parapsychology to determine what these circumstances are, minds interact directly with the external environment, either extracting information from the world, as in ESP, or, as in PK, producing physical effects. In the latter case, however, it is not necessary to suppose that the mind exerts a force in doing so or generates psychic energy; it is simpler to suppose that the paraphysical effects come about by dint of changing the entropy of the system, that is by extracting order out of random noise. In this way mind would intervene in the real world not by violating the conservation laws of physics but by controlling the flow of information.

NOTES

1. Alan Gauld, "ESP and Attempts to Explain It," in *Philosophy and Psychical Research,* ed. S. C. Thakur (London: Allen & Unwin, 1976), see Chap. 1, p. 36.

2. See Arthur Koestler, *The Roots of Coincidence* (London: Hutchinson, 1972). Also A. Hardy, R. Harvie, and A. Koestler, *The Challenge of Chance* (London: Hutchinson, 1973).

3. Arthur Koestler, *The Case of the Midwife Toad* (London: Hutchinson, 1971). See esp. Append. I, "The Law of Seriality."

4. See my "Psi Phenomena: Causal versus Acausal Interpretation." *JSPR* (in press).

5. See M. Gauquelin, *Cosmic Influences on Human Behaviour* (London: Garnstone, 1974), or other works by this author. Gauquelin himself, as it happens, does not countenance a synchronicity interpretation and still hopes that, in due course, an acceptable scientific explanation will be forthcoming.

6. In a paper delivered at the Internation Conference of the Society for Psychical Research in April 1977. Cf. his *Superminds* (London: Macmillan, 1975), in which he defends the electromagnetic hypothesis.

7. See E. Harris Walker, "Consciousness and Quantum Theory," in Edgar D. Mitchell and John White, *Psychic Exploration* (New York: Putnam's, 1974), or for a more technical treatment, "Foundations of Paraphysical and Parapsychological Phenomena," in *Quantum Physics and Parapsychology*: Proceedings of an International Conference held at Geneva, Aug. 1974, ed. Laura Oteri (New York: Parapsychology Foundation, 1975).

8. See Helmut Schmidt, "A Logically Consistent Model of a World with Psi Interaction," in *Quantum Physics and Parapsychology* (*op. cit.*). Also his "Towards a Mathematical Theory of Psi," *JASPR*, 69, (1975): 301-322.

9. J. B. Hasted, "An Experimental Study of the Validity of Metal Bending Phenomena," *JSPR*, 48, (1976): 365-384.

10. See my "On Making Sense of the Paranormal" (Presidential Address) *PSPR*, 56, (1976): 173-195, or my "Mind-Body Interactionism in the Light of Parapsychological Evidence," *Theoria to Theory*, 10, (1976): 125-137.

H. H. Price[1]

Parapsychology and Human Nature

INTRODUCTION

This lecture is concerned mainly with paranormal cognition[2] and its bearings on theories of human personality. The importance of the phenomena from a philosophical point of view is that they do not fit in with the current Western educated outlook. This is not because they cast any doubt on the validity of scientific method. But they do conflict with the materialistic conception of human personality. The theory which they suggest is a dualistic interaction theory, but a different one from the dualistic theory of Descartes.

Parapsychology, or psychical research as we usually call it in my country, may be roughly defined as the scientific investigation of paranormal phenomena. These phenomena have usually been divided into two main classes—mental and physical. The mental phenomena include the various forms of paranormal cognition: telepathy, clairvoyance, precognition. The physical phenomena include what is called psychokinesis or telekinesis—where some human being causes physical objects to move without bodily contact and without the use of any known physical intermediary.

In this lecture, however, it is the implications of the mental group of phenomena which I chiefly wish to discuss. Telepathy, clairvoyance, and precognition are the best established of all paranormal phenomena; and if

Reprinted from the *Journal of Parapsychology*, volume 23 (1959), pp. 178-195, by permission of the author and editors.

he will allow me to say so in his presence, I think that Prof. Rhine has done more than any other living man to put them in that position. Whether we like it or not, telepathy, clairvoyance, and precognition do occur. The universe might be a neater and tidier place if they did not, and human personality also might be a neater and tidier thing. But we must put up with the facts as best we may; and if we have any philosophical curiosity, we must consider the bearings which they have on our theories of human personality.

Perhaps I should first say a word about the difference between telepathy and clairvoyance. It may be that the distinction is not in the end a hard and fast one. But it does seem on the face of it that there are two different types of paranormal cognition. In the first, information is paranormally acquired about some other person's mind: either about some experience of his or about other contents of his mind—for instance, his memories (including his subconscious memories). This is what happens in telepathy. Telepathy may be described as the mind-to-mind variety of paranormal cognition.

Secondly, there is the matter-to-mind variety of paranormal cognition, where information is paranormally acquired about some material object—for example, about a playing card in the middle of the pack, or about the contents of a sealed letter, or the whereabouts of some lost object. This is what happens in clairvoyance.

Precognition, I think, is best regarded, not as an independent cognitive power, but as one of the dimensions, so to speak, of telepathy and clairvoyance. It would seem that both telepathy and clairvoyance are in some degree independent of the physical time order. In telepathy, information may be got about something which is going to be in another person's mind at a later date. In clairvoyance, information may be got about some physical event which is going to happen but has not yet happened. Moreover, it would appear that both telepathy and clairvoyance are capable of going backwards in time as well as forward. They may be retrocognitive as well as precognitive.

I now turn to an important point about paranormal cognition in general. I must confess that I have always felt a little uncomfortable about Prof. Rhine's term "extrasensory perception." It is a very convenient term (especially in its abbreviated form, ESP). We could hardly get on without it, and I constantly use it myself, as almost all students of the subject do. But I think it would be a mistake to suppose that paranormal cognition is at all like seeing or touching or hearing, though it does sometimes manifest itself in consciousness in the form of a sensory hallucination; for example, in a hallucination of sight or hearing.

It seems to me that paranormal cognition is best regarded as a two-stage process. In the first stage, some piece of information is paranormally acquired at an unconscious level of the person's mind. In the second stage, this information manifests itself in one way or another in his consciousness. I say "in one way or another" because it is important to notice that this second stage of the process may take many different forms. The paranormally acquired information may present itself in the form of mental imagery; in the form of a dream; or a "hunch" (an unreasoned but subsequently verified belief); or of an equally unreasoned impulse (for instance an impulse to go and see Mr. X or write a letter to him). Again, the telepathically or clairvoyantly acquired idea may make use of the neurological mechanism of hallucination to "get itself across" into the percipient's consciousness. That is what happens when an apparition is experienced, if the telepathic theory of apparitions is correct. But the hallucination need not take the form of an apparition. It might take the form of hallucinatory words conveying the paranormally acquired information, either spoken words or written ones. Or again, the paranormally acquired idea may manifest itself not so much in the percipient's consciousness as in his bodily behavior. This happens in automatic writing and also in the automatic speech which occurs in some forms of mediumistic trance.

It looks as if this second stage of the process was the difficult one, the stage of manifestation or emergence. The very fact that there are so many different ways in which a paranormally acquired idea may manifest itself suggests that there is some kind of barrier or censorship or resistance which has to be overcome. To speak anthropomorphically and metaphorically, it looks as if a paranormally received idea had an impulse or urge to manifest itself or make itself known in some manner, and chooses whatever way is easiest in the circumstances. This view of the matter is strengthened when we notice that sometimes the paranormally acquired idea can only "get itself across" in a disguised or symbolic form; or it can only get itself across when it is mixed in with other items which do not have a paranormal origin but are products of the percipient's own memory or imagination (thus a dream may be partly telepathic and partly not); or it does not itself succeed in getting into consciousness at all, but some other idea which is closely associated with it does. These seem to be ways of avoiding the vigilance of the "censor"; and in such cases we need to use something like the Freudian technique of dream interpretation to discover just what piece of paranormally acquired information is trying (so to speak) to get itself into consciousness in this oblique manner.

In view of all this, it is not at all surprising that paranormal cognition is very far from being infallible. Even if the information received were always infallibly correct at the first or unconscious stage, all sorts of errors and distortions could still creep in at the second stage when it is "getting itself across" into consciousness. Moreover, telepathy and clairvoyance are not at present subject to voluntary control, or hardly at all. Some day, perhaps, they will be, when we have learned more about them. But at present these paranormal cognitive processes cannot be turned on or shut off at will, any more than artistic inspiration can, which appears to work in the same unconscious and uncontrollable manner. The most that can be done at present is to provide conditions which are favorable for their operation and then hope for the best. This is probably the point of various traditional practices like crystal-gazing which seem so utterly silly to hard-headed persons. I have read somewhere that Mongolian lamas use a rather similar method. They gaze at a lichen-covered stone and "read" Chinese characters in the wavy lines and patterns which they see. Such practices are probably rough-and-ready methods for encouraging unconscious mental contents to come to the surface. It may even be that some degree of telepathy and clairvoyance is going on all the time in all of us, and that what we need is not so much a method of turning them on and off at will (as I put it just now), but rather a reliable and voluntarily controllable method for ensuring that the information they give us will get into consciousness when we need it.

THE PHILOSOPHICAL IMPLICATIONS

So much for some of the empirical facts about paranormal cognition. Now let us consider the philosophical implications of the facts. The phenomena which parapsychologists have discovered are important from a philosophical point of view just because it is so very difficult to devise a conceptual framework, a system of explanatory ideas, which will render the facts intelligible. On the face of it, the facts which have been discovered appear "not to fit in anywhere." Indeed, that is what we mean by calling them paranormal. This word would no longer be needed if there were some generally accepted system of explanatory ideas which would render the facts intelligible.

The task of inventing a suitable conceptual framework is surely one in which philosophers should take a hand, as their predecessors did in the seventeenth century, when a new conceptual framework had to be invented (or the old one drastically revised) to make sense of the then newly discovered facts about the physical world. The new facts would not fit into the medieval-Aristotelian conception of the universe. A kind of conceptual revolution was needed, and it may be that something like it is needed now.

What is required is, first, a set of concepts which will unify the paranormal facts themselves, what might be called a working philosophy of psychical research itself. That is the first stage, and so far, we are only at the beginning of it. But secondly, and still more difficult, we need a more comprehensive set of concepts which will unify the whole paranormal field with the rest of our knowledge, bringing it into intelligible relations with what we have learned from the established sciences and from everyday experience and observation. When this second stage of conceptual unification has been achieved, and not until then, words like "paranormal" and "supernormal" will no longer be necessary.

But why is it so difficult to devise the new system of explanatory ideas which is needed? It is because the facts which parapsychologists have discovered conflict in certain ways with what is called "the modern Western educated outlook." (They do not conflict to anything like the same degree with the medieval European outlook, nor with the educated outlook of the ancient Greco-Roman world, nor yet with the educated Hindu or Buddhist outlook, either ancient or modern.)

I use the word "outlook," for lack of a better one, to describe a set of assumptions or presuppositions (often unconscious and unformulated) which determine one's intellectual attitude to the facts or reported facts which are brought to one's notice. We use these presuppositions as standards of credibility and incredibility, of intelligibility and of unintelligibility.[3]

TWO ELEMENTS IN THE MODERN EDUCATED OUTLOOK

What I have called the modern educated Western outlook is no doubt very complex. But for the purposes of the present discussion it will be enough to mention two of the most important elements in it. The first is the belief in scientific method. The second is something entirely different. It is a set of rather general beliefs or assumptions concerning human personality and its relation to the rest of the universe, beliefs about "the mind and its place in Nature," if I may borrow a phrase which Prof. C. D. Broad has used as the title of a well-known book. These beliefs about the mind and its place in Nature are logically independent of the belief in scientific method. They might conceivably be mistaken, or partly mistaken, even though the belief in scientific method was completely justified. But for historical reasons, going back to the eighteenth century or earlier, there has come to be a very close psychological connection between the two things—between the belief in scientific method on the one hand, and the beliefs concerning "the mind and its place in Nature" on the other.

I said just now that the facts which psychical researchers have discovered conflict in certain ways with the modern Western outlook. At what points do they conflict with it? First, do they conflict in any way with the belief in scientific method? I think they do not. It would be very strange if they did, because they have themselves been discovered by the use of that method. All the same, the question is not altogether free from difficulty, and it requires some discussion.

We generally assume that the mental attitude of the observer or experimenter makes no difference to the facts he is investigating, except indeed in introspective psychology, and that is one reason why the scientific status of introspective psychology has fallen under suspicion. For example, we assume that the state of mind of a chemist makes no difference to what is going on in his test tube, or that the thoughts or emotions of an astronomer make no difference to the behavior of the planets or the stars. But once we admit the existence of telepathy, it would seem that the mental attitude of the observer might very well make a considerable difference to the facts which he is observing—at any rate when he is observing or experimenting upon living creatures, especially other human beings. And another observer whose mental attitude is different might very well reach a different result.

We should all agree that the mental attitude of the observer might make such a difference if it was overtly expressed by words or gestures or by other forms of bodily behavior (for example, bodily symptoms of annoyance or fear or surprise) and that in psychological investigations carried out upon human beings or animals, or even sometimes in physiological ones, the observer must take precautions against this danger.

But if telepathy is occurring between the observer and the human being or animal he is investigating, or if we have no means of being certain that it is not occurring, these ordinary precautions will not be adequate.

Even though he takes great care not to express his mental attitude by any overt symptoms, it may well be influencing the facts he is investigating; and another observer whose mental attitude is different might still reach a different result. This is the reason, I suppose, for the remark attributed to Wundt, that if the reality of telepathy were once admitted, experimental psychology would be dead. But experimental psychology is not the only science which would be affected. The same difficulty arises in all the sciences which investigate living creatures.

But there is another consideration which is still more disturbing, because it affects the purely physical sciences as well. It concerns telekinesis or psychokinesis. If once we admit the reality of this process, it becomes conceivable that even in the purely physical sciences the state of mind of the observer might make a difference in the occurrences he is investigating. The mental attitude of a chemist might after all make a difference to what is going on in his test tube. The *de facto* success which the physical sciences have had, the "objectivity" or public verifiability of their results, might then seem to be dependent on a piece of good luck. It might be due to the fortunate fact that psychokinetic powers are rare and that the people who have them do not in general become scientists. Physical mediums are not commonly found in scientific laboratories; nor are the psychopathic adolescents who seem to be responsible for at least some poltergeist phenomena. Or again, it might be that the attitude of impartial and disinterested investigation itself prevents one's psychokinetic powers from being exercised if one has them. When a person is being trained as a scientist, perhaps he is also being trained (unconsciously) to inhibit any psychokinetic powers that he has.

What is to be said about these difficulties? Should we really have to admit that phenomena which have themselves been discovered by the use of scientific method cast doubt upon the assumptions underlying that method? An obscure and half-conscious fear that we might have to say something of the kind may account for the suspicion which many scientifically educated people show towards parapsychology, and for their unwillingness to examine the empirical evidence which parapsychologists have collected.

But fortunately the situation is not quite as bad as it may seem. In spite of what I have said about the implications of telepathy and psychokinesis, we can still use the test of public verifiability. If the discoveries which scientist X claims to have made do turn out to be publicly confirmable—if they are confirmed by all other investigators who take the trouble to repeat his observations or experiments—then we have very good ground for concluding that the occurrences which X observed really were independent of the thoughts, emotions, or wishes he had when he observed them; for the mental states of the other investigators who confirm his results are likely to have been different in each case—different from his and also different from one another. The more widespread this public confirmation is, the more likely it becomes that any telepathic or psychokinetic power which X might possess had nothing to do with the results he arrived at.

There is, however, an awkward fact, or apparent fact, which I confess has sometimes troubled me, and perhaps it has troubled other investigators too. It concerns the use of scientific method in psychical research itself. I shall purposely state the difficulty in rather an extravagant way. In some branches of psychical research, and most notably perhaps in the investigation of mediumship, it would seem that *faith* on the investigator's part is a necessary condition for achieving positive results; and sometimes not only faith but a considerable degree of hope and charity too. Every student of mediumship has noticed that there are not only good and bad mediums, but also good and bad sitters. But surely these Christian virtues are not required in the physical sciences? There the results which a man gets surely do not depend in any way upon his moral character.

One might reply, no doubt, that some moral virtues are required in the orthodox sciences too, distressing as it may be to admit it: common honesty, for instance, and also a certain humility, as Thomas Huxley pointed out long ago. But this reply does not help much. Nor will it help to point out that in all the sciences a certain degree of faith is required—faith in the orderliness of the universe, or something of the kind—for that is quite a different sort of faith from the one we are here concerned with. Faith in the orderliness of the universe does not make the universe orderly; at the most, it is merely a precondition for finding out the kind of orderliness which the universe actually has. But the faith which the parapsychologist needs, in some of his investigations at any rate, would appear to be a precondition for the very existence of the phenomena he is investigating. If the faith is lacking, it would seem that the phenomena are thereby prevented from occurring.

But I would suggest that even in this case we can still use the test of public verifiability. If, or so far as, it is true that absence of faith (or of hope or charity either) tends to prevent the phenomena from happening, this fact, like any other, must be capable of being publicly established to the satisfaction of all observers. Suppose that faith is needed for getting positive results in the investigation of mediumship, or indeed that hope and charity are needed too: the reasons for accepting this fact, if it is one, must surely be empirical reasons. We should have to conduct what logicians would call a "second order" investigation, an investigation of what happens in mediumistic investigations. We should have to establish empirically, by observation, that when people investigate the phenomena of mediumship the results which they get vary with the degree of faith (or hope or charity) which they have, and that the results are completely negative when the investigator is very deficient in those qualities. The people who observe this correlation between the investigator's faith, or other qualities of character, and the results which he gets need not themselves have any faith at all, nor any hope or charity either. The only moral qualities they need are that modicum of common honesty and humility which are required for all scientific investigation whatever.

THE MATERIALISTIC CONCEPTION OF HUMAN PERSONALITY

If I am right so far, the paranormal facts do not conflict with scientific method, the belief which is the first and most important of the assumptions or presuppositions which make up the modern Western educated outlook. What the paranormal facts do appear to conflict with is the second element which I distinguished in the modern educated Western outlook; namely, certain deep-rooted assumptions about "the mind and its place in Nature," or about human personality and its relation to the rest of the universe. It is assumed by the majority of modern Western educated people that in some form or other the materialistic conception of human personality must be the right one. Historically, there have been several different versions of this conception of human personality. The classical version of it is the theory which philosophers call epiphenomenalism, the theory that mental processes are unilaterally dependent upon brain processes, and are "epiphenomenal" in the sense that they are effects but never causes. Another and more modern version of the materialistic conception of human personality is behaviorism, of which, again, there are several different versions. Still another is the Marxian theory of human personality. An adherent of the modern educated outlook would not necessarily commit himself to any one of these theories as it stands. He might be willing to admit that no completely satisfactory formulation of materialism has yet been suggested. But what he takes to be unquestionable is that in some form or other the materialistic conception of human personality must be right, that in one way or another all mental processes must be completely explicable in terms of brain processes.

Behind this assumption there is perhaps another more general assumption which is seldom formulated clearly, the assumption that what is publicly observable is in some sense "more real" than what is not. It is assumed, perhaps, that either there is nothing at all which is not publicly observable, at least in principle; or that if there are some events or entities which are irremediably private—mental images, for instance, or thought processes or voluntary decisions—then somehow they have only a sort of second-class reality; and that such private events or entities, even though they do exist in a way, are no part of "the executive order of Nature" (to borrow a phrase from Whitehead) and in predicting and controlling what goes on in the world no account need be taken of them. Bodily behavior, on the other hand, and also the brain processes which determine it, certainly are part of "the executive order of Nature"; and of course we must take full account of them in our attempts to control and predict events, at any rate so far as events on this planet are concerned. I am not suggesting that this preference for the publicly observable is something conscious and explicitly formulated—except in a very few philosophers. But I suspect that it has an unconscious influence on the minds of many modern educated people, and is one of the things which leads them to assume without question that in some form or other the materialistic concept of human personality must be the correct one.

Now I wish to suggest that the queer facts which parapsychologists have discovered are very difficult to reconcile with the materialistic conception of human personality in any of its forms. This is because of the extrasensory character of paranormal cognition. You may remember that some time ago I ventured to express a certain amount of discomfort about the term "extrasensory perception" on the ground that telepathy and clairvoyance have very little resemblance to what is ordinarily called perception. A better analogy or explanatory model for them might be provided by the Freudian theory of dreams. But though the *noun* "perception" does not seem to me to fit the facts very well, the *adjective* "extrasensory" does.

In paranormal cognition a person obtains non-inferential information concerning some event or state of affairs outside his own organism. Now according to the materialistic conception of human personality, there is only one way in which non-inferential information can be acquired concerning external matters of fact, namely as the result of the physical stimulation of one or another of our sense organs. It is assumed that for such information to be acquired there must first be a long and complex causal chain, beginning with an event outside the percipient's body and ending with an event in his brain, and it is assumed that the reception of a physical stimulus by a sense organ must always be included in this causal chain. But in paranormal cognition we seem to have a startling exception to this rule. Here we find that non-inferential information about some extra-somatic event or state of affairs is acquired by some process which is independent of this causal chain, and the stimulation of a sense organ plays no part in the process.

Attempts have been made to get out of this difficulty by supposing that paranormal cognition is nothing more nor less than successful guessing. This very radical suggestion has been put forward by students of experimental paranormal cognition (such experiments are of course often called "card-guessing" experiments). After all, if we fix our attention on the basic experimental facts, what do they amount to but this, that with a number of subjects there is an above-chance correspondence between the symbols they mark down on the score sheet and the symbols which are printed on the target cards? Moreover, guessing is of course a very familiar phenomenon in daily life. In everyday experiences we have all met or heard of people who are unusually good at guessing. That is, their guesses are surprisingly often correct. Surely there is nothing paradoxical in the phenomenon of successful guessing, and it can have no bearing, one way or the other, on anyone's theories about human personality?

I have two comments to make on this. First, if someone's guesses are consistently correct over a long period, we are no longer willing to describe them as mere guesses. We think that there must be some explanation of his success, though he himself cannot tell us by introspection what the explanation is. (All he is conscious of is that this particular guess occurs to him, perhaps with a "feeling of rightness" attached to it.) For example, if a person is particularly successful at guessing the right answer to a certain sort of puzzle or riddle, it might be because he is very familiar with the mental habits of the people who invent puzzles or riddles of that sort, or it might be that he just happens to have similar mental habits himself. In the first case, his successful guesses are really a kind of inferences, though unconscious or subconscious ones. And what concerns us in discussing paranormal cognition is non-inferential information. The second explanation (similarity of mental habits) does not help us either, if the target cards or other target objects are selected by a random procedure. I think that the suggestion that paranormal cognition is merely successful guessing is just a refusal to look for any explanation of a set of surprising and paradoxical phenomena. At the best, it is just a way of describing the problem which has to be solved, and not a solution of it.

But secondly, it is not even a good way of describing the problem when we take spontaneous cases into account, as well as experimental ones. It is true that there are some spontaneous cases where paranormal cognition does look like guessing; for instance, when someone has a veridical "hunch" about the location of some missing object or a sudden veridical conviction that one of his relatives is ill or in danger. But when the paranormal cognition takes the form of a dream or of vivid and detailed mental imagery, or of a hallucinatory voice, or (best of all) when a telepathic apparition occurs, it would be strangely inadequate to describe these experiences as examples of "guessing."

If someone wishes to argue that the facts of paranormal cognition can after all be reconciled with the materialistic conception of human personality, how is he to set about it? I think the only way which looks at all plausible is to postulate some new and hitherto unknown kind of matter, or some new and hitherto unknown causal properties in ordinary matter, or both.

Attempts have, of course, been made to explain telepathy and clairvoyance by means of physical radiations. But it must be pointed out that this is a process of pure postulation as far as our present knowledge goes. There is no independent evidence for the existence of the supposed radiations. They are not capable of being detected by any known physical instrument. There is no known way of intercepting them or diverting them. Nor is there any known receptor organ in the human body for receiving them. (I shall have more to say about this last point presently.)

Again, it is not easy to see how any physical radiation theory could account for precognition or (if you prefer to put it so) for the precognitive character which telepathy and clairvoyance sometimes have. What kind of a physical process could it be in which the effect is earlier in time than the cause? It would almost seem that we should be forced to postulate an additional physical world, over and above the ordinary one, and to suppose that it already contains duplicates of some of the future events which are going to occur later in our ordinary physical world.

The conclusion, so far, is this: the difficulties confronting a physical radiation theory of paranormal cognition can only be overcome, if at all, by transforming the ordinary scientific world picture in a pretty thorough-going way. We should be driven to postulate strange entities and even stranger processes which are certainly not part of the publicly observable world as we now know it; whereas the whole purpose of such a theory is to preserve the ordinary scientific world-picture and the materialistic conception of human nature which is a part of it.

Still further difficulties arise, as I have hinted already, when we consider the recipient's end of the process. In ordinary sense perception there have to be highly specialized and very complex receptor organs for receiving various kinds of physical stimuli. Otherwise, whatever radiations may be impinging on our bodies, they will not produce any experiences in us; they will not provide us with any non-inferential information about what is happening outside us. But in the human organism, so far as it is a publicly observable object, observable by anatomists and physiologists, there is no trace of any receptor organ which might be affected by the postulated telepathic or clairvoyant radiations.

I am inclined to think that if we are determined to preserve the materialistic conception of human personality we shall be compelled to postulate some sort of "astral body" or "hyperphysical" body. We shall have to suppose that the human organism is not merely what anatomists and physiologists declare it to be, but that it somehow contains in addition other sense organs (and presumably other nerves and brain centers) which are made of some "higher" kind of matter, capable of being affected by the postulated radiations in a way that our ordinary familiar sense organs are not. Conceivably, there might be a new version of the materialistic conception of human personality, what might be called occultistic materialism, or astral body materialism. Or perhaps it already exists in some quarters. There might, for instance, be a new version of epiphenomenalism in which some mental events (paranormal ones in particular) are held to be "epiphenomena" of processes in the astral body, while others—ordinary sense experiences, for instance—are held to be "epiphenomena" of processes in the familiar physical body.

But this is no consolation to ordinary materialists. What they have to do is to account for telepathy and clairvoyance in terms of what goes on in ordinary publicly observable human organisms which anatomists can dissect and physiologists can experiment upon. We may notice also that this "higher body" materialism would be compatible with the possibility of survival after death, a possibility which ordinary materialism excludes.

My conclusion so far is that the facts of paranormal cognition could only be reconciled with the materialistic conception of human personality by postulating new kinds of matter, both inside the human organism and outside it, and new kinds of physical and physiological processes—entities and processes which are certainly not part of the publicly observable world.

The facts which have been established by parapsychologists do seem to me to suggest strongly that there is something wrong with the materialistic conception of human personality and that this conception of human nature can only be saved (if at all) by abandoning the principle which is one of the main motives for holding it; that is, by giving up the principle that the publicly observable material world is the only reality there is, or at least the only reality in which causally relevant events occur.

But to be fair to all parties, there is something more I should like to add. People who are inclined to postulate new kinds of matter, either inside the human organism or outside it, may be feeling after something which does, I believe, deserve serious discussion; namely, the hypothesis of a *tertium quid* which is intermediate between mind and matter as traditionally conceived, and has some of the properties of both—something which is extended in space (or in some sort of space) and yet also has mental or quasi-mental properties. Some such hypothesis has been suggested by various speculative persons at various times from the seventeenth century to the present day. Indeed, if I am not mistaken, something like it was suggested by some of the Neoplatonist philosophers in the last century or two of the Roman Empire.

But whatever merits or demerits such a theory might have, it is utterly different from ordinary materialism, and it would be misleading to call it a materialistic theory at all. For the whole point of it is to suggest that the traditional disjunction between "materialistic" and "anti-materialistic" theories is not exhaustive, and that there is a third alternative between the two.

THE DUALISTIC INTERACTION THEORY

Perhaps these remarks have already been long enough, and controversial enough. But before I end, I must say a few words about the theory of a two-sided interaction between the mind and brain. This theory, sometimes called psycho-physical dualism, is of course the traditional alternative to the materialistic conception of human personality. It has often been rejected on purely a priori grounds. It has been said that psycho-physical interaction would be something inconceivable or unintelligible and therefore cannot possibly occur. These a priori objections seem to me to have no force at all. They derive, I think, from a mistaken conception of causation, in which the relation of cause to effect is confused with the quite different relation between ground and consequent, or premise and conclusion, an error which one would have hoped had been exploded once and for all by David Hume more than two hundred years ago. What kinds of causation there are in the world is a purely empirical question, not to be settled by a priori methods. I think that Hume was right when he said that for all we can tell a priori "anything can cause anything." Nothing but experience can teach us what sorts of causal laws do in fact prevail in the world and what sorts do not.

But if we are inclined to go back to some sort of dualistic interaction theory, we must be very careful what sort of dualistic theory it is. Traditionally, the dualistic interaction theory is associated with the doctrine that every human mind is a substance, a psychical or spiritual substance, what Descartes called a *res cogitans*. And each of these mental substances was supposed to be indivisible, and moreover to be incapable of combining with any other. The world of minds, if I may put it so, was supposed to have an irreducibly pluralistic structure, though the world of matter might have a monistic one. This is the view of Descartes, whose formulation of the interaction theory is generally regarded as the classical one.

It seems to me that we shall never get anywhere in the philosophy of parapsychology (or in the philosophy of psychopathology either) unless we firmly reject this Cartesian conception of indivisible and uncombinable mental substances. And so far as I can see, it is in no way a necessary consequence of the hypothesis of two-way mind-body interaction.

The phenomena of telepathy seem to me to show that a human mind is not an insulated mental substance. On the contrary, they suggest that at the unconscious level, there is no clear-cut boundary between one human mind and another. And the phenomena of psychopathology seem to me to show that the human mind is not an indivisible entity either. We must not ignore the strange and rather disconcerting facts of dissociated and alternating personality; and it seems likely that there is some degree of dissociation in every one of us, however sane and normal he may appear.

So if we do wish to accept the hypothesis of two-sided mind-body interaction, our theory of mind must be something much less neat and tidy than the theory of Descartes. It must not be a mental substance theory, but something more like the theory of Hume and of the Buddhists, in which the unity of a mind is regarded as a matter of degree, and not a matter of all or none; and a mind, such as your mind or mine, is regarded as a very complex series of interlinked mental events, some of which are conscious experiences, and others subconscious or unconscious. This suggestion would be compatible with the tripartite division of human nature into Body, Mind and Spirit which some religious thinkers, both eastern and western, have advocated. On this tripartite theory, the remarks in the text would apply to mind, but not to spirit.

My conclusion, then, is this: if the paranormal facts compel us to abandon the materialistic conception of human personality, and if we are therefore inclined to adopt a dualistic interaction theory instead, we must be careful to dissociate the interaction theory from the substantialist conception of mind which has been historically associated with it. If we do retain the substantialist conception of mind, our dualistic theory will be as irreconcilable with the paranormal facts as any of the materialistic theories are. Indeed, I am inclined to think that the unconscious influence which the indivisible-mental-substance theory still has upon our thinking is at present the greatest single obstacle to the progress of parapsychology on its theoretical side. It has an inhibiting influence on our inventive powers and prevents us from constructing the new and no doubt very strange explanatory ideas which we need for making sense of the new and strange facts which parapsychologists have discovered.

NOTES

1. This article was delivered as a public lecture at Duke University on April 13, 1959, under the auspices of the Parapsychology Laboratory.
2. Extrasensory perception.
3. These presuppositions have been described by Prof. C. D. Broad as "limiting principles." [See pp. 43-63 for Broad's discussion of these matters—Ed.]

Michael Scriven[1]

New Frontiers of the Brain

The banquet speech provides a suitable occasion for a survey of the whole or some part of our field. I shall use it to argue that this year sees parapsychology facing a serious crisis, a double crisis in fact, although this is not, I believe, apparent to everyone within the field. I intend to explain my grounds for my belief that such a crisis is on us, to indicate one way in which we can better prepare ourselves to meet it, and to provide some of the material necessary for a defense of the kind I think necessary. It is with some care that I do not say parapsychology is *again* facing a severe crisis: of its kind this is either the first, or at least much the most serious crisis the subject has faced.

Of course, parapsychology has often faced severe financial crises and in this respect it is perhaps now better off than in most preceding years— but it is not of these that I am speaking. A cynic might indeed say that we are about due to face the first of the crises that affluence brings, the wealth that has brought such teething trouble to the social sciences in this country. But whatever the economic interpretation, the crisis itself is an intellectual one. The evidential foundations of our subject, or at least the major branches of it, are severely threatened, in a way they have not previously been threatened, not by Spencer Brown nor by the exposure of medium after medium, nor by the devastation of Hettinger's work, or the elimina-

Reprinted from the *Journal of Parapsychology*, volume 25 (1961), pp. 305-318, by permission of the author and editors.

tion of the claims to seriousness of the healer-diagnostician de la Warr, the telepathic horse Clever Hans, the cloud-buster, the retrocognitive story of *An Adventure,* the ghost of Borley Rectory, and possibly the claims of the water and metal-diviners—or by any other of the similarly arduous, often brilliant and often unpopular pieces of scientific research that have frequently made me feel that we number in our midst the only competent and open-minded critics of parapsychological material, and feel proud that this was so.

The crisis that I now see upon us is not indeed due to any single issue or attack. It is due to the cumulative effect of two trends. One is what I shall call the evaporation tendency or trend, of which I have just given examples, the trend towards the reduction in the number of independent paranormal phenomena of whose existence there seems a substantial possibility. This negative trend is supported not only by examples of *disproof:* in evaluating it one must not forget the number of phenomena that have persistently *failed to recur* in the period of high-powered parapsychology, which I would take to be the last twenty-five years. Of these, ghosts are only the most famous; levitation, the rope trick, materialization, many of the old-time physical mediumistic phenomena, death by pointing the bone, many of the voodoo, mana, and witchcraft phenomena, and many others must be included. Honesty compels me to add that I would add to this list—despite the contrary opinion of those whose ability I greatly respect—the poltergeist. The field of the paranormal appears to have dwindled away under the scientific microscope of the parapsychologists. It is well worth noting again that evaporation has been achieved, not by the critics of parapsychology but by good scientific parapsychologists.

Apart from this negative trend—towards the evaporation of the paranormal supernatural—there is an almost equally significant trend in some areas towards its reduction to the normal. What we at first took to be paranormal phenomena turned out on closer examination to be only special cases of perfectly ordinary phenomena—and I do not mean that we *simply* became accustomed to something and thus extended the range of what we took to be normal. The classic example of this trend, which I shall call the absorption trend, is the fate of hypnosis which was originally a subject of special interest to our ancestors in the founding days of the Societies for Psychical Research. To begin with I believe this *was* merely a case of familiarity breeding content, but today I think we can see most, though not all, of the connections between the normal psychological phenomena of habituation, conditioning, and neural resonance, and genuine hypnotic effects. Notice incidentally the concomitant reduction in the field of accepted hypnotic phenomena, by comparison with the original accounts, beginning with the excessively skeptical early work of Clark Hull: thus we have here a combination of the evaporative and absorptive trends. Another example from the field of suggestibility effects is the history of miraculous cures and the faith-healers. The careful analytical work of men like D. J. West has provided the destructive, evaporative beginning and we then see revealed only the commonplaces of psychotherapy which by absorption takes over our field. Again, the subject is far from closed even now, though apparently christening faith-healing "the placebo effect" has made it an entirely respectable subject for ordinary scientific inquiry! Closed or not, it is no longer part of the paranormal. The eventual disposition of the homing phenomenon in pigeons, etc. is not yet clear: if a natural account emerges, we shall be able to point once more to the contribution of the parapsychologists.

Perhaps the best examples of the absorptive trend, from my point of view, would be the fate of firewalking (where realism and physiology have taken over from exaggeration and parapsychology) and automatic writing, now a standard dissociative phenomenon.

Notice the way in which physiology figures in each of these absorptive examples. It is probably the development of this subject, and of neurophysiology in particular, which has been principally responsible for the narrowing of the field of parapsychology. This is one of the two reasons for the title of this paper. Think for a moment of Grey Walter's important Fourteenth Myers Memorial Lecture, which has just been published under the title "The Neurophysiological Aspects of Hallucinations and Illusory Experience." Grey Walter does not explicitly draw the following conclusions from his work, but they are plain enough. First, there are now excellent reasons for supposing that a very large number of people will occasionally have startling lifelike hallucinations (or dreams) whose subject matter is likely to be people or circumstances of great emotional importance to them. This seriously weakens one step in the usual inferences to the paranormal significance of a veridical experience. For we usually ask—in investigating alleged veridical phantasms—whether the subject *commonly* has startling experiences or dreams, our idea being that one "hit" among many "trials" is proportionately less significant. This question is not the only one we should ask, however, for there is also the possibility—now seen to be highly probable—that the frequency of such experiences may be very high *across* people even where it is unusual for any one person. And if this "interperson frequency" is high, the fact that in one or two cases per 100,000 we get a correspondence to reality is just as insignificant as it would be if one person had 100,000 such experiences with one or two successes. In my judgment, the work of neurophysiologists, such as Grey Walter, has completely and finally undercut the possibility of drawing any conclusions about the existence *or* nature of telepathy and clairvoyance from spontaneous phenomena. Of course, the theoretical possibility remains open that some quantitative measure might be devised which would show a disproportion between the natural expectancy of success calculated from the normal base-rate of such experiences and the actual number of successes. But I believe all our work on evaluation supports me when I say that such a possibility is fantastically remote.

The second conclusion which follows from his work illustrates the absorptive trend in its most powerful form. I think we should probably now view our data on spontaneous phenomena as only data for the neurophysiologist and psychologist in their work on the mechanisms of projection and neural aberration and breakdown. Our conclusions undercut and our data appropriated!

This is a severe comment, and there is one perfectly rational reply which I myself thought adequate until recently. It might be said that the spontaneous phenomena could not be thought of as constituting the *grounds* of scientific belief in ESP, but they can serve to illustrate its mechanisms and suggest further laboratory experiments. Alas, even supposing we have unquestioned independent evidence for ESP the spontaneous phenomena could virtually never be reliably identified as instances of that rather than of coincidence plus neurological accident. Hence we could virtually never be sure we were identifying the mechanisms of ESP rather than those of normal psychology and physiology.

Nevertheless, one might respond to the whole tenor of my remarks so far along similar lines. One might say that whereas the over-all number of fields of parapsychology has shrunk under the scientific microscope, we have simply shed the dross and refined and expanded the yield from the fields of good ore, i.e., the field of laboratory ESP, so that actually there has been no over-all diminution in the field. This is indeed the only possible line of defense. The trouble with it lies simply in the vulnerability of the key work here. By "key work" I mean the few experiments with overwhelmingly positive results. There are good reasons for assessing the evidential value of these as higher than that of many less striking experiments even when the combined mathematical probability from the latter is the same as from the key work. (See my "Modern Experiments in Telepathy" in *Philosophical Review,* April, 1956.) Now there has simply not been enough of these key experiments *in recent years* to stifle a feeling of uneasiness in many of us which has partly manifested itself in the search for a "repeatable" experiment. That feeling of uneasiness is now brought to a head by C. E. M. Hansel's attacks.[2] It is easy to react negatively to the occasionally intemperate tone, to some of the definitely unjustified remarks or the extremely dubious philosophical framework of his remarks. It is exactly this kind of reaction we must studiously avoid, for it is exactly this kind of reaction to the work of Mesmer, Freud, and Rhine that has so often in the past identified the unscientific scientist. We must not make the mistakes that have often made our critics ridiculous. The question of importance is not "Do I like the man?" nor "Is he absolutely correct?" but "Can we learn something from him?" From Hansel I think we had better learn, because Hansel has propounded what I take to be the first really serious criticism of the key work. From George Price[3] and David Spencer Brown—or, more accurately, from the discussions they precipitated—there was something to be learned, but it was of a general, philosophical kind, about the nature of evidence and randomness. Hansel has discovered *internal* evidence which lends some support to a counter-hypothesis. He takes that counterhypothesis—I speak on the basis of his earlier articles and without having seen the manuscript of his book—to be fraud. It is clear that there are other possible ways of interpreting his data, perfectly consistent with the ESP hypothesis, but in any case he has exposed an Achilles heel in the data that we had not previously fully recognized. It is too highly dependent on too small a family of key successes. The effect of this is to make it too susceptible to being explained away by a single counterhypothesis, whether it involves fraud or not. At the stage when we realize this, we should become more seriously concerned by the relative rarity and antiquity of our key experiments. It is in my view now inescapable that we reverse, or at least partly suspend, what was until now the sensible trend in parapsychological experimenting, the trend away from proving the existence of phenomena, towards proving something about their fine-structure. I am afraid we must go back to our primers, or at least arrange our work so as to include some work on them.

It is important to stress that the concern with repeatability is *not* the crucial matter. The Lisbon earthquake is not repeatable but its occurrence is extremely well established. *If* we can get repeatability, all the better; and eventually it is highly desirable. But it is not a requirement of all scientific claims that they be subject to test by repetition. It is only if they involve a claim with an unrestricted time variable, e.g., that Basil Shackleton is *always* able to score on $(+ 1)$ GESP [4] tests, or that most school children (i.e., now as well as in the past) display ESP rapport with their teachers. Our proper concern is with finding several subjects who—possibly under quite different conditions—do in fact maintain a score at around 30-50% above MCE [5] as Mrs. Stewart did with her best agents.

The need for reconfirmation arises, not because repeatability is always a requirement, but for quite other reasons. The comparison we should have in mind is with the observation of the canals on Mars: the colossal difference between what is observable under exceptionally good and under normal seeing conditions was quite enough to account for the absence of confirmation for a long time, even with more powerful telescopes. But with the passage of time, we became increasingly aware of several kinds of counterhypothesis—for example, the optical illusions which lead an observer to "see" lines where in fact there are only dots. Today the feeling is one of general skepticism though not of complete disregard. I believe we must face the unwelcome fact that time and Hansel have undermined the key work in a way not unlike in kind, though importantly different in degree, from the way in which time and Dingwall have undercut our confidence in many of the best earlier séance reports in which we still cannot identify any specific weaknesses. This is not mere failure of nerve. It is a combination of two judgments—first, that even though the claims themselves *were* restricted in time, if phenomena of that kind ever occurred it is probable that *something like them* would occur somewhere else in some way. If it has not, and if we have been looking hard, this makes it slightly less probable with every passing year that the original reports were correct. I do not say the possibility diminishes to zero, but it does, and should, diminish.

Second, there are good grounds for supposing that our critical faculties are steadily improving in this field, so that we eventually have grounds for suspecting that if *we* had been present in the earlier days, we might well have detected some loophole not apparent to the less sophisticated workers of, say, the last generation. Will these arguments, which evidently affect most of us in evaluating the early séance data, apply to Dr. Soal's much more recent work with Shackleton and Stewart? Hansel's suggestions make it clear that they do, because we can now see certain ways in which it would have been desirable to tighten up the control of his experiments. (I say nothing of Soal's latest work *The Mind Readers*[6] because it is all too clear that a tremendous loophole exists in those experiments. However they do demonstrate exactly how *not* to run experiments with any new high-scoring subjects, i.e., do the experiments and then publish the design for open discussion.)

There is another respect in which we must learn from Hansel's attack, distasteful though it is to mention it. Whatever may be said about the manner in which he treated his hosts at Duke and Dr. Soal, there is no doubt that he was not always fully and freely accorded access to all the data in England at least, and there is no doubt that some of his perfectly valid criticisms of the records were "hushed-up" or held back instead of being given every kind of acknowledgment in the journals. The full facts of the various issues are not yet before us and I may have to change my conclusions about where the blame lies—but I shall not have to change them much because it is the absence of a proper discussion—early, open, and with replies all around—which is principally culpable, and that absence is quite indisputable. (In England public discussion has been essentially nil; here, recent and still incomplete.) A subject loses its claims to scientific respectability when it closes its publications to bitter or radical criticism; there are already too many examples of this behavior to be found around us, in the scientifically moribund field of psychoanalysis for example. Again, it seems a mistake to produce ad hominem arguments against critics who do not employ them. Hansel's papers in the *Journal of Parapsychology* are models of temperance; the replies are not. Certainly it is Hansel who is alleging fraud and some indignation is understandable. It is neither necessary nor desirable.

Notice the difference between the kind of evaluation I am making and that of George Price. He argued from external grounds to the impossibility of ESP: I argue from internal grounds to the need for new foundations. One should not be alarmed by the inconsistency of ESP with current physics (even if that inconsistency existed, which I doubt); if one has valid experiments yielding odds of 10^{70} to 1 for ESP, then goodbye physics! But one *should* be alarmed the moment a shadow of doubt grows about the validity of those key experiments. It will be a test of the reader's detachment if he is surprised to find that I am myself in no doubt about the existence of ESP: and nothing that I have said above implies that I am or should be. Of course, it may be expected to set off the usual emotional reactions among those who think in terms of allegiances or antagonisms instead of logic, for it *is* critical. But I think it clear that Hansel's arguments, though significant in the way mentioned, are simply not as strong as his conclusions, nor as strong as those of Pratt and others in the discussion so far. (*Journal of Parapsychology,* June, 1961.)

This paper is an exercise in what one might call long-term logic, i.e., the structure of arguments involving long-range extrapolations, the conclusions being probability *modifications* rather than demonstrations or eliminations. So far it has been concerned with the conclusions that one might draw from noticing the shrinkage in the number of parapsychological phenomena, and I have suggested that this puts *added pressure* on the remaining fields to counteract the normal extrapolations of this trend. It could not possibly be grounds for outright rejection of perfectly good evidence: I have also suggested that these remaining fields are themselves suffering from certain internal extrapolations due to lack of recent key experiments. The added pressure from this further source unfortunately comes at the same time as discoveries which to some degree affect our confidence in some of the key experiments. I consider that this total situation constitutes a serious crisis and I have proposed certain measures to deal with it: a wider search for key subjects, a greater willingness to face the deterioration of evidence with age, and increased analytical skills.

I now wish to turn to a closely related though somewhat more philosophical set of problems within parapsychology where it seems to me our defenses are very poor and in need of a concerted effort at repair. Anyone picking up recent issues of the *Journal of the S.P.R.* and the *Journal of Parapsychology* would be struck by the pervasiveness of debate or comment on the relations between the phenomena of physics and those of psychology and parapsychology. Interestingly enough, this has an extremely close bearing on the present evidential status of parapsychological phenomena. The service I hope to perform here is to set out some of the issues and the location on the battlefield of some of the forces, introduce you to a new force about which parapsychologists have not been fully informed despite the extensive discussion of it in journals, explain the relevance of the engagement to the problem of evidence and to certain general claims about the significance of parapsychological findings, and suggest my own conclusions.

On the major issue of the relation of the mind to the body and in particular to the brain, there are—as you know—two main schools of thought, the monists and the dualists. The monists, who believe there is only one fundamental substance or type of entity involved, may decide that it is mental (the idealists), physical (the physicalists—sometimes the term "materialist" is used synonymously with physical), or of some third kind (the "neutral" monists). In any case, it appears that they have no problem of explaining how the mind and brain affect each other; since there is only one thing involved, there cannot be a problem about any causal relation, which would involve two things. Their problem is to explain why there *seems* to be a distinction between mind and body, and a correlation or causal connection between them.

The dualists accept the existence of two fundamentally different kinds of entity, and are then faced with the problem of deciding how they are related. The parallelists maintain there is a constant correlation or synchronicity between mental and physical events, but not a causal connection between them, although within each separate sequence of events there may be causal connection; the epiphenomenalists believe that all mental events are caused by physical ones, though not vice versa, and that, unlike physical events, no mental events cause other mental events; and the interactionists (as I shall interpret their position, which is some-times ambiguous) believe that both mental and physical phenomena can cause phenomena of the same and of the other kind. I assume that *mechanism* means much the same as physicalism and materialism in contemporary philosophical parlance, but I shall try to avoid the term.

In our own field, we find Smythies as a monist, sub-species physicalist (he thinks sense-data are "end products of the causal chain of perception" and in the brain), with most of the rest being dualists; Zorab and Grey Walter being epiphenomenalists; Pratt, Rhine, Broad and Burt being —probably—interactionists. I am pleased to say that everyone seems to agree on two rather important propositions (1) that there is an external world, which rules out idealism, and (2) that some mental states are caused by some physical ones, e.g., headaches by excessive drinking, which rules out parallelism.

At this stage the disagreements start. In order to keep our feet on the ground I shall take four putative phenomena, two normal and two para-normal, and examine their implications for the mind-body problem, rather than talking at the theoretical level.

As the first phenomenon, consider the existence of a correlation between mental and physical states such that every variation in the former is accompanied by a variation in the latter (though not necessarily vice versa). This is a fundamental premise for physicalism and epiphenome-nalism and is not usually denied by interactionists, hence its *truth* does not decide the dispute. But if it were *false,* only interactionism could still hold. So a great deal hangs on its truth in this sense. *Is* is true? We shall return to that question in a moment. I shall also comment on the exercise of the will to command the body, which R. H. Thouless and Cyril Burt take to be the everyday case of PK,[7] and which the epiphenomenalists and physicalists take to be an illusion; on telepathy, which Rhine and Pratt take to disprove physicalism; and on survival which is thought by Broad and Zorab to disprove both physicalism and epiphenomenalism. Let us turn to the first putative phenomenon.

Is there a separate brain-state for every mental state? We have a quite negligible amount of direct evidence for this Hypothesis of Neurophysiological Determinism, as it is sometimes called, but we certainly have no evidence to the contrary, and there is a reasonable though not overwhelming presumption in its favor stemming from the immense, though not unrestricted, success of determinism in general. It could apparently be disproved only if we could perform the physically virtually impossible experiment of observing the brain state to remain unchanged while the subject's thoughts changed. This is physically virtually impossible because the brain is never static and it is not only sustaining but also functional circuits that are in constant flux; moreover, the brain stem is almost inaccessible from complete observation, being masked by the outer layers.

Nevertheless, it appears conceivable that we might decide to abandon the Hypothesis of Neurophysiological Determinism (HND). Suppose, for example, that examination of the brain processes of individuals who come to a decision after meditation displays a condition during the meditation absolutely indistinguishable from the process during any other reflections, problem-solving, etc., terminating in a burst of activity in the centers appropriate for implementing the decision. In that case, interactionism would be in and the rest out. (I may add that it is in fact rather hard to reconcile interactionism with the HND, though interactionists rarely see this.)

Now, unless this unlikely and wholly nonparapsychological discovery is substantiated, the usual arguments in our journals will not suffice to defeat physicalism. Telepathy, for example, may be *thought* of as the influence of mind on mind, but then being in love is often thought of as a communion of souls and neither phenomenon has the least logical force against a carefully thought out position by those who are skeptical about minds or souls. For if physicalism is true, then telepathy is simply an example of a hitherto unknown interbrain reaction which could be regarded as analogous to the discovery of magnetism. Of course, telepathy might be a useful accessory in an assault on the Hypothesis of Neurophysiological Determinism: a super telepath might be able to provide an independent check on whether a given subject *was* actually thinking when his electroencephalogram remained constant. But *only* through disproving that hypothesis could physicalism—materialism be disproved.

The same discouraging remarks must be made about the exercise of the will. If this is a case of mind affecting matter (the brain) and if interactionism is true, then it is or it could be a model for the PK effect, but until those premises are established (by disproof of HND) it can be perfectly well accounted for by the physicalists and the epiphenomenalists. It is most undesirable for parapsychologists as scientists to commit themselves to a theory of extrasensory perception which requires the falsehood of the basic tenet of neurophysiological psychology, when all our phenomena can perfectly well be handled within a framework which is consistent with it. We should not fight at the new frontiers of the brain unless we have to.

Now surely there is *one* parapsychological phenomenon which has the most direct bearing on the mind-body problem. Broad, Thouless, and Ian Stevenson have recently argued that the IPA[8] phenomenon, or survival, demonstrates the independence of the mind from the body. Broad indeed puts it by saying that this is the absolutely crucial and only parapsychological phenomenon which counts against monism and hence materialism. To this I would say, first, that it is then quite essential we apply to the evidence here the same "back-to-bedrock" attitude I have recommended with respect to the ESP work, noticing particularly how very long it is since we had good evidence and viewing the cross-correspondences as long overdue for critical reassessment. Secondly, I would say that we must not imagine we can show water vapor is fundamentally different from water by showing that it continues to exist when we remove the saucepan of water from which it originated. The mind may be a kind of field or emanation or related form of the brain which is eventually and rarely capable of independent temporary existence. This would not prove materialism to be false or dualism true in the supposed sense. I would myself think this kind of hypothesis inherently *more* likely than a radical two-substance dualism, partly because we have many analogs for it in nature and it would permit of explanation without the introduction of special correlation laws.

I am thus suggesting that we have often been too quick to think in a stereotyped way about the interpretation of parapsychological phenomena; carefully evaluated, they count less in favor of dualism than has been usually supposed among parapsychologists, if indeed they count in that direction at all. I view this as fortunate since I think we may expect an advance of the frontiers of the brain, of materialism if you will, which could well be of the greatest service to us and should not be thought of as a threat to ESP in the way in which the advance of electromagnetic technology, exemplified by the snooperscope, was a threat to the physical mediums. There is no need to suppose that the identification of an ESP organ, or of an ESP mechanism perhaps analogous to known fields, would constitute either absorption or evaporation of our field. To discover that ESP is just as brain-dependent as abstract thought is not to discover it does not exist. Surely that point must be clear and we must not arouse opposition among neurophysiologists by behaving as if we were fundamentalists facing the development of evolutionary biologists. So far from being threatened by the subject, it can—and already has—afforded us new ideas and tools of great value. I think we have only a limited chance of survival as a science if we commit ourselves on what I see as purely dogmatic grounds to the denial of materialism. This would be the more tragic since I believe there are perfectly good logical grounds for rejecting monistic materialism. Moreover they apply to and overpower a much more sophisticated form of materialism than is usually discussed in parapsychological circles, a version which has replaced behaviorism as the philosophically "in" physicalist thesis. I add two cautions in case this sounds more exciting than it is: the weaknesses in this new version (known as the Identity Theory) are neither very novel nor in any way related to parapsychology. The plain facts of our own experience, logically analyzed, demonstrate the irreducibility of sensations to brain states. The development of the Identity Theory recently has been largely in the hands of Feigl and Smart and I shall not attempt to do more than bring it to your attention. Feigl's article "The Mental and the Physical" in *Minnesota Studies in the Philosophy of Science* (Volume II, ed. H. Feigl et al.) provides the most comprehensive exposition and a stupendous bibliography. (My own detailed comments will be found in the forthcoming Feigl Festschrift volume for Feigl, edited by P. K. Feyerabend.)[9]

Dualism is true, but two questions remain. The obvious one: Which version of dualism? And an important but subtle one: How can science ever explain the fact dualism apparently must take as fundamental; viz., the existence of an enormous number of basic correlations of certain sensations, e.g., sharp shooting pain, with certain brain states? Cyril Burt sees this problem but answers it by saying these correlations would be inexplicable—just some more of the basic postulated correlations in science. But I can think of only one or two such, compared with the *embarras des richesses* psychophysical dualism yields. This is contrary to the spirit of scientific economy and yet apparently inescapable. There is just one ray of hope here. The correlations are not between two independently identifiable properties, a fact recognized in the old "Perhaps when you see green, you see what I see when I see red" puzzle. I believe this ray of hope actually sheds enough light to get us out of the dualistic darkness and into the (dualistic) light. Similarly, I think we can demonstrate the truth of inter-actionism as an answer to the first question—which kind of dualism should we adopt. But I only *think* this: I have not yet found or constructed such a proof.

To conclude then, let me remind you of a development in the history of biology of great importance to us. For a long time there was a popular school of theoretical biology—it still has its supporters—the entelechists, which maintained that purposive behavior in organisms clearly demon-strated the falsehood of mechanism. This was simply a logical error, but it had serious scientific and social consequences for the entelechists. Scien-tifically, it misled them into fruitless theorizing about *élan vital* etc.; socio-logically, it made them the reactionaries of the continuing scientific revolu-tion in biology—they became the old men, the foes of progress. We cannot afford those consequences. At the very least we should recognize the primacy of the facts about ESP phenomena over any metaphysical frame-work commitments we may have, and their compatibility with several al-ternative frameworks. It is particularly tempting for the worker in an un-popular field to see the prevalent ideology of the conventional scientist as culpable for the unpopularity and the criticisms; and he may be supported in this view by the conventional scientist. Both are usually, and in the present case definitely, incorrect.

Thus I believe we face a double danger; over the evidence and over the interpretation of the evidence. If we do not exhibit a willingness to redo old work and rethink old thoughts I am afraid we shall find that the processes of evaporation and absorption will remove our subject matter.

NOTES

1. An address delivered at the fourth annual meeting of the Parapsychological Association, Sept. 8, 1961.
2. [Culminating in: *ESP: A Scientific Evaluation,* by C. E. M. Hansel (New York: Scrib-ner's, 1966).—Ed.]

3. [See Section II above. pp. 143-204—Ed.]
4. [*General Extra-Sensory Perception*—Ed.]
5. [*Mean Chance Expectation*—Ed.]
6. [London: Faber and Faber, 1959—Ed.]
7. [I.e., psychokinesis—Ed.]
8. [I.e., *Incorporeal Personal Agency*—Ed.]
9. [See: Michael Scriven, "The Limitations of the Identity Theory," pp. 191-197 in: Paul K. Feyerabend and Grover Maxwell [Eds.], *Mind, Matter, and Method* (Minneapolis: University of Minnesota Press, 1966).—Ed.]

John W. Godbey, Jr.

Central-State Materialism and Parapsychology

It is sometimes argued that Central-State Materialism (CSM) would be falsified if the existence of parapsychological phenomena were established. For example, Keith Campbell has written that "if even a single example of . . . paranormal phenomena is genuine, Central-State Materialism is false."[1] Similarly, D. M. Armstrong gives several possible ways of 'explaining away' the data of parapsychology, and then remarks that "If these ways of escape prove unsatisfactory, Central-State Materialism cannot be the whole truth about the mind."[2] It is these assertions which I wish to refute in this paper.

CSM is one form of the Identity Theory of mind and body (IT). By the 'Identity Theory' I mean the theory which holds that all mental states are as a matter of fact identical with states of the body. Some philosophers, such as Smart and Armstrong, believe that the bodily states in question are states of the central nervous system, and this is why they call their materialism 'Central-State Materialism.' Their theory is a version of *materialism* because they believe that the central nervous system and all of its states and properties are physical or material, or physical neutral. (States or properties are 'physical neutral' if, even though they are not physical, non-living physical bodies can be in them, or have them. *Being beautiful* or *being the third member of a series* are examples of physical

Reprinted from *Analysis*, volume 36 (1975), pp. 22-25, by permission of the author.

neutral properties.) The beliefs that mental states are identical with states of the central nervous system and that the central nervous system is solely physical or physical neutral are the heart of CSM. In order, then, to demonstrate the consistency of CSM and parapsychology I must (a) show that parapsychological phenomena do not imply the falsity of any of the identities asserted by the IT; and (b) show that these phenomena do not imply that the central nervous system is not solely physical.

(a) A number of parapsychological phenomena involve a person's allegedly coming to know something by a means other than reasoning, memory, sense perception or some combination of these. If the person comes to be aware of another person's mental states the phenomenon is called telepathy; if he comes to be aware of an event which will take place in the future it is called precognition; and so on. Let us suppose that precognition occurs: how could this refute the IT? Since the IT is only a claim that mental states are identical with bodily states, if precognition can refute the IT then from a description of a precognitive event it must follow that one or more of the identity statements are false. The one most relevant to precognition is

To know such and such is to be in brain state such and such.

But a statement asserting the existence of precognition is compatible with any statement which asserts that to know something is to be in a certain state. The existence of precognition could only show that one came to be in that state in a peculiar way. When we assert the existence of precognition we are asserting the existence or non-existence of certain causal relations; and since the IT neither asserts nor denies any causal claims, it cannot be falsified by the existence of precognition.

This argument can be generalized fairly easily. The vast majority of parapsychological phenomena can be placed in one of two mutually exclusive categories: the mind either comes to be in the state it is in (knowledge, belief, etc.) by paranormal means (e.g., precognition), or it causes something else to be in the state it is in by paranormal means (e.g., psychokinesis). But the acceptance of either of these kinds of phenomena, though it may cause a large revision or even rejection of parts of science or the philosophy of science, is compatible with the claim that the mental state in question is a brain state. Thus they are compatible with the IT.

(b) It follows that if parapsychological phenomena are incompatible with CSM it can only be because the phenomena are incompatible with mental states being physical or physical neutral states—for this is all that CSM adds to the IT. And since all that the existence of the parapsychological phenomena would show is that certain causal chains do or do not occur, if Campbell's or Armstrong's arguments are sound they must show that physical or physical neutral states cannot enter into the appropriate causal chains. Neither of them—nor any other writer with whom I am familiar—has even attempted to show this. Rather, they argue that parapsychological phenomena are incompatible with modern science. Campbell's argument is typical:

> Parapsychological phenomena, by definition, demonstrate capacities of mind which exceed any capacities of brain. The brain is receptive only to information which arrives by neural pathways, and so is confined to perception by way of the senses. If some people can learn more about distant, hidden, or future fact than memory and inference from present sense perception can teach them, then their minds are not just brains. (p. 91.)

Campbell is mistaken. The fact that people can learn about distant facts other than by present sense perception, memory and inference does not show that their minds are not just brains. Such data would be consistent with, and in fact would seem to imply, merely that these people can acquire information in ways other than normal. Parapsychological data only demonstrate capacities of the mind which exceed any known capacities of the brain. Campbell acknowledges as much in his summary of his discussion:

> Even if some paranormal results were established as genuine, they might of course be accommodated in a new, expanded, physical science. . . . Television is paranormal with respect to Newton's physics, but not to ours.

But then he goes on:

> The fact that some neomaterialism might survive the establishment of paranormal truths would not vindicate Central-State Materialism. For Central-State Materialism is a materialism based on our present physical and chemical science. If that science is inadequate, the materialism based on it is false. (Pp. 96-7.)

What Campbell is apparently saying is that if present-day science is not completely true then CSM is false, because it is 'based' on present-day science. But in order to explain or define CSM no mention was made of science, or scientific theories, present-day or otherwise.

JOHN W. GODBEY, JR.

Campbell needed to show that if parapsychological phenomena occur, then the central nervous system cannot be material. The most he has shown is that if these phenomena occur, then present-day science cannot explain them. For his argument to have any force he would have to show both that the phenomena could be not explained using present-day conceptions of the physical and that they could be explained under the hypothesis that humans are partly non-physical, or immaterial. Lacking a convincing argument for these two propositions, there is no reason to suppose that, even if they should be accepted as genuine, any of the phenomena under discussion could refute CSM. The likelihood of anyone producing arguments for these propositions appears to me to be remote. What could cause us to accept an unknown immaterial substance or property over an unknown physical one in explaining some phenomenon?

The parapsychological phenomena I have been discussing all, as I have said, fall into two classes: those phenomena in which the mind comes to be in some state by paranormal means, and those in which it causes something else to come to be in some state by paranormal means. Since I have shown that the existence of any or all of these phenomena is consistent with CSM, Campbell and those philosophers who agree with him are wrong in their belief that the existence of even a 'single example' of parapsychological phenomena would refute CSM.

I have not shown other possible kinds of parapsychological phenomena are compatible with CSM. However, until someone produces data to support a belief in the existence of another kind of phenomenon, and an argument to show its inconsistency with CSM, there is no reason to think that the results of parapsychological research are incompatible with CSM.

NOTES

1. *Mind and Body* (Garden City, New York, 1970), pp. 91-92. Page references to Campbell are to this book.
2. *A Materialist Theory of the Mind* (London and New York, 1968), p. 364.

Section VI

Historical Postscript

William James[1]

Final Impressions of a Psychical Researcher

The late Professor Henry Sidgwick was celebrated for the rare mixture of ardor and critical judgment which his character exhibited. The liberal heart which he possessed had to work with an intellect which acted destructively on almost every particular object of belief that was offered to its acceptance. A quarter of a century ago, scandalized by the chaotic state of opinion regarding the phenomena now called by the rather ridiculous name of "psychic"—phenomena, of which the supply reported seems inexhaustible, but which scientifically trained minds mostly refuse to look at—he established, along with Professor Barrett, Frederic Myers, and Edmund Gurney, the Society for Psychical Research. These men hoped that if the material were treated rigorously, and, as far as possible, experimentally, objective truth would be elicited, and the subject rescued from sentimentalism on the one side and dogmatizing ignorance on the other. Like all founders, Sidgwick hoped for a certain promptitude of result; and I heard him say, the year before his death, that if anyone had told him at the outset that after twenty years he would be in the same identical state of doubt and balance that he started with, he would have deemed the prophecy incredible. It appeared impossible that that amount of handling evidence should bring so little finality of decision.

My own experience has been similar to Sidgwick's. For twenty-five

Reprinted from William James, *Memories and Studies* (New York: Longmans, Green, and Co., 1911), pp. 173-206.

years I have been in touch with the literature of psychical research, and have had acquaintance with numerous "researchers." I have also spent a good many hours (though far fewer than I ought to have spent) in witnessing (or trying to witness) phenomena. Yet I am theoretically no "further" than I was at the beginning; and I confess that at times I have been tempted to believe that the Creator has eternally intended this department of nature to remain *baffling,* to prompt our curiosities and hopes and suspicions all in equal measure, so that, although ghosts and clairvoyances, and raps and messages from spirits, are always seeming to exist and can never be fully explained away, they also can never be susceptible of full corroboration.

The peculiarity of the case is just that there are so many sources of possible deception in most of the observations that the whole lot of them *may* be worthless, and yet that in comparatively few cases can aught more fatal than this vague general possibility of error be pleaded against the record. Science meanwhile needs something more than bare possibilities to build upon; so your genuinely scientific inquirer—I don't mean your ignoramus "scientist"—has to remain unsatisfied. It is hard to believe, however, that the Creator has really put any big array of phenomena into the world merely to defy and mock our scientific tendencies; so my deeper belief is that we psychical researchers have been too precipitate with our hopes, and that we must expect to mark progress not by quarter-centuries, but by half-centuries or whole centuries.

I am strengthened in this belief by my impression that just at this moment a faint but distinct step forward is being taken by competent opinion in these matters. "Physical phenomena" (movements of matter without contact, lights, hands and faces "materialized," etc.) have been one of the most baffling regions of the general field (or perhaps one of the least baffling *prima facie,* so certain and great has been the part played by fraud in their production); yet even here the balance of testimony seems slowly to be inclining towards admitting the supernaturalist view. Eusapia Paladino, the Neapolitan medium, has been under observation for twenty years or more. Schiaparelli, the astronomer, and Lombroso were the first scientific men to be converted by her performances. Since then innumerable men of scientific standing have seen her, including many "psychic" experts. Every one agrees that she cheats in the most barefaced manner whenever she gets an opportunity. The Cambridge experts, with the Sidgwicks and Richard Hodgson at their head, rejected her *in toto* on that account. Yet her credit has steadily risen, and now her last converts are the eminent psychiatrist, Morselli, the eminent physiologist, Botazzi, and our own psychical researcher, Carrington, whose book on "The Physical Phenomena of Spiritualism" (*against* them rather!) makes his conquest strategically important. If Mr. Podmore, hitherto the prosecuting attorney of the S. P. R., so far as physical phenomena are concerned becomes converted also, we may indeed sit up and look around us. Getting a good health bill from "Science," Eusapia will then throw retrospective credit on Home and Stainton Moses, Florence Cook (Prof. Crookes' medium), and all similar wonder-workers. The balance of *presumptions* will be changed in favor of genuineness being possible at least, in all reports of this particularly crass and low type of supernatural phenomena.

* * *

Not long after Darwin's "Origin of Species" appeared I was studying with that excellent anatomist and man, Jeffries Wyman, at Harvard. He was a convert, yet so far a half-hesitating one, to Darwin's views; but I heard him make a remark that applies well to the subject I now write about. When, he said, a theory gets propounded over and over again, coming up afresh after each time orthodox criticism has buried it, and each time seeming solider and harder to abolish, you may be sure that there is truth in it. Oken and Lamarck and Chambers had been triumphantly despatched and buried, but here was Darwin making the very same heresy seem only more plausible. How often has "Science" killed off all spook philosophy, and laid ghosts and raps and "telepathy" away underground as so much popular delusion. Yet never before were these things offered us so voluminously, and never in such authentic-seeming shape or with such good credentials. The tide seems steadily to be rising, in spite of all the expedients of scientific orthodoxy. It is hard not to suspect that here may be something different from a mere chapter in human gullibility. It may be a genuine realm of natural phenomena.

Falsus in uno, falsus in omnibus, once a cheat, always a cheat, such has been the motto of the English psychical researchers in dealing with mediums. I am disposed to think that, as a matter of policy, it has been wise. Tactically, it is far better to believe much too little than a little too much; and the exceptional credit attaching to the row of volumes of the S.P.R.'s Proceedings, is due to the fixed intention of the editors to proceed very slowly. Better a little belief tied fast, better a small investment *salted down,* than a mass of comparative insecurity.

But, however wise as a policy the S.P.R.'s maxim may have been, as a test of truth, I believe it to be almost irrelevant. In most things human the accusation of deliberate fraud and falsehood is grossly superficial. Man's character is too sophistically mixed for the alternative of "honest or dishonest" to be a sharp one. Scientific men themselves will cheat—at public lectures—rather than let experiments obey their well-known tendency towards failure. I have heard of a lecturer on physics, who had taken over the apparatus of the previous incumbent, consulting him about a certain machine intended to show that, however the peripheral parts of it might be agitated, its centre of gravity remained immovable. "It *will* wobble," he complained. "Well," said the predecessor, apologetically, "To tell the truth, whenever *I* used that machine I found it advisable to *drive a nail* through the centre of gravity." I once saw a distinguished physiologist, now dead, cheat most shamelessly at a public lecture, at the expense of a poor rabbit, and all for the sake of being able to make a cheap joke about its being an "American rabbit"—for no other, he said, could survive such a wound as he pretended to have given it.

To compare small men with great, I have myself cheated shamelessly. In the early days of the Sanders Theater at Harvard, I once had charge of a heart on the physiology of which Professor Newell Martin was giving a popular lecture. This heart, which belonged to a turtle, supported an index-straw which threw a moving shadow, greatly enlarged, upon the screen, while the heart pulsated. When certain nerves were stimulated, the lecturer said, the heart would act in certain ways which he described. But the poor heart was too far gone and, although it stopped duly when the nerve of arrest was excited, that was the final end of its life's tether. Presiding over the performance, I was terrified at the fiasco, and found myself suddenly acting like one of those military geniuses who on the field of battle convert disaster into victory. There was no time for deliberation; so, with my forefinger under a part of the straw that cast no shadow, I found myself impulsively and automatically imitating the rhythmical movements which my colleague had prophesied the heart would undergo. I kept the experiment from failing; and not only saved my colleague (and the turtle) from a humiliation that but for my presence of mind would have been their lot, but I established in the audience the true view of the subject. The lecturer was stating this; and the misconduct of one half-dead specimen of heart ought not to destroy the impression of his words. "There is no worse lie than a truth misunderstood," is a maxim which I have heard ascribed to a former venerated President of Harvard. The heart's

failure would have been misunderstood by the audience and given the lie
to the lecturer. It was hard enough to make them understand the subject
anyhow; so that even now as I write in cool blood I am tempted to think
that I acted quite correctly. I was acting for the *larger* truth, at any rate,
however automatically; and my sense of this was probably what prevented
the more pedantic and literal part of my conscience from checking the
action of my sympathetic finger. To this day the memory of that critical
emergency has made me feel charitable towards all mediums who make
phenomena come in one way when they won't come easily in another. On
the principles of the S.P.R., my conduct on that one occasion ought to
discredit everything I ever do, everything, for example, I may write in this
article,—a manifestly unjust conclusion.

Fraud, conscious or unconscious, seems ubiquitous throughout the
range of physical phenomena of spiritism, and false pretence, prevarica-
tion and fishing for clues are ubiquitous in the mental manifestations of
mediums. If it be not everywhere fraud simulating reality, one is tempted
to say, then the reality (if any reality there be) has the bad luck of being
fated everywhere to simulate fraud. The suggestion of humbug seldom
stops, and mixes itself with the best manifestations. Mrs. Piper's control,
"Rector," is a most impressive personage, who discerns in an
extraordinary degree his sitter's inner needs, and is capable of giving
elevated counsel to fastidious and critical minds. Yet in many respects he
is an arrant humbug—such he seems to me at least—pretending to a
knowledge and power to which he has no title, nonplussed by contradiction, yielding to suggestion, and covering his tracks with plausible excuses.
Now the non-"researching" mind looks upon such phenomena simply
according to their face-pretension and never thinks of asking what they
may signify below the surface. Since they profess for the most part to be
revealers of spirit life, it is either as being absolutely that, or as being
absolute frauds, that they are judged. The result is an inconceivably
shallow state of public opinion on the subject. One set of persons, emotionally touched at hearing the names of their loved ones given, and consoled
by assurances that they are "happy," accept the revelation, and consider
spiritualism "beautiful." More hard-headed subjects, disgusted by the
revelation's contemptible contents, outraged by the fraud, and prejudiced
beforehand against all "spirits," high or low, avert their minds from
what they call such "rot" or "bosh" entirely. Thus do two opposite
sentimentalisms divide opinion between them! A good expression of the
"scientific" state of mind occurs in Huxley's "Life and Letters":

"I regret," he writes, "that I am unable to accept the invitation of the Committee of the Dialectical Society. . . . I take no interest in the subject. The only case of 'Spiritualism' I have ever had the opportunity of examining into for myself was as gross an imposture as ever came under my notice. But supposing these phenomena to be genuine—they do not interest me. If anybody would endow me with the faculty of listening to the chatter of old women and curates in the nearest provincial town, I should decline the privilege, having better things to do. And if the folk in the spiritual world do not talk more wisely and sensibly than their friends report them to do, I put them in the same category. The only good that I can see in the demonstration of the 'Truth of Spiritualism' is to furnish an additional argument against suicide. Better live a crossing-sweeper, than die and be made to talk twaddle by a 'medium' hired at a guinea a *Seance.*" [2]

Obviously the mind of the excellent Huxley has here but two whole-souled categories, namely revelation or imposture, to apperceive the case by. Sentimental reasons bar revelation out, for the messages, he thinks, are not romantic enough for that; fraud exists anyhow; therefore the whole thing is nothing but imposture. The odd point is that so few of those who talk in this way realize that they and the spiritists are using the same major premise and differing only in the minor. The major premise is: "Any spirit-revelation must be romantic." The minor of the spiritist is: "This *is* romantic"; that of the Huxleyan is: "this is dingy twaddle"—whence their opposite conclusions!

Meanwhile the first thing that anyone learns who attends seriously to these phenomena is that their causation is far too complex for our feelings about what is or is not romantic enough to be spiritual to throw any light upon it. The causal factors must be carefully distinguished and traced through series, from their simplest to their strongest forms, before we can begin to understand the various resultants in which they issue. Myers and Gurney began this work, the one by his serial study of the various sorts of "automatism," sensory and motor, the other by his experimental proofs that a split-off consciousness may abide after a post-hypnotic suggestion has been given. Here we have subjective factors; but are not transsubjective or objective forces also at work? Veridical messages, apparitions, movements without contact, seem *prima facie* to be such. It was a good stroke on Gurney's part to construct a theory of apparitions which brought the subjective and the objective factors into harmonious co-operation. I doubt whether this telepathic theory of Gurney's will hold along the whole line of apparitions to which he applied it, but it is unquestionable that some theory of that mixed type is required for the explanation of all mediumistic phenomena; and that when all the psychological factors and elements involved have been told off—and they are many—the question still forces itself upon us: Are these all, or are there indications of any residual forces acting on the subject from beyond, or of any "metapsychic" faculty (to use Richet's useful term), exerted by him? This is the problem that requires real expertness, and this is where the simple sentimentalisms of the spiritist and scientist leave us in the lurch completely.

"Psychics" form indeed a special branch of education, in which experts are only gradually becoming developed. The phenomena are as massive and wide-spread as is anything in Nature, and the study of them is as tedious, repellent and undignified. To reject it for its unromantic character is like rejecting bacteriology because *penicillium glaucum* grows on horse-dung and *bacterium termo* lives in putrefaction. Scientific men have long ago ceased to think of the dignity of the materials they work in. When imposture has been checked off as far as possible, when chance coincidence has been allowed for, when opportunities for normal knowledge on the part of the subject have been noted, and skill in "fishing" and following clues unwittingly furnished by the voice or face of bystanders have been counted in, those who have the fullest acquaintance with the phenomena admit that in good mediums *there is a residuum of knowledge displayed* that can only be called supernormal: the medium taps some source of information not open to ordinary people. Myers used the word "telepathy" to indicate that the sitter's own thoughts or feelings may be thus directly tapped. Mrs. Sidgwick has suggested that if living minds can be thus tapped telepathically, so possibly may the minds of spirits be similarly tapped—if spirits there be. On this view we should have one distinct theory of the performances of a typical test-medium. They would be all originally due to an odd *tendency to personate,* found in her dream life as it expresses itself in trance. [Most of us reveal such a tendency whenever we handle a "ouija-board" or a "planchet," or let ourselves write automatically with a pencil.] The result is a "control," who purports to be speaking; and all the resources of the automatist, including his or her trance-faculty of telepathy, are called into play in building this fictitious personage out plausibly. On such a view of the control, the medium's *will to personate* runs the whole show; and if spirits be involved in it at all, they are passive beings, stray bits of whose memory she is able to seize and use for her purposes, without the spirit being any more aware of it than the sitter is aware of it when his own mind is similarly tapped.

This is one possible way of interpreting a certain type of psychical phenomenon. It uses psychological as well as "spiritual" factors, and quite obviously it throws open for us far more questions than it answers, questions about our subconscious constitution and its curious tendency to humbug, about the telepathic faculty, and about the possibility of an existent spirit-world.

I do not instance this theory to defend it, but simply to show what complicated hypotheses one is inevitably led to consider, the moment one looks at the facts in their complexity and turns one's back on the *naïve* alternative of "revelation or imposture," which is as far as either spiritist thought or ordinary scientist thought goes. The phenomena are endlessly complex in their factors, and they are so little understood as yet that off-hand judgments, whether of "spirits" or of "bosh" are the one as silly as the other. When we complicate the subject still farther by considering what connection such things as rappings, apparitions, poltergeists, spirit-photographs, and materializations may have with it, the bosh end of the scale gets heavily loaded, it is true, but your genuine inquirer still is loath to give up. He lets the data collect, and bides his time. He believes that "bosh" is no more an ultimate element in Nature, or a really explanatory category in human life than "dirt" is in chemistry. Every kind of "bosh" has its own factors and laws; and patient study will bring them definitely to light.

The only way to rescue the "pure bosh" view of the matter is one which has sometimes appealed to my own fancy, but which I imagine few readers will seriously adopt. If, namely, one takes the theory of evolution radically, one ought to apply it not only to the rock-strata, the animals and the plants, but to the stars, to the chemical elements, and to the laws of nature. There must have been a far-off antiquity, one is then tempted to suppose, when things were really chaotic. Little by little, out of all the haphazard possibilities of that time, a few connected things and habits arose, and the rudiments of regular performance began. Every variation in the way of law and order added itself to this nucleus, which inevitably grew more considerable as history went on; while the aberrant and inconstant variations, not being similarly preserved, disappeared from being, wandered off as unrelated vagrants, or else remained so imperfectly connected with the part of the world that had grown regular as only to manifest their existence by occasional lawless intrusions, like those which "psychic" phenomena now make into our scientifically organized world.

On such a view, these phenomena ought to remain "pure bosh" forever, that is, they ought to be forever intractable to intellectual methods, because they should not yet be organized enough in themselves to follow any laws. Wisps and shreds of the original chaos, they would be connected enough with the cosmos to affect its periphery every now and then, as by a momentary whiff or touch or gleam, but not enough ever to be followed up and hunted down and bagged. Their relation to the cosmos would be tangential solely.

Looked at dramatically, most occult phenomena make just this sort of impression. They are inwardly as incoherent as they are outwardly wayward and fitful. If they express anything, it is pure "bosh," pure discontinuity, accident, and disturbance, with no law apparent but to interrupt, and no purpose but to baffle. They seem like stray vestiges of that primordial irrationality, from which all our rationalities have been evolved.

To settle dogmatically into this bosh-view would save labor, but it would go against too many intellectual prepossessions to be adopted save as a last resort of despair. Your psychical researcher therefore bates no jot of hope, and has faith that when we get our data numerous enough, some sort of rational treatment of them will succeed.

When I hear good people say (as they often say, not without show of reason), that dabbling in such phenomena reduces us to a sort of jelly, disintegrates the critical faculties, liquifies the character, and makes of one a *gobe-mouche* generally, I console myself by thinking of my friends Frederic Myers and Richard Hodgson. These men lived exclusively for psychical research, and it converted both to spiritism. Hodgson would have been a man among men anywhere; but I doubt whether under any other baptism he would have been that happy, sober and righteous form of energy which his face proclaimed him in his later years, when heart and head alike were wholly satisfied by his occupation. Myers' character also grew stronger in every particular for his devotion to the same inquiries. Brought up on literature and sentiment, something of a courtier, passionate, disdainful, and impatient naturally, he was made over again from the day when he took up psychical research seriously. He became learned in science, circumspect, democratic in sympathy, endlessly patient, and above all, happy. The fortitude of his last hours touched the heroic, so completely were the atrocious sufferings of his body cast into insignificance by his interest in the cause he lived for. When a man's pursuit gradually makes his face shine and grow handsome, you may be sure it is a worthy one. Both Hodgson and Myers kept growing ever handsomer and stronger-looking.

Such personal examples will convert no one, and of course they ought not to. Nor do I seek at all in this article to convert any one to my belief that psychical research is an important branch of science. To do that, I should have to quote evidence; and those for whom the volumes of S.P.R. "Proceedings" already published count for nothing would remain in their dogmatic slumber, though one rose from the dead. No, not to convert readers, but simply to *put my own state of mind upon record publicly* is the purpose of my present writing. Some one said to me a short time ago, that after my twenty-five years of dabbling in "Psychics," it would be rather shameful were I unable to state any definite conclusions whatever as a consequence. I had to agree; so I now proceed to take up the challenge and express such convictions as have been engendered in me by that length of experience, be the same true or false ones. I may be dooming myself to the pit in the eyes of better-judging posterity; I may be raising myself to honor; I am willing to take the risk, for what I shall write is *my* truth, as I now see it.

* * *

I began this article by confessing myself baffled. I *am* baffled, as to spirit-return, and as to many other special problems. I am also constantly baffled as to what to think of this or that particular story, for the sources of error in any one observation are seldom fully knowable. But weak sticks make strong faggots; and when the stories fall into consistent sorts that point each in a definite direction, one gets a sense of being in presence of genuinely natural types of phenomena. As to there being such real natural types of phenomena ignored by orthodox science, I am not baffled at all, for I am fully convinced of it. One cannot get demonstrative proof here. One has to follow one's personal sense, which, of course, is liable to err, of the dramatic probabilities of nature. Our critics here obey their sense of dramatic probability as much as we do. Take "raps" for example, and the whole business of objects moving without contact. "Nature," thinks the scientific man, is not so unutterably silly. The cabinet, the darkness, the tying, suggest a sort of human rat-hole life exclusively and "swindling" is for him the dramatically sufficient explanation. It probably is, in an indefinite majority of instances; yet it is to me dramatically improbable that the swindling should not have accreted round some originally genuine nucleus. If we look at human imposture as a historic phenomenon, we find it always imitative. One swindler imitates a previous swindler, but the first swindler of that kind imitated some one who was honest. You can no more create an absolutely new trick than you can create a new word without any previous basis.—You don't know how to go about it. Try, reader, yourself, to invent an unprecedented kind of "physical phenomenon of spiritualism." When *I* try, I find myself mentally turning over the regular medium-stock, and thinking how I might improve some item. This being the dramatically probable human way, I think differently of the whole type, taken collectively, from the way in which I may think of the single instance. I find myself believing that there is "something in" these never ending reports of physical phenomena, although I haven't yet the least positive notion of the something. It becomes to my mind simply a very worthy problem for investigation. Either I or the scientist is of course a fool, with our opposite views of probability here; and I only wish he might feel the liability, as cordially as I do, to pertain to both of us.

I fear I look on Nature generally with more charitable eyes than his, though perhaps he would pause if he realized as I do, how vast the fraudulency is which in consistency he must attribute to her. Nature is brutal enough, Heaven knows; but no one yet has held her non-human side to be *dishonest,* and even in the human sphere deliberate deceit is far rarer than the "classic" intellect, with its few and rigid categories, was ready to acknowledge. There is a hazy penumbra in us all where lying and delusion meet, where passion rules beliefs as well as conduct, and where the term "scoundrel" does not clear up everything to the depths as it did for our forefathers. The first automatic writing I ever saw was forty years ago. I unhesitatingly thought of it as deceit, although it contained vague elements of supernormal knowledge. Since then I have come to see in automatic writing one example of a department of human activity as vast as it is enigmatic. Every sort of person is liable to it, or to something equivalent to it; and whoever encourages it in himself finds himself personating someone else, either signing what he writes by fictitious name, or spelling out, by ouija-board or table-tips, messages from the departed. Our subconscious region seems, as a rule, to be dominated either by a crazy "will to make-believe," or by some curious external force impelling us to personation. The first difference between the psychical researcher and the inexpert person is that the former realizes the commonness and typicality of the phenomenon here, while the latter, less informed, thinks it so rare as to be unworthy of attention. *I wish to go on record for the commonness.*

The next thing I wish to go on record for is *the presence,* in the midst of all the humbug, *of really supernormal knowledge.* By this I mean knowledge that cannot be traced to the ordinary sources of information—the senses namely, of the automatist. In really strong mediums this knowledge seems to be abundant, though it is usually spotty, capricious and unconnected. Really strong mediums are rarities; but when one starts with them and works downwards into less brilliant regions of the automatic life, one tends to interpret many slight but odd coincidences with truth as possibly rudimentary forms of this kind of knowledge.

What is one to think of this queer chapter in human nature? It is odd enough on any view. If all it means is a preposterous and inferior monkey-like tendency to forge messages, systematically embedded in the soul of all of us, it is weird; and weirder still that it should then own all this super-normal information. If on the other hand the supernormal information be the key to the phenomenon, it ought to be superior; and then how ought we to account for the "wicked partner," and for the undeniable mendacity and inferiority of so much of the performance? We are thrown, for our conclusions, upon our instinctive sense of the dramatic probabilities of nature. My own dramatic sense tends instinctively to picture the situation as an interaction between slumbering faculties in the automatist's mind and a cosmic environment of *other consciousness* of some sort which is able to work upon them. If there were in the universe a lot of diffuse soul-stuff, unable of itself to get into consistent personal form, or to take permanent possession of an organism, yet always craving to do so, it might get its head into the air, parasitically, so to speak, by profiting by weak spots in the armor of human minds, and slipping in and stirring up there the sleeping tendency to personate. It would induce habits in the subconscious region of the mind it used thus, and would seek above all things to prolong its social opportunities by making itself agreeable and plausible. It would drag stray scraps of truth with it from the wider environment, but would betray its mental inferiority by knowing little how to weave them into any important or significant story.

This, I say, is the dramatic view which my mind spontaneously takes, and it has the advantage of falling into line with ancient human traditions. The views of others are just as dramatic, *for the phenomenon is actuated by will of some sort anyhow,* and wills give rise to dramas. The spiritist view, as held by Messrs. Hyslop and Hodgson, sees a "will to communicate," struggling through inconceivable layers of obstruction in the conditions. I have heard Hodgson liken the difficulties to those of two persons who on earth should have only dead-drunk servants to use as their messengers. The scientist, for his part, sees a "will to deceive," watching its chance in all of us, and able (possibly?) to use "telepathy" in its service.

Which kind of will, and how many kinds of will are most inherently probable? Who can say with certainty? The only certainty is that the phenomena are enormously complex, especially if one includes in them such intellectual flights of mediumship as Swedenborg's, and if one tries in any way to work the physical phenomena in. That is why I personally am as yet neither a convinced believer in parasitic demons, nor a spiritist, nor a scientist, but still remain a psychical researcher waiting for more facts before concluding.

Out of my experience, such as it is (and it is limited enough) one fixed conclusion dogmatically emerges, and that is this, that we with our lives are like islands in the sea, or like trees in the forest. The maple and the pine may whisper to each other with their leaves, and Conanicut and Newport hear each other's foghorns. But the trees also commingle their roots in the darkness underground, and the islands also hang together through the ocean's bottom. Just so there is a continuum of cosmic consciousness, against which our individuality builds but accidental fences, and into which our several minds plunge as into a mother-sea or reservoir. Our "normal" consciousness is circumscribed for adaptation to our external earthly environment, but the fence is weak in spots, and fitful influences from beyond leak in, showing the otherwise unverifiable common connection. Not only psychic research, but metaphysical philosophy, and speculative biology are led in their own ways to look with favor on some such "panpsychic" view of the universe as this. Assuming this common reservoir of consciousness to exist, this bank upon which we all draw, and in which so many of earth's memories must in some way be stored, or mediums would not get at them as they do, the question is, What is its own structure? What is its inner topography? This question, first squarely formulated by Myers, deserves to be called "Myers' problem" by scientific men hereafter. What are the conditions of individuation or insulation in this mother-sea? To what tracts, to what active systems functioning separately in it, do personalities correspond? Are individual "spirits" constituted there? How numerous, and of how many hierarchic orders may these then be? How permanent? How transient? And how confluent with one another may they become?

What again, are the relations between the cosmic consciousness and matter? Are there subtler forms of matter which upon occasion may enter into functional connection with the individuations in the psychic sea, and then, and then only, show themselves?—So that our ordinary human experience, on its material as well as on its mental side, would appear to be only an extract from the larger psychophysical world?

Vast, indeed, and difficult is the inquirer's prospect here, and the most significant data for his purpose will probably be just these dingy little mediumistic facts which the Huxleyan minds of our time find so unworthy of their attention. But when was not the science of the future stirred to its conquering activities by the little rebellious exceptions to the science of the present? Hardly, as yet, has the surface of the facts called "psychic" begun to be scratched for scientific purposes. It is through following these facts, I am persuaded, that the greatest scientific conquests of the coming generations will be achieved. *Kühn ist das Mühen, herrlich der Lohn!*

NOTES

1. Published under the title "Confidences of a Psychical Researcher" in the *American Magazine,* October, 1909. For a more complete and less popular statement of some theories suggested in this article see the last pages of a "Report on Mrs. Piper's Hodgson-Control" in *Proceedings of the [Eng.] Society for Psychical Research,* 1909, 470; also printed in *Proc. of Am. Soc. for Psychical Research* for the same year.
2. T. H. Huxley, "Life and Letters," I, 240.

Bibliography

The literature of parapsychology is massive and very uneven in quality. Much the best of it is to be found in periodicals, and there is at present no bibliography of the periodical literature in the field. I have especially tried to locate periodical articles relevant to the philosophy of parapsychology, and to be reasonably selective as to the quality and seriousness of the materials included below. In order better to serve the needs of scholars, I have given analytical entries for the contents of the major anthologies dealing with philosophical issues in parapsychology. Works not included in the bibliography to James M. O. Wheatley and Hoyt L. Edge [editors], *Philosophical Dimensions of Parapsychology* are particularly stressed here. My bibliography is by no means exhaustive of the serious literature; in particular, no attempt has been made to survey the literature in languages other than English.

The best general guide to books in the field of parapsychology is Rhea A. White and Laura A. Dale, *Parapsychology: Sources of Information* (Metuchen, New Jersey: The Scarecrow Press, 1973), which ought to be consulted with regard to non-philosophical works. George Zorab, *Bibliography of Parapsychology* (New York: Parapsychology Foundation, 1957) includes Continental literature and some periodical articles, but it is sparse in its coverage and has for most purposes been superseded by

White and Dale. Other bibliographies of use to the student of parapsychology are listed in White and Dale under the heading "Reference Books," and in Appendix 3. Some access to periodical articles may be gained by consulting the *Philosopher's Index* and *Psychological Abstracts*, but much relevant material lies outside the scope of these publications. In the end, the serious student of parapsychology must have available complete runs of the major professional journals in the field, which unfortunately are held by only a few libraries.

In the bibliographic entries below the following abbreviations have been utilized:

ANTHOLOGIES

Angoff — Allan Angoff and Betty Shapin. *Parapsychology and the Sciences* (New York: Parapsychology Foundation, 1974).

French — Peter A. French. *Philosophers in Wonderland: Philosophy and Psychical Research* (Saint Paul, Minnesota: Llewellyn Publications, 1975).

Murchison — Carl Murchison. *The Case For and Against Psychical Belief* (Worcester, Massachusetts: Clark University, 1927).

Smythies — J. R. Smythies. *Science and ESP* (New York: Humanities Press, 1967).

Thakur — Shivesh C. Thakur. *Philosophy and Psychical Research* (London: George Allen & Unwin, 1976).

Wheatley — James M. O. Wheatley and Hoyt L. Edge. *Philosophical Dimensions of Parapsychology* (Springfield, Illinois: Charles C. Thomas, 1976).

PERIODICALS*

IJP — *International Journal of Parapsychology*

JASPR — *Journal of the American Society for Psychical Research*

*Abbreviations here follow those of White and Dale, Appendix 6.

JP   *Journal of Parapsychology*

JSPR   *Journal of the Society for Psychical Research* [London]

PASPR   *Proceedings of the American Society for Psychical Research*

PSPR   *Proceedings of the Society for Psychical Research* [London]

BIBLIOGRAPHY

Armstrong, D. M. *A Materialist Theory of the Mind.* (London: Routledge and Kegan Paul, 1968).

Ayer, A. J. "ESP". *The Listener,* 90 (1973): 375.

Balfour, Gerald. "Psychical Research and Current Doctrines of Mind and Body." *Hibbert Journal,* 8 (1910): 543-561.

———. "Telepathy and Metaphysics." *Hibbert Journal,* 11 (1913): 544-562.

Beloff, John. "ESP: The Search for a Physiological Index." *JSPR*, 47 (1974): 403-420.

———. *The Existence of Mind.* (New York: Citadel, 1965).

———. "Matter and Manner." *IJP,* 6 (1964): 93-99.

———. *New Directions in Parapsychology.* (London: Elek Science, 1974).

———. "On Trying to Make Sense of the Paranormal." *PSPR*, 56 (1976): 173-195.

———. "Parapsychology and Its Neighbors." *JP*, 34 (1970): 129-142. [Reprinted *in* Wheatley: 374-387.]

———. "Parapsychology As Science." *IJP,* 9 (1967): 91-97.

———. "The Subliminal and the Extrasensory." *in* Angoff: 103-115.

———. "What Are We Up To?" *JP*, 28 (1964): 302-309.

Bennett, Edward T. *The Society for Psychical Research.* (London: R. Brimley Johnson, 1903).

Bergson, Henri. *Matter and Memory.* (London: Allen and Unwin, 1910).

―――. *Mind-Energy: Lectures and Essays.* (New York: Holt, 1920).

―――. "Presidential Address." *PSPR*, 27 (1914-15): 157-175.

Black, Max. "Why Cannot an Effect Precede Its Cause?" *Analysis*, 16 (1956): 49-58.

Blanshard, Brand. "Proof in Psychical Research." *JASPR,* 51 (1957): 3-24.

Brann, Henry W. "The Role of Parapsychology in Schopenhauer's Philosophy." *IJP,* 8 (1966): 397-415.

Brier, Bob. "Magicians, Alarm Clocks, and Backward Causation." *Southern Journal of Philosophy,* 11 (1973): 359-364. [Reprinted, in slightly altered form, *in* Wheatley: 235-244.]

―――. "The Metaphysics of Parapsychology: Towards a Magical Conception of the Universe." *in Lectures by the Faculty of C. W. Post Center of Long Island University,* Series Four (1975), edited by Richard R. Griffith. (n.p.: Faculty of the C. W. Post Center, 1976): 9-23.

―――. "The Metaphysics of Precognition." *in* Thakur: 46-58.

―――. "Methodology in Parapsychology and Other Sciences." *in* Angoff: 15-25.

―――. *Precognition and the Philosophy of Science.* (New York: Humanities Press, 1974).

―――, and James Giles. "Philosophy, Psychical Research, and Parapsychology: A Survey." *Southern Journal of Philosophy,* 13 (1975): 393-405.

Broad, C. D. "The Antecedent Probability of Survival." *Hibbert Journal,* 17 (1919): 561-578.

―――. "Discussion of Prof. Rhine's Paper and the Foregoing Comments

Upon It." *PSPR,* 48 (1946): 20-25.

Broad, C. D. "Discussion: The Experimental Establishment of Telepathic Precognition." *Philosophyy*, 19 (1944): 261-275.

———. "Dreaming, and Some of Its Implications." *PSPR,* 52 (1959): 53-78.

———. "A Half-Century of Psychical Research." *JP,* 20 (1956): 209-228.

———. "Henry Sidgwick and Psychical Research." *PSPR,* 45 (1938): 131-161.

———. *Human Personality and the Possibility of Its Survival.* (Berkeley: University of California Press, 1955).

———. "Immanuel Kant and Psychical Research." *PSPR,* 49 (1949-52): 79-104.

———. "In What Sense Is Survival Desirable?" *Hibbert Journal,* 17 (1918): 7-20.

———. *Lectures on Psychical Research.* (London: Routledge and Kegan Paul, 1962).

———. *The Mind and Its Place in Nature.* (New York: Harcourt, Brace, 1929).

———. "Mr. Dunne's Theory of Time in *An Experiment with Time.*" *Philosophy,* 10 (1935): 168-185.

———. "Normal Cognition, Clairvoyance and Telepathy." *PSPR,* 43 (1935): 397-438. [Reprinted *in* French: 244-274.]

———. "The Notion of Precognition." *IJP,* 10 (1968): 165-195. [Originally published *in* Smythies: 165-196.]

———. *Personal Identity and Survival.* (London: Society for Psychical Research, 1958).

———. "Personal Identity and Survival." *Newsletter* of the Parapsychology Foundation, Inc., 1958. [Reprinted *in* Wheatley: 348-365.]

———. "Phantasms of the Living and the Dead." *PSPR,* 50 (1953): 51-66.

———. "The Phenomenology of Mrs. Leonard's Mediumship." *JASPR,* 49 (1955): 47-63.

———. "Philosophical Implications of Precognition." *The Listener,* 37 (1947): 709-710.

———. "The Philosophical Implications of Precognition. A Discussion Between C. D. Broad and H. H. Price." *Proceedings of the Aristotelian Society,* Supplementary volume 16 (1937): 229-245. [Pages 211-245 published separately.]

———. *Religion, Philosophy, and Psychical Research.* (New York: Harcourt, Brace, 1953).

———. [Replies to Ducasse and Flew]. *in The Philosophy of C. D. Broad,* edited by P. A. Schilpp. (New York: Tudor, 1959): 774-786; 794-796.

———. "Science and Psychical Phenomena." *Philosophy,* 13 (1938): 466-475.

———. "Some Notes on Mr. Roll's 'The Problem of Precognition' and On the Comments Evoked by It." *JSPR,* 41 (1962): 225-234.

———. "Trinity College and Psychical Research." *Trinity Magazine,* June 1947: 13-17.

Brooks, Richard. "PT + PC = GESP." *in Research in Parapsychology 1973* (Metuchen: Scarecrow Press, 1974): 94-98.

Brown, G. Spencer. *Probability and Scientific Inference.* (London: Longmans, 1957).

———. "Statistical Significance in Psychical Research." *Nature,* 172 (1953): 154-156.

Burt, Cyril. "Evolution and Parapsychology." *JSPR,* 43 (1966): 391-422.

———. "The Implications of Parapsychology for General Psychology." *JP,* 31 (1967): 1-18.

———. "Parapsychology and Its Implications." *International Journal of Neuropsychiatry,* 2 (1966): 363-377.

———. "Psychology and Parapsychology." *in* Smythies: 61-141.

———. *Psychology and Psychical Research.* (London: Society for Psychical Research, 1968).

———. "Theories of Mind." *JSPR*, 41 (1961): 55-60.

Campbell, Keith. *Body and Mind.* (Garden City, N.Y.: Doubleday, 1970).

———. "Materialism." *in The Encyclopedia of Philosophy*, edited by Paul Edwards. (New York: Macmillan and Free Press, 1967): volume 5: 179-188.

Carington, Whately. *Matter, Mind and Meaning.* (London: Methuen, 1949).

———. *The Meaning of "Survival".* (London: Society for Psychical Research, 1935).

———. *Telepathy: An Outline of Its Facts, Theory, and Implications.* (London: Methuen, 1945). [Also an American edition under the title, *Thought Transference* (New York: Creative Age Press, 1946).]

Carrington, Hereward. "Possible and Impossible: What Constitutes 'Impossibility'?" *JASPR*, 45 (1951): 55-61.

Chari, C. T. "The Challenge of Psi: New Horizons of Scientific Research." *JP*, 38 (1974): 1-15.

———. "Discussion: Psychical Research and Philosophy." *Philosophy*, 28 (1953): 72-74.

———. "ESP and 'Semantic Information'." *JASPR*, 61 (1967): 47-63.

———. "ESP and the 'Theory of Resonance'." *British Journal for the Philosophy of Science*, 15 (1964): 137-140.

———. "The Mystical and the Paranormal." *JASPR*, 48 (1954): 96-107.

———. "A Note on Precognition." *JSPR*, 36 (1951): 509-518.

Chauvin, Rémy. "To Reconcile Psi and Physics." *JP*, 34 (1970): 215-218. [Reprinted *in* Wheatley: 409-412.]

Churchman, C. W. "Perception and Deception." *Science*, 153 (1966): 1088-1090.

Cooper, David E. "ESP and the Materialist Theory of Mind." *in* Thakur: 59-80.

Coover, John Edgar. *Experiments in Psychical Research at Leland Stanford Junior University.* (Stanford University, California: Published by the University, 1917).

———. "Metapsychics and the Incredulity of Psychologists." *in* Murchison: 229-264.

Crumbaugh, James C. "Parapsychology and the Repeatability Issue." *Research Journal of Philosophy and Social Science,* 2 (1965): 60-64.

———. "A Scientific Critique of Parapsychology." *International Journal of Neuropsychiatry,* 2 (1966): 523-531.

Dean, E. D. "Techniques and Status of Modern Parapsychology." *Science,* 170 (1970): 1237-1238.

Devereux, George [editor]. *Psychoanalysis and the Occult.* (New York: International Universities Press, n.d.).

Dingwall, Eric J. "Is Modern Parapsychology a Science?" *Parapsychology Review,* 3 (1972): 1-2; 23-26.

Dobbs, Adrian. "The Feasibility of a Physical Theory of ESP." *in* Smythies: 225-254.

Dobbs, H. A. "Time and Extrasensory Perception." *PSPR,* 54 (1965): 249-361.

Dodds, E. R. "Supernormal Phenomena in Classical Antiquity." *PSPR,* 55 (1971): 189-237.

———. "Why I Do Not Believe in Survival." *PSPR,* 42 (1934): 147-172.

Dommeyer, Frederick C. "Parapsychology—An Evaluation." *Research Journal of Philosophy and Social Science,* 3 (1966): 20-30.

———. "Parapsychology: Old Delusion or New Science?" *International Journal of Neuropsychiatry,* 2 (1966): 539-555.

———. "Philosophical and Other Perspectives of Parapsychology." *Research Journal of Philosophy and Social Science,* 4 (1974): 1-22.

Driesch, Hans. "Psychical Research and Philosophy." *in* Murchison: 163-178.

———. *Psychical Research: The Science of the Supernormal.* (London: G. Bell and Sons, 1933).

Ducasse, C. J. "Broad on the Relevance of Psychical Research to Philosophy." *in The Philosophy of C. D. Broad,* edited by P. A. Schilpp. (New York: Tudor, 1959): 375-410. [Partially reprinted *in* Wheatley: 227-234.]

———. "Broad's Lectures on Psychical Research." *Philosophy and Phenomenological Research,* 24 (1964): 561-566.

———. "Causality and Parapsychology." *JP,* 23 (1959): 90-96.

———. *A Critical Examination of the Belief in Life After Death.* (Springfield, Illinois: Charles C. Thomas, 1961).

———. *Is Life After Death Possible?* (Berkeley: University of California Press, 1948).

———. "Knowing the Future." *Tomorrow,* 3 (1955): 13-16. [Reprinted *in* Wheatley: 193-197.]

———. *Nature, Mind, and Death.* (LaSalle, Illinois: Open Court, 1951).

———. "Paranormal Phenomena, Nature, and Man." *JASPR,* 45 (1951): 129-148.

———. *Paranormal Phenomena, Science, and Life After Death.* (New York: Parapsychology Foundation, 1969).

———. "Physical Phenomena in Psychical Research." *JASPR,* 52 (1958): 3-23.

———. "Science, Scientists, and Psychical Research." *JASPR,* 50 (1956): 142-147.

———. "Some Questions Concerning Psychical Phenomena." *JASPR,* 48 (1954): 3-20.

———. "What Would Constitute Conclusive Evidence of Survival After Death?" *JSPR,* 41 (1962): 401-406.

Ducasse, C. J., C. W. K. Mundle, G. Zorab, and G. F. Dalton. "The Problem of Precognition: Comments on W. G. Roll's Paper." *JSPR*, 41 (1961): 173-183.

Dunne, J. W. *An Experiment With Time.* (New York: Macmillan, 1927).

———. *The Serial Universe.* (London: Faber and Faber, 1934).

Edge, Hoyt L. "Do Spirits Matter?: Naturalism and Disembodied Survival." *JASPR,* 70 (1976): 293-301.

Edgeworth, F. Y. "The Calculus of Probabilities Applied to Psychical Research." *PSPR,* 3 (1885): 190-199.

———. "The Calculus of Probabilities Applied to Psychical Research II." *PSPR*, 4 (1886): 189-208.

Ehrenwald, Jan. "Human Personality and the Nature of Psi Phenomena." *JASPR,* 62 (1968): 366-380.

———. *Telepathy and Medical Psychology.* (New York: W. W. Norton, 1948).

Estabrooks, G. H. *Spiritism.* (New York: E. P. Dutton, 1947).

Eysenck, H. J. "Personality and Extrasensory Perception." *JSPR,* 44 (1967): 55-71.

Fisher, R. A. "The Statistical Method in Psychical Research." *PSPR,* 39 (1929-31): 189-192.

Flew, Antony [editor]. *Body, Mind and Death.* (New York: Macmillan, 1964).

———. "Broad and Supernormal Precognition." *in The Philosophy of C. D. Broad,* edited by P.A. Schilpp. (New York: Tudor, 1959): 411-435.

———. "Can a Man Witness His Own Funeral?" *Hibbert Journal*, 54 (1956): 242-250.

———. "The Challenge of Precognition." *in* Angoff: 174-182.

———. "Coincidence and Synchronicity." *JSPR,* 37 (1953): 198-201.

———. "Effects Before Their Causes?—Addenda and Corrigenda."

Analysis, 16 (1956): 104-110.

———. "Is There a Case for Disembodied Survival?" *JASPR,* 66 (1972): 129-144. [Reprinted *in* Wheatley: 330-347.]

———. "Minds and Mystification." *The Listener,* 46 (1951): 501-502; 515. [Reprinted *in* French: 163-167.]

———. *A New Approach to Psychical Research.* (London: C. A. Watts, 1953).

———. "Philosophical Implications of Precognition." *in The Encyclopedia of Philosophy,* edited by Paul Edwards. (New York: Macmillan and Free Press, 1967): volume 6: 436-441.

———. "Something Very Unsatisfactory . . ." *IJP,* 6 (1964): 101-105.

———. "The Sources of Serialism." *in* Thakur: 81-96.

Flournoy, Théodore. *Spiritism and Psychology.* (New York: Harper and Brothers, 1911).

Foster, Lewis. "Fatalism and Precognition." *Philosophy and Phenomenological Research,* 31 (1971): 341-351.

Garnett, A. "Matter, Mind and Precognition." *JP,* 29 (1965): 19-26.

Garrett, Eileen J. [editor]. *Does Man Survive Death?: A Symposium.* (New York: Helix Press, 1957).

Gauld, A. *The Founders of Psychical Research.* (New York: Schocken Books, 1968).

Greenbank, R. K. "Can ESP Be Explained?" *International Journal of Neuropsychiatry,* 2 (1966): 532-538.

Greenwald, Anthony G. "Significance, Nonsignificance, and Interpretation of an ESP Experiment." *Journal of Experimental Social Psychology,* 11 (1975): 180-191.

Greenwood, J. A. "Analysis of a Large Chance Control Series of ESP Data." *JP,* 2 (1938): 138-146.

———, and C. E. Stuart. "Mathematical Techniques Used in ESP Research." *JP,* 1 (1937): 206-225.

Gregory, Anita. "Ethics and Psychical Research." *JSPR,* 47 (1974): 283-305.

Gudas, Fabian [editor]. *Extrasensory Perception.* (New York: Scribner's, 1961).

Gulliksen, H. O. "Extra-Sensory Perception—What Is It?" *American Journal of Sociology,* 43 (1938): 623-631.

Gurney, Edmund, Frederic W. H. Myers, and Frank Podmore. *Phantasms of the Living.* (London: Rooms of the Society for Psychical Research, Trübner and Co., 1886). Two volumes.

Hansel, C. E. M. *ESP: A Scientific Evaluation.* (New York: Scribner's, 1966).

Hardy, Alister. "Biology and ESP." *in* Smythies: 143-164.

———. "Biology and Psychical Research." *PSPR,* 50 (1953): 96-134.

———. "Psychic Research and Civilization." *PSPR,* 55 (1966): 1-21.

———, Robert Harvie, and Arthur Koestler. *The Challenge of Chance: A Mass Experiment in Telepathy and Its Unexpected Outcome.* (New York: Random House, 1975).

Harrison, Jonathan. "Religion and Psychical Research." *in* Thakur: 97-121.

Hart, H. "Creative Discussion in Psychical Research: A Rejoinder to Professor Wheatley." *JASPR,* 61 (1967): 72-75.

———. "Psychical Research and the Methods of Science." *JASPR,* 51 (1957): 85-105.

———. *Toward a New Philosophical Basis for Parapsychological Phenomena.* (New York: Parapsychology Foundation, 1965).

Heinlein, C. P., and J. H. Heinlein. "Critique of the Premises and Statistical Methodology of Parapsychology." *Journal of Psychology,* 5 (1938): 135-148.

Herr, D. L. "A Mathematical Analysis of the Experiments in Extra-Sensory Perception." *Journal of Experimental Psychology,* 22 (1938): 491-496.

Heywood, Rosalind. *Beyond the Reach of Sense: An Inquiry into Extra-Sensory Perception.* (New York: E. P. Dutton, 1961). [English title: *The Sixth Sense: An Inquiry* . . . (London: Chatto and Windus, 1959).]

Hinton, C. Howard. *The Fourth Dimension.* (London: Swan Sonnenschein, 1904).

Huby, Pamela M. "Some Aspects of the Problem of Survival." *in* Thakur: 122-141.

Huntington, E. V. "Exact Probabilities in Certain Card-Matching Problems." *Science,* 86 (1937): 499-500.

———. "Is It Chance or ESP?" *American Scholar,* 7 (1938): 201-210.

"In Memoriam: Professor C. D. Broad 1887-1971." *JSPR,* 46 (1971): 103-113.

James, William. "Mrs. Piper 'the Medium'." *Science,* 7 (1898): 640-641.

———. "Presidential Address." *PSPR,* 12 (1896): 2-10. [Also *in: Science,* 3 (1896): 881-888.]

———. "Psychical Research." *Psychological Review,* 3 (1896): 649-652.

———. "Report on Mrs. Piper's Hodgson-Control." *PSPR,* 23 (1909): 1-121. [Also in: *PASPR,* 3, (1909): 470-589.]

———. "Review of F. W. H. Myers, *Human Personality and Its Survival of Bodily Death.*" *PSPR,* 18 (1903): 22-33.

———. "Review of Gurney, Myers, and Podmore, *Phantasms of the Living.*" *Science,* 9 (1887) [old series]: 18-20.

———. "What Psychical Research Has Accomplished." *in The Will To Believe and Other Essays in Popular Philosophy.* (New York: Longmans, Green and Co., 1897): 299-327.

Joad, C. E. M. *Guide to Modern Thought.* (New York: Frederick A. Stokes Co., 1933).

Jonas, A. D., and D. F. Klein. "The Logic of ESP." *American Journal of Psychiatry,* 126 (1970): 1173-1177.

Jung, C. G., and W. Pauli. *The Interpretation of Nature and the Psyche.* (New York: Pantheon Books, 1955).

Kellogg, C. E. "Dr. J. B. Rhine and Extra-Sensory Perception." *Journal of Abnormal and Social Psychology,* 31 (1936): 190-193.

————. "New Evidence (?) for Extra-Sensory Perception." *Scientific Monthly,* 45 (1937): 331-341.

Kennedy, John L. "A Methodological Review of Extra-Sensory Perception." *Psychological Bulletin,* 36 (1939): 59-103. [Includes bibliography of early critical studies of experimental parapsychology.]

Koestler, Arthur. *The Roots of Coincidence.* (New York: Random House, 1972).

Kooy, J. M. J. "Space, Time, and Consciousness." *JP,* 21 (1957): 259-272.

Lambert, G. W. "The Use of Evidence in Psychical Research." *PSPR,* 50 (1956): 275-293.

LeClair, R. [editor]. *The Letters of William James and Théodore Flournoy.* (Madison: University of Wisconsin Press, 1966).

Lemmon, V. W. "Extra-Sensory Perception." *Journal of Psychology,* 4 (1937): 227-238.

LeShan, Lawrence. *The Medium, the Mystic, and the Physicist.* (New York: Viking Press, 1974).

————. "Parapsychology and the Concept of the Repeatable Experiment." *IJP,* 8 (1966): 133-142.

————. "Some Psychological Hypotheses on the Non-Acceptance of Parapsychology as a Science." *IJP,* 8(1966): 367-385.

————. *Toward a General Theory of the Paranormal: A Report of Work in Progress.* (New York: Parapsychology Foundation, 1969).

Leuba, Clarence. "An Experiment to Test the Role of Chance in ESP Research." *JP,* 2 (1938): 217-221.

Lewis, Hywel D. "Religion and the Paranormal." *in* Thakur: 142-156.

Lewy, Casimir. "Is the Notion of Disembodied Existence Self-Contradictory?" *Proceedings of the Aristotelian Society,* 43 (1942-43): 59-78.

Littlewood, J. E. "Statistical Analysis in Card-Guessing." *JSPR,* 44 (1968): 321-26.

McConnell, R. A. "ESP and Credibility in Science." *American Psychologist,* 24 (1969): 531-538.

———. *ESP: Curriculum Guide.* (New York: Simon and Schuster, 1971).

McCreery, Charles. *Science, Philosophy and ESP.* (London: Faber and Faber, 1967).

McVaugh, Michael R., and Seymour Mauskopf. "Historical Perspective and Parapsychology." *JP,* 38 (1974): 312-323.

———. "J. B. Rhine's *Extra-Sensory Perception* and Its Background in Psychical Research." *Isis,* 67 (1976): 160-189.

Mace, C. A. "Supernormal Faculty and the Structure of the Mind." *PSPR,* 44 (1937): 279-302.

Marcel, Gabriel. *The Influence of Psychic Phenomena on My Philosophy.* (London: Society for Psychical Research, 1956).

Margenau, Henry. "ESP in the Framework of Modern Science." *JASPR,* 60 (1966): 214-228. [Also *in* Smythies: 209-224.]

Marshall, N. "ESP and Memory: A Physical Theory." *British Journal for the Philosophy of Science,* 10 (1960): 265-286. [See also: Response by H. A. C. Dobbs and rejoinder by Marshall in the same journal, 12 (1961): 65-70.]

Medhurst, R. G. "The Fraudulent Experimenter: Professor Hansel's Case Against Psychical Research." *JSPR,* 44 (1968): 217-232.

Miller, G. A. "Concerning Psychical Research." *Scientific American,* 209 (1963): 171-177.

Mundle, C. W. K. "Philosophical Implications of ESP Phenomena." in *The Encyclopedia of Philosopy,* edited by Paul Edwards. (New York: Macmillan and Free Press, 1967): volume 3: 49-58.

———. "The Explanation of ESP." *IJP,* 7 (1965): 221-230. [Reprinted *in* Smythies: 197-207.]

———. "On the 'Psychic' Powers of Nonhuman Animals." *in* Thakur: 157-180.

———. "Professor Rhine's Views About PK." *Mind,* 59 (1950): 372-379.

———. "Review: The Philosophy of C. D. Broad." *JSPR,* 41 (1961): 1-11.

———. "Some Philosophical Perspectives for Parapsychology." *JP,* 16 (1952): 257-272.

———. "Strange Facts in Search of a Theory." *PSPR,* 56 (1973): 1-20. [Reprinted *in* Wheatley: 76-97.]

Murphy, Gardner. "Are There Any Solid Facts in Psychical Research?" *JASPR,* 64 (1970): 3-17. [Reprinted *in* Wheatley: 388-404.]

———. "Direct Contacts with Past and Future: Retro- and Precognition." *JASPR,* 61 (1967): 3-23.

———. "Dr. Rhine and the Mind's Eye." *American Scholar,* 7(1938): 189-200.

———. "Lawfulness versus Caprice: Is There a 'Law of Psychic Phenomena'." *JASPR,* 58 (1964): 238-249.

———. "The Natural, the Mystical, and the Paranormal." *JASPR,* 46 (1952): 125-142.

———. "The Place of Parapsychology Among the Sciences." *JP,* 13(1949): 62-71.

———. "Psychical Research and Personality." *JASPR,* 44(1950): 3-20.

———. "Psychical Research and the Mind-Body Relation." *JASPR,* 40(1946): 189-207.

———. "Psychology and Psychical Research." *PSPR,* 50(1953): 26-49.

———. *Three Papers on the Survival Problem: An Outline of Survival Evidence; Difficulties Confronting the Survival Hypothesis; Field Theory and Survival.* (New York: American Society for Psychical Research, [1955]). [Previously published *in: JASPR,* 39(1945): 2-34; 67-94; 181-209.]

———. "Triumphs and Defeats in the Study of Mediumship." *JASPR,* 51(1957): 125-135.

————, with Laura A. Dale. *Challenge of Psychical Research: A Primer of Parapsychology.* (New York: Harper and Row, 1961).

————, and Robert O. Ballou [editors]. *William James on Psychical Research.* (New York: Viking Press, 1960).

Myers, Frederic W. H. *Human Personality and Its Survival of Bodily Death.* (London: Longmans, Green and Co., 1903). Two volumes.

Nash, Carroll B. "Note on Precognition of the Percipient's Calls as an Alternative Hypothesis to Telepathy." *JP,* 39(1975): 21-23.

————. "Physical and Metaphysical Parapsychology." *JP,* 27(1963): 283-300.

————. "The Unorthodox Science of Parapsychology." *IJP,* 1(1959): 5-23.

Nayak, G. C. "Survival, Reincarnation, and the Problem of Personal Identity." *Journal of the* [Indian] *Philosophical Association,* 11(1968): 131-143. [Reprinted *in* Wheatley: 295-307.]

Nicol, J. Fraser. "C. D. Broad on Psychical Research." *IJP,* 6(1964): 261-281.

————. "Randomness: The Background, and Some New Investigations." *JSPR,* 38 (1955): 71-87.

Odegard, D. "Disembodied Existence and Central State Materialism." *Australasian Journal of Philosophy,* 48(1970): 256-260.

Oram, A. T. "An Experiment with Random Numbers." *JSPR,* 37(1954): 369-377.

Orme, J. E. "Precognition and Time." *JSPR,* 47(1974): 351-365.

Parker-Rhodes, A. F. "On Causation in Psi Phenomena." *JSPR,* 37(1953): 85-89.

Penelhum, Terence. "Personal Identity, Memory, and Survival." *Journal of Philosophy,* 56(1959): 882-903.

————. *Survival and Disembodied Existence.* (New York: Humanities Press, 1970).

Podmore, Frank. *Apparitions and Thought-Transference: An Examination of the Evidence for Telepathy.* (London: Walter Scott Ltd., 1894).

———. *Studies in Psychical Research.* (London: Kegan Paul, Trench, Trübner and Co., 1897).

Pope, Dorothy H., and J. G. Pratt. "The ESP Controversy." *JP,* 6(1942): 174-189.

Poynton, John. "Parapsychology and the Biological Sciences." *Parapsychology Review,* 4(1973): 10-12; 23-26.

Pratt, J. G. "The Case for Psychokinesis." *JP,* 24(1960): 171-188.

———. *ESP Research Today: A Study of Developments in Parapsychology Since 1960.* (Metuchen: Scarecrow Press, 1973).

———. *Parapsychology: An Insider's View of ESP.* (New York: Doubleday and Co., 1964).

———. "Some Notes for the Future Einstein for Parapsychology." *JASPR,* 68(1974): 133-155.

———, and others. *Extra-sensory Perception After Sixty Years: A Critical Appraisal of the Research in Extra-sensory Perception.* (New York: Holt, 1940). [Reprinted: Boston: Bruce Humphries, 1967.]

Pratt, V. "The Inexplicable and the Supernatural." *Philosophy,* 43(1968): 248-257.

Price, H. H. "Apparitions: Two Theories." *JP,* 24(1960): 110-128.

———. "Mediumship and Human Survival." *JP,* 24(1960): 199-219. [Reprinted *in* Wheatley: 262-281.]

———. "The Philosophical Implications of Precognition. Discussion Between C. D. Broad and H. H. Price." *Proceedings of the Aristotelian Society,* Supplementary volume 16(1937): 211-228. [Pages 211-245 published separately.]

———. "Professor C. D. Broad's *Religion, Philosophy and Psychical Research.*" *JASPR,* 48(1954): 56-68.

———. "Psychical Research and Human Personality." *Hibbert Journal,* 47(1948-49): 105-113. [Reprinted *in* Smythies: 33-45.]

———. "Some Philosophical Questions About Telepathy and Clairvoyance." *Philosophy,* 15(1940): 363-385. [Reprinted *in* Wheatley: 105-132.]

———. "Survival and the Idea of 'Another World'." *PSPR,* 50(1953): 1-25.

———, Robert H. Thouless, C. W. K. Mundle, C. C. Stevens, Antony G. N. Flew, and C. T. K. Chari. " 'The Extension of Mind': Comments on Dr. J. R. Smythies' Paper." *JSPR,* 36(1952): 537-569. [Reply by Smythies.]

Randall, J. L. "Psi Phenomena and Biological Theory." *JSPR,* 46(1971): 151-165.

Ransom, Champe. "Recent Criticisms of Parapsychology: A Review." *JASPR,* 65(1971): 289-307.

Rao, K. R. "Consideration of Some Theories in Parapsychology." *JP,* 25(1961): 32-54.

———. *Experimental Parapsychology: A Review and Interpretation.* (Springfield, Illinois: Charles C. Thomas, 1966).

Read, Ronald C. "Card Guessing with Information—A Problem of Probability." *American Mathematical Monthly,* 69(1962): 506-511.

Rees, D. A. "The Meaning of 'Survival'." *Analysis,* 12(1951-52): 94-98.

Rhine, J. B. "The Bearing of Parapsychology on Human Potentiality." *JP,* 30(1966): 243-258.

———. *Extra-Sensory Perception.* Revised edition. (Boston: Bruce Humphries, 1964). [Originally published in 1934.]

———. *New Frontiers of the Mind.* (New York: Farrar and Rinehart, 1937).

———. *New World of the Mind.* (New York: William Sloane Associates, 1953).

———. "On Parapsychology and the Nature of Man." *in Dimensions of Mind,* edited by Sidney Hook. (New York: New York University Press, 1960): 74-78.

———. "Parapsychology and Man." *JP,* 36(1972): 101-121. [Also *in: Human Values and the Mind of Man,* edited by E. Laszlo and J. B. Wilbur. (New York: Gordon and Breach, 1971): 3-20.]

———. *Parapsychology from Duke to FRNM.* (Durham: Parapsychology

Press, [1965]).

———. *Progress in Parapsychology.* (Durham: Parapsychology Press, 1971).

———. "Psi and Psychology: Conflict and Solution." *JP,* 32(1968): 101-128.

———. "The Question of Sensory Cues and the Evidence." *JP,* 1 (1937): 276-291.

———. *The Reach of the Mind.* (New York: William Sloane Associates, 1947).

———. "Research on Spirit Survival Re-Examined." *JP,* 20(1956): 121-131.

———. "Some Guiding Concepts for Parapsychology." *JP,* 32(1968): 190-218.

———. "Telepathy and Clairvoyance Reconsidered." *PSPR,* 48(1946): 1-7.

———. *Telepathy and Human Personality.* (London: Society for Psychical Research, 1950).

———. "Telepathy and Other Untestable Hypotheses." *JP,* 38(1974): 137-153.

———, and Robert Brier [editors]. *Parapsychology Today.* (New York: Citadel, 1968).

———, and J. G. Pratt. *Parapsychology, Frontier Science of the Mind: A Survey of the Field, the Methods, and the Facts of ESP and PK Research.* (Springfield, Illinois: Charles C. Thomas, 1957).

Rhine, Louisa E. *ESP in Life and Lab.* (New York: Macmillan, 1967).

———. "The Establishment of Basic Concepts and Terminology in Parapsychology." *JP,* 35(1971): 34-56.

———. *Hidden Channels of the Mind.* (New York: William Morrow and Co., 1961).

———. *Mind Over Matter: Psychokinesis.* (New York: Macmillan, 1970).

Richet, Charles. "La suggestion mentale et le calcul des probabilités." *Revue philosophique,* 18(1884): 609-674.

———. *Thirty Years of Psychical Research: Being a Treatise on Metapsychics.* (New York: Macmillan, 1923).

Robertson, L. C. "The Logical and Scientific Implications of Precognition, Assuming This To Be Established Statistically from the Work of Card-Guessing Subjects." *JSPR,* 39(1957): 134-139.

Rogosin, H. "An Evaluation of Extra-Sensory Perception." *Journal of General Psychology,* 21(1939): 203-217.

———. "Probability Theory and Extra-Sensory Perception." *Journal of Psychology,* 5(1938): 265-270.

Roll, W. G. "ESP and Memory." *International Journal of Neuropsychiatry,* 2(1966): 505-521. [Reprinted *in* Wheatley: 154-184.]

———. "The Problem of Precognition." *JSPR,* 41(1961): 115-128.

Salter, W. H. *ZOAR, or Evidence of Psychical Research Concerning Survival.* (London: Sidgwick and Jackson, 1961).

Saltmarsh, H. F. *Foreknowledge.* (London: Bell and Sons, 1938).

———. "Report on Cases of Apparent Precognition." *PSPR,* 42(1934): 49-103. [Partially reprinted *in* French: 106-114.]

Schiller, F. C. S. "Philosophy, Science, and Psychical Research." *PSPR,* 27(1914-15): 191-220.

———. "Review of *Experiments in Psychical Research* by J. E. Coover." *PSPR,* 30(1918): 261-273.

———. "Some Logical Aspects of Psychical Research." *in* Murchison: 215-226.

Schmeidler, Gertrude [editor]. *Extra Sensory Perception.* (New York: Atherton Press, 1969).

———, and R. A. McConnell. *ESP and Personality Patterns.* (New Haven: Yale University Press, 1958).

Scott, Christopher. "G. Spencer Brown and Probability: A Critique."

JSPR, 39 (1958): 217-234.

———. "In Search of a Repeatable ESP Experiment." *JSPR*, 40(1959): 174-185.

Scriven, Michael. "Explanations of the Supernatural." *in* Thakur: 181-194.

———. "The Frontiers of Psychology: Psychoanalysis and Parapsychology." *in Frontiers of Science and Philosophy,* edited by R. Colodny. (Pittsburgh: University of Pittsburgh Press, 1962): 79-129. [Partially reprinted *in* Wheatley: 46-75.

———. "Modern Experiments in Telepathy." *Philosophical Review,* 65 (1956): 231-253.

———. "New Experimental Designs for Psi Research." *JSPR*, 38(1956): 231-237.

———. "Personal Identity and Parapsychology." *JASPR*, 59(1965): 309-317.

———. "Physicality and Psi: Symposium and a Forum Discussion." *JP*, 25(1961): 13-31. [Also: responses to the symposiasts, *JP*, 25(1961): 214-218.]

———. "Randomness and the Causal Order." *Analysis,* 17(1956): 5-9.

———. "Some Theoretical Possibilities in Psi Research." *JSPR*, 39(1957): 78-83.

Shaffer, Jerome. *Philosophy of Mind.* (Englewood Cliffs: Prentice-Hall, 1968).

Shewmaker, Kenneth L., and Carlton W. Berenda. "Science and the Problem of Psi." *Philosophy of Science,* 29(1962): 195-203. [Reprinted *in* Wheatley: 413-424.]

Sidgwick, Henry. "Presidential Addresses." *PSPR*, 1(1882-83): 7-12; 65-69; 245-250.

Sinclair, Upton. *Mental Radio.* Second revised edition. (Springfield, Illinois: Charles C. Thomas, 1962). [Originally published in 1930.]

Smart, B. "Can Disembodied Persons Be Spatially Located?" *Analysis,* 31 (1970-71): 133-138.

Smythies, J. R. [editor]. *Brain and Mind: Modern Concepts of the Nature of Mind.* (New York: Humanities Press, 1965).

———. "ESP Fact or Fiction: A Sidelight on Soal." *PSPR*, 56(1974): 130-131.

———. "The Extension of Mind: A New Theoretical Basis for Psi Phenomena." *JSPR*, 36(1951): 477-502.

———. "Is ESP Possible." *in* Smythies: 1-14.

———. "Three Classical Theories of Mind." *JSPR*, 40(1960): 385-397.

Soal, S. G. "Methods in Experimental Telepathy." *JSPR*, 27(1931): 130-135.

———. "My Thirty Years of Psychical Research." *PSPR*, 50(1953): 67-95.

———. "A Repetition of Dr. J. B. Rhine's Work in Extra-Sensory Perception." *JSPR*, 30(1937): 55-58.

———, and F. Bateman. *Modern Experiments in Telepathy.* (New Haven: Yale University Press, 1954). [Also: London: Faber and Faber, 1954.]

Society for Psychical Research (London). *Presidential Addresses to the Society for Psychical Research 1882-1911.* (Glasgow: Robert Maclehose and Co., 1912).

Stanford, R. G. "Parapsychology and the Method of Science." *Journal of the Foundation for Research in Parapsychology,* 1(1961): 11-22.

Sterne, T. E. "The Solution of a Problem in Probability." *Science,* 86 (1937): 500-501.

Stevenson, Ian. "An Antagonist's View of Parapsychology: A Review of Professor Hansel's *ESP: A Scientific Evaluation.*" *JASPR,* 61(1967): 254-267.

———, and W. G. Roll. "Criticism in Parapsychology: An Informal Statement of Some Guiding Principles." *JASPR,* 60 (1966): 347-356.

Stuart, C. E., and J. A. Greenwood. "A Review of Criticisms of the Mathematical Evaluation of ESP Data." *JP,* 1(1937): 295-304.

Sudre, R. "Clairvoyance and the Theory of Probabilities." *JASPR,* 22 (1928): 63-69.

———. *Parapsychology.* (New York: Citadel, 1960).

Swiggart, Peter. "A Note on Telepathy." *Analysis,* 22(1961-62): 42-43. [Reprinted *in* Wheatley: 139-141.]

Thakur, Shivesh C. "Telepathy, Evolution and Dualism." *in* Thakur: 195-210.

Thalberg, I. "Telepathy." *Analysis,* 21(1960-61): 49-53. [Revised version entitled, "Telepathic Awareness of Another's Feelings," *in* Wheatley: 133-138.]

Thouless, Robert H. "Dr. Rhine's Recent Experiments on Telepathy and Clairvoyance and a Reconsideration of J. E. Coover's Conclusions on Telepathy." *PSPR,* 43(1935): 24-37.

———. *From Anecdote to Experiment in Psychical Research.* (London: Routledge and Kegan Paul, 1972).

———. "Parapsychology During the Last Quarter of a Century." *JP,* 33 (1969): 283-299.

———. "Problems of Design in Parapsychological Experiments." *JSPR,* 37(1954): 299-307.

———. "Where Does Parapsychology Go Next?" *JSPR,* 40(1960): 207-219.

———, and B. P. Wiesner. "The Psi Process in Normal and 'Paranormal' Psychology." *PSPR,* 48(1946-49): 177-196.

Tischner, Rudolf. *Telepathy and Clairvoyance.* (New York: Harcourt, Brace, 1925).

Turner, Ralph H. "Parapsychology: A Topic Illustrating Basic Concepts in Psychology." *Psychological Record,* 20(1970): 505-508.

Tyrrell, G. N. M. *Apparitions.* (London: Duckworth, 1953).

———. "The *Modus Operandi* of Paranormal Cognition." *PSPR,* 48 (1947): 65-120.

———. *The Nature of Human Personality.* (London: Allen and Unwin, 1954).

————. *The Personality of Man.* (Baltimore: Penguin Books, 1947).

————. *Science and Psychical Phenomena.* (London: Methuen, 1938).

Ullman, Montague, and Stanley Krippner, with Alan Vaughn. *Dream Telepathy.* (New York: Macmillan, 1973).

Wade, N. "Psychical Research: The Incredible in Search of Credibility." *Science,* 181(1973): 138-143.

Walker, R. "Parapsychology and Dualism." *Scientific Monthly,* 79(1954): 1-9.

Warcollier, René. *Experiments in Telepathy.* (New York: Harper and Brothers, 1938).

————. "Methods in Experimental Telepathy." *JSPR,* 27(1932): 205-207.

Ware, Mark, and Mary A. Butler. "Chance: An Adequate Control for Clairvoyant Research?" *Psychology,* 8(1971): 44-52.

Warner, Lucien. "Is 'Extra-Sensory Perception' Extra-Sensory?" *Journal of Psychology,* 7(1939): 71-77.

————. "The Role of Luck in ESP Data." *Journal of Psychology,* 1(1937): 84-92.

Wassermann, G. D. "Some Comments on Methods and Statements in Parapsychology and Other Sciences." *British Journal for the Philosophy of Science,* 6(1955): 122-140.

West, D. J. *Psychical Research Today.* (London: Duckworth, 1954).

Wheatley, James M. O. "Is Telepathy a Faculty?" *IJP,* 7(1965): 117-128.

————. "Knowledge, Empiricism and ESP." *IJP,* 3(1961): 7-19. [Reprinted, with minor alterations, *in* Wheatley: 142-153.]

————. "The Necessity for Bodies: An Appreciation of Professor Terence Penelhum's *Survival and Disembodied Existence." JASPR,* 66(1972): 321-328.

————. "The Question of Survival: Some Logical Reflections." *JASPR,* 59 (1965): 202-210. [Reprinted *in* Wheatley: 252-261.]

Bibliography

Whiteman, J. H. M. "Quantum Theory and Parapsychology." *JASPR,* 67 (1973): 341-360.

Willoughby, R. R. "A Critique of Rhine's *Extra-Sensory Perception.*" *Journal of Abnormal and Social Psychology,* 30(1936): 199-207.

———."Prerequisites for a Clairvoyance Hypothesis." *Journal of Applied Psychology,* 19(1935): 543-550.

———. "The Use of Probable Error in Evaluating Clairvoyance." *Character and Personality,* 4(1935): 79-80.

Wilson, Richard. "Deviations from Randomness in ESP Experiments." *IJP,* 8(1966): 387-396.

Wolfle, D. L. "A Review of the Work on Extra-Sensory Perception." *American Journal of Psychiatry,* 94 (1938): 943-955.

Zorab, George. "The Use of the Word 'Paranormal' in Medicine." *JSPR,* 38(1956): 212-215.

Contributors

HAROLD W. BALDWIN is assistant professor of philosophy at the University of South Alabama, where he is developing a philosophy of science course incorporating parapsychological issues. His current research is in the philosophy of social science.

JOHN BELOFF is professor of psychology at The University of Edinburgh. His writings include *The Existence of Mind* (1962) and *New Directions in Parapsychology* (1974), as well as many contributions to parapsychological journals. Dr. Beloff is a past president of the Society for Psychical Research.

STEPHEN E. BRAUDE is associate professor of philosophy at the University of Maryland—Baltimore County. A specialist in the philosophy of language, Professor Braude has written papers on temporal notions in logic and language which have appeared in *Philosophical Studies, Analysis,* and *The Philosophical Review.*

PERCY WILLIAMS BRIDGMAN (1882-1961) took his Ph.D. in physics from Harvard University and taught there for forty-four years. His book, *The Logic of Modern Physics* (1927), introduced the notion of operational definition into discussions of scientific method.

BOB BRIER is associate professor of philosophy at C.W. Post College. He was a research fellow at the Institute for Parapsychology and coeditor of *Parapsychology Today* (1968) with J.B. Rhine. A frequent contributor to philosophical and parapsychological journals, Professor Brier is also the author of *Precognition and the Philosophy of Science* (1974).

CHARLIE DUNBAR BROAD (1887-1971) was Knightbridge professor of moral philosophy at the University of Cambridge and one of the foremost philosophers of parapsychology in this century. He was twice president of the Society for Psychical Research and a major contributor to its *Journal* and *Proceedings*. Perhaps best known for *The Mind and Its Place in Nature* (1929), Professor Broad was the author of other books, including *Religion, Philosophy, and Psychical Research* (1953), and *Lectures on Psychical Research* (1962).

CURT JOHN DUCASSE (1881-1969) was professor of philosophy at Brown University and a major American advocate of the philosophical study of parapsychology. In addition to his contributions to philosophical and parapsychological periodicals, Professor Ducasse authored many books, including *Nature, Mind, and Death* (1951) and *A Critical Examination of the Belief in Life After Death* (1961).

ANTONY G. N. FLEW is professor of philosophy at the University of Reading. He has also served as a visiting professor at a number of American universities. Professor Flew's first book, *A New Approach to Psychical Research* (1953), broke new ground in the philosophy of parapsychology. His many other books and articles deal with an extraordinarily wide range of philosophical issues.

LEWIS A. FOSTER, JR. is professor of philosophy at The College of William and Mary. His primary interests are comparative East-West philosophy and the philosophy of parapsychology. A member of the American Society for Psychical Research, Professor Foster has published articles on the philosophical problems of precognition.

JOHN W. GODBEY, JR. received his Ph.D. in philosophy from Duke University. Primarily interested in epistemology and the philosophy of mind, he has taught at the University of South Carolina and is currently an Andrew Mellon Postdoctoral Fellow at Duke.

WILLIAM JAMES (1842-1910) was the son of an eccentric Swedenborgian, the brother of a psychological novelist, and the foremost spokesman of his time for the philosophical movement called American pragmatism. He taught anatomy, physiology, psychology and philosophy at Harvard University from 1872 until 1907. An early supporter of the American

Society for Psychical Research, Professor James was a serious student of parapsychology throughout his career and served as president of the Society for Psychical Research from 1895 to 1897.

MARTHA HURST KNEALE is a fellow emeritus of Lady Margaret Hall, Oxford University, where she was a tutor from 1939 until 1966. Mrs. Kneale co-authored *The Development of Logic* (1962) with her husband, William C. Kneale.

JAN K. LUDWIG is associate professor and chairperson of the Philosophy Department at Union College (Schenectady, New York), where he teaches a course on the history and philosophy of parapsychology. Professor Ludwig has published articles on the early philosophy of Wittgenstein.

PAUL E. MEEHL is Regents professor of psychology at the University of Minnesota. He is also a professor of psychiatry, law, and philosophy; in the latter capacity he is a member of the Minnesota Center for the Philosophy of Science and a frequent contributor to publications in the philosophy of science.

CLEMENT W. K. MUNDLE recently retired as professor and chairman of the Philosophy Department, University College of North Wales. The author of a number of articles on topics in the philosophy of parapsychology, Professor Mundle contributed the article, "Philosophical Implications of ESP Phenomena," to *The Encyclopedia of Philosophy* (1967).

GARDNER MURPHY is one of the most influential contemporary spokespersons for the serious study of parapsychology. The author of *Challenge of Psychical Research* (1961, with Laura A. Dale) and of many contributions to parapsychological journals, Dr. Murphy is currently professor emeritus of psychology at The George Washington University.

GEORGE ROBERT PRICE (1922-1975) received his Ph.D. in physical and analytical chemistry from The University of Chicago. He served as Research Associate in Medicine at the University of Minnesota and later as a science writer and as a member of the staff of IBM Corporation.

HENRY HABBERLEY PRICE is professor emeritus of logic at Oxford University. Twice president of the Society for Psychical Research, Professor

Price has published many articles on the philosophy of parapsychology. His books include *Perception* (1932), *Thinking and Experience* (1953; Second edition 1969), and *Belief* (1969).

JOSEPH BANKS RHINE received his doctorate in botany, but spent most of his career in the experimental study of parapsychology at Duke University, where he was director of the Parapsychology Laboratory from 1940 until 1965. His first book, *Extra-Sensory Perception* (1934), precipitated both extensive criticism and the continuing tradition of serious research in parapsychology. Dr. Rhine is currently executive director of the Foundation for Research in the Nature of Man (Durham, North Carolina).

RICHARD G. F. ROBINSON taught philosophy from 1947 to 1969 at Oxford University, where he was a fellow of Oriel College. His books include *Plato's Earlier Dialectic* (1941; Second edition 1953), *Definition* (1950), and *Essays in Greek Philosophy* (1969).

MICHAEL SCRIVEN is professor of philosophy at the University of California at Berkeley. In addition to making important contributions to the philosophy of science and, more recently, the philosophy of education, Professor Scriven is an influential analyst of philosophical issues in parapsychology. His books include *Primary Philosophy* (1966) and *Reasoning* (1976).

SAMUEL G. SOAL, who died in 1975 at the age of eighty-five, was an early critic of J.B. Rhine's research who later uncovered precognition effects in his own work with Basil Shackleton. This work and its continuation was reported in *Modern Experiments in Telepathy* (1954, with F. Bateman). Dr. Soal received his D.Sc. in parapsychology from the University of London.

JAMES M. O. WHEATLEY is associate professor of philosophy at the University of Toronto. A member of the American Society for Psychical Research and a frequent contributor to its *Journal*, Professor Wheatley recently co-edited, with Hoyt L. Edge, *Philosophical Dimensions of Parapsychology* (1976). His work has also appeared in *Analysis, Philosophy of Science,* and the *International Journal of Parapsychology*.